Table of Contents

studysync®

Reading & Writing Companion

GRADE 11 UNITS

We the People • The Individual
Modern Times • Seeking Romance

::studysync®

studysync.com

Send all inquiries to:
BookheadEd Learning, LLC
610 Daniel Young Drive
Sonoma, CA 95476

1 2 3 4 5 6 7 8 9 QVR 20 19 18 17 16 15 B

2015 G11

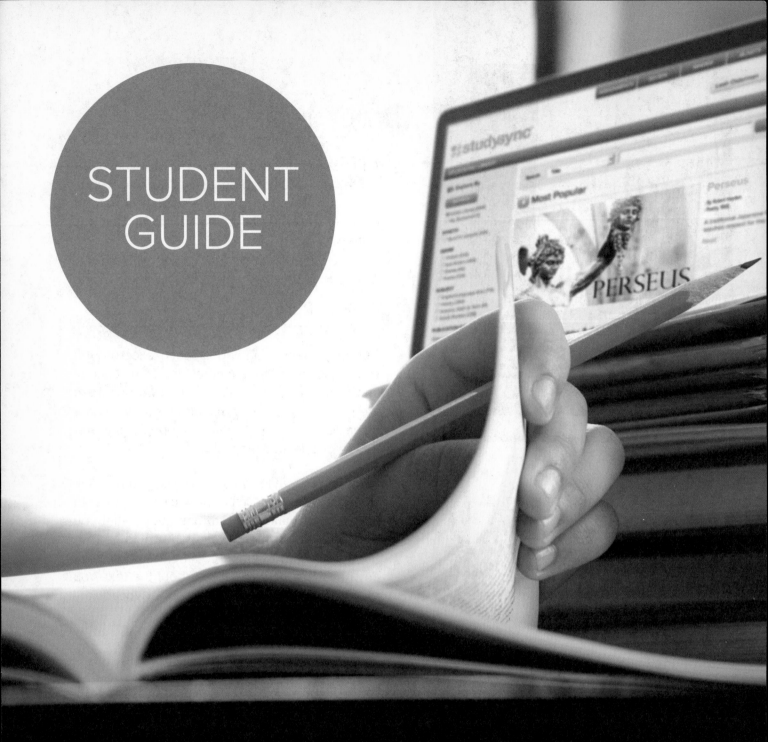

STUDENT GUIDE

GETTING STARTED

Welcome to the StudySync Reading and Writing Companion! In this booklet, you will find a collection of readings based on the theme of the unit you are studying. As you work through the readings, you will be asked to answer questions and perform a variety of tasks designed to help you closely analyze and understand each text selection. Read on for an explanation of each section of this booklet.

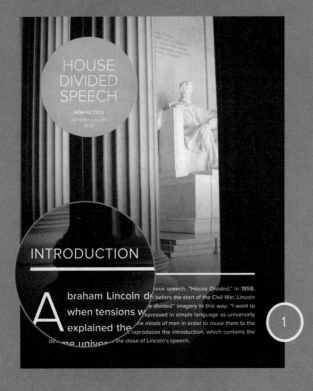

1 INTRODUCTION

An Introduction to each text provides historical context for your reading as well as information about the author. You will also learn about the genre of the excerpt and the year in which it was written.

2 FIRST READ

During your first reading of each excerpt, you should just try to get a general idea of the content and message of the reading. Don't worry if there are parts you don't understand or words that are unfamiliar to you. You'll have an opportunity later to dive deeper into the text.

Many times, while working through the Think Questions after your first read, you will be asked to **annotate** or **make annotations** about what you are reading. This means that you should use the "Notes" column to make comments or jot down any questions you may have about the text. You may also want to note any unfamiliar vocabulary words here.

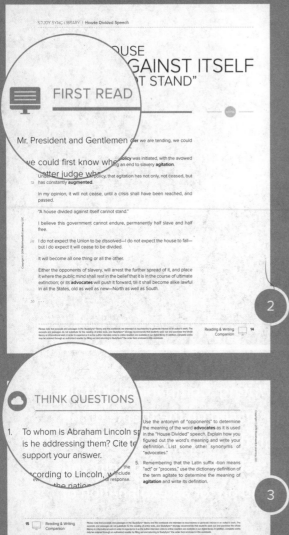

3 THINK QUESTIONS

These questions will ask you to start thinking critically about the text, asking specific questions about its purpose, and making connections to your prior knowledge and reading experiences. To answer these questions, you should go back to the text and draw upon specific evidence that you find there to support your responses. You will also begin to explore some of the more challenging vocabulary words used in the excerpt.

4   CLOSE READ & FOCUS QUESTIONS

After you have completed the First Read, you will then be asked to go back and read the excerpt more closely and critically. Before you begin your Close Read, you should read through the Focus Questions to get an idea of the concepts you will want to focus on during your second reading. You should work through the Focus Questions by making annotations, highlighting important concepts, and writing notes or questions in the "Notes" column. Depending on instructions from your teacher, you may need to respond online or use a separate piece of paper to start expanding on your thoughts and ideas.

5   WRITING PROMPT

Your study of each excerpt or selection will end with a writing assignment. To complete this assignment, you should use your notes, annotations, and answers to both the Think and Focus Questions. Be sure to read the prompt carefully and address each part of it in your writing assignment.

6   EXTENDED WRITING PROJECT

After you have read and worked through all of the unit text selections, you will move on to a writing project. This project will walk you through steps to plan, draft, revise, edit, and finally publish an essay or other piece of writing about one or more of the texts you have studied in the unit. Student models and graphic organizers will provide guidance and help you organize your thoughts as you plan and write your essay. Throughout the project, you will also study and work on specific writing skills to help you develop different portions of your writing.

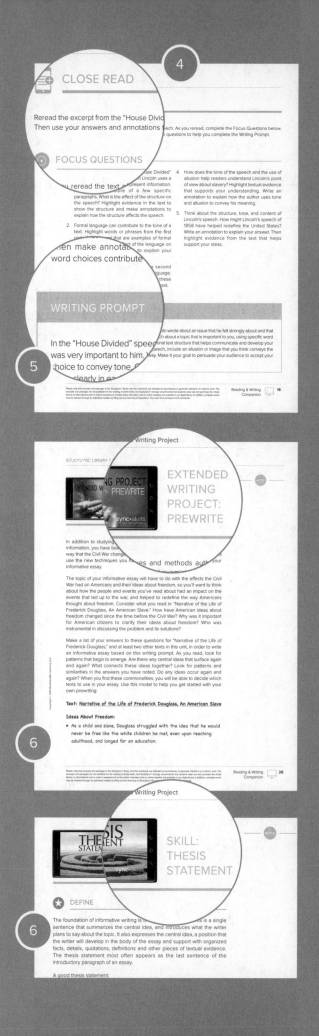

studysync®

Reading & Writing Companion

What shaped America's early identity?

We the People

We the People

TEXTS

TEXTS

EXTENDED WRITING PROJECT

Reading & Writing
Companion

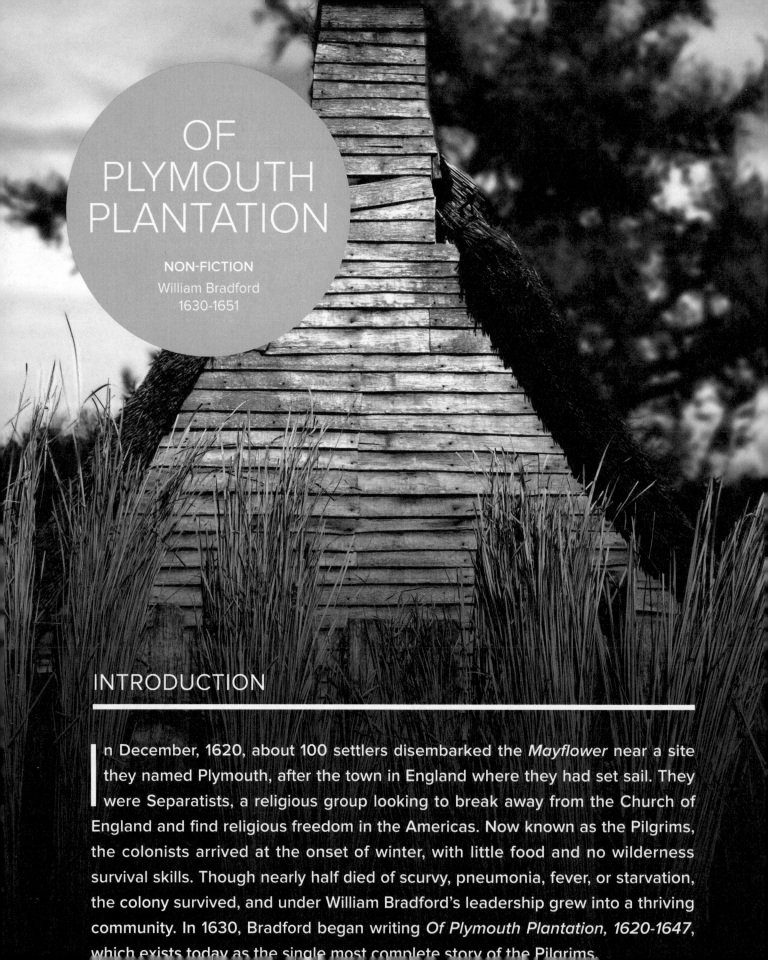

OF PLYMOUTH PLANTATION

NON-FICTION
William Bradford
1630-1651

INTRODUCTION

In December, 1620, about 100 settlers disembarked the *Mayflower* near a site they named Plymouth, after the town in England where they had set sail. They were Separatists, a religious group looking to break away from the Church of England and find religious freedom in the Americas. Now known as the Pilgrims, the colonists arrived at the onset of winter, with little food and no wilderness survival skills. Though nearly half died of scurvy, pneumonia, fever, or starvation, the colony survived, and under William Bradford's leadership grew into a thriving community. In 1630, Bradford began writing *Of Plymouth Plantation, 1620-1647*, which exists today as the single most complete story of the Pilgrims,

"...brought safe to land, they fell upon their knees and blessed the God of Heaven..."

 FIRST READ

 NOTES

From Chapter 9: Of Their Voyage, and How They Passed the Sea; and of Their Safe Arrival at Cape Cod (September, 1620)

1 In **sundry** of these storms the winds were so fierce and the seas so high, as they could not bear a knot of sail, but were forced to hull for divers days together. And in one of them, as they thus lay at hull in a mighty storm, a lusty young man called John Howland, coming upon some occasion above the gratings was, with a seele of the ship, thrown into sea; but it pleased God that he caught hold of the topsail halyards which hung overboard and ran out at length. Yet he held his hold (though he was sundry fathoms under water) till he was hauled up by the same rope to the brim of the water, and then with a boat hook and other means got into the ship again and his life saved. And though he was something ill with it, yet he lived many years after and became a profitable member both in church and commonwealth. In all this voyage there died but one of the passengers, which was William Butten, a youth, servant to Samuel Fuller, when they drew near the coast.

...

2 Being thus arrived in a good harbor, and brought safe to land, they fell upon their knees and blessed the God of Heaven who had brought them over the vast and furious ocean, and delivered them from all the perils and miseries thereof, again to set their feet on the firm and stable earth, their proper element. And no marvel if they were thus joyful, seeing wise Seneca was so affected with sailing a few miles on the coast of his own Italy, as he affirmed, that he had rather remain twenty years on his way by land than pass by sea to any place in a short time, so tedious and dreadful was the same unto him.

3 But here I cannot but stay and make a pause, and stand half amazed at this poor people's present condition; and so I think will the reader, too, when he well considers the same. Being thus passed the vast ocean, and a sea of

Reading & Writing Companion

troubles before in their preparation (as may be remembered by that which went before), they had now no friends to welcome them nor inns to entertain or refresh their weatherbeaten bodies; no houses or much less towns to repair to, to seek for succor. It is recorded in Scripture as a mercy to the Apostle and his shipwrecked company, that the barbarians showed them no small kindness in refreshing them, but these savage barbarians, when they met with them (as after will appear) were readier to fill their sides full of arrows than otherwise. And for the season it was winter, and they that know the winters of that country know them to be sharp and violent, and subject to cruel and fierce storms, dangerous to travel to known places, much more to search an unknown coast.

From Chapter 11: The Starving Time (Winter, 1620–1621)

4   But that which was most sad and lamentable was, that in two or three months' time half of their company died, especially in January and February, being the depth of winter, and wanting houses and other comforts; being infected with the scurvy and other diseases which this long voyage and their inaccommodate condition had brought upon them. So as there died some times two or three of a day in the foresaid time, that of 100 and odd persons, scarce fifty remained. And of these, in the time of most distress, there was but six or seven sound persons who to their great **commendations,** be it spoken, spared no pains night nor day, but with abundance of toil and hazard of their own health, fetched them wood, made them fires, dressed them meat, made their beds, washed their loathsome clothes, clothed and unclothed them. In a word, did all the homely and necessary offices for them which dainty and queasy stomachs cannot endure to hear named; and all this willingly and cheerfully, without any grudging in the least, showing herein their true love unto their friends and brethren; a rare example and worthy to be remembered. Two of these seven were Mr. William Brewster, their reverend Elder, and Myles Standish, their Captain and military commander, unto whom myself and many others were much beholden in our low and sick condition. And yet the Lord so upheld these persons as in this general calamity they were not at all infected either with sickness or lameness. . . .

Indian Relations

5   All this while the Indians came **skulking** about them, and would sometimes show themselves **aloof** off, but when any approached near them, they would run away; and once they stole away their tools where they had been at work and were gone to dinner. But about the 16th of March, a certain Indian came boldly amongst them and spoke to them in broken English, which they could well understand but marveled at it. At length they understood by discourse with him, that he was not of these parts, but belonged to the eastern parts where some English ships came to fish, with whom he was acquainted and

could name sundry of them by their names, amongst whom he had got his language. He became profitable to them in acquainting them with many things concerning the state of the country in the east parts where he lived, which was afterward profitable unto them; as also of the people here, of their names, number and strength, of their situation and distance from this place, and who was chief amongst them. His name was Samoset. He told them also of another Indian whose name was Squanto, a native of this place, who had been in England and could speak better English than himself.

6   Being, after some time of entertainment and gifts dismissed, a while after he came again, and five more with him, and they brought again all the tools that were stolen away before, and made way for the coming of their great Sachem, called Massasoit. Who, about four or five days after, came with the chief of his friends and other attendance, with the aforesaid Squanto. With whom, after friendly entertainment and some gifts given him, they made a peace with him (which hath now continued this 24 years) in these terms:

1.   That neither he nor any of his should injure or do hurt to any of their people.

2.   That if any of his did hurt to any of theirs, he should send the offender, that they might punish him.

3.   That if anything were taken away from any of theirs, he should cause it to be restored; and they should do the like to his.

4.   If any did unjustly war against him, they would aid him; if any did war against them, he should aid them.

5.   He should send to his neighbors confederates to certify them of this, that they might not wrong them, but might be likewise comprised in the conditions of peace.

6.   That when their men came to them, they should leave their bows and arrows behind them.

7   After these things he returned to his place called Sowams, some 40 miles from this place, but Squanto continued with them and was their interpreter and was a special instrument sent of God for their good beyond their expectation. He directed them how to set their corn, where to take fish, and to **procure** other commodities, and was also their pilot to bring them to unknown places for their profit, and never left them till he died.

From Chapter 12: First Thanksgiving (Fall, 1621)

8   They began now to gather in the small harvest they had, and to fit up their houses and dwellings against winter, being all well recovered in health and

Please note that excerpts and passages in the StudySync® library and this workbook are intended as touchstones to generate interest in an author's work. The excerpts and passages do not substitute for the reading of entire texts, and StudySync® strongly recommends that students seek out and purchase the whole literary or informational work in order to experience it as the author intended. Links to online resellers are available in our digital library. In addition, complete works may be ordered through an authorized reseller by filling out and returning to StudySync® the order form enclosed in this workbook.

Reading & Writing
Companion

7

NOTES

strength and had all things in good plenty. For as some were thus employed in affairs abroad, others were exercised in fishing, about cod and bass and other fish, of which they took good store, of which every family had their portion. All the summer there was no want; and now began to come in store of fowl, as winter approached, of which this place did abound when they came first (but afterward decreased by degrees). And besides waterfowl there was great store of wild turkeys, of which they took many, besides venison, etc. Besides they had about a peck of meal a week to a person, or now since harvest, Indian corn to that proportion. Which made many afterward write so largely of their plenty here to their friends in England, which were not **feigned** but true reports.

THINK QUESTIONS

1. How do the Pilgrims demonstrate their values in their daily effort to survive in a harsh environment? Cite one example from the text and explain how this reflects the Pilgrims' beliefs and values.

2. How does Bradford's diction (choice of words) reveal his own thoughts and feelings about the events or the individuals described in the excerpt? Cite one example from the text and explain how this reflects Bradford's point of view.

3. How did Bradford initially view the Native Americans? Do you think that his first impressions were completely accurate? Remember to cite evidence from the text to explain your response.

4. Use context to determine what Bradford means by the word **feigned** in the last paragraph. How might you define this word? Explain what context clue helped you determine the meaning.

5. The word *commend* is a verb that means "to praise formally or officially." The addition of the suffix *-tion* changes the part of speech. Write a definition and identify the part of speech for the word *commendations,* as it is used in paragraph 4. Explain how breaking down the word into its word parts helped you determine the meaning.

CLOSE READ

Reread the excerpt from *Of Plymouth Plantation*. As you reread, complete the Focus Questions below. Then use your answers and annotations from the questions to help you complete the Writing Prompt.

 FOCUS QUESTIONS

1. In the first paragraph of Chapter 9, Bradford tells the story of John Howland. Annotate some of the language that distinguishes this account from a simple, fact-based retelling of the tale. How does Bradford's analysis of the events relate to the purpose of the book? Use the annotation tool to write your response to this question.

2. How does the clause "that which was most sad and lamentable" build upon the idea of the chapter title, "The Starving Time"? To what, exactly, is Bradford referring? How does this compare to the mood of the start of Chapter 9? Highlight evidence in the text that addresses these questions. Use the annotation tool to write your response to the questions.

3. What enabled the Pilgrims to survive "the Starving Time"? What do Bradford's comments reveal about the Pilgrims' character and beliefs? Highlight evidence in the text that addresses these questions. Use the annotation tool to write your response to the questions.

4. In the chapter "Indian Relations," highlight words and phrases that Bradford used to describe Squanto. Which of these provide evidence of the Pilgrims' religious perspective of his arrival? Use the annotation tool to write your response to this question.

5. Did Bradford think that the peace agreement between the Pilgrims and the native peoples was favorable or detrimental? Highlight evidence in the text that addresses this question. Use the annotation tool to write your response to the question.

6. Reread the final paragraph and think about the reports the Pilgrims sent back to England. What effect might these letters have had on their friends and relatives overseas? How might their reports have shaped America's early identity?

WRITING PROMPT

Write a response in which you describe two distinct themes, or central ideas, in *Of Plymouth Plantation*. Cite evidence from the text to support your understanding of these themes. In your response, include examples of rhetoric from the text and explain how the use of rhetoric helps to support the themes.

THE SCARLET LETTER
(CHAPTER 2)

FICTION

Nathaniel Hawthorne
1850

INTRODUCTION

The Scarlet Letter is Nathaniel Hawthorne's 1850 novel of Hester Prynne, a young mother of a newborn baby living in the Puritan settlement of Boston in 17th century New England. Branded as an adulteress and sentenced to wear a scarlet "A" as her badge of shame, Hester must endure the judgment of strict, mean-spirited townspeople. In this excerpt, after defiantly refusing to disclose the identity of the baby's father, Hester is led to the town square for public shaming.

"On the breast of her gown, in fine red cloth...appeared the letter A."

FIRST READ

NOTES

Chapter II. THE MARKET-PLACE

1   The grass-plot before the jail, in Prison Lane, on a certain summer morning, not less than two centuries ago, was occupied by a pretty large number of the inhabitants of Boston, all with their eyes intently fastened on the iron-clamped oaken door. Amongst any other population, or at a later period in the history of New England, the grim rigidity that petrified the bearded physiognomies of these good people would have augured some awful business in hand. It could have betokened nothing short of the anticipated execution of some noted culprit, on whom the sentence of a legal tribunal had but confirmed the verdict of public sentiment. But, in that early severity of the Puritan character, an inference of this kind could not so indubitably be drawn. It might be that a sluggish bond-servant, or an undutiful child, whom his parents had given over to the civil authority, was to be corrected at the whipping-post. It might be that an Antinomian, a Quaker, or other heterodox religionist, was to be scourged out of the town, or an idle or vagrant Indian, whom the white man's firewater had made riotous about the streets, was to be driven with stripes into the shadow of the forest. It might be, too, that a witch, like old Mistress Hibbins, the bitter-tempered widow of the magistrate, was to die upon the gallows. In either case, there was very much the same **solemnity** of demeanour on the part of the spectators, as befitted a people among whom religion and law were almost identical, and in whose character both were so thoroughly interfused, that the mildest and severest acts of public discipline were alike made venerable and awful....

2   "Goodwives," said a hard-featured dame of fifty, "I'll tell ye a piece of my mind. It would be greatly for the public behoof if we women, being of mature age and church-members in good repute, should have the handling of such malefactresses as this Hester Prynne. What think ye, gossips? If the hussy stood up for judgment before us five, that are now here in a knot together,

would she come off with such a sentence as the worshipful magistrates have awarded? Marry, I trow not."

3   "People say," said another, "that the Reverend Master Dimmesdale, her godly pastor, takes it very **grievously** to heart that such a scandal should have come upon his congregation."

4   "The magistrates are God-fearing gentlemen, but merciful overmuch—that is a truth," added a third autumnal matron. "At the very least, they should have put the brand of a hot iron on Hester Prynne's forehead. Madame Hester would have winced at that, I warrant me. But she—the naughty baggage— little will she care what they put upon the bodice of her gown! Why, look you, she may cover it with a brooch, or such like heathenish adornment, and so walk the streets as brave as ever!"

5   "Ah, but," interposed, more softly, a young wife, holding a child by the hand, "let her cover the mark as she will, the pang of it will be always in her heart."

6   "What do we talk of marks and brands, whether on the bodice of her gown or the flesh of her forehead?" cried another female, the ugliest as well as the most pitiless of these self-constituted judges. "This woman has brought shame upon us all, and ought to die; is there not law for it? Truly there is, both in the Scripture and the statute-book. Then let the magistrates, who have made it of no effect, thank themselves if their own wives and daughters go astray."

7   "Mercy on us, goodwife!" exclaimed a man in the crowd, "is there no virtue in woman, save what springs from a wholesome fear of the gallows? That is the hardest word yet! Hush now, gossips for the lock is turning in the prison-door, and here comes Mistress Prynne herself."

8   The door of the jail being flung open from within there appeared, in the first place, like a black shadow emerging into sunshine, the grim and gristly presence of the town-beadle, with a sword by his side, and his staff of office in his hand. This personage prefigured and represented in his aspect the whole **dismal** severity of the Puritanic code of law, which it was his business to administer in its final and closest application to the offender. Stretching forth the official staff in his left hand, he laid his right upon the shoulder of a young woman, whom he thus drew forward, until, on the threshold of the prison-door, she repelled him, by an action marked with natural dignity and force of character, and stepped into the open air as if by her own free will. She bore in her arms a child, a baby of some three months old, who winked and turned aside its little face from the too vivid light of day; because its existence, heretofore, had brought it acquaintance only with the grey twilight of a dungeon, or other darksome apartment of the prison.

9   When the young woman—the mother of this child—stood fully revealed before the crowd, it seemed to be her first impulse to clasp the infant closely to her bosom; not so much by an impulse of motherly affection, as that she might thereby conceal a certain token, which was wrought or fastened into her dress. In a moment, however, wisely judging that one token of her shame would but poorly serve to hide another, she took the baby on her arm, and with a burning blush, and yet a **haughty** smile, and a glance that would not be abashed, looked around at her townspeople and neighbours. On the breast of her gown, in fine red cloth, surrounded with an elaborate embroidery and fantastic flourishes of gold thread, appeared the letter A. It was so artistically done, and with so much fertility and gorgeous **luxuriance** of fancy, that it had all the effect of a last and fitting decoration to the apparel which she wore, and which was of a splendour in accordance with the taste of the age, but greatly beyond what was allowed by the sumptuary regulations of the colony.

 THINK QUESTIONS

1. Where and when does the opening scene of this chapter take place? Is Hawthorne writing about his own society or a different time period? Refer to details from the text and the introduction to support your answer.

2. How do the women of Boston feel about Hester Prynne in this scene? Quote specific words from the text to support your response.

3. What does Hawthorne mean when he writes "one token of her shame would but poorly serve to hide another" in the final paragraph? Cite details that support your response.

4. What context clues might help you to determine the meaning of the word *luxuriance* in the last paragraph? What do you think *luxuriance* means?

5. How can you figure out the part of speech and the meaning of the word *grievously* by breaking it down to its word parts?

CLOSE READ

Reread the excerpt from *The Scarlet Letter*. As you reread, complete the Focus Questions below. Then use your answers and annotations from the questions to help you complete the Writing Prompt.

FOCUS QUESTIONS

1. In the first paragraph, what does the reader learn about the Puritans' beliefs regarding sin and punishment? How does Hawthorne present the Puritanical approach to punishment? Highlight textual evidence that helps you answer these questions. Use the annotation tool to write your response to the questions.

2. How do Hawthorne's depictions of individual characters relate to the general description of Puritan society in the first paragraph? Choose two characters and explain how these characters reflect ideas about Puritan society. Highlight textual evidence that helps you answer this question. Use the annotation tool to write your response to the question.

3. Reread the second to last paragraph. How does Hawthorne describe the town-beadle and Hester Prynne? How do his descriptions shape the way readers are supposed to think and feel about these characters? What do these descriptions suggest about the story's conflict? Highlight textual evidence that helps you answer these questions. Use the annotation tool to write your response to the questions.

4. Why does the author wait so long to have Hester Prynne physically appear in the doorway to the jail? Highlight textual evidence that helps you answer this question. Use the annotation tool to write your response to the question.

5. In the last paragraph, what does the fancy embroidery of the letter A as well as her overall style of dress suggest about Hester? Highlight textual evidence that helps you answer this question. Use the annotation tool to write your response to the question.

WRITING PROMPT

How does a combination of plot, character, and setting in this excerpt from *The Scarlet Letter* reveal Hawthorne's view of the Puritans? Use your understanding of story elements to analyze the passage and describe the significance of the choices that Hawthorne made in his depiction of the plot, the characters, and the setting.

THE CRUCIBLE

DRAMA
Arthur Miller
1953

INTRODUCTION

studysync tv

Modeled after the Salem witchcraft trials of 1692, Arthur Miller's *The Crucible* is an allegory of the anti-Communist "witch-hunts" of the 1950s carried out by Senator Joseph McCarthy and the House Committee on Un-American Activities. In this opening scene, Samuel Parris' daughter Betty is unconscious after a night of dancing in the woods with several girls and the family

"...the rumor of witchcraft is all about..."

NOTES

FIRST READ

From Act I (An Overture)

A small upper bedroom in the home of Reverend Samuel Parris, Salem, Massachusetts, in the spring of the year 1692.

1   There is a narrow window at the left. Through its leaded panes the morning sunlight streams. A candle still burns near the bed, which is at the right. A chest, a chair, and a small table are the other furnishings. At the back a door opens on the landing of the stairway to the ground floor. The room gives off an air of clean spareness. The roof rafters are exposed, and the wood colors are raw and unmellowed.

2   As the curtain rises, Reverend Parris is discovered kneeling beside the bed, evidently in prayer. His daughter, Betty Parris, aged ten, is lying on the bed, inert.

    ...

3   [H]is niece, Abigail Williams, seventeen, enters—a strikingly beautiful girl, an orphan, with an endless capacity for dissembling. Now she is all worry and apprehension and propriety.

4   ABIGAIL: Uncle? *He looks to her.* Susanna Walcott's here from Doctor Griggs.

5   PARRIS: Oh? Let her come, let her come.

6   ABIGAIL, *leaning out the door to call to Susanna, who is down the hall a few steps:* Come in, Susanna.

7   *Susanna Walcott, a little younger than Abigail, a nervous, hurried girl, enters.*

8   PARRIS, *eagerly:* What does the doctor say, child?

NOTES

9   SUSANNA, *craning around Parris to get a look at Betty:* He bid me come and tell you, reverend sir, that he cannot discover no medicine for it in his books.

10   PARRIS: Then he must search on.

11   SUSANNA: Aye, sir, he have been searchin' his books since he left you, sir. But he bid me tell you, that you might look to unnatural things for the cause of it.

12   PARRIS, *his eyes going wide:* No—no. There be no unnatural cause here. Tell him I have sent for Reverend Hale of Beverly, and Mr. Hale will surely confirm that. Let him look to medicine and put out all thought of unnatural causes here. There be none.

13   SUSANNA: Aye, sir. He bid me tell you. *She turns to go.*

14   ABIGAIL: Speak nothin' of it in the village, Susanna.

15   PARRIS: Go directly home and speak nothing of unnatural causes.

16   SUSANNA: Aye, sir. I pray for her. *She goes out.*

17   ABIGAIL: Uncle, the rumor of witchcraft is all about; I think you'd best go down and deny it yourself. The parlor's packed with people, sir. I'll sit with her.

18   PARRIS, *pressed, turns on her:* And what shall I say to them? That my daughter and my niece I discovered dancing like **heathen** in the forest?

19   ABIGAIL: Uncle, we did dance; let you tell them I confessed it—and I'll be whipped if I must be. But they're speaking of witchcraft. Betty's not witched.

20   PARRIS: Abigail, I cannot go before the congregation when I know you have not opened with me. What did you do with her in the forest?

21   ABIGAIL: We did dance, uncle, and when you leaped out of the bush so suddenly, Betty was frightened and then she fainted. And there's the whole of it.

22   PARRIS: Child. Sit you down.

23   ABIGAIL, *quivering, as she sits:* I would never hurt Betty. I love her dearly.

24   PARRIS: Now look you, child, your punishment will come in its time. But if you **trafficked** with spirits in the forest I must know it now, for surely my enemies will, and they will ruin me with it.

25   ABIGAIL: But we never conjured spirits.

NOTES

26   PARRIS: Then why can she not move herself since midnight? This child is desperate! *Abigail lowers her eyes.* It must come out—my enemies will bring it out. Let me know what you done there. Abigail, do you understand that I have many enemies?

27   ABIGAIL: I have heard of it, uncle.

28   PARRIS: There is a faction that is sworn to drive me from my pulpit. Do you understand that?

29   ABIGAIL: I think so, sir.

30   PARRIS: Now then, in the midst of such disruption, my own household is discovered to be the very center of some obscene practice. **Abominations** are done in the forest—

31   ABIGAIL: It were sport, uncle!

32   PARRIS, *pointing at Betty:* You call this sport? She lowers her eyes. *He pleads:* Abigail, if you know something that may help the doctor, for God's sake tell it to me. *She is silent.* I saw Tituba waving her arms over the fire when I came on you. Why was she doing that? And I heard a screeching and gibberish coming from her mouth. She were swaying like a dumb beast over that fire!

33   ABIGAIL: She always sings her Barbados songs, and we dance.

34   PARRIS: I cannot blink what I saw, Abigail, for my enemies will not blink it. I saw a dress lying on the grass.

35   ABIGAIL, *innocently:* A dress?

36   PARRIS—*it is very hard to say:* Aye, a dress. And I thought I saw—someone naked running through the trees!

37   ABIGAIL, *in terror:* No one was naked! You mistake yourself, uncle!

38   PARRIS, *with anger:* I saw it! He moves from her. *Then, resolved:* Now tell me true, Abigail. And I pray you feel the weight of truth upon you, for now my ministry's at stake, my ministry and perhaps your cousin's life. Whatever abomination you have done, give me all of it now, for I dare not be taken unaware when I go before them down there.

39   ABIGAIL: There is nothin' more. I swear it, uncle.

40   PARRIS, *studies her, then nods, half convinced:* Abigail, I have fought here three long years to bend these stiff-necked people to me, and now, just now when some good respect is rising for me in the parish, you compromise my

very character. I have given you a home, child, I have put clothes upon your back—now give me upright answer. Your name in the town—it is entirely white, is it not?

41 ABIGAIL, *with an edge of resentment:* Why, I am sure it is, sir. There be no blush about my name.

42 PARRIS, *to the point:* Abigail, is there any other cause than you have told me, for your being discharged from Goody Proctor's service? I have heard it said, and I tell you as I heard it, that she comes so rarely to the church this year for she will not sit so close to something soiled. What signified that remark?

43 ABIGAIL: She hates me, uncle, she must, for I would not be her slave. It's a bitter woman, a lying, cold, sniveling woman, and I will not work for such a woman!

44 PARRIS: She may be. And yet it has troubled me that you are now seven month out of their house, and in all this time no other family has ever called for your service.

45 ABIGAIL: They want slaves, not such as I. Let them send to Barbados for that. I will not black my face for any of them! *With ill-concealed resentment at him:* Do you begrudge my bed, uncle?

46 PARRIS: No—no.

47 ABIGAIL, *in a temper:* My name is good in the village! I will not have it said my name is soiled! Goody Proctor is a gossiping liar!

48 *Enter Mrs. Ann Putnam. She is a twisted soul of forty-five, a death-ridden woman, haunted by dreams.*

49 PARRIS, *as soon as the door begins to open:* No—no, I cannot have anyone. *He sees her, and a certain deference springs into him, although his worry remains.* Why, Goody Putnam, come in.

50 MRS. PUTNAM, *full of breath, shiny-eyed:* It is a marvel. It is surely a stroke of hell upon you.

51 PARRIS: No, Goody Putnam, it is—

52 MRS. PUTNAM, *glancing at Betty:* How high did she fly, how high?

53 PARRIS: No, no, she never flew—

54 MRS. PUTNAM, *very pleased with it:* Why, it's sure she did. Mr. Collins saw her goin' over Ingersoll's barn, and come down light as bird, he says!

Please note that excerpts and passages in the StudySync® library and this workbook are intended as touchstones to generate interest in an author's work. The excerpts and passages do not substitute for the reading of entire texts, and StudySync® strongly recommends that students seek out and purchase the whole literary or informational work in order to experience it as the author intended. Links to online resellers are available in our digital library. In addition, complete works may be ordered through an authorized reseller by filling out and returning to StudySync® the order form enclosed in this workbook.

Reading & Writing
Companion

19

NOTES

55 PARRIS: Now, look you, Goody Putnam, she never—*Enter Thomas Putnam, a well-to-do, hard-handed landowner, near fifty.* Oh, good morning, Mr. Putnam.

56 PUTNAM: It is a **providence** the thing is out now! It is a providence. *He goes directly to the bed.*

57 PARRIS: What's out, sir, what's—?

58 *Mrs. Putnam goes to the bed.*

59 PUTNAM, *looking down at Betty:* Why, *her* eyes is closed! Look you, Ann.

60 MRS. PUTNAM: Why, that's strange. *To Parris:* Ours is open.

61 PARRIS, *shocked:* Your Ruth is sick?

62 MRS. PUTNAM, *with vicious certainty:* I'd not call it sick; the Devil's touch is heavier than sick. It's death, y'know, it's death drivin' into them, forked and hoofed.

63 PARRIS: Oh, pray not! Why, how does Ruth ail?

64 MRS. PUTNAM: She ails as she must—she never waked this morning, but her eyes open and she walks, and hears naught, sees naught, and cannot eat. Her soul is taken, surely.

65 *Parris is struck.*

66 PUTNAM, *as though for further details:* They say you've sent for Reverend Hale of Beverly?

67 PARRIS, *with dwindling conviction now:* A precaution only. He has much experience in all demonic arts, and I—

68 MRS. PUTNAM: He has indeed; and found a witch in Beverly last year, and let you remember that.

69 PARRIS: Now, Goody Ann, they only thought that were a witch, and I am certain there be no element of witchcraft here.

70 PUTNAM: No witchcraft! Now look you, Mr. Parris—

71 PARRIS: Thomas, Thomas, I pray you, leap not to witchcraft. I know that you—you least of all, Thomas, would ever wish so disastrous a charge laid upon me. We cannot leap to witchcraft. They will howl me out of Salem for such corruption in my house.

72 A word about Thomas Putnam. He was a man with many grievances, at least one of which appears justified. Some time before, his wife's brother-in-law, James Bayley, had been turned down as minister of Salem. Bayley had all the qualifications, and a two-thirds vote into the bargain, but a faction stopped his acceptance, for reasons that are not clear.

73 Thomas Putnam was the eldest son of the richest man in the village. He had fought the Indians at Narragansett, and was deeply interested in parish affairs. He undoubtedly felt it poor payment that the village should so blatantly disregard his candidate for one of its more important offices, especially since he regarded himself as the intellectual superior of most of the people around him.

74 His vindictive nature was demonstrated long before the witchcraft began. A former Salem minister, George Burroughs, had had to borrow money to pay for his wife's funeral, and, since the parish was remiss in his salary, he was soon bankrupt. Thomas and his brother John had Burroughs jailed for debts the man did not owe. The incident is important only in that Burroughs succeeded in becoming minister where Bayley, Thomas Putnam's brother-in-law, had been rejected; the motif of resentment is clear here. Thomas Putnam felt that his own name and the honor of his family had been smirched by the village, and he meant to right matters however he could.

75 Another reason to believe him a deeply embittered man was his attempt to break his father's will, which left a disproportionate amount to a stepbrother. As with every other public cause in which he tried to force his way, he failed in this.

76 So it is not surprising to find that so many accusations against people are in the handwriting of Thomas Putnam, or that his name is so often found as a witness corroborating the supernatural testimony, or that his daughter led the crying-out at the most opportune junctures of the trials, especially when—But we'll speak of that when we come to it.

77 PUTNAM—*at the moment he is intent upon getting Parris, for whom he has only contempt, to move toward the abyss:* Mr. Parris, I have taken your part in all contention here, and I would continue; but I cannot if you hold back in this. There are hurtful, vengeful spirits layin' hands on these children.

78 PARRIS: But, Thomas, you cannot—

79 PUTNAM: Ann! Tell Mr. Parris what you have done.

80 MRS. PUTNAM: Reverend Parris, I have laid seven babies unbaptized in the earth. Believe me, sir, you never saw more hearty babies born. And yet, each would wither in my arms the very night of their birth. I have spoke nothin', but

my heart has clamored intimations. And now, this year, my Ruth, my only—I see her turning strange. A secret child she has become this year, and shrivels like a sucking mouth were pullin' on her life too. And so I thought to send her to your Tituba—

81   PARRIS: To Tituba! What may Tituba—?

82   MRS. PUTNAM: Tituba knows how to speak to the dead, Mr. Parris.

83   PARRIS: Goody Ann, it is a **formidable** sin to conjure up the dead!

84   MRS. PUTNAM: I take it on my soul, but who else may surely tell us what person murdered my babies?

85   PARRIS, *horrified:* Woman!

86   MRS. PUTNAM: They were murdered, Mr. Parris! And mark this proof! Mark it! Last night my Ruth were ever so close to their little spirits; I know it, sir. For how else is she struck dumb now except some power of darkness would stop her mouth? It is a marvelous sign, Mr. Parris!

87   PUTNAM: Don't you understand it, sir? There is a murdering witch among us, bound to keep herself in the dark. *Parris turns to Betty, a frantic terror rising in him.* Let your enemies make of it what they will, you cannot blink it more.

88   PARRIS, *to Abigail:* Then you were conjuring spirits last night.

89   ABIGAIL, *whispering:* Not I, sir—Tituba and Ruth.

90   PARRIS *turns now, with new fear, and goes to Betty, looks down at her, and then, gazing off:* Oh, Abigail, what proper payment for my charity! Now I am undone.

From THE CRUCIBLE by Arthur Miller, copyright 1952, 1953, 1954, renewed (c) 1980, 1981, 1982 by Arthur Miller. Used by permission of Viking Penguin, a division of Penguin Group (USA) LLC.

THINK QUESTIONS

1. What role does Parris play in the community? Use details from the text to explain how this might influence the future action of the story.

2. What is Parris trying to learn from Abigail? Why is he so intent on getting a truthful response? Cite text evidence to support your answer.

3. What do you learn about Ann Putnam's beliefs regarding witchcraft in this excerpt? Cite evidence in the text that supports your answer.

4. What context clues can you identify for the word **trafficked?** What do you think that *trafficked* might mean? Look up the meaning of *trafficked* and compare the dictionary definition with your guess.

5. Identify the word parts that make up the word **abomination.** What context clue can you identify for the word *abomination?* Using word parts and context, what do you think *abomination* might mean?

Please note that excerpts and passages in the StudySync® library and this workbook are intended as touchstones to generate interest in an author's work. The excerpts and passages do not substitute for the reading of entire texts, and StudySync® strongly recommends that students seek out and purchase the whole literary or informational work in order to experience it as the author intended. Links to online resellers are available in our digital library. In addition, complete works may be ordered through an authorized reseller by filling out and returning to StudySync® the order form enclosed in this workbook.

Reading & Writing Companion   **23**

CLOSE READ

Reread the excerpt from *The Crucible*. As you reread, complete the Focus Questions below. Then use your answers and annotations from the questions to help you complete the Writing Prompt.

FOCUS QUESTIONS

1. There are two settings that are relevant to this excerpt—Betty's bedroom and the forest. Highlight textual evidence that provides information about the two settings. Use the annotation tool to explain what each setting represents in terms of religious beliefs.

2. Review Parris's and Abigail's descriptions of what happened in the woods the previous night. How does Parris's description of what he saw differ from Abigail's account? How does this affect the atmosphere of the scene? Highlight textual evidence and make annotations to explain how the textual evidence you've chosen addresses these questions.

3. Why do you think Arthur Miller choose to have Parris and Abigail discuss what happened in the forest the previous night rather than begin the play with the girls in the woods? How does this create uncertainty in the text and why do you think Miller left matters uncertain? Highlight textual evidence and make annotations to explain how the textual evidence you've chosen addresses these questions.

4. Do you think Parris is being paranoid or has good reason to fear that his reputation will be ruined and that he will be driven from his pulpit? Highlight textual evidence and make annotations to explain how the textual evidence you've chosen addresses these questions.

5. What does the reader learn about Thomas Putnam from the historical note that Miller inserted in the middle of the dialogue? How does this background information help support the theme of revenge in the text? Highlight textual evidence and make annotations to explain how the textual evidence you've chosen addresses these questions.

6. What negative aspects of the early American identity are revealed in this scene? Highlight textual evidence that supports your response.

WRITING PROMPT

Explain how the events, the characters, and the setting described in the excerpt contribute to an atmosphere of fear and paranoia. Then tell how this atmosphere relates to the period of McCarthyism in the 1950s, when Miller wrote the play. (During this time, Senator Joseph McCarthy, believing that Communists were hiding even in the U.S. government, held hearings in which people were accused without evidence of being Communists and if thought guilty, fired from their jobs or blacklisted. Through fear and intimidation, some people even felt forced to falsely accuse others of being Communists.)

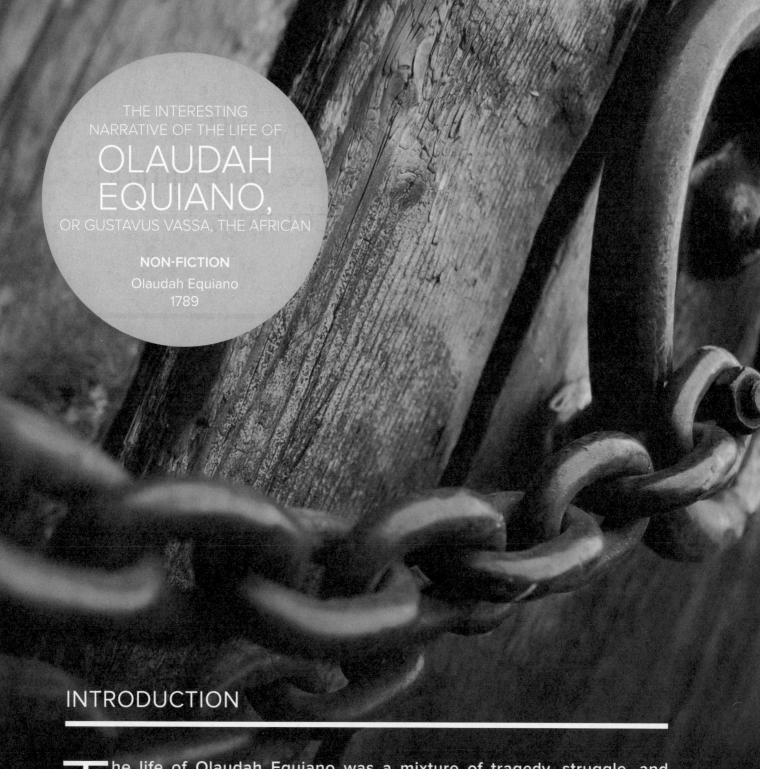

THE INTERESTING
NARRATIVE OF THE LIFE OF
OLAUDAH EQUIANO,
OR GUSTAVUS VASSA, THE AFRICAN

NON-FICTION
Olaudah Equiano
1789

INTRODUCTION

The life of Olaudah Equiano was a mixture of tragedy, struggle, and achievement. When Equiano was eleven, he was kidnapped by slave traders in Africa and forced onto a ship to the Caribbean. What he witnessed while on board the slave ship haunted him for the rest of his life. Eventually, Equiano was able to purchase his freedom and settle in England, where he became an ardent abolitionist. His greatest contribution to the anti-slavery movement was his autobiography, in which he provided graphic and powerful descriptions of the inhumanity he and other slaves suffered.

"I now saw myself deprived of all chance of returning to my native country…"

 FIRST READ

1   The first object which saluted my eyes when I arrived on the coast was the sea, and a slave ship, which was then riding at anchor, and waiting for its cargo. These filled me with astonishment, which was soon converted into terror when I was carried on board. I was immediately handled and tossed up to see if I were sound by some of the crew; and I was now persuaded that I had gotten into a world of bad spirits, and that they were going to kill me.

2   Their complexions too differing so much from ours, their long hair, and the language they spoke, (which was very different from any I had ever heard) united to confirm me in this belief. Indeed such were the horrors of my views and fears at the moment, that, if ten thousand worlds had been my own, I would have freely parted with them all to have exchanged my condition with that of the meanest slave in my own country. When I looked round the ship too and saw a large furnace of copper boiling, and a multitude of black people of every description chained together, every one of their countenances expressing dejection and sorrow, I no longer doubted of my fate; and, quite overpowered with horror and anguish, I fell motionless on the deck and fainted.

3   When I recovered a little I found some black people about me, who I believed were some of those who brought me on board, and had been receiving their pay; they talked to me in order to cheer me, but all in vain. I asked them if we were not to be eaten by those white men with horrible looks, red faces, and loose hair. They told me I was not; and one of the crew brought me a small portion of spirituous liquor in a wine glass; but, being afraid of him, I would not take it out of his hand. One of the blacks therefore took it from him and gave it to me, and I took a little down my palate, which, instead of reviving me, as they thought it would, threw me into the greatest **consternation** at the strange feeling it produced, having never tasted any such liquor before. Soon after this the blacks who brought me on board went off, and left me abandoned to despair.

4   I now saw myself deprived of all chance of returning to my native country, or even the least glimpse of hope of gaining the shore, which I now considered as friendly; and I even wished for my former slavery in preference to my present situation, which was filled with horrors of every kind, still heightened by my ignorance of what I was to undergo. I was not long suffered to indulge my grief; I was soon put down under the decks, and there I received such a salutation in my nostrils as I had never experienced in my life: so that, with the loathsomeness of the stench, and crying together, I became so sick and low that I was not able to eat, nor had I the least desire to taste any thing. I now wished for the last friend, death, to relieve me; but soon, to my grief, two of the white men offered me eatables; and, on my refusing to eat, one of them held me fast by the hands, and laid me across I think the windlass, and tied my feet, while the other flogged me severely. I had never experienced any thing of this kind before; and although, not being used to the water, I naturally feared that element the first time I saw it, yet nevertheless, could I have got over the nettings, I would have jumped over the side, but I could not; and, besides, the crew used to watch us very closely who were not chained down to the decks, lest we should leap into the water: and I have seen some of these poor African prisoners most severely cut for attempting to do so, and hourly whipped for not eating. This indeed was often the case with myself. In a little time after, amongst the poor chained men, I found some of my own nation, which in a small degree gave ease to my mind. I inquired of these what was to be done with us; they gave me to understand we were to be carried to these white people's country to work for them. I then was a little revived, and thought, if it were no worse than working, my situation was not so desperate: but still I feared I should be put to death, the white people looked and acted, as I thought, in so savage a manner; for I had never seen among any people such instances of brutal cruelty; and this not only shewn towards us blacks, but also to some of the whites themselves. One white man in particular I saw, when we were permitted to be on deck, flogged so unmercifully with a large rope near the foremast, that he died in consequence of it; and they tossed him over the side as they would have done a brute. This made me fear these people the more; and I expected nothing less than to be treated in the same manner. I could not help expressing my fears and **apprehensions** to some of my countrymen: I asked them if these people had no country, but lived in this hollow place (the ship): they told me they did not, but came from a distant one. 'Then,' said I, 'how comes it in all our country we never heard of them?' They told me because they lived so very far off. I then asked where were their women? had they any like themselves? I was told they had: 'and why,' said I, 'do we not see them?' they answered, because they were left behind. I asked how the vessel could go? they told me they could not tell; but that there were cloths put upon the masts by the help of the ropes I saw, and then the vessel went on; and the white men had some spell or magic they put in the water when they liked in order to stop the vessel. I was exceedingly amazed at this account, and really thought they were spirits.

Reading & Writing Companion

I therefore wished much to be from amongst them, for I expected they would sacrifice me: but my wishes were vain; for we were so quartered that it was impossible for any of us to make our escape.

5 While we stayed on the coast I was mostly on deck; and one day, to my great astonishment, I saw one of these vessels coming in with the sails up. As soon as the whites saw it, they gave a great shout, at which we were amazed; and the more so as the vessel appeared larger by approaching nearer. At last she came to an anchor in my sight, and when the anchor was let go I and my countrymen who saw it were lost in astonishment to observe the vessel stop; and were not convinced it was done by magic. Soon after this the other ship got her boats out, and they came on board of us, and the people of both ships seemed very glad to see each other. Several of the strangers also shook hands with us black people, and made motions with their hands, signifying I suppose we were to go to their country; but we did not understand them.

6 At last, when the ship we were in had got in all her cargo, they made ready with many fearful noises, and we were all put under deck, so that we could not see how they managed the vessel. But this disappointment was the least of my sorrow. The stench of the hold while we were on the coast was so intolerably **loathsome,** that it was dangerous to remain there for any time, and some of us had been permitted to stay on the deck for the fresh air; but now that the whole ship's cargo were confined together, it became absolutely pestilential. The closeness of the place, and the heat of the climate, added to the number in the ship, which was so crowded that each had scarcely room to turn himself, almost suffocated us. This produced copious perspirations, so that the air soon became unfit for respiration, from a variety of loathsome smells, and brought on a sickness among the slaves, of which many died, thus falling victims to the improvident **avarice,** as I may call it, of their purchasers. This wretched situation was again aggravated by the galling of the chains, now become insupportable; and the filth of the necessary tubs, into which the children often fell, and were almost suffocated. The shrieks of the women, and the groans of the dying, rendered the whole a scene of horror almost inconceivable. Happily perhaps for myself I was soon reduced so low here that it was thought necessary to keep me almost always on deck; and from my extreme youth I was not put in fetters. In this situation I expected every hour to share the fate of my companions, some of whom were almost daily brought upon deck at the point of death, which I began to hope would soon put an end to my miseries. Often did I think many of the inhabitants of the deep much more happy than myself. I envied them the freedom they enjoyed, and as often wished I could change my condition for theirs. Every circumstance I met with served only to render my state more painful, and heighten my apprehensions, and my opinion of the cruelty of the whites.

7　One day they had taken a number of fishes; and when they had killed and satisfied themselves with as many as they thought fit, to our astonishment who were on the deck, rather than give any of them to us to eat as we expected, they tossed the remaining fish into the sea again, although we begged and prayed for some as well as we could, but in vain; and some of my countrymen, being pressed by hunger, took an opportunity, when they thought no one saw them, of trying to get a little privately; but they were discovered, and the attempt procured them some very severe floggings. One day, when we had a smooth sea and moderate wind, two of my wearied countrymen who were chained together (I was near them at the time), preferring death to such a life of misery, somehow made through the nettings and jumped into the sea: immediately another quite dejected fellow, who, on account of his illness, was suffered to be out of irons, also followed their example; and I believe many more would very soon have done the same if they had not been prevented by the ship's crew, who were instantly alarmed. Those of us that were the most active were in a moment put down under the deck, and there was such a noise and confusion amongst the people of the ship as I never heard before, to stop her, and get the boat out to go after the slaves. However two of the wretches were drowned, but they got the other, and afterwards flogged him unmercifully for thus attempting to prefer death to slavery. In this manner we continued to undergo more hardships than I can now relate, hardships which are inseparable from this accursed trade. Many a time we were near suffocation from the want of fresh air, which we were often without for whole days together. This, and the stench of the necessary tubs, carried off many.

8　During our passage I first saw flying fishes, which surprised me very much: they used frequently to fly across the ship, and many of them fell on the deck. I also now first saw the use of the quadrant; I had often with astonishment seen the mariners make observations with it, and I could not think what it meant. They at last took notice of my surprise; and one of them, willing to increase it, as well as to gratify my curiosity, made me one day look through it. The clouds appeared to me to be land, which disappeared as they passed along. This heightened my wonder; and I was now more persuaded than ever that I was in another world, and that every thing about me was magic. At last we came in sight of the island of Barbadoes, at which the whites on board gave a great shout, and made many signs of joy to us. We did not know what to think of this; but as the vessel drew nearer we plainly saw the harbour, and other ships of different kinds and sizes; and we soon anchored amongst them off Bridge Town. Many merchants and planters now came on board, though it was in the evening. They put us in separate parcels, and examined us attentively. They also made us jump, and pointed to the land, signifying we were to go there. We thought by this we should be eaten by these ugly men, as they appeared to us; and, when soon after we were all put down under the deck again, there was much dread and trembling among us, and nothing but bitter cries to be heard all the night from these apprehensions, insomuch that at last the white people got some old slaves from the land to pacify us. They told us we were not to be eaten, but to work, and were soon to go on land, where we should see many of our country people. This report eased us much; and sure enough, soon after we were landed, there came to us Africans of all languages.

9   We were conducted immediately to the merchant's yard, where we were all pent up together like so many sheep in a fold, without regard to sex or age. As every object was new to me every thing I saw filled me with surprise. What struck me first was that the houses were built with stories, and in every other respect different from those in Africa: but I was still more astonished on seeing people on horseback. I did not know what this could mean; and indeed I thought these people were full of nothing but magical arts. While I was in this astonishment one of my fellow prisoners spoke to a countryman of his about the horses, who said they were the same kind they had in their country. I understood them, though they were from a distant part of Africa, and I thought it odd I had not seen any horses there; but afterwards, when I came to converse with different Africans, I found they had many horses amongst them, and much larger than those I then saw.

10   We were not many days in the merchant's custody before we were sold after their usual manner, which is this:—On a signal given, (as the beat of a drum) the buyers rush at once into the yard where the slaves are confined, and make choice of that parcel they like best. The noise and clamour with which this is attended, and the eagerness visible in the countenances of the buyers, serve not a little to increase the apprehensions of the terrified Africans, who may well be supposed to consider them as the ministers of that destruction to which they think themselves devoted. In this manner, without scruple, are relations and friends separated, most of them never to see each other again. I remember in the vessel in which I was brought over, in the men's apartment, there were several brothers, who, in the sale, were sold in different lots; and it was very moving on this occasion to see and hear their cries at parting. O, ye nominal Christians! might not an African ask you, learned you this from your God, who says unto you, Do unto all men as you would men should do unto you? Is it not enough that we are torn from our country and friends to toil for your luxury and lust of gain? Must every tender feeling be likewise sacrificed to your avarice? Are the dearest friends and relations, now rendered more dear by their separation from their kindred, still to be parted from each other, and thus prevented from cheering the gloom of slavery with the small comfort of being together and mingling their sufferings and sorrows? Why are parents to lose their children, brothers their sisters, or husbands their wives? Surely this is a new refinement in cruelty, which, while it has no advantage to **atone** for it, thus aggravates distress, and adds fresh horrors even to the wretchedness of slavery.

THINK QUESTIONS

1. In the 4th paragraph, why might Equiano have included a description of the flogging of a white man? Cite evidence from the text to support your response.

2. In the 3rd paragraph from the end, Equiano describes his fascination with a quadrant, a tool that sailors use to see far away and measure distances. What can you infer about Equiano based on this passage? Does this passage make you feel differently about the slave traders? Provide textual evidence to support your response.

3. How is the last paragraph different from the rest of the narrative? Why do you think Equiano makes this change? Support your answer with evidence from the text.

4. Based on the meaning of the prefix *con-*, would you predict that the vocabulary word *consternation* has a positive or a negative connotation? Look for any context clues that support your response. Then explain how the prefix and the context helped you decide whether the word has a positive or negative connotation.

5. What word parts make up the word *loathsome*? What context clues can help you determine the meaning of the word *loathsome*? (Note that the word *loathsome* appears twice in the 6th paragraph. Look for context clues around both instances of the word.) Explain how using word parts and context clues can help you determine the definition for *loathsome*.

Please note that excerpts and passages in the StudySync® library and this workbook are intended as touchstones to generate interest in an author's work. The excerpts and passages do not substitute for the reading of entire texts, and StudySync® strongly recommends that students seek out and purchase the whole literary or informational work in order to experience it as the author intended. Links to online resellers are available in our digital library. In addition, complete works may be ordered through an authorized reseller by filling out and returning to StudySync® the order form enclosed in this workbook.

Reading & Writing Companion   **31**

CLOSE READ

Reread the excerpt from *The Interesting Narrative of the Life of Olaudah Equiano, or Gustavus Vassa, the African*. As you reread, complete the Focus Questions below. Then use your answers and annotations from the questions to help you complete the Writing Prompt.

FOCUS QUESTIONS

1. Why would Equiano's story have been useful to the cause of abolition? Explain your answer and support it with evidence from the text.

2. Provide an example from the text of an appeal to emotion. How does this appeal help make readers aware of slavery's injustice? Provide examples from the text to support your response.

3. Provide an example from the text of an appeal to shared beliefs and values. How does this appeal help make readers aware of slavery's injustice? Provide examples from the text to support your response.

4. In the final paragraph, why does Equiano tell the story of the two brothers? How is this story an example of the use of rhetoric? How does the story relate to the **rhetorical questions** (questions that are not meant to be answered but asked only to make a point) at the end of the paragraph? Provide evidence from the text to support your response.

5. In the final paragraph, why does Equiano quote the Bible? How does this reference to the Bible support his purpose? How does it connect to other ideas in the paragraph? Do you think this reference is an effective use of rhetoric? Explain your answer, citing evidence from the text to support your response.

6. Reread the final paragraph. What effect does Equiano hope that his narrative will have on shaping the identity of early America? Highlight words, phrases, and sentences that support your response. In your annotations, explain how this textual evidence relates to Equiano's appeal.

WRITING PROMPT

How successful is Equiano in making readers aware of slavery's injustice? Select two examples from the text that you found to be particularly powerful and persuasive. How does each passage reflect Equiano's purpose for writing and his point of view, or his thoughts and feelings, about the events being narrated? How does Equiano's writing style, including his choice of words and his use of rhetoric, contribute to the persuasiveness of the text? Provide textual evidence to support your response.

ON BEING BROUGHT FROM AFRICA TO AMERICA

POETRY
Phillis Wheatley
1773

INTRODUCTION

Seized from her home in West Africa in 1761, when she was about 7 years old, Phillis Wheatley was named after the slave ship that carried her to her new country and eventual owners. Recognizing her intelligence, the Wheatleys taught Phillis to read and write, exposing her to the Bible and classic works of literature. She began writing poetry, and became the first published African-American poet, though at the time many disputed a slave's capacity to write with such sophistication.

"Some view our sable race with scornful eye..."

 FIRST READ

1 'Twas mercy brought me from my **Pagan** land,
2 Taught my **benighted** soul to understand
3 That there's a God, that there's a *Saviour* too:
4 Once I redemption neither sought nor knew.
5 Some view our **sable** race with **scornful** eye,
6 "Their colour is a **diabolic** die."
7 Remember, *Christians*, *Negros*, black as *Cain*,
8 May be refin'd, and join th' angelic train.

 THINK QUESTIONS

1. What is the "*Pagan* land" mentioned in the first line? Tell where in the poem you found the answer.

2. What are the first four lines about? Cite textual evidence to support your answer.

3. What new topic is introduced in the last four lines of the poem? Cite textual evidence to support your answer.

4. Identify and explain how the word parts in the vocabulary word **benighted** can help you determine its meaning. Then identify and explain how to use a context clue in the same line to check your preliminary determination of the word's meaning.

5. Review the last three lines. Identify and explain the context clue for the meaning of the vocabulary word **diabolic**.

CLOSE READ

Reread the poem "On Being Brought from Africa to America." As you reread, complete the Focus Questions below. Then use your answers and annotations from the questions to help you complete the Writing Prompt.

FOCUS QUESTIONS

1. Look at the title of the poem and the poem itself and highlight details that provide information about the speaker of the poem. What do we learn about the speaker's past and present life? Write notes to explain what the evidence you've highlighted reveals about the speaker's identity.

2. Annotate and respond to the final image in the poem. What do you think Wheatley means by the phrase "th' angelic train"?

3. Highlight the words "black as Cain" in the second to last line of the poem. Explain this reference.

4. Highlight the words "diabolic" and "angelic" near the end of the poem. How do these terms relate to one another? What do these terms suggest about how the Africans were viewed? What do they suggest about religion?

5. How does the speaker use religious faith in an argument for racial equality? How might this, in turn, relate to the question of national identity? Highlight textual evidence and note how the evidence you've chosen helps you respond to this question.

WRITING PROMPT

How do the themes of religion and identity develop over the course of the poem and interact or build on one another to produce a complex account? Refer to evidence found in the poem as well as any relevant details from Wheatley's life that might help explain your analysis.

Please note that excerpts and passages in the StudySync® library and this workbook are intended as touchstones to generate interest in an author's work. The excerpts and passages do not substitute for the reading of entire texts, and StudySync® strongly recommends that students seek out and purchase the whole literary or informational work in order to experience it as the author intended. Links to online resellers are available in our digital library. In addition, complete works may be ordered through an authorized reseller by filling out and returning to StudySync® the order form enclosed in this workbook.

Reading & Writing Companion   **35**

ON THE EMIGRATION TO AMERICA AND PEOPLING THE WESTERN COUNTRY

POETRY

Philip Freneau
1785

INTRODUCTION

Philip Freneau was a prolific 18th century American poet and nationalist who is often referred to as the "Poet of the American Revolution." A 1771 graduate of Princeton, Freneau later became the editor of the *National Gazette*, a partisan newspaper promoted by the likes of Thomas Jefferson and James Madison. In this poem, Freneau celebrates America's virtues, and predicts a bright

"What wonders there shall freedom show…"

FIRST READ

1   To western woods, and lonely plains,
2   Palemon from the crowd departs,
3   Where Nature's wildest genius reigns,
4   To tame the soil, and plant the arts—
5   What wonders there shall freedom show,
6   What mighty states successive grow!

7   From Europe's proud, **despotic** shores
8   Hither the stranger takes his way,
9   And in our new found world explores
10 A happier soil, a milder sway,
11 Where no proud despot holds him down,
12 No slaves insult him with a crown.

13 What charming scenes attract the eye,
14 On wild Ohio's savage stream!
15 There Nature reigns, whose works outvie
16 The boldest pattern art can frame;
17 There ages past have rolled away,
18 And forests bloomed but to decay.

19 From these fair plains, these rural seats,
20 So long concealed, so lately known,
21 The unsocial Indian far retreats,
22 To make some other clime his own,
23 When other streams, less pleasing flow,
24 And darker forests round him grow.

25 Great sire of floods! whose varied wave
26 Through climes and countries takes its way,
27 To whom creating Nature gave
28 Ten thousand streams to swell thy sway!
29 No longer shall they useless prove,
30 Nor idly through the forests rove;

31 Nor longer shall your princely flood
32 From distant lakes be swelled in vain,
33 Nor longer through a darksome wood
34 Advance, unnoticed to the main,
35 Far other ends, the heavens decree—
36 And **commerce** plans new freights for thee.

37 While virtue warms the generous breast,
38 There heaven-born freedom shall reside,
39 Nor shall the voice of war molest,
40 Nor Europe's all-aspiring pride—
41 There Reason shall new laws devise,
42 And order from confusion rise.

43 Forsaking kings and regal state,
44 With all their **pomp** and fancied bliss,
45 The traveler owns, convinced though late,
46 No realm so free, so blessed as this—
47 The east is half to slaves **consigned,**
48 Where kings and priests enchain the mind.

49 O come the time, and haste the day,
50 When man shall man no longer crush,
51 When Reason shall enforce her sway,
52 Nor these fair regions raise our blush,
53 Where still the African complains,
54 And mourns his yet unbroken chains.

55 Far brighter scenes a future age,
56 The muse predicts, these states will hail,
57 Whose genius may the world engage,
58 Whose deeds may over death prevail,
59 And happier systems bring to view,
60 Than all the eastern **sages** knew.

THINK QUESTIONS

1. Freneau's poem guides the reader through a journey. Where does the journey begin? Where does the journey take the reader? Provide evidence from the text to support your response.

2. How does the poem portray the "Western Country"? Provide evidence from the text to support your response.

3. How does the poem portray Europe? How does that portrayal differ from the description of America, the Western Country? Provide evidence from the text to support your response.

4. Locate the word **consigned** at the end of the eighth stanza. How do context clues and the appearance of the word *slaves* before it and the word *enchain* in line 48 help you to predict the word's meaning? State what you think the definition of *consigned* might be.

5. Locate the word **pomp** in stanza 8. How do context clues help you to predict the word's meaning? State what you think the definition of *pomp* might be. Then look up the word in a dictionary and explain how the definition relates to the context clues.

Please note that excerpts and passages in the StudySync® library and this workbook are intended as touchstones to generate interest in an author's work. The excerpts and passages do not substitute for the reading of entire texts, and StudySync® strongly recommends that students seek out and purchase the whole literary or informational work in order to experience it as the author intended. Links to online resellers are available in our digital library. In addition, complete works may be ordered through an authorized reseller by filling out and returning to StudySync® the order form enclosed in this workbook.

Reading & Writing Companion **39**

CLOSE READ

Reread the poem "On the Emigration to America and Peopling the Western Country." Then use your answers and annotations from the questions to help you complete the Writing Prompt.

FOCUS QUESTIONS

1. Reread stanza 6. Highlight the reference to "heaven." What is Freneau suggesting by this reference?

2. Recall from the Unit 1 introduction "Early America to 1800" that during the 1700s America came under the influence of the European cultural movement known as the Enlightenment. Enlightenment thinkers emphasized reason and individualism over tradition and believed that human beings possessed certain natural and basic rights that should never be taken away, including the right to freedom. Then reread stanza 7. Highlight any references that reflect Enlightenment ideals. How do these references relate to the Enlightenment? How do they provide a contrast to the ideas underlying European governments?

3. How does this poem describe European government? What words reveal the poet's view of European government? What does the last stanza suggest about the new country and the old system of government? Highlight textual evidence, and write notes to explain how the text you've highlighted helps you answer these questions.

4. Reread the poem, and look for words associated with royalty used to describe the natural landscape in America. Highlight those words, and write notes to explain why Freneau may have decided to use such language to describe nature.

5. Reread stanzas 8 and 9. What irony is described in these stanzas? Highlight textual evidence, and write notes to explain how the text you've highlighted helps you answer this question.

WRITING PROMPT

Write a response in which you compare and contrast the treatment of a similar topic or theme in Philip Freneau's "On the Emigration to America and Peopling the Western Country" and in one of these other selections from this unit: *Of Plymouth Plantation, The Interesting Narrative of the Life of Olaudah Equiano,* or "On Being Brought from Africa to America." Include examples from both texts to support your ideas.

LETTERS TO JOHN ADAMS

NON-FICTION

Abigail Adams
1776

INTRODUCTION

Abigail Adams was known to the world as the loyal wife of John Adams, second president of the United States, but she actively participated in the events of some of the most tumultuous years of the nation, including the American Revolution. Adams wrote about her experiences in a series of letters that have endured over time, her words vibrating with personality. She could be unapologetically opinionated, seeking to enlarge her husband's sense of morality on topics like slavery and women's rights. She sent the letters here to her husband while he was serving as a Massachusetts delegate at the Continental Congresses in Philadelphia.

"I will not despair, but will believe that our cause being good we shall finally prevail."

FIRST READ

Letter to John Adams
September 22, 1774
Boston Garrison, Massachusetts

1   I have just returned from a visit to my Brother, with my Father who carried me there the day before yesterday, and called here in my return to see this much injured Town. I view it with much the same sensations that I should the body of a departed Friend, only put off its present Glory, for to rise finally to a more happy State. I will not despair, but will believe that our cause being good we shall finally prevail. The Maxim 'In time of peace prepare for war' (if this may be called a time of peace) resounds throughout the Country. Next Tuesday they are warned at Braintree all above 15 and under 60 to attend with their arms, and to train once a fortnight from that time, is a Scheme which lays much at heart with many.

2   Scot has arrived, and brings news that he expected to find all peace and Quietness here as he left them at home. You will have more particulars than I am able to send you, from much better hands. There has been in Town a conspiracy of the Negroes. At present it is kept pretty private and was discovered by one who endeavored to dissuade them from it—he being threatened with his life, applied to Justice Quincy for protection. They conducted in this way—got an Irishman to draw up a petition to the Governor telling him they would fight for him provided he would arm them and engage to liberate them if he conquered, and it is said that he attended so much to it as to consult Percy upon it, and one Lieut. Small has been very busy and active. There is but little said, and what Steps they will take in consequence of it I know not. I wish most sincerely there was not a Slave in the province. It always appeared a most **iniquitous** Scheme to me—fight ourselves for what we are daily robbing and **plundering** from those who have as good a right to freedom as we have. You know my mind upon this Subject.

3 I left all our little ones well, and shall return to them to night. I hope to hear from you by the return of the bearer of this and by Revere. I long for the Day of your return, yet look upon you much safer where you are, but know it will not do for you. Not one action has been brought to this court, no business of any sort in your way. All law ceases, and the Gospel will soon follow, for they are supporters of each other. Adieu. My Father hurries me. Yours most sincerely,

Abigail

Letter to John Adams
March 31, 1776
Braintree, Massachusetts

4 The town in general is left in a better state than we expected, more owing to a **precipitate** flight than any regard to the inhabitants, though some individuals discovered a sense of honor and justice and have left the rent of the houses in which they were for the owners and the furniture unhurt, or if damaged sufficient to make it good.

5 Others have committed abominable ravages. The mansion house of your president* is safe and the furniture unhurt, whilst both the house and the furniture of the Solicitor General have fallen a prey to their own merciless party. Surely the very fiends feel a reverential awe for virtue and patriotism, whilst they detest the parricide and traitor.

6 I feel very differently at the approach of spring to which I did a month ago. We knew not then whether we could plant or sow with safety, whether when we had toiled we could reap the fruits of our own industry, whether we should not be driven from the sea coasts to seek shelter in the wilderness, but now we feel as if we might sit under our own vine and eat the good of the land.

7 I feel a *gaiete de coeur* to which before I was a stranger. I think the sun looks brighter, the birds sing more melodiously, and nature put on a more cheerful countenance. We feel a temporary peace, and the poor fugitives are returning to their deserted habitations.

8 Though we felicitate ourselves, we sympathize with those who are trembling lest the lot of Boston should be theirs. But they cannot be in similar circumstances unless pusillanimity [cowardliness] and cowardice should take possession of them. They have time and warning given them to see the evil and shun it.—I long to hear that you have declared an independency—and by the way, in the new Code of Laws which I suppose it will be necessary for you to make, I desire you would remember the ladies, and be more generous and favorable to them than your ancestors. Do not put such unlimited power into

NOTES

Please note that excerpts and passages in the StudySync® library and this workbook are intended as touchstones to generate interest in an author's work. The excerpts and passages do not substitute for the reading of entire texts, and StudySync® strongly recommends that students seek out and purchase the whole literary or informational work in order to experience it as the author intended. Links to online resellers are available in our digital library. In addition, complete works may be ordered through an authorized reseller by filling out and returning to StudySync® the order form enclosed in this workbook.

Reading & Writing
Companion

43

NOTES

the hands of the husbands. Remember, all men would be tyrants if they could. If particular care and attention is not paid to the ladies, we are determined to foment a rebellion, and will not hold ourselves bound by any laws in which we have no voice, or representation.

9   That your sex are naturally tyrannical is truth so thoroughly established as to admit no dispute, but such of you as wish to be happy willingly give up the harsh title of master for the more tender and endearing one of friend. Why, then, not put it out of the power of the vicious and the lawless to use us with cruelty and indignity with **impunity.** Men of sense in all ages abhor those customs which treat us only as the **vassals** of your sex. Regard us then as beings placed by providence under your protection, and in imitation of the Supreme Being, make use of that power only for our happiness.

Abigail

*Referring to John Hancock, president of the Continental Congress. When the British occupied Boston, General William Howe took Hancock's house as his headquarters.

 THINK QUESTIONS

1. At the start of the first letter, how does Abigail Adams describe her feelings about the state of the town? Cite evidence from the text to support your answer.

2. Briefly summarize the "conspiracy" Abigail Adams mentions in the second paragraph of her first letter. Cite evidence from the text to support your answer.

3. In the second letter, what does Abigail Adams ask her husband to do as he works with others to draw up the nation's founding documents? Provide a quotation from the text that supports your response.

4. Use context to determine the meaning of **plundering** as it is used in the letter. Write what you think *plundering* means. Explain how context helped you guess at the meaning.

5. Look up the word **impunity** in a dictionary, and then explain how its word parts reflect its meaning.

CLOSE READ

Reread the text *Letters to John Adams.* As you reread, complete the Focus Questions below. Then use your answers and annotations from the questions to help you complete the Writing Prompt.

 FOCUS QUESTIONS

1. In the first paragraph of the first letter, highlight the passage in which Abigail Adams uses a religious analogy. Explain the meaning of this analogy and how it relates to the cause of the Revolutionary War.

2. Annotate key ideas related to slavery in Adams's first letter. How do her views on colonial freedom relate to the issue of slavery? What specific words does she use to indicate the wrongness of slavery? Why do you think she chose such words?

3. Adams describes a changed mood in Boston at the start of her second letter. Highlight details from the text that relate to that change. Based on your findings, what has caused the shift in mood among the Massachusetts colonists?

4. In the second to last paragraph of the March 31, 1776, letter, Abigail Adams uses the language of the American Revolution to argue for women's rights and representation in government. Highlight some examples of this revolutionary language. Explain how the use of this language might strengthen her argument.

5. Reread the last paragraph. What analogy is Abigail Adams using to describe the relationship between men and women? How does this analogy strengthen her argument for women's rights? Highlight evidence from the text, and explain how the text you've highlighted helps you answer these questions.

WRITING PROMPT

Write a response in which you analyze the rhetoric that Abigail Adams uses to support the opinions she expresses in these letters. Recall that rhetoric is the art of using language to influence others. It can include appeals to logic, emotions, and morality. It might also include rhetorical devices, such as analogies, to strengthen an argument. Remember to use evidence from the text to support your response.

Please note that excerpts and passages in the StudySync® library and this workbook are intended as touchstones to generate interest in an author's work. The excerpts and passages do not substitute for the reading of entire texts, and StudySync® strongly recommends that students seek out and purchase the whole literary or informational work in order to experience it as the author intended. Links to online resellers are available in our digital library. In addition, complete works may be ordered through an authorized reseller by filling out and returning to StudySync® the order form enclosed in this workbook.

Reading & Writing Companion   **45**

THE CRISIS

NON-FICTION
Thomas Paine
1776

INTRODUCTION

I n January 1776, American revolutionary Thomas Paine anonymously published the pamphlet *Common Sense*, arguing in favor of independence from Britain. The pamphlet quickly sold more than 100,000 copies. After that, Paine enlisted in George Washington's army and began to write the first pamphlet of a series of sixteen called *The Crisis*. Washington ordered that the first pamphlet be read aloud at every military campground. In this excerpt from that pamphlet, Paine presents an impassioned argument calling for war against Britain to end British rule in the American colonies.

"What we obtain too cheap, we esteem too lightly: it is dearness only that gives every thing its value."

 FIRST READ

 NOTES

December 23, 1776

1   THESE are the times that try men's souls. The summer soldier and the sunshine patriot will, in this crisis, shrink from the service of their country; but he that stands by it now, deserves the love and thanks of man and woman. Tyranny, like hell, is not easily conquered; yet we have this consolation with us, that the harder the conflict, the more glorious the triumph. What we obtain too cheap, we esteem too lightly: it is dearness only that gives every thing its value. Heaven knows how to put a proper price upon its goods; and it would be strange indeed if so celestial an article as FREEDOM should not be highly rated. Britain, with an army to enforce her tyranny, has declared that she has a right (not only to TAX) but "to BIND us in ALL CASES WHATSOEVER" and if being bound in that manner, is not slavery, then is there not such a thing as slavery upon earth. Even the expression is **impious;** for so unlimited a power can belong only to God.

2   Whether the independence of the continent was declared too soon, or delayed too long, I will not now enter into as an argument; my own simple opinion is, that had it been eight months earlier, it would have been much better. We did not make a proper use of last winter, neither could we, while we were in a dependent state. However, the fault, if it were one, was all our own; we have none to blame but ourselves. But no great deal is lost yet. All that Howe has been doing for this month past, is rather a ravage than a conquest, which the spirit of the Jerseys, a year ago, would have quickly **repulsed,** and which time and a little resolution will soon recover.

3   I have as little superstition in me as any man living, but my secret opinion has ever been, and still is, that God Almighty will not give up a people to military destruction, or leave them unsupportedly to perish, who have so earnestly and so repeatedly sought to avoid the calamities of war, by every decent method which wisdom could invent. Neither have I so much of the **infidel** in

me, as to suppose that He has relinquished the government of the world, and given us up to the care of devils; and as I do not, I cannot see on what grounds the king of Britain can look up to heaven for help against us: a common murderer, a highwayman, or a house-breaker, has as good a pretence as he.

4   'Tis surprising to see how rapidly a panic will sometimes run through a country. All nations and ages have been subject to them. Britain has trembled like an ague at the report of a French fleet of flat-bottomed boats; and in the fourteenth [fifteenth] century the whole English army, after ravaging the kingdom of France, was driven back like men petrified with fear; and this brave exploit was performed by a few broken forces collected and headed by a woman, Joan of Arc. Would that heaven might inspire some Jersey maid to spirit up her countrymen, and save her fair fellow sufferers from ravage and ravishment! Yet panics, in some cases, have their uses; they produce as much good as hurt. Their duration is always short; the mind soon grows through them, and acquires a firmer habit than before. But their peculiar advantage is, that they are the touchstones of sincerity and hypocrisy, and bring things and men to light, which might otherwise have lain forever undiscovered. In fact, they have the same effect on secret traitors, which an imaginary apparition would have upon a private murderer. They sift out the hidden thoughts of man, and hold them up in public to the world. Many a disguised Tory has lately shown his head, that shall **penitentially** solemnize with curses the day on which Howe arrived upon the Delaware.

...

5   I shall conclude this paper with some miscellaneous remarks on the state of our affairs; and shall begin with asking the following question, Why is it that the enemy have left the New England provinces, and made these middle ones the seat of war? The answer is easy: New England is not infested with Tories, and we are. I have been tender in raising the cry against these men, and used numberless arguments to show them their danger, but it will not do to sacrifice a world either to their folly or their baseness. The period is now arrived, in which either they or we must change our sentiments, or one or both must fall. And what is a Tory? Good God! What is he? I should not be afraid to go with a hundred Whigs against a thousand Tories, were they to attempt to get into arms. Every Tory is a coward; for servile, slavish, self-interested fear is the foundation of Toryism; and a man under such influence, though he may be cruel, never can be brave.

...

6   Quitting this class of men, I turn with the warm ardor of a friend to those who have nobly stood, and are yet determined to stand the matter out: I call not upon a few, but upon all: not on this state or that state, but on every state: up

and help us; lay your shoulders to the wheel; better have too much force than too little, when so great an object is at stake. Let it be told to the future world, that in the depth of winter, when nothing but hope and virtue could survive, that the city and the country, alarmed at one common danger, came forth to meet and to repulse it. Say not that thousands are gone, turn out your tens of thousands; throw not the burden of the day upon Providence, but "show your faith by your works," that God may bless you. It matters not where you live, or what rank of life you hold, the evil or the blessing will reach you all. The far and the near, the home counties and the back, the rich and the poor, will suffer or rejoice alike. The heart that feels not now is dead; the blood of his children will curse his cowardice, who shrinks back at a time when a little might have saved the whole, and made them happy. I love the man that can smile in trouble, that can gather strength from distress, and grow brave by reflection. 'Tis the business of little minds to shrink; but he whose heart is firm, and whose conscience approves his conduct, will pursue his principles unto death. My own line of reasoning is to myself as straight and clear as a ray of light. Not all the treasures of the world, so far as I believe, could have induced me to support an **offensive** war, for I think it murder; but if a thief breaks into my house, burns and destroys my property, and kills or threatens to kill me, or those that are in it, and to "bind me in all cases whatsoever" to his absolute will, am I to suffer it? What signifies it to me, whether he who does it is a king or a common man; my countryman or not my countryman; whether it be done by an individual villain, or an army of them? If we reason to the root of things we shall find no difference; neither can any just cause be assigned why we should punish in the one case and pardon in the other. Let them call me rebel and welcome, I feel no concern from it; but I should suffer the misery of devils, were I to make a whore of my soul by swearing allegiance to one whose character is that of a sottish, stupid, stubborn, worthless, brutish man. I conceive likewise a horrid idea in receiving mercy from a being, who at the last day shall be shrieking to the rocks and mountains to cover him, and fleeing with terror from the orphan, the widow, and the slain of America.

THINK QUESTIONS

1. What exactly is the "crisis" to which Paine refers in both the title and the first paragraph of this essay? What is Paine's purpose in writing this essay about the crisis? Use evidence from the text to support your answer.

2. In the third paragraph, what does Paine say about God in terms of this conflict between the colonists and the British? Use evidence from the text to explain your response.

3. In the last paragraph, how does Paine justify going to war? Use evidence from the text to explain your response.

4. The Latin root of **infidel** is *fidelis,* the noun for *faithful*. Combine this information with your knowledge of the prefix *-in* to predict the word's meaning. Then locate the word in the text and use context to determine the word's part of speech and to check your prediction about the word's meaning.

5. Look up the word **offensive** in a dictionary and notice that it's a multiple-meaning word. Then locate the word in the text. Using context clues, explain which meaning is relevant to the text.

CLOSE READ

Reread the text "The Crisis." As you reread, complete the Focus Questions below. Then use your answers and annotations from the questions to help you complete the Writing Prompt.

FOCUS QUESTIONS

1. In paragraph 3, what hyperbole (exaggeration) does Paine use to describe the king, and what is the purpose of this hyperbole? Highlight evidence from the text, and write notes to explain how the text you've highlighted supports your response to this question.

2. An allusion is a reference to a well-known person, event, or text in order to draw comparisons and make a point. Highlight the allusion in paragraph 4. Explain how this allusion is used as a rhetorical device to strengthen Paine's argument.

3. In paragraph 4, what does Thomas Paine say about panics? How does his argument about panics relate to his rhetorical appeal to morality? Highlight evidence from the text, and write notes to explain how the text you've highlighted supports your response to these questions.

4. Reread the last paragraph. What kinds of citizens does Paine criticize? What kinds does he praise? How do these descriptions provide another example of a rhetorical appeal to morality? Highlight evidence from the text, and write notes to explain how the text you've highlighted supports your response to these questions.

5. An analogy is an extended comparison that shows similarities between two things that are otherwise dissimilar. Highlight the analogy in the last paragraph. Explain the analogy and describe what it implies about Enlightenment ideas regarding the natural rights of an individual and how this relates to the role of government.

WRITING PROMPT

What concepts about citizenship and government does Paine's essay present? How do those concepts reflect ideas from the Enlightenment, the cultural movement that influenced American revolutionaries? (Before responding, you may wish to reread the unit introduction "Early America to 1800" in StudySync.) Provide examples from the text to support your response.

THE WHISTLE

NON-FICTION
Benjamin Franklin
1779

INTRODUCTION

B enjamin Franklin (1706-1790) was a scientist, a writer, a publisher, an inventor, a statesman, a musician, a philosopher, and a Founding Father of the United States. A gifted and prolific storyteller, Ben Franklin drew on incidents from his boyhood in Boston to illustrate moral points. Some of his writings are collected in *Poor Richard's Almanack,* a yearly publication Franklin wrote, compiled, and published for over 25 years. The following letter, written to a friend in 1779, contains elements of the humor and integrity that mark Franklin's unique style.

"...the reflection gave me more chagrin than the whistle gave me pleasure."

FIRST READ

1   To Madame Brillon,

2   ...I am charmed with your description of Paradise, and with your plan of living there; and I approve much of your conclusion, that, in the meantime, we should draw all the good we can from this world. In my opinion we might all draw more good from it than we do, and suffer less evil, if we would take care not to give too much for whistles. For to me it seems that most of the unhappy people we meet with are become so by neglect of that caution.

3   You ask what I mean? You love stories, and will excuse my telling one of myself.

4   When I was a child of seven years old, my friends, on a holiday, filled my pocket with coppers. I went directly to a shop where they sold toys for children; and being charmed with the sound of a whistle, that I met by the way in the hands of another boy, I voluntarily offered and gave all my money for one. I then came home, and went whistling all over the house, much pleased with my whistle, but disturbing all the family. My brothers, and sisters, and cousins, understanding the bargain I had made, told me I had given four times as much for it as it was worth; put me in mind what good things I might have bought with the rest of the money; and laughed at me so much for my folly, that I cried with **vexation;** and the reflection gave me more **chagrin** than the whistle gave me pleasure.

5   This, however, was afterwards of use to me, the impression continuing on my mind; so that often, when I was tempted to buy some unnecessary thing, I said to myself, Don't give too much for the whistle; and I saved my money.

6   As I grew up, came into the world, and observed the actions of men, I thought I met with many, very many, who gave too much for the whistle.

7   When I saw one too ambitious of court favor, sacrificing his time in attendance on levees, his repose, his liberty, his virtue, and perhaps his friends, to attain it, I have said to myself, this man gives too much for his whistle.

8   When I saw another fond of popularity, constantly employing himself in political bustles, neglecting his own affairs, and ruining them by that neglect, "He pays, indeed," said I, "too much for his whistle."

9   If I knew a miser, who gave up every kind of comfortable living, all the pleasure of doing good to others, all the esteem of his fellow-citizens, and the joys of **benevolent** friendship, for the sake of accumulating wealth, "Poor man," said I, "you pay too much for your whistle."

10 When I met with a man of pleasure, sacrificing every **laudable** improvement of the mind, or of his fortune, to mere **corporeal** sensations, and ruining his health in their pursuit, "Mistaken man," said I, "you are providing pain for yourself, instead of pleasure; you give too much for your whistle."

11 If I see one fond of appearance, or fine clothes, fine houses, fine furniture, fine equipages, all above his fortune, for which he contracts debts, and ends his career in a prison, "Alas!" say I, "he has paid dear, very dear, for his whistle."

12 When I see a beautiful sweet-tempered girl married to an ill-natured brute of a husband, "What a pity," say I, "that she should pay so much for a whistle!"

13 In short, I conceive that great part of the miseries of mankind are brought upon them by the false estimates they have made of the value of things, and by their giving too much for their whistles.

14 Yet I ought to have charity for these unhappy people, when I consider that, with all this wisdom of which I am boasting, there are certain things in the world so tempting, for example, the apples of King John, which happily are not to be bought; for if they were put to sale by auction, I might very easily be led to ruin myself in the purchase, and find that I had once more given too much for the whistle.

15 Adieu, my dear friend, and believe me ever yours very sincerely and with unalterable affection.

THINK QUESTIONS

1. In the first paragraph, what does Franklin identify as his central idea? How do you know that Franklin intended to initially puzzle the reader? What do you think was his purpose in structuring the opening paragraph this way? Use evidence from the text to support your response.

2. What childhood event upset Franklin so much that he "cried with vexation"? Use specific details from the text to support your answer.

3. How does Franklin connect the characters of the miser, the man of pleasure, and the man who is fond of appearance? Refer to evidence in the text to support your response.

4. Explain how you can use context to predict the meaning of word **chagrin**.

5. Consider that the root of the word **corporeal** is the Latin word *corpus,* which means "body." How can you use this knowledge and context clues to help you guess at the meaning of the word *corporeal*?

CLOSE READ

Reread the excerpt from the text "The Whistle." As you reread, complete the Focus Questions below. Then use your answers and annotations from the questions to help you complete the Writing Prompt.

FOCUS QUESTIONS

1. Look back over the full text of the letter. Where does Franklin utilize repetition about "the whistle" in his letter? Highlight examples of words or phrases that are repeated. What conclusion can you draw about the structure of Franklin's paragraphs? Do you find this repetition effective? Explain how the passages you've highlighted help you respond to these questions.

2. Reread the sections about the people who have "paid too much for their whistles." Do you sense a pattern in how Franklin describes them? What effect does the internal structure of these paragraphs have on the reader? Highlight evidence from the text. Explain how the passages you've highlighted help you respond to these questions.

3. **Parallelism** is the use of a series of words, phrases, or sentences that have similar grammatical structure. Parallelism shows the relationship between ideas and helps emphasize certain points. Highlight examples of grammatical parallelism in the sentences that Franklin uses to describe people who have "paid too much for their whistles." Explain how these examples of parallelism help to emphasize Franklin's points.

4. Why does Franklin bring up "the apples of King John" in the paragraph before the closing? How does this paragraph provide an extension of the lesson taught in the letter? Highlight evidence from the text. Explain how the passages you've highlighted help you respond to these questions.

5. Franklin's letter gives examples of people who are driven by ambition, seek popularity, value saving money, enjoy sensual pleasures, and appreciate the finer things in life. Is Franklin implying that these things are always detrimental and should be avoided? If not, what point is he exactly trying to express? Highlight evidence from the text. Explain how the passages you've highlighted help you respond to these questions.

WRITING PROMPT

Do you think that Benjamin Franklin's advice is still relevant today? Imagine that you are writing a letter to an advice columnist about a time you "paid too much for a whistle." Write a letter, telling your personal story and asking for advice. Then respond to the letter as if you were the advice columnist. Provide advice consistent with the lesson expressed in "The Whistle." Structure your response so that it is clear, convincing, and engaging and respectful of the advice seeker.

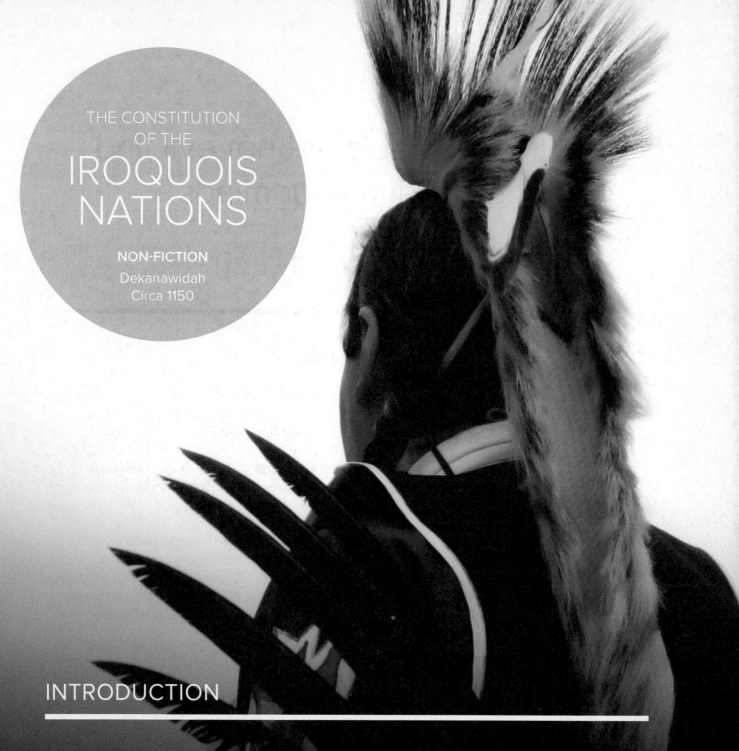

THE CONSTITUTION OF THE IROQUOIS NATIONS

NON-FICTION
Dekanawidah
Circa 1150

INTRODUCTION

According to tradition, when the Iroquois tribes in present-day New York state were torn apart by fighting, Dekanawidah stepped in to instill peace and unite the Iroquois nation. The oral constitution that followed represented an alliance among five tribes: the Seneca, Cayuga, Oneida, Onondaga, and Mohawk; a sixth tribe—the Tuscarora—later joined the union. Most historians believe that the democratic ideals of the Iroquois Constitution inspired the framers of the U.S. Constitution. The excerpt here includes about a dozen of the 117 total articles.

"United people, let not evil find lodging in your minds."

FIRST READ

The Great Binding Law, Gayanashagowa

1   1. I am Dekanawidah and with the Five Nations' Confederate Lords I plant the Tree of Great Peace. I plant it in your territory, Adodarhoh, and the Onondaga Nation, in the territory of you who are Firekeepers.

2   I name the tree the Tree of the Great Long Leaves. Under the shade of this Tree of the Great Peace we spread the soft white feathery down of the globe thistle as seats for you, Adodarhoh, and your cousin Lords.

3   We place you upon those seats, spread soft with the feathery down of the globe thistle, there beneath the shade of the spreading branches of the Tree of Peace. There shall you sit and watch the Council Fire of the **Confederacy** of the Five Nations, and all the affairs of the Five Nations shall be transacted at this place before you, Adodarhoh, and your cousin Lords, by the Confederate Lords of the Five Nations.

4   2. Roots have spread out from the Tree of the Great Peace, one to the north, one to the east, one to the south and one to the west. The name of these roots is The Great White Roots and their nature is Peace and Strength.

5   If any man or any nation outside the Five Nations shall obey the laws of the Great Peace and make known their disposition to the Lords of the Confederacy, they may trace the Roots to the Tree and if their minds are clean and they are obedient and promise to obey the wishes of the Confederate Council, they shall be welcomed to take shelter beneath the Tree of the Long Leaves. We place at the top of the Tree of the Long Leaves an Eagle who is able to see afar. If he sees in the distance any evil approaching or any danger threatening he will at once warn the people of the Confederacy.

6   10. In all cases the procedure must be as follows: when the Mohawk and Seneca Lords have **unanimously** agreed upon a question, they shall report their decision to the Cayuga and Oneida Lords who shall deliberate upon the question and report a unanimous decision to the Mohawk Lords. The Mohawk Lords will then report the standing of the case to the Firekeepers, who shall render a decision as they see fit in case of a disagreement by the two bodies, or confirm the decisions of the two bodies if they are identical. The Fire Keepers shall then report their decision to the Mohawk Lords who shall announce it to the open council.

7   11. If through any misunderstanding or **obstinacy** on the part of the Fire Keepers, they render a decision at variance with that of the Two Sides, the Two Sides shall reconsider the matter and if their decisions are jointly the same as before they shall report to the Fire Keepers who are then compelled to confirm their joint decision.

Rights, Duties and Qualifications of Lords

8   19. If at any time it shall be manifest that a Confederate Lord has not in mind the welfare of the people or disobeys the rules of this Great Law, the men or women of the Confederacy, or both jointly, shall come to the Council and **upbraid** the erring Lord through his War Chief. If the complaint of the people through the War Chief is not heeded the first time it shall be uttered again and then if no attention is given a third complaint and warning shall be given. If the Lord is contumacious the matter shall go to the council of War Chiefs. The War Chiefs shall then divest the erring Lord of his title by order of the women in whom the titleship is vested. When the Lord is **deposed** the women shall notify the Confederate Lords through their War Chief, and the Confederate Lords shall sanction the act. The women will then select another of their sons as a candidate and the Lords shall elect him. Then shall the chosen one be installed by the Installation Ceremony. When a Lord is to be deposed, his War Chief shall address him as follows:

9   "So you, _____, disregard and set at naught the warnings of your women relatives. So you fling the warnings over your shoulder to cast them behind you. "Behold the brightness of the Sun and in the brightness of the Sun's light I depose you of your title and remove the sacred emblem of your Lordship title. I remove from your brow the deer's antlers, which was the emblem of your position and token of your nobility. I now depose you and return the antlers to the women whose heritage they are."

10   25. If a Lord of the Confederacy should seek to establish any authority independent of the jurisdiction of the Confederacy of the Great Peace, which is the Five Nations, he shall be warned three times in open council, first by the women relatives, second by the men relatives and finally by the Lords of the

Please note that excerpts and passages in the StudySync® library and this workbook are intended as touchstones to generate interest in an author's work. The excerpts and passages do not substitute for the reading of entire texts, and StudySync® strongly recommends that students seek out and purchase the whole literary or informational work in order to experience it as the author intended. Links to online resellers are available in our digital library. In addition, complete works may be ordered through an authorized reseller by filling out and returning to StudySync® the order form enclosed in this workbook.

Reading & Writing Companion   **59**

Confederacy of the Nation to which he belongs. If the offending Lord is still obdurate he shall be dismissed by the War Chief of his nation for refusing to conform to the laws of the Great Peace. His nation shall then install the candidate nominated by the female name holders of his family.

11   26. It shall be the duty of all of the Five Nations Confederate Lords, from time to time as occasion demands, to act as mentors and spiritual guides of their people and remind them of their Creator's will and words. They shall say:

12   "Hearken, that peace may continue unto future days! "Always listen to the words of the Great Creator, for he has spoken. "United people, let not evil find lodging in your minds. "For the Great Creator has spoken and the cause of Peace shall not become old. "The cause of peace shall not die if you remember the Great Creator."

13   Every Confederate Lord shall speak words such as these to promote peace.

14   27. All Lords of the Five Nations Confederacy must be honest in all things. They must not idle or gossip, but be men possessing those honorable qualities that make true royaneh. It shall be a serious wrong for anyone to lead a Lord into trivial affairs, for the people must ever hold their Lords high in estimation out of respect to their honorable positions.

Names, Duties and Rights of War Chiefs

15   37. There shall be one War Chief for each Nation and their duties shall be to carry messages for their Lords and to take up the arms of war in case of emergency. They shall not participate in the proceedings of the Confederate Council but shall watch its progress and in case of an erroneous action by a Lord they shall receive the complaints of the people and convey the warnings of the women to him. The people who wish to convey messages to the Lords in the Confederate Council shall do so through the War Chief of their Nation. It shall ever be his duty to lay the cases, questions and propositions of the people before the Confederate Council.

Official Symbolism

16   57. Five arrows shall be bound together very strong and each arrow shall represent one nation. As the five arrows are strongly bound this shall symbolize the complete union of the nations. Thus are the Five Nations united completely and enfolded together, united into one head, one body and one mind. Therefore they shall labor, legislate and council together for the interest of future generations. The Lords of the Confederacy shall eat together from one bowl the feast of cooked beaver's tail. While they are eating they are to use no sharp utensils for if they should they might accidentally cut one

another and bloodshed would follow. All measures must be taken to prevent the spilling of blood in any way.

Religious Ceremonies Protected

17   99. The rites and festivals of each nation shall remain undisturbed and shall continue as before because they were given by the people of old times as useful and necessary for the good of men.

 THINK QUESTIONS

1. Do you think that the "Tree of the Great Peace" is real or symbolic or some combination? Support your interpretation with evidence from the text.

2. According to Articles 1 and 10, how did the role of the Onondaga people differ from the roles of the other four tribes of the Iroquois nation? Provide details from the text to support your answer.

3. What does the bundle of arrows in Article 57 symbolize? What does this symbolism suggest is the main purpose of the Iroquois Constitution? Provide details from the text to support your answer.

4. Use context to determine the meaning of the word **upbraid** as it is used in "The Constitution of the Iroquois Nations." Write your definition of *upbraid* here and tell how you got it.

5. Consider the usage of the word *unanimously* within the text in Article 10. Do you think that the initial letters *un* in *unanimously* refer to the Latin prefix for "one" (as in *unicycle*) or "not" (as in *uncooperative*)? How does the context support your answer?

CLOSE READ

Reread the excerpt from *The Constitution of the Iroquois Nations*. As you reread, complete the Focus Questions below. Then use your answers and annotations from the questions to help you complete the Writing Prompt.

FOCUS QUESTIONS

1. Search online for a map of the five Iroquois nations. How do you think their geographic locations influenced the decisions and procedures outlined in Articles 1 and 10? What does this suggest about the ideas underlying the Iroquois Constitution? Highlight evidence in the text, and explain how that evidence helps you respond to these questions.

2. How does the word *confederacy* relate to one of the central ideas of the Iroquois Constitution? Highlight evidence in the text, and explain how that evidence helps you respond to this question.

3. Why do you think the Constitution of the Iroquois Nations includes scripts for leaders to say aloud in certain situations? What does this suggest about how the Iroquois wished to handle certain situations? Highlight evidence in the text, and explain how that evidence helps you respond to these questions.

4. Highlight the following related words in the text: *obstinacy, contumacious,* and *obdurate.* How do these words relate back to one of the central ideas of the articles? Write notes to explain your response.

5. What were important leadership qualities in the Confederacy? How do the ideas presented about leadership interact with and build on another main idea in the articles to produce a complex account? Highlight evidence in the text, and explain how that evidence helps you respond to these questions.

6. Reflect on the entire reading selection. Which section of the Constitution of the Iroquois Nation reminded you most of ideas that would eventually shape the early American identity? Highlight evidence in the text and, in your annotation notes, explain how that evidence has influenced your response to this question. As part of your response, summarize the chosen section in your own words.

WRITING PROMPT

The introduction notes that some historians claim a connection between the Constitution of the Iroquois Nations and the representative government of the United States of America. Based on what you have read, do you agree or disagree with this claim? To support your response, compare what you know about the U.S. government to details and information from the text. Cite specific instances in which the central ideas of both governments are either similar or different.

THE DECLARATION OF INDEPENDENCE

NON-FICTION

Thomas Jefferson

1776

INTRODUCTION

On June 11, 1776, the delegates of the Second Continental Congress had appointed a five-member committee to draft a statement declaring independence from Britain. The committee included Benjamin Franklin, John Adams, and Thomas Jefferson, and Jefferson was called upon to do the writing. Some of his ideas were not new. According to English political philosopher John Locke's theory of "natural law," which Jefferson had studied, human beings are "by nature free, equal and independent." Following Locke, Jefferson stressed that the American Revolution was a struggle for the rights of all people.

"We hold these truths to be self-evident, that all men are created equal..."

FIRST READ

In Congress, July 4, 1776
The unanimous Declaration of the thirteen united States of America

1   When in the Course of human events, it becomes necessary for one people to dissolve the political bands which have connected them with another, and to assume, among the Powers of the earth, the separate and equal station to which the Laws of Nature and of Nature's God entitle them, a decent respect to the opinions of mankind requires that they should declare the causes which impel them to the separation.

2   We hold these truths to be self-evident, that all men are created equal, that they are endowed by their Creator with certain unalienable Rights, that among these are Life, Liberty, and the pursuit of Happiness.—That to secure these rights, Governments are instituted among Men, deriving their just powers from the consent of the governed,—That whenever any Form of Government becomes destructive of these ends, it is the Right of the People to alter or to abolish it, and to institute new Government, laying its foundation on such principles and organizing its powers in such form, as to them shall seem most likely to effect their Safety and Happiness. **Prudence,** indeed, will dictate that Governments long established should not be changed for light and transient causes; and accordingly all experience hath shown, that mankind are more disposed to suffer, while evils are sufferable, than to right themselves by abolishing the forms to which they are accustomed. But when a long train of abuses and usurpations, pursuing invariably the same Object evinces a design to reduce them under absolute Despotism, it is their right, it is their duty, to throw off such Government, and to provide new Guards for their future security.—Such has been the patient sufferance of these Colonies; and such is now the necessity which constrains them to alter their former Systems of Government. The history of the present King of Great Britain is a history of repeated injuries and usurpations, all having in direct object the

establishment of an absolute Tyranny over these States. To prove this, let Facts be submitted to a candid world.

3   He has refused his Assent to Laws, the most wholesome and necessary for the public good.

4   He has forbidden his Governors to pass Laws of immediate and pressing importance, unless suspended in their operation till his Assent should be obtained; and when so suspended, he has utterly neglected to attend to them.

5   He has refused to pass other Laws for the accommodation of large districts of people, unless those people would relinquish the right of Representation in the Legislature, a right inestimable to them and formidable to tyrants only.

6   He has called together legislative bodies at places unusual, uncomfortable, and distant from the depository of their Public Records, for the sole purpose of fatiguing them into compliance with his measures.

7   He has dissolved Representative Houses repeatedly, for opposing with manly firmness his invasions on the rights of the people.

8   He has refused for a long time, after such dissolutions, to cause others to be elected; whereby the Legislative Powers, incapable of Annihilation, have returned to the People at large for their exercise; the State remaining in the mean time exposed to all the dangers of invasion from without, and convulsions within.

9   He has endeavoured to prevent the population of these States; for that purpose obstructing the Laws of Naturalization of Foreigners; refusing to pass others to encourage their migration hither, and raising the conditions of new Appropriations of Lands.

10 He has obstructed the Administration of Justice, by refusing his Assent to Laws for establishing Judiciary Powers.

11 He has made judges dependent on his Will alone, for the tenure of their offices, and the amount and payment of their salaries.

12 He has erected a multitude of New Offices, and sent hither swarms of Officers to harass our People, and eat out their substance.

13 He has kept among us, in times of peace, Standing Armies without the Consent of our legislatures.

14 He has affected to render the Military independent of and superior to the Civil Power.

15 He has combined with others to subject us to a jurisdiction foreign to our constitution, and unacknowledged by our laws; giving his Assent to their Acts of pretended legislation:

16 For quartering large bodies of armed troops among us:

17 For protecting them, by a mock Trial, from Punishment for any Murders which they should commit on the Inhabitants of these States:

18 For cutting off our Trade with all parts of the world:

19 For imposing taxes on us without our Consent:

20 For depriving us, in many cases, of the benefits of Trial by Jury:

21 For transporting us beyond Seas to be tried for pretended offences:

22 For abolishing the free System of English Laws in a neighbouring Province, establishing therein an Arbitrary government, and enlarging its Boundaries so as to render it at once an example and fit instrument for introducing the same absolute rule into these Colonies:

23 For taking away our Charters, abolishing our most valuable Laws, and altering fundamentally the Forms of our Governments:

24 For suspending our own Legislatures and declaring themselves invested with Power to legislate for us in all cases whatsoever.

25 He has abdicated Government here, by declaring us out of his Protection and waging War against us.

26 He has plundered our seas, ravaged our Coasts, burnt our towns, and destroyed the lives of our people.

27 He is at this time transporting large armies of foreign mercenaries to complete the works of death, desolation and tyranny, already begun with circumstances of Cruelty & **perfidy** scarcely paralleled in the most barbarous ages, and totally unworthy of the Head of a civilized nation.

28 He has constrained our fellow Citizens taken Captive on the high Seas to bear Arms against their Country, to become the executioners of their friends and Brethren, or to fall themselves by their Hands.

29   He has excited domestic insurrections amongst us, and has endeavoured to bring on the inhabitants of our frontiers, the merciless Indian Savages, whose known rule of warfare is an undistinguished destruction of all ages, sexes and conditions.

30   In every stage of these Oppressions We have Petitioned for Redress in the most humble terms: Our repeated Petitions have been answered only by repeated injury. A Prince, whose character is thus marked by every act which may define a Tyrant, is unfit to be the ruler of a free People.

31   Nor have We been wanting in attention to our British brethren. We have warned them from time to time of attempts by their legislature to extend an unwarrantable jurisdiction over us. We have reminded them of the circumstances of our emigration and settlement here. We have appealed to their native justice and magnanimity, and we have conjured them by the ties of our common kindred to disavow these usurpations, which would inevitably interrupt our connections and correspondence. They too have been deaf to the voice of justice and of **consanguinity.** We must, therefore, **acquiesce** in the necessity, which denounces our Separation, and hold them, as we hold the rest of mankind, Enemies in War, in Peace Friends.

32   We, therefore, the Representatives of the United States of America, in General Congress, Assembled, appealing to the Supreme Judge of the world for the **rectitude** of our intentions, do, in the Name, and by the Authority of the good People of these Colonies, solemnly publish and declare, That these United Colonies are, and of Right ought to be Free and Independent States; that they are Absolved from all Allegiance to the British Crown, and that all political connection between them and the State of Great Britain, is and ought to be totally dissolved; and that as Free and Independent States, they have full Power to levy War, conclude Peace, contract Alliances, establish Commerce, and to do all other Acts and Things which Independent States may of right do. And for the support of this Declaration, with a firm reliance on the Protection of Divine Providence, we mutually pledge to each other our Lives, our Fortunes and our sacred Honor.

THINK QUESTIONS

1. According to the first paragraph, what is the purpose of the Declaration of Independence beyond simply claiming freedom from British rule? Identify the phrase that states this purpose most clearly and relate it to the rest of the document.

2. In paragraph 2, what does Jefferson say about the treatment of the colonists under the King of Great Britain? According to Jefferson, what justifies a revolt against the existing government? Use evidence from the text to support your response.

3. Where in the document does Jefferson officially declare independence and how does he define independence for the states? Use evidence from the text to support your response.

4. Consider the Latin root of the word **consanguinity:** *sanguis,* which means "blood." Combine this with the knowledge that the prefix *con-* means "with" to come up with a reasonable definition of the word in the context of this document. Can you find any supporting evidence of your definition within the same paragraph?

5. Consider the meaning of the Latin root *rect-:* "right" or "straight." Use what you know about word roots and affixes to come up with a definition for the word **rectitude.** Then check your prediction of the word's meaning in context. What other words can be made from this Latin root?

CLOSE READ

Reread the excerpt from "The Declaration of Independence." As you reread, complete the Focus Questions below. Then use your answers and annotations from the questions to help you complete the Writing Prompt.

 FOCUS QUESTIONS

1. Highlight words and phrases in the second paragraph that relate to government. How might Thomas Jefferson define the ideal form of government? Write notes about the textual evidence to explain your response to this question.

2. The rhetorical device of **anaphora** involves the repetition of words at the beginning of a series of sentences. Highlight examples of anaphora in Jefferson's list of grievances. What is the overall effect of this long listing of grievances? Write notes to explain your response to these questions.

3. Why did Jefferson present such a long list of grievances? Highlight a statement of purpose in the second paragraph that might explain why Jefferson included such a long list. Write a note to explain your answer to this question.

4. Highlight examples in the document of appeals to emotion. Write notes to explain how these appeals help support Jefferson's argument.

5. Reread the last paragraph. Highlight any references that represent an appeal to ethics. Write notes to explain how these references support Jefferson's argument.

6. Reread the final paragraph again. What words and phrases does Jefferson use to describe the newly declared country? Highlight the relevant textual evidence and write notes that explain how the highlighted text relates to America's identity as a new nation in the late 1700s.

WRITING PROMPT

Write an essay about The Declaration of Independence in which you explain how the document reflects ideas from the Enlightenment. Then analyze the rhetorical appeals and rhetorical devices that are used to support these ideas. Before you write your response, you may wish to reread the unit introduction "Early America to 1800."

FOUNDING DOCUMENTS
OF THE UNITED STATES OF AMERICA

NON-FICTION
Thomas Jefferson and
Gouverneur Morris, et al.
1776 and 1787

INTRODUCTION

The Founding Fathers of the United States used both words and weapons to create a nation. Pamphlets such as *The Crisis* and *Common Sense*, and documents such as *The Federalist Papers*, helped to drive public opinion around the time of the Revolutionary War. The most important of these documents are the Declaration of Independence, The Constitution of the United States of America, and the Bill of Rights (the first ten amendments to the United States Constitution). These documents set forth the reasoning behind the American Colonists' decision to revolt against the King of England and British rule and provided the basis of how they intended to form their new government. Carefully, they defined and established how that government would function—what it could

"We, the People of the United States..."

FIRST READ

IN CONGRESS, July 4, 1776.

1   The unanimous Declaration of the thirteen united States of America,

2   When in the Course of human events, it becomes necessary for one people to dissolve the political bands which have connected them with another, and to assume among the powers of the earth, the separate and equal station to which the Laws of Nature and of Nature's God entitle them, a decent respect to the opinions of mankind requires that they should declare the causes which impel them to the separation.

3   We hold these truths to be self-evident, that all men are created equal, that they are endowed by their Creator with certain **unalienable** Rights, that among these are Life, Liberty and the pursuit of Happiness.—That to secure these rights, Governments are instituted among Men, deriving their just powers from the consent of the governed,—That whenever any Form of Government becomes destructive of these ends, it is the Right of the People to alter or to abolish it, and to institute new Government, laying its foundation on such principles and organizing its powers in such form, as to them shall seem most likely to effect their Safety and Happiness.

Preamble to the United States Constitution and First Ten Amendments (The Bill of Rights) 1787–1791.

4   Preamble:
We, the People of the United States, in Order to form a more perfect Union, establish Justice, insure domestic **Tranquility,** provide for the common defence, promote the general Welfare, and secure the Blessings of Liberty to ourselves and our **Posterity,** do ordain and establish this Constitution of the United States of America.

5   Amendment I:

Congress shall make no law respecting the establishment of religion, or prohibiting the free exercise thereof; or abridging the freedom of speech, or of the press; or the right of people peaceably to assemble, and to petition the Government for a **redress** of grievances.

6   Amendment II:

A well regulated Militia, being necessary to the security of a free State, the right of the people to keep and bear Arms, shall not be infringed.

7   Amendment III:

No Soldier shall, in time of peace be quartered in any house, without the consent of the Owner, nor in time of war, but in a manner to be prescribed by law.

8   Amendment IV:

The right of the people to be secure in their persons, houses, papers, and effects, against unreasonable searches and seizures, shall not be violated, and no Warrants shall issue, but upon probable cause, supported by Oath or affirmation, and particularly describing the place to be searched, and the persons or things to be seized.

9   Amendment V:

No person shall be held to answer for a capital, or otherwise infamous crime, unless on a presentment or indictment of a Grand Jury, except in cases arising in the land or naval forces, or in the Militia, when in actual service in time of War or public danger; nor shall any person be subject for the same offence to be twice put in jeopardy of life or limb; nor shall be compelled in any criminal case to be a witness against himself, nor be deprived of life, liberty, or property, without due process of law; nor shall private property be taken for public use, without just compensation.

10   Amendment VI:

In all criminal prosecutions, the accused shall enjoy the right to a speedy and public trial, by an impartial jury of the State and district wherein the crime shall have been committed, which district shall have been previously ascertained by law, and to be informed of the nature and cause of the accusation; to be confronted with the witnesses against him; to have compulsory process for obtaining witnesses in his favor, and to have the Assistance of Counsel for his defence.

11   Amendment VII:

In Suits at common law, where the value in controversy shall exceed twenty dollars, the right of trial by jury shall be preserved, and no fact tried by a jury, shall be otherwise re-examined in any Court of the United States, than according to the rules of the common law.

12 Amendment VIII:

Excessive bail shall not be required, nor excessive fines imposed, nor cruel and unusual punishments inflicted.

13 Amendment IX:

The enumeration in the Constitution, of certain rights, shall not be construed to deny or disparage others retained by the people.

14 Amendment X:

The powers not delegated to the United States by the Constitution, nor prohibited by it to the States, are reserved to the States respectively, or to the people.

 THINK QUESTIONS

1. According to the Declaration of Independence, what are the natural rights that belong to citizens? What is the government's role in protecting these rights?

2. Identify the use of parallelism in the Preamble. What is effect of this example of parallelism?

3. Identify a central theme or idea that is common in all three excerpts. Cite evidence from the text to support your response.

4. Look at the word **preamble.** How does the prefix *pre-* relate to the context in which this word is used?

5. Explain how you can use context to guess at the meaning of the word **redress.**

Please note that excerpts and passages in the StudySync® library and this workbook are intended as touchstones to generate interest in an author's work. The excerpts and passages do not substitute for the reading of entire texts, and StudySync® strongly recommends that students seek out and purchase the whole literary or informational work in order to experience it as the author intended. Links to online resellers are available in our digital library. In addition, complete works may be ordered through an authorized reseller by filling out and returning to StudySync® the order form enclosed in this workbook.

Reading & Writing Companion **73**

CLOSE READ

Reread the excerpts from "Founding Documents of the United States of America." As you reread, complete the Focus Questions below. Then use your answers and annotations from the questions to help you complete the Writing Prompt.

FOCUS QUESTIONS

1. Highlight three individual words in the text that you think help to support the central ideas of the text. Write notes to explain why you selected those words.

2. Reread the first amendment of the Bill of Rights. How does it reflect the idea that governments should not be all powerful but derive their power from the people? Highlight details in the text that support your answer, and write a note to support your response.

3. Reread the fifth amendment. How does it reflect ideas from The Declaration of Independence or the Preamble? Highlight details in the text, and write a note to support your response.

4. Reread the ninth and tenth amendments. Do you think that the Founding Fathers believed in a system of government that was rigid and permanent, or one that was more fluid and flexible? Highlight details in the text, and write a note to support your response.

5. Note the style of language in each of the three documents. Which one has the simplest, most easy-to-understand language? Why do you think that is? Highlight examples, and write notes to explain your response to these questions.

WRITING PROMPT

What were some of the central ideas of the Declaration of Independence, the Preamble, and the Bill of Rights? Write a response in which you identify two central ideas. Explain how they are stated as principles and applied as law in the text. Cite evidence from the text to support your explanation.

THE FEDERALIST PAPERS: NO. 10

NON-FICTION
James Madison
1787

INTRODUCTION

Although the United States is a democracy in the sense that its government derives power from the people, the U.S. Constitution establishes a republic in which elected officials make policy decisions, and not a democracy in which citizens decide on policy matters directly. James Madison addressed that topic in *The Federalist Papers*, a collection of 85 articles and essays published by Madison, Alexander Hamilton and John Jay in 1787 and 1788 to promote ratification of the Constitution, and in turn create a strong central government that could raise revenue through taxation and maintain law and order at a time when people feared political instability. Here, in Federalist No. 10, Madison argues that only a strong republican government will protect its citizens against dangerous factions of individuals motivated by their own political self-interests.

"There are two methods of curing the mischiefs of faction..."

NOTES

FIRST READ

Federalist No 10. The Same Subject Continued
The Union as a Safeguard Against Domestic Faction and Insurrection
From the New York Packet. Friday, November 23, 1787.

MADISON
To the People of the State of New York:

1   Among the numerous advantages promised by a well-constructed Union, none deserves to be more accurately developed than its tendency to break and control the violence of faction. ... Complaints are everywhere heard from our most considerate and virtuous citizens, equally the friends of public and private faith, and of public and personal liberty, that our governments are too unstable, that the public good is disregarded in the conflicts of rival parties, and that measures are too often decided, not according to the rules of justice and the rights of the minor party, but by the superior force of an interested and overbearing majority....

2   By a faction, I understand a number of citizens, whether amounting to a majority or a minority of the whole, who are united and actuated by some common impulse of passion, or of interest, adversed to the rights of other citizens, or to the permanent and aggregate interests of the community.

3   There are two methods of curing the mischiefs of faction: the one, by removing its causes; the other, by controlling its effects.

4   There are again two methods of removing the causes of faction: the one, by destroying the liberty which is essential to its existence; the other, by giving to every citizen the same opinions, the same passions, and the same interests.

5   It could never be more truly said than of the first remedy, that it was worse than the disease. Liberty is to faction what air is to fire, an aliment without

NOTES

which it instantly expires. But it could not be less folly to abolish liberty, which is essential to political life, because it nourishes faction, than it would be to wish the annihilation of air, which is essential to animal life, because it imparts to fire its destructive agency.

6   The second **expedient** is as impracticable as the first would be unwise. As long as the reason of man continues fallible, and he is at liberty to exercise it, different opinions will be formed. As long as the connection subsists between his reason and his self-love, his opinions and his passions will have a **reciprocal** influence on each other; and the former will be objects to which the latter will attach themselves. The diversity in the faculties of men, from which the rights of property originate, is not less an insuperable obstacle to a uniformity of interests. The protection of these faculties is the first object of government. From the protection of different and unequal faculties of acquiring property, the possession of different degrees and kinds of property immediately results; and from the influence of these on the sentiments and views of the respective proprietors, ensues a division of the society into different interests and parties.

7   The latent causes of faction are thus sown in the nature of man; and we see them everywhere brought into different degrees of activity, according to the different circumstances of civil society. A zeal for different opinions concerning religion, concerning government, and many other points, as well of speculation as of practice; an attachment to different leaders ambitiously contending for pre-eminence and power; or to persons of other descriptions whose fortunes have been interesting to the human passions, have, in turn, divided mankind into parties, inflamed them with mutual animosity, and rendered them much more disposed to vex and oppress each other than to co-operate for their common good. So strong is this propensity of mankind to fall into mutual animosities, that where no substantial occasion presents itself, the most frivolous and fanciful distinctions have been sufficient to kindle their unfriendly passions and excite their most violent conflicts. But the most common and durable source of factions has been the various and unequal distribution of property. Those who hold and those who are without property have ever formed distinct interests in society. Those who are creditors, and those who are debtors, fall under a like discrimination. A landed interest, a manufacturing interest, a mercantile interest, a moneyed interest, with many lesser interests, grow up of necessity in civilized nations, and divide them into different classes, actuated by different sentiments and views. The regulation of these various and interfering interests forms the principal task of modern legislation, and involves the spirit of party and faction in the necessary and ordinary operations of the government.

...

8　The inference to which we are brought is, that the CAUSES of faction cannot be removed, and that relief is only to be sought in the means of controlling its EFFECTS.

9　If a faction consists of less than a majority, relief is supplied by the republican principle, which enables the majority to defeat its sinister views by regular vote. It may clog the administration, it may convulse the society; but it will be unable to execute and mask its violence under the forms of the Constitution. When a majority is included in a faction, the form of popular government, on the other hand, enables it to sacrifice to its ruling passion or interest both the public good and the rights of other citizens. To secure the public good and private rights against the danger of such a faction, and at the same time to preserve the spirit and the form of popular government, is then the great object to which our inquiries are directed.

...

10　A republic, by which I mean a government in which the scheme of representation takes place, opens a different prospect, and promises the cure for which we are seeking. Let us examine the points in which it varies from pure democracy, and we shall comprehend both the nature of the cure and the efficacy which it must derive from the Union.

11　The two great points of difference between a democracy and a republic are: first, the **delegation** of the government, in the latter, to a small number of citizens elected by the rest; secondly, the greater number of citizens, and greater sphere of country, over which the latter may be extended.

12　The effect of the first difference is, on the one hand, to refine and enlarge the public views, by passing them through the medium of a chosen body of citizens, whose wisdom may best discern the true interest of their country, and whose patriotism and love of justice will be least likely to sacrifice it to temporary or partial considerations. Under such a regulation, it may well happen that the public voice, pronounced by the representatives of the people, will be more **consonant** to the public good than if pronounced by the people themselves, convened for the purpose....

13　The other point of difference is, the greater number of citizens and extent of territory which may be brought within the compass of republican than of democratic government; and it is this circumstance principally which renders factious combinations less to be dreaded in the former than in the latter. The smaller the society, the fewer probably will be the distinct parties and interests composing it; the fewer the distinct parties and interests, the more frequently will a majority be found of the same party; and the smaller the number of individuals composing a majority, and the smaller the compass within which they are placed, the more easily will they concert and execute their plans of

NOTES

oppression. Extend the sphere, and you take in a greater variety of parties and interests; you make it less probable that a majority of the whole will have a common motive to invade the rights of other citizens; or if such a common motive exists, it will be more difficult for all who feel it to discover their own strength, and to act in unison with each other. Besides other impediments, it may be remarked that, where there is a consciousness of unjust or dishonorable purposes, communication is always checked by distrust in proportion to the number whose concurrence is necessary.

...

14 The influence of factious leaders may kindle a flame within their particular States, but will be unable to spread a general conflagration through the other States. A religious sect may degenerate into a political faction in a part of the Confederacy; but the variety of sects dispersed over the entire face of it must secure the national councils against any danger from that source. A rage for paper money, for an abolition of debts, for an equal division of property, or for any other improper or wicked project, will be less apt to pervade the whole body of the Union than a particular member of it; in the same proportion as such a malady is more likely to taint a particular county or district, than an entire State.

15 In the extent and proper structure of the Union, therefore, we behold a republican remedy for the diseases most incident to republican government. And according to the degree of pleasure and pride we feel in being republicans, ought to be our zeal in cherishing the spirit and supporting the character of Federalists.

 THINK QUESTIONS

1. Reread the first paragraph. What are the three undesirable effects of factions?

2. Reread paragraphs 3 through 6. What are the two ways of controlling factions? Which method does Madison favor and why?

3. Reread the paragraph that begins "The effect of the first difference is." Why does Madison believe that chosen government representatives can control the effects of factions?

4. Locate the word *expedient* in the text. How does the adjective *second* in front of the word help you locate clues elsewhere in the text that can help you define the word? Follow that line of thinking and write a definition for *expedient*.

5. Locate the word *concert* in the next-to-last paragraph. You may recognize the word, but the most familiar definition from today doesn't match its use in this historical document. How might you determine its meaning in this passage if its usage is unfamiliar to you?

Please note that excerpts and passages in the StudySync® library and this workbook are intended as touchstones to generate interest in an author's work. The excerpts and passages do not substitute for the reading of entire texts, and StudySync® strongly recommends that students seek out and purchase the whole literary or informational work in order to experience it as the author intended. Links to online resellers are available in our digital library. In addition, complete works may be ordered through an authorized reseller by filling out and returning to StudySync® the order form enclosed in this workbook.

Reading & Writing Companion **79**

CLOSE READ

Reread the excerpts from "Federalist Papers No. 10." As you reread, complete the Focus Questions below. Then use your answers and annotations from the questions to help you complete the Writing Prompt.

FOCUS QUESTIONS

1. Highlight any passages that present an analogy about disease and cure. How does this analogy relate to Madison's central argument?

2. Reread the paragraphs that begin "The second expedient is..." and "The latent causes of faction." What do these paragraphs suggest about human nature? Do you agree with Madison's assessment of human nature? Highlight evidence in the text that will help you respond to these questions, and comment on that evidence.

3. Reread the paragraph that begins "The effect of the first difference is..." What is Madison's opinion of elected representatives? Does he provide any evidence to justify this opinion? Is his characterization of elected representatives consistent with his earlier observations about human nature? Highlight evidence in the text that will help you respond to these questions, and comment on that evidence.

4. Reread the paragraph that begins "The other point of difference is..." What is Madison saying about small democracies versus larger republics? Highlight evidence in the text that will help you respond to this question, and comment on that evidence.

5. Reread the paragraph that begins "The influence of factious leaders..." Highlight the analogy related to fire in that paragraph. Explain this analogy. Do you think the point that Madison is making about the threat to the nation's early identity is still true today?

WRITING PROMPT

Do you think Madison's arguments are still relevant today? For example, do you think that factions, or groups that represent people who share the same interests and have a common political cause, are necessarily a threat to the public good? Do you agree with Madison's descriptions about human nature and the natural formation of factions? Do you agree that elected politicians are enlightened individuals who can be trusted to make decisions for the public good? Do you think that Madison was right in saying that the larger the society, the less likely a faction will unite members across the country? Select two points from Madison's essay and write a response in which you explain whether you think the points are still valid in today's society.

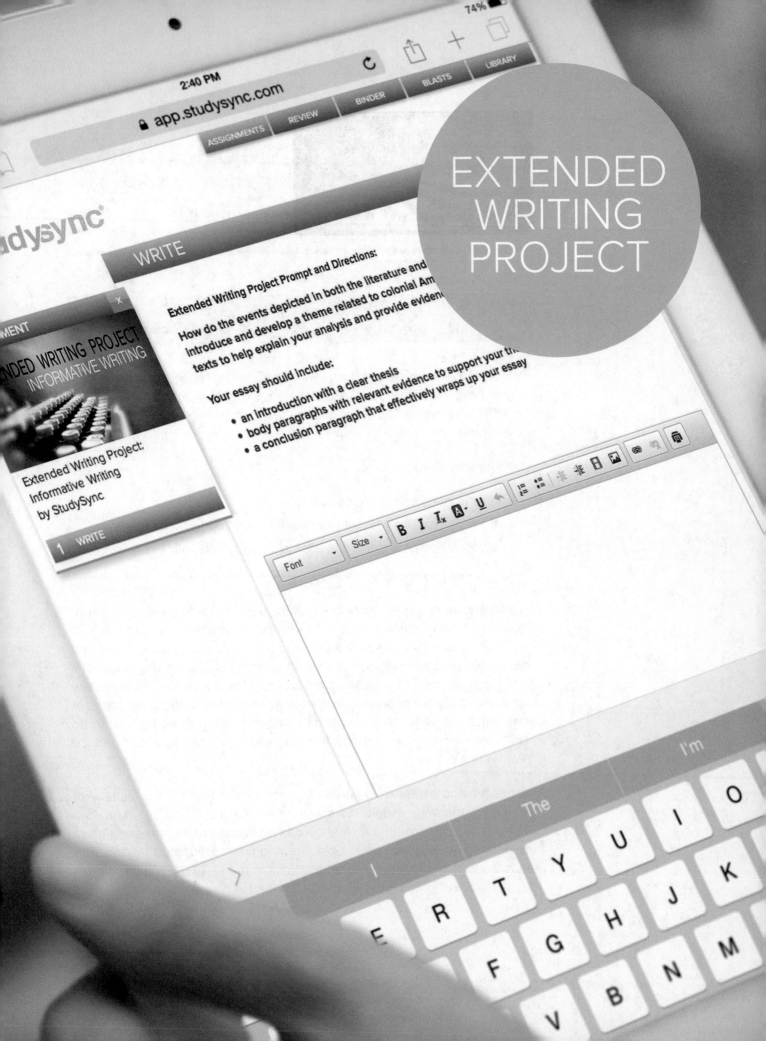

EXTENDED
WRITING
PROJECT

WRITE

Extended Writing Project Prompt and Directions:

How do the events depicted in both the literature and
Introduce and develop a theme related to colonial Am
texts to help explain your analysis and provide evide

Your essay should include:

- an introduction with a clear thesis
- body paragraphs with relevant evidence to support your th
- a conclusion paragraph that effectively wraps up your essay

Extended Writing Project:
Informative Writing
by StudySync

1   WRITE

INFORMATIVE/ EXPLANATORY WRITING

WRITING PROMPT

How do the events depicted in both the literature and historical documents you have read introduce and develop a theme related to colonial America's identity? Select two of these texts to help explain your analysis and provide evidence for your response.

Your essay should include:

- an introduction with a clear thesis
- body paragraphs with relevant evidence to support your thesis
- a conclusion paragraph that effectively wraps up your essay

An **informative or explanatory essay** is a type of nonfiction writing in which the writer presents ideas, concepts, and information in an organized style to the reader. Often the writer will examine complex or complicated ideas and convey them with the purpose of educating or instructing the reader about a particular topic, such as explaining the events leading up to the Revolutionary War or exploring the economic factors that contributed to the slave trade. At other times, the writer may simply be trying to teach the reader how to do something, such as loading and firing a musket or making butter and ice cream with a churn.

Informative and explanatory writing focuses on the facts of the matter. For that reason, the writer usually stays well in the background (third-person point of view is usually favored over first-person point of view) and presents his or her details and evidence in an objective and non-opinionated fashion. This lends the writing a formal style that assures the reader that the author knows the material well enough to provide a clear and accurate analysis.

The features of informative/explanatory writing include:

- a strong introduction with a clear thesis statement
- clear and logical organizational structure
- supporting details
- precise language and domain-specific vocabulary
- citations of sources
- an effective and efficient conclusion

As you continue with this extended writing project, you'll receive more instructions and practice to help you craft each of the elements of informative/explanatory writing in your own essay.

 ## STUDENT MODEL

Education as a Survival Tactic in Early America

When some of the first European settlers arrived in North America, they were unprepared for the challenges that lay ahead of them. The competent crew of the *Mayflower* could transport the Pilgrims across the stormy Atlantic with only one fatality, but neither they nor their passengers were equipped to handle the lack of food and deadly New England winter that awaited them at their destination. Clearly, if they were going to survive in the New World and lay down the building blocks of the America we know today, they would have to learn new skills and strategies. This commitment to education which is apparent in two classic American texts, William Bradford's *Of Plymouth Plantation* and Arthur Miller's *The Crucible*, would serve the colonists well and help to shape America's emerging identity over the years ahead.

In *Of Plymouth Plantation*, William Bradford demonstrates that many of the Pilgrims were already quite well educated, especially in the areas of religion and philosophy. Bradford himself can quote from the Bible as well as from the ancient Roman philosopher Seneca, whose sailing trip along coastal Italy paled in comparison to the ordeal the Pilgrims had just endured (Bradford 69). Unfortunately, such theoretical knowledge hadn't prepared him or his fellow Pilgrims well for hunting game and planting corn in the foreign wilderness. For this, the Puritans relied on Squanto and his fellow Indians, who "directed them how to set their corn, where to take their fish, and to procure other commodities"

Please note that excerpts and passages in the StudySync® library and this workbook are intended as touchstones to generate interest in an author's work. The excerpts and passages do not substitute for the reading of entire texts, and StudySync® strongly recommends that students seek out and purchase the whole literary or informational work in order to experience it as the author intended. Links to online resellers are available in our digital library. In addition, complete works may be ordered through an authorized reseller by filling out and returning to StudySync® the order form enclosed in this workbook.

Reading & Writing
Companion

83

NOTES

(Bradford 89). The value of this information was perhaps best represented by the bounty of the next fall's harvest, which occasioned the nation's first Thanksgiving feast, a tradition that continues to play a major role in defining the American identity.

Like William Bradford, the character of Reverend Parris in Arthur Miller's play *The Crucible* stands at the intersection of reason and religion. Though he, too, is well educated and able to provide religious remedies to problems, he finds himself looking for more scientific or logical answers when a seemingly supernatural crisis takes hold of his own household. Early in the play, he receives a response from Doctor Griggs, who, according to the messenger Susanna, has "been searchin' his books" for a reasonable solution (Miller 9). When Griggs can't find one, Parris insists that he try again: "Let him look to medicine and put out all thoughts of unnatural causes" (Miller 9). When many of the citizens of Salem accepted "unnatural causes" as an explanation his daughter's illness, Parris sought logical or scientific explanation.

As the reader can see in both of the texts mentioned, nature remained something of a mystery to the earliest American colonists. The natural world—and, by extension, the unnatural world—was a great unknown that needed to be learned and understood in order to survive. Without such knowledge, it would remain a "vacant wilderness," as one of Bradford's fellow Pilgrims later called it (Clap 3). In this context, Parris's sense of urgency in *The Crucible* is understandable, even though his fellow townspeople did not face the wilderness challenges endured by the Pilgrims in *Of Plymouth Plantation*.

Whether they were confronting the unknown in the untamed landscape around them or the hearts and suspicious minds of their own community members, the early Americans knew that they didn't know enough to survive. Bradford's Pilgrims had to learn how to live off the land, and Parris's Puritan townspeople had to learn, perhaps the hard way, to replace their fears and suspicions with a more rational approach to the world. There was, and would always be, much more to learn about life on the continent they now called their home. Education would prove to be an essential cornerstone in the foundation of this new country, and would thus establish itself as a crucial part of any subsequent American identity.

Works Cited

Clap, Roger. "Surviving the First Year of the Massachusetts Bay Colony,

1630–1631." *American Beginnings*. National Humanities Center, n.d. Web.

21 July 2014.

Bradford, William, and Harold Paget. *Of Plymouth Plantation*. Mineola, NY: Dover

Publications, 2006. Print.

Miller, Arthur. *The Crucible*. New York: Penguin Books, 2003. Print.

 THINK QUESTIONS

1. What does the title tell you about how this writer chose to respond to the prompt?

2. Where does the writer state the main idea of the essay? How might you restate it in your own words?

3. Which two main texts does the author of the essay look to for evidence? In what ways does the author include evidence from these texts?

4. Reflect on the writing prompt. Which selections, Blasts, or other resources do you think would provide the strongest material and evidence to develop a thorough response to the prompt?

5. Focus on the final part of the writing prompt. What themes from literature and informational texts do you think are most closely related to the theme of identity? Which one excites you most as a possible topic for your essay?

Please note that excerpts and passages in the StudySync® library and this workbook are intended as touchstones to generate interest in an author's work. The excerpts and passages do not substitute for the reading of entire texts, and StudySync® strongly recommends that students seek out and purchase the whole literary or informational work in order to experience it as the author intended. Links to online resellers are available in our digital library. In addition, complete works may be ordered through an authorized reseller by filling out and returning to StudySync® the order form enclosed in this workbook.

Reading & Writing Companion   **85**

NOTES

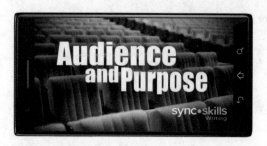

SKILL:
AUDIENCE AND
PURPOSE

 ## DEFINE

Before any writer begins writing, he or she needs to think about who will be reading the work. An **audience** may be the subscribers to a magazine, the employees of a company, the owners of a new piece of software or machinery, the admissions board of a college, or any number of groups of people who may be interested in the text. As you can see from the examples, the **purpose** of a piece of writing, or the reason for its creation, is often directly related to the audience. The writer may be seeking to provide information to the audience, explain a process, set forth a convincing argument, or simply entertain the readers with a story, screenplay, or poem. This clarification of audience and purpose has major impacts on the writing process, from start to finish. For example, if you're assigned to write a recipe book for kindergarteners, you'll need to consider foods that are easy to prepare, contain limited ingredients, and avoid using any dangerous tools, such as sharp knives or kitchen blowtorches. Likewise, you'll need to consider the complexity of your steps and structure, the reading level of the vocabulary, and the inclusion of any helpful elements such as graphics, headings, and numbered lists. All of these decisions stem from an initial understanding of the audience and purpose.

 ## IDENTIFICATION AND APPLICATION

- **Identifying the audience** means answering the question, "Who will be reading this?" If you can describe the typical reader in some way (intelligent, young, mainly female, urban, etc.), you may better understand what kind of writing might engage and satisfy them more fully.

- The audience for a piece of writing may be **explicitly stated** in a writing prompt or assignment, such as a sports report for the high school newspaper.

- **Informative/explanatory writing** often communicates **ideas and information** that a group of readers may not know. This may place extra demands on the writer to **define terms** and provide **additional explanation or examples.**

- An audience may expect **clear, context-based structures** from a particular kind of writing, such as lists of ingredients in a recipe and numbered steps for preparation. The writer should anticipate these needs and meet them as thoroughly as possible.

- The **purpose** for writing may also be **explicitly stated** in the prompt or assignment, such as a light humor column for a church bulletin, in which the purpose is to entertain and make readers laugh about something related to religion.

- The purpose dictates the **type or form of writing** to be done, including narrative stories, informative/explanatory essays, and arguments. Each of these has **text features and elements** that may be similar, but they also include features and elements, such as numbered steps, that are specific to the task.

- Both the audience and purpose are often stated or implied in the **introduction** to the writing, which establishes the complexity of the topic, tone, style, and structure of the text ahead.

- The purpose may also create expectations of a particular kind of **vocabulary,** such as **academic language or domain-specific terminology.** A chemistry lab report might list types of equipment without describing them, while a history paper might contain references to periods and movements specific to the topic.

 MODEL

The intended audience and purpose of a text can sometimes be determined in the initial paragraph. In the student model, for example, we can consider something as basic as the length and complexity of the first sentence to know that the writer intends this essay to be read by someone who can comprehend an introductory clause:

> When some of the first European settlers arrived in North America, they were unprepared for the challenges that lay ahead of them. The competent crew of the *Mayflower* could transport the Pilgrims across the stormy Atlantic with only one fatality, but neither they nor their passengers were equipped to handle the lack of food and deadly New England winter that awaited them at their destination. Clearly, if they were going to survive in the New World and lay down the building blocks of the America we know today, they would have to learn new skills and strategies. This commitment to education which is apparent in two classic American texts, William Bradford's *Of Plymouth Plantation* and Arthur Miller's *The Crucible*, would

serve the colonists well and help to shape America's emerging identity over the years ahead.

In addition to the somewhat advanced sentence structure and syntax, the author obviously assumes that the audience has some basic knowledge of American history. If not, the writer may have felt the need to provide more background information about the first European settlers and establish the actual dates or period of time in question. Likewise, the author provides no background information about the geographical location of New England, so the intended reader is most likely from the United States or familiar with the country's regions.

As we read further, we come to understand that the purpose of this writing is not merely to provide factual information, such as historical dates and locations. The author intends to undertake an analysis of themes in historical literature pertaining to colonial America. The last sentence of the paragraph directly states the topic that will be discussed. It is neither a work of fictional literature nor a statement of opinion to be argued; the writer clearly seeks to explain something to the reader.

With that established, the audience has a better sense of what to expect in the paragraphs ahead. Hopefully, the snippets of information already mentioned, such as the dangerous transatlantic journey, and the writing style itself has also engaged the audience's interest enough to keep them reading.

 ## PRACTICE

Write a brief, three- or four-sentence paragraph that states the audience and purpose for the writing prompt. Relate this as closely as possible to the ideas you are currently considering for your essay. When you are finished, trade with a partner and offer each other feedback. How well does the intended audience and purpose for writing match your intended response? Can you foresee any difficulties or challenges, such as necessary text features or domain-specific vocabulary that may need to be defined? Remember to be considerate and respectful as you offer constructive suggestions to one another.

PREWRITE

WRITING PROMPT

How do the events depicted in both the literature and historical documents you have read introduce and develop a theme related to colonial America's identity? Select two of these texts to help explain your analysis and provide evidence for your response.

Your essay should include:

- an introduction with a clear thesis
- body paragraphs with relevant evidence to support your thesis
- a conclusion paragraph that effectively wraps up your essay

As you look back over the texts you'll be considering for this prompt, look for any annotations or notes you made that relate to theme. Which of these might also be related to the topic of identity, which is the main focus of the prompt? As you review the texts, do you see any details or examples that also relate back to the prompt? In the box below, list the ideas and information that you would like to include in your essay. Try to select only the most significant and relevant details, examples, and quotations. Also note any thoughts you may have about the audience for your essay and how this might relate back to your purpose in writing. Make a note of any other research you plan to do in order to find additional relevant information.

As you brainstorm and prewrite, keep in mind the specific requirements of the prompt. You may want to break them down into a helpful list of questions, such as the sample below. Once you begin to answer questions and make connections between texts, you'll find your ideas developing and suggesting new paths and avenues for consideration in your essay.

NOTES

What events did I read about that shaped colonial identity in America? *the arrival of the Pilgrims in New England*

What other themes or topics are related to identity? *religion, education, government*

How might I develop two or more of those themes in an essay? *I might demonstrate the need to learn new things, such as survival techniques in the early settlements. I might also relate education to religious upbringing to explore how the two topics interact with one another.*

Which two texts will I focus on in my essay?

1. *Of Plymouth Plantation*
2. *The Crucible*

NOTES

SKILL: THESIS STATEMENT

⭐ DEFINE

The foundation of informative/explanatory writing is the thesis statement. This is a single sentence that summarizes the central idea or position that the writer will develop in the body of the essay through organized facts, details, quotations, definitions and other pieces of textual evidence. It also briefly introduces what the writer plans to say about the topic. The thesis statement most often appears as the last sentence of the introductory paragraph of an essay.

••• IDENTIFICATION AND APPLICATION

A good thesis statement:

- makes a clear statement about the central idea of the essay
- lets the reader know what to expect in the body of the essay
- is presented in the introductory paragraph
- responds completely to the writing prompt

MODEL

Before considering the thesis statement from the Student Model essay, have another look at the writing prompt:

How do the events depicted in both the literature and historical documents you have read introduce and develop a theme related to colonial America's identity? Select two of these texts to help explain your analysis and provide evidence for your response.

NOTES

The following is the introductory paragraph from the Student Model essay "Education as a Survival Tactic in Early America":

> When some of the first European settlers arrived in North America, they were unprepared for the challenges that lay ahead of them. The competent crew of the Mayflower could transport the Pilgrims across the stormy Atlantic with only one fatality, but neither they nor their passengers were equipped to handle the lack of food and deadly New England winter that awaited them at their destination. **Clearly, if they were going to survive in the New World and lay down the building blocks of the America we know today, they would have to learn new skills and strategies. This commitment to education which is apparent in two classic American texts, William Bradford's *Of Plymouth Plantation* and Arthur Miller's *The Crucible*, would serve the colonists well and help to shape America's emerging identity over the years ahead.**

Notice the bold-faced thesis statement. Note that in this example, because of the complexity of the topic, the writer uses two sentences for the thesis statement. This student's thesis statement meets the requirements of an effective thesis statement. First, it reminds readers of the topic of the essay: the beginning of colonial American identity. Then it specifically states the writer's central or main idea about this topic: that learning new skills and strategies was necessary to the survival and identity of colonial America. A strong thesis will always have both of these aspects. When developing your own thesis ask yourself these two questions:

- Have I clearly stated the topic of the essay?
- Have I clearly stated the central or main idea that I will explore in the body paragraphs to follow?

 PRACTICE

Write a thesis statement for your informative essay that articulates your central idea in relation to the essay prompt. When you are finished, trade with a partner and offer each other feedback. How clear was the writer's main point or idea? Is it obvious what this essay will focus on? Does it specifically address the prompt? Offer each other suggestions, and remember that they are most helpful when they are constructive.

SKILL:
ORGANIZE
INFORMATIVE
WRITING

 DEFINE

There are many choices available for **organizing informative writing.** All of them share one common goal: to structure the analysis, explanation, or process in a clear and logical fashion appropriate to the task or purpose for writing. This will allow the writer to better understand how the relevant information should fall into place within the article or essay. If the purpose is to depict a series of historical events, a **chronological structure** might work best. If the purpose is to describe steps in a process, a **sequential structure** might be more appropriate to the task. If the purpose is to show how these events build upon one another, a **cause-and-effect structure,** which can be quite similar to the chronological structure, might be more effective. If two or more texts or ideas are being analyzed together, a **compare-and-contrast structure** would help the reader understand how one group of ideas and information relates to another group of ideas and information.

 IDENTIFICATION AND APPLICATION

- Quite often, the writer of an essay will offer something like an outline or roadmap of the organizational structure in the introduction. This helps to orient the reader and prepare him or her for the sequence of the analysis or explanation that will follow.

- When selecting an organizational structure, writers must consider the purpose of their writing. They often ask themselves questions about the kind of information they are writing about. They might consider:

  › "What is the main idea I'd like to convey?"
  › "Would it make sense to relay events in the order they occurred?"
  › "What is the problem?"
  › "What solutions seem likely answers to the problem?"
  › "Is there a natural cause-and-effect relationship in my information?"
  › "Can I compare and contrast different examples of my thesis statement?"
  › "Am I teaching readers how to do something?"

Please note that excerpts and passages in the StudySync® library and this workbook are intended as touchstones to generate interest in an author's work. The excerpts and passages do not substitute for the reading of entire texts, and StudySync® strongly recommends that students seek out and purchase the whole literary or informational work in order to experience it as the author intended. Links to online resellers are available in our digital library. In addition, complete works may be ordered through an authorized reseller by filling out and returning to StudySync® the order form enclosed in this workbook.

Reading & Writing Companion | 93

NOTES

- Writers often choose words that create connections between details and hint at the organizational structure being used:
  - › Sequential or chronological order: *first, next, then, finally, at last, initially, ultimately*
  - › Cause and effect: *because, accordingly, as a result, effect, so*
  - › Compare and contrast: *like, unlike, also, both, similarly, although, while, but, however*

- Sometimes, within the overall structure, writers may find it necessary to organize individual paragraphs using other structures, such as a case study presented in a narrative or chronological structure. This should not affect the overall organization of the essay as a whole.

 MODEL

Olaudah Equiano sets out to tell his life story with the purpose or main idea of informing his readers about the disorienting horrors and cruelties of the slave trade. In the early stages of his captivity, Equiano is often confused by what is happening around him. He has no context in which to place his kidnapping and transport from Africa, and so he tries to make sense of the objective facts as they present themselves to him, however unnatural they may seem. A strict adherence to **chronological order** helps the reader avoid the sense of confusion and mystification that Equiano himself felt at the time without losing sight of that theme overall.

An analysis of one particular paragraph shows how deftly and effectively Equiano describes the arrival of another ship bearing mysterious passengers near the beginning of his transatlantic journey:

> While we stayed on the coast I was mostly on deck; and **one day,** to my great astonishment, I saw one of these vessels coming in with the sails up. **As soon as** the whites saw it, they gave a great shout, at which we were amazed; and the more so as the vessel appeared larger by approaching nearer. **At last** she came to an anchor in my sight, and when the anchor was let go I and my countrymen who saw it were **lost in astonishment** to observe the vessel stop; and were not convinced it **was done by magic. Soon after** this the other ship got her boats out, and they came on board of us, and the people of both ships seemed very glad to see each other. Several of the strangers also shook hands with us black people, and made motions with their hands, signifying **I suppose we were to go to their country; but we did not understand them.**

Copyright © BookheadEd Learning, LLC

The details of this event are organized chronologically, words and phrases such as "one day," "as soon as," "at last," and "soon after" helping the reader to follow the sequence of events quite clearly. Even so, Equiano is able to work in the themes of confusion and suspicion of magic. He describes his fellow countrymen being "lost in astonishment" and wondering if the second ship's sudden stop "was done by magic."

The paragraph ends with a reinforcement of the overall theme of confusion when he says, "I suppose we were to go to their country, but we did not understand them." Equiano has explained this quite well in the preceding paragraph, showing his former confused self without confusing the reader. The chronological structure functions effectively with this purpose in mind.

 ## PRACTICE

Identify a possible organizational structure among the notes and evidence you have gathered during the Prewrite stage of your informative/explanatory essay. Then choose an appropriate graphic organizer and use it to structure your information. Here are some ideas:

- Sequential structure: Chain of Events chart
- Chronological structure: Chain of Events chart
- Logical steps: Chain of Events chart
- Cause-and-effect structure: Cause and Effect chart
- Problem and Solution: Problem and Solution chart
- Compare-and-contrast structure: Venn diagram

SUPPORTING DETAILS

sync•skills
Writing

SKILL: SUPPORTING DETAILS

 DEFINE

In a piece of informative/explanatory writing, writers need to include **supporting details** that support the central or main idea with relevant information. This information can take the form of:

- Facts important to understanding the topic
- Research related to the main idea or thesis
- Quotations from experts, eyewitnesses, or other source material
- Conclusions of scientific findings and studies
- Definitions from reference material

The quantity and quality of this information should be related to the audience's knowledge of the topic. For example, a writer crafting an emergency weather report might not need to define or explain *isobars* (from the dictionary: "lines on a weather map depicting the same atmospheric pressure") to an audience of meteorologists, but a general reader might need a more detailed definition or explanation of what they are and why people should be evacuating the coastline because of the rapid air pressure changes and hurricane-force winds they might be predicting.

 IDENTIFICATION AND APPLICATION

- To identify **relevant information** to use as supporting details, ask yourself if the material relates back to the central or main idea of your informative/ explanatory essay. Is it a direct reference, perhaps using some of the same words or concepts, or is it an indirect reference, one that would require a great deal of explanation to connect it back to the theme?

- A **concept map** can help writers organize relevant information. With a central or main idea stated in the middle of the map, the writer can branch out and record related information either close to or farther away from the center.

- Along these same lines, the writer needs to reject information that is unrelated or irrelevant to the central or main idea. Such extraneous

NOTES

details can clutter up an informative/explanatory essay and distract the reader. They can also lead the writer off on tangents that are unrelated to the main topic. Think of it as driving your car off the road and getting lost in the forest. If the reader can't follow you, you may be stuck in there all by yourself for a very long time.

- **Facts** are the most objective form of relevant information to include on a concept map. They also provide support for any **inferences** that the writer might make. In many forms of informative/explanatory writing, facts are the preferred kind of relevant information.

- **Definitions** are sometimes essential when writing about complex topics for an audience that may not be familiar with the vocabulary or terminology. An **extended definition** will seek to place the word's meaning within the context of the central or main idea in order to explain its relevance further. This is particularly helpful with historical terminology, since some words may have multiple meanings or unexpected connotations in their original contexts.

- **Examples** help to explain or demonstrate a topic or central idea. They can take the form of factual relationships (a terrier is an example of a dog, for instance), analogies or metaphors (true happiness is like playing with puppies, for instance), or thought experiments (imagine you were starving in the jungle, for instance, and had nothing to eat for days).

- **Concrete details** are specific words or phrases from the text that relate back to the central or main idea in some way. An analysis of fruit imagery in a text might want to make mention of the "apples, pears, and cherries strewn about the picnic blanket" in a story, for example.

- **Text excerpts,** such as the one in the last point, offer firsthand evidence of the information in the text. In this respect, it is somewhat stronger than **paraphrasing,** which is the writer's restatement of the events or ideas. To paraphrase the excerpt above, the writer might say, "There was fruit at the scene," which isn't as convincing but may serve to shorten an otherwise lengthy description.

- **Quotations** can include direct excerpts from a text or refer to other **primary sources,** such as a person being interviewed about the main topic. Primary sources provide original material; they do not retell or filter the stories or ideas of others.

 ## MODEL

In order to discuss education in "Education as a Survival Tactic in Early America," the writer of the essay needed to provide **details and examples** of the theme's appearance within the texts being analyzed. To do that, the writer looks for **relevant information** about William Bradford's scholarly background:

In *Of Plymouth Plantation*, William Bradford demonstrates that many of the Pilgrims were already quite well educated, especially in the areas of religion and philosophy. Bradford himself can quote from the Bible as well as from the ancient Roman philosopher Seneca, whose sailing trip along coastal Italy paled in comparison to the ordeal the Pilgrims had just endured (Bradford 69). Unfortunately, such theoretical knowledge hadn't prepared him or his fellow Pilgrims well for hunting game and planting corn in the foreign wilderness. For this, the Puritans relied on Squanto and his fellow Indians, who "directed them **how to set their corn, where to take their fish, and to procure other commodities**" (Bradford 89). The value of this information was perhaps best represented by the bounty of the next fall's harvest, which occasioned the nation's first Thanksgiving feast, a tradition that continues to play **a major role in defining the American identity.**

In this excerpt, the details of the Bible and the Roman philosopher Seneca both point not only to Bradford's ability to read, but also to his ability to understand complex texts and apply them to his current situation. The writer of the essay **paraphrases** this application, giving us just enough information from the text to support the central idea of the paragraph. Additionally, the author distinguishes Bradford's "theoretical" knowledge from the more practical knowledge of agriculture. A **quotation** from the text provides a further example of what that practical knowledge might entail: "how to set their corn, where to take their fish," and so on. The writer hasn't provided irrelevant details about how the Pilgrims met Squanto or how long it took for them all to become friends. He or she describes only the moment that is related to the central or main idea of education.

Likewise, the writer has no real need to define Thanksgiving for the audience of the essay. Even so, he or she includes an **extended definition** that places the familiar holiday squarely within the context of another major theme of the essay, identity, noting that Thanksgiving is a tradition that plays "a major role in defining the American identity."

 PRACTICE

Using the reading selections or other sources, write a few supporting details for your informative essay that help develop your main idea. Then trade your details with a partner when you are finished. Offer feedback about the details. Engage in a peer review to determine which details are most relevant and strengthen your thesis statement.

PLAN

WRITING PROMPT

How do the events depicted in both the literature and historical documents you have read introduce and develop a theme related to colonial America's identity? Select two of these texts to help explain your analysis and provide evidence for your response.

Your essay should include:

- an introduction with a clear thesis
- body paragraphs with relevant evidence to support your thesis
- a conclusion paragraph that effectively wraps up your essay

Review the information and ideas you identified and developed over the past writing and skills lessons. Check them against the original writing prompt to make sure that you've addressed all of the requirements for this assignment. You can then use this organized information and your thesis to generate the main ideas and topics for individual paragraphs. You can also use the StudySync graphic organizer for *Informative/Explanatory Writing* to help you better visualize and arrange the various parts of your essay.

Start by restating your thesis statement. Then ask yourself:

- How might I expand upon my thesis statement in my introduction?
- Which texts will I use as my sources for relevant evidence?
- What kind of organizational structure might be most useful or effective?
- How will I determine the order in which I write about events and ideas?
- Which text excerpts or pieces of evidence support my individual ideas?
- Are any of my sources connected to one another in some way?

Please note that excerpts and passages in the StudySync® library and this workbook are intended as touchstones to generate interest in an author's work. The excerpts and passages do not substitute for the reading of entire texts, and StudySync® strongly recommends that students seek out and purchase the whole literary or informational work in order to experience it as the author intended. Links to online resellers are available in our digital library. In addition, complete works may be ordered through an authorized reseller by filling out and returning to StudySync® the order form enclosed in this workbook.

Reading & Writing Companion   99

Finally, jot down some ideas about what you might include in your conclusion. You may think of other ideas when you start to write your draft in the next step of the writing process.

You may also use the model below to help create an outline or road map for your essay. Depending on your thesis statement and the texts you have chosen to discuss, you may need to include additional information or evidence in each paragraph or map out additional paragraphs.

Informative/Explanatory Essay Road Map

Introduction
Thesis statement:

Paragraph 1 Topic:
Organizational Strategy:
    Textual Evidence #1:
    Textual Evidence #2:

Paragraph 2 Topic:
Organizational Strategy:
    Textual Evidence #1:
    Textual Evidence #2:

Paragraph 3 Topic:
Organizational Strategy:
    Textual Evidence #1:
    Textual Evidence #2:

Conclusion

SKILL: INTRODUCTIONS

 DEFINE

The **introduction** to an informative/explanatory text usually states the **central or main idea** that will be examined or conveyed in the subsequent paragraphs. In addition, the writer may try to engage or "hook" the reader with an interesting piece of relevant information that sets up the significance of the analysis or the process to be described. For example, a scientific article might pique the reader's interest by promising to explain how an archeological discovery relates to our current understanding of backaches, or a recipe will entice the reader with pictures of a luscious chocolate cake and a teasing line about how it looks rich but costs next-to-nothing to make. The introduction may also set forth the basic structure of the text that will follow, providing readers with a roadmap of sorts before the trip officially begins.

 IDENTIFICATION AND APPLICATION

- An introduction is more than simply the first paragraph of a text. It establishes the **author's purpose** in writing and will often provide the reader with some insight into the organizational structure of the writing.

- The introduction contains an explicit **thesis** statement of the **central or main idea,** usually at either the beginning or the end of the paragraph.

- The writer of an informative/explanatory text will often establish a **formal style** and **clear, objective tone** in the first paragraph. More often than not, this means writing from a **third-person point of view** and avoiding any personal reference to the author himself or herself. The formal style will also convey to the reader a sense of the writer's authority and trustworthiness on the topic.

- The writer may also provide an interesting **"hook"** or entry point for consideration in order to engage the reader and provoke interest in the subject at hand. For example, the writer may ask an intriguing question that he or she hopes to answer in the text, such as: How do they get those amazingly detailed ships inside those tiny bottles?

MODEL

Though the title of the essay "Education as a Survival Tactic in Early America" seems somewhat academic, the introduction opens with some powerful and relevant details about a stormy passage by sea and the deadly winter ahead for the first settlers:

> When some of the first European settlers arrived in North America, they were unprepared for the challenges that lay ahead of them. The competent crew of the *Mayflower* could transport the Pilgrims across the stormy Atlantic with only one fatality, but neither they nor their passengers were equipped to handle the lack of food and deadly New England winter that awaited them at their destination. Clearly, if they were going to survive in the New World and lay down the building blocks of the America we know today, they would have to learn new skills and strategies. This commitment to education which is apparent in two classic American texts, William Bradford's *Of Plymouth Plantation* and Arthur Miller's *The Crucible*, would serve the colonists well and help to shape America's emerging identity over the years ahead.

Once the dramatic opening has hooked the reader's attention, the writer introduces the **central or main idea** of the text. This is directly linked to the story of the settlers' arrival and leads the reader to trust that the writer will be sharing an interesting and enlightening analysis of the texts under discussion. The writer also clearly employs an **objective tone** to tell us his or her **purpose** for writing this particular informative/explanatory text. In the final sentence, there is a hint about the **organization plan** of the essay: the writer will analyze two texts that build upon the theme of education contributing to identity. From this, the reader can infer that a compare-and-contrast structure will most likely follow.

 PRACTICE

Write an introduction for your informative/explanatory essay that clearly states a thesis or main idea, includes a hook to grab the reader's attention, gives readers a preview of the main points that will be made in the essay, and establishes a formal tone for the essay. When you are finished, trade with a partner and offer each other feedback. How strong is the language of your partner's thesis statement? How clear is the topic? Were you hooked? Offer each other suggestions, and remember that advice is most helpful when it is constructive.

SKILL: SOURCES AND CITATIONS

⭐ **DEFINE**

When writing an informative/explanatory essay, writers cannot simply make up information or rely on their own subjective experiences or opinions. To thoroughly support the treatment and analysis of their topics, writers need to include information from relevant, accurate, and reliable sources and to cite, or give credit to, their research sources.

When incorporating the ideas of others into their own research papers, writers can **quote** the exact words of an author or expert by enclosing all the borrowed words in quotation marks to make it clear that the ideas belong to someone else. They may also **paraphrase,** that is, restate the researched information, in their own words, though they still need to cite the original source of the information. Through experience, writers can develop a good sense of when it is more effective to quote or to paraphrase researched information. Sometimes quoting is better because the actual wording is especially interesting or comes from an important source. Other times, it is more elegant to pull out a few key words or phrases from the source and integrate them into the flow of original writing.

Writers should keep track of all their sources as they research and plan their work. When it comes time to write, they can use this information to acknowledge the sources they've used. Failure to acknowledge those sources is **plagiarism,** or stealing someone else's words and ideas. In some academic texts, writers may be asked to provide sources and citations in **footnotes** or **endnotes,** which link specific references within the essay to the correlating pages or chapters in an outside source. In addition to internal citations, writers may also need to provide a full list of sources in a **Works Cited** section or standard **bibliography.**

💬 **IDENTIFICATION AND APPLICATION**

- You should gather information relevant to your research topic from multiple print and digital sources, avoiding overreliance on one source.

Please note that excerpts and passages in the StudySync® library and this workbook are intended as touchstones to generate interest in an author's work. The excerpts and passages do not substitute for the reading of entire texts, and StudySync® strongly recommends that students seek out and purchase the whole literary or informational work in order to experience it as the author intended. Links to online resellers are available in our digital library. In addition, complete works may be ordered through an authorized reseller by filling out and returning to StudySync® the order form enclosed in this workbook.

Reading & Writing Companion

103

- When performing research online using a search engine, remember to use accurate keywords and online filters to narrow the results and limit the number of distracting and irrelevant results. Try a variety of words for different searches in order to come up with the widest range of options.

- Wikipedia is an extremely popular source of information, but it is not a primary source as it provides summaries of other sources and common knowledge. Although you should avoid using it as source itself for a formal research paper, it can be a helpful tool to jumpstart research. You can look up information on Wikipedia and follow the links to the original sources cited as Wikipedia references.

- Before you decide to use a source, consider the following factors to evaluate its credibility:

  › **Authority** — Is the source material written by a recognized expert or experts on the topic? Authors who have written several books or articles about a subject for informed audiences in the field and who are frequently quoted may be considered authorities.

  › **Reliability** — Has the source material been published in a trustworthy book, periodical, or website? Use materials from scholarly journals or from well-respected magazines and newspapers. Keep in mind that websites of well-known experts, universities, and organizations are more reliable than those of unknown individuals.

  › **Objectivity** — Is the source material connected with persons or organizations that are biased? Does it present only a single perspective or point of view? If the person or organization has something to gain by presenting information in a certain way, the source might not be objective. Subjective information is told from only one point of view.

  › **Currency** — Is the source material up to date or based on the most current information? In general, use the most recent material available, particularly for subjects of current importance. Check the publication date of books, magazines, and websites. However, depending on the topic, the source material may not need to be current. For example, currency is not an issue in primary source material such as documents and letters and may not be important in secondary source material such as biographies of historical figures.

- As you use a source, take a closer look at it. Consider the following questions to evaluate its accuracy:

  › **Is the information presented verified by other sources?** If you find conflicting information, check a third or even a fourth source.

  › **Is the source itself based on other reliable sources?** This is particularly important with secondary sources. See if the document lists its sources in a bibliography or links to reliable primary sources if it is an online source.

Copyright © BookheadEd Learning, LLC

> › **Does the document explain how the information was gathered or obtained?** You might want to determine whether the author did a thorough research job or only a quick study. You might want to know whether the author used only the Internet for research or also used special libraries and museum holdings. Sometimes the preface of the book or article will tell you this.

- When gathering sources and information for an informative/explanatory text, writers should take note of as much of the following information as possible:
  - › Title of the work or website
  - › Author(s) or editor(s) of the work
  - › Pages referenced, if available (relate this to specific quotations or information)
  - › Date of publication
  - › Publisher name and address (city, state, and/or country)
  - › Medium of publication (web or print)
  - › Version numbers (revisions, issue numbers, volumes, editions)
  - › Date of access

- Always avoid plagiarism by either quoting the original text directly or paraphrasing the original and crediting the author.

- Different organizations and references, such as the Modern Language Association (MLA), the American Psychological Association (APA), and the *Chicago Manual of Style,* recommend different ways of handling the proper formatting of citations and sources. When you receive an assignment, always check for and follow the proper formatting requirements.

MODEL

Modern Language Association (MLA) guidelines for citing research sources is the style mostly used in English classes. For detailed guidelines, refer to the *MLA Handbook for Writers of Research Papers* or a reliable online source such as the Purdue Online Writing Lab (OWL).

MLA style for citing sources takes a two-pronged approach. Writers following MLA style provide both a Works Cited page and in-text citations. The Works Cited page appears at the end of the essay and lists all the sources cited in the paper. The in-text citations, which appear at the end of sentences that contain researched information, link to the entries on the Works Cited page. These citations often contain **signal words.** Signal words correspond to the first word or first few words of the related entry on the Works Cited page and are typically the author's last name or the first few words of the title.

These are the rules for in-text citations:

- After a quotation or a paraphrase of researched information, insert in parentheses the author's last name and the page number where the information was found. For instance:

  Without such knowledge, it would remain a "vacant wilderness," as one of Bradford's fellow Pilgrims later called it (Clap 3).

- If you mention the author's name in the sentence, you do not need to use a signal word in the parentheses:

  Without such knowledge, it would remain a "vacant wilderness," as Roger Clap, one of Bradford's fellow Pilgrims, later called it in his memoir (3).

- If the source does not indicate the author, use the first few words of the title or if it is short title, the entire title to identify the piece:

  Without such knowledge, it would remain a "vacant wilderness," as one of Bradford's fellow Pilgrims later called it ("Surviving the First Year" 3).

For the Works Cited page, follow these general formatting guidelines:

- The title Works Cited should be centered at the top of the page and appear in regular font. (It should not be bold or underlined, nor should it be in a font larger than that of the surrounding text.)
- Arrange the entries alphabetically by author's last name or by the first word in the title, if no author is mentioned.
- Long entries, that is, entries that take up more than one line, should be indented half an inch every line after the first.
- The entire list should be double spaced. Some writers mistakenly use single spacing for long entries and then use double spacing between entries. That is not correct. Double spacing should be used between all lines of text.

The format for each entry in the Works Cited list depends on the type of source. Here are two of the most commonly used formats:

<u>Book</u>

Structure:

Last, First M., and First M. Last (for additional author or editor), *Book Title.* City,

State: Publisher, Year Published. Medium.

Example:

Bradford, William, and Harold Paget. *Of Plymouth Plantation*. Mineola, NY:

Dover Publications, 2006. Print.

Website

Structure:

Last, First M. "Article or Page Title." *Website Title*. Website Publisher. Date

Month Year Published (if available). Web. Date Month Year Accessed.

Example:

Clap, Roger. "Surviving the First Year of the Massachusetts Bay Colony,

1630–1631" *American Beginnings*. National Humanities Center, n.d. Web.

21 July 2014.

The Purdue OWL site can serve as a quick reference for examples for many different types of formats, including books, periodicals, electronic sources, and other common sources.

 PRACTICE

Write citations for your in-text references and Works Cited page for any researched information in your informative essay. When you are finished, trade with a partner and offer each other feedback. How successful was the writer in citing sources for the essay? How well did the writer make use of varied sources? Offer each other suggestions, and remember that suggestions are most helpful when they are constructive.

Please note that excerpts and passages in the StudySync® library and this workbook are intended as touchstones to generate interest in an author's work. The excerpts and passages do not substitute for the reading of entire texts, and StudySync® strongly recommends that students seek out and purchase the whole literary or informational work in order to experience it as the author intended. Links to online resellers are available in our digital library. In addition, complete works may be ordered through an authorized reseller by filling out and returning to StudySync® the order form enclosed in this workbook.

Reading & Writing Companion   **107**

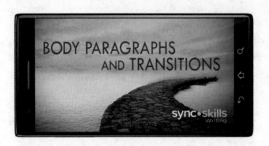

SKILL: BODY PARAGRAPHS AND TRANSITIONS

 DEFINE

Body paragraphs are the sections of the essay between the introduction and conclusion paragraphs. This is where you support your thesis statement by developing your main points with evidence from the text and analysis. Typically, each body paragraph will focus on one main point or idea to avoid confusing their reader. The main point of each body paragraph must support the thesis statement.

It's important to structure your body paragraph clearly. One strategy for structuring the body paragraph for an informational essay is the following:

Topic sentence: The topic sentence is the first sentence of your body paragraph and clearly states the main point of the paragraph. It's important that your topic sentence develop the main assertion or statement you made in your thesis statement.

Evidence #1: It's important to support your topic sentence with evidence. Evidence can be relevant facts, definitions, concrete details, quotations, or other information and examples.

Analysis/Explanation #1: After presenting evidence to support your topic sentence, you will need to analyze that evidence and explain how it supports your topic sentence and, in effect, your thesis.

Evidence #2: Continue to develop your topic sentence with a second piece of evidence.

Analysis/Explanation #2: Analyze this second piece of evidence and explain how it supports your topic sentence and, in effect, your thesis.

Concluding sentence: After presenting your evidence you need to wrap up your main idea and transition to the next paragraph in your conclusion sentence.

Transitions are words or phrases that guide a reader from one idea to the next or from one paragraph to the next. As they do, they establish either explicit or implicit links between major sections of the text, create a sense of overall cohesion to the organizational structure, and clarify the relationships among complex ideas and concepts. In addition, transition words and phrases help authors make connections between words within a sentence. Conjunctions such as *and, or,* and *but* and prepositions such as *with, beyond, inside,* show the relationships between words.

 IDENTIFICATION AND APPLICATION

- Body paragraphs provide the evidence and analysis/explanation needed to support the thesis statement from the introduction. Typically, writers develop one main idea per body paragraph.
  - › Topic sentences clearly state the main idea of that paragraph. In most instances, they are the first sentence in a body paragraph.
  - › Evidence consists of relevant facts, definitions, concrete details, quotations, or other information and examples.
  - › Analysis and explanation are needed to explain how the evidence supports the topic sentence.
  - › The final sentence wraps up the main point and transitions to the next body paragraph.

- Transition words are a necessary element of a successful piece of informative writing.
  - › Transition words help readers understand the text structure of an informative text. Here are some transition words that are frequently used in three different text structures:
    - › Cause and effect: *because, accordingly, as a result, effect, so, for, since*
    - › Compare and contrast: *like, unlike, also, both, similarly, although, while, but, however, whereas, conversely, meanwhile, on the contrary, and yet, still*
    - › Chronological order: *first, next, then, finally, last, initially, ultimately*

- Transition words help readers understand the flow of ideas and concepts in a text. Some of the most useful transitions are words that indicate that the ideas in one paragraph are building on or adding to those in another. Examples include: *furthermore, therefore, in addition, moreover, by extension, in order to,* etc.

Please note that excerpts and passages in the StudySync® library and this workbook are intended as touchstones to generate interest in an author's work. The excerpts and passages do not substitute for the reading of entire texts, and StudySync® strongly recommends that students seek out and purchase the whole literary or informational work in order to experience it as the author intended. Links to online resellers are available in our digital library. In addition, complete works may be ordered through an authorized reseller by filling out and returning to StudySync® the order form enclosed in this workbook.

Reading & Writing Companion **109**

NOTES

 MODEL

In this third body paragraph from "Education as a Survival Tactic in Early America," the student author is making a transition from a discussion of William Bradford's *Of Plymouth Plantation* to a consideration of Arthur Miller's *The Crucible*. In order to avoid the abrupt shift that might occur within a compare-and-contrast organizational structure, the author refers one last time to Bradford before moving on, establishing a connection between the two paragraphs by acknowledging the impending comparison:

> **Like** William Bradford, the character of Reverend Parris in Arthur Miller's play *The Crucible* stands at **the intersection of reason and religion. Though** he, **too,** is well educated and able to provide religious remedies to problems, he finds himself looking for more scientific or logical answers when a seemingly supernatural crisis takes hold of his own household.

Here, the word "like," though somewhat informal in tone, establishes right away that a comparison will take place within this paragraph. The writer then reminds the reader of what is being compared: *Of Plymouth Plantation* and *The Crucible*. In the first sentence, the writer restates the topic, which will be developed with further details and evidence in this body paragraph: "the intersection of reason and religion." The word "too" later in the paragraph reinforces this connection, even as the writer has introduced a contrast with the transitional word "though" in the second sentence. These guide words can be most helpful in a complex analysis such as this one, helping the reader to keep track of the similarities and differences being analyzed in each body paragraph.

Later in the same paragraph, the author of the student essay provides an example to support the central idea. Since the writer is describing an event from the play, chronological transitions aid the reader in following the action:

> **Early in the play,** he receives a response from Doctor Griggs, who, according to the messenger Susanna, has "been searchin' his books" for a reasonable solution (Miller 9). **When Griggs can't find one,** Parris insists that he try again: "Let him look to medicine and put out all thoughts of unnatural causes" (Miller 9).

The phrase "early in the play" helps the reader understand where in the text this particular action takes place. The clause "When Griggs can't find one" serves as a transition to show that some time has elapsed since the Doctor was first asked to look for a solution. The writer of the student model has condensed both explicit and implicit action from the play into this short, one-sentence summary. The transitional words help to keep the reader from becoming overly confused. With this summary, the writer further explains how the evidence supports the main idea of the intersection of reason and religion.

 PRACTICE

Write one body paragraph for your informative essay that follows the format suggested in the definition. When you are finished, trade with a partner and offer each other feedback. How effective is the topic sentence at stating the main point of the paragraph? How strong is the evidence used to support the topic sentence? Are all quotes and paraphrased evidence cited properly? Did the explanation and analysis thoroughly support the topic sentence? Offer each other helpful suggestions. Remember to be considerate and respectful of one another as you offer constructive advice.

DRAFT

WRITING PROMPT

How do the events depicted in both the literature and historical documents you have read introduce and develop a theme related to colonial America's identity? Select two of these texts to help explain your analysis and provide evidence for your response.

Your essay should include:

- an introduction with a clear thesis
- body paragraphs with relevant evidence to support your thesis
- a conclusion paragraph that effectively wraps up your essay

You've already made substantial progress toward writing your own informative/explanatory text. You've thought about your purpose, audience, and topic. You've carefully examined the unit's texts and selected relevant evidence to include in your response to the prompt. Based on your consideration of these resources, you've determined how to organize your information in an effective structure, which includes a strong introduction and a logical sequence of body paragraphs. You've also learned how to cite the sources you'll be referencing in your essay. Now it's time to write a draft of your essay.

Use the prewriting and planning you have done, including your ideas, sources, supporting evidence, and your outline to draft your informative/explanatory essay. Your essay should explain how a theme from two of the texts you've read relates to the identity of early America. Be sure to include a clear thesis statement in your introductory paragraph that states your main or central idea. As you write, follow a well-organized structure to help guide the reader along in your analysis and include relevant textual evidence to support your ideas throughout the essay. Transitions can help readers understand the logical relationships among your ideas and follow the flow of information. Use your concluding paragraph to restate or reinforce your thesis statement. An effective conclusion can also leave a lasting impression on your readers. Finally, remember to maintain a formal style and objective tone throughout your essay to create a sense of authority and trustworthiness in the reader.

When drafting, ask yourself these questions:

- What can I do to further clarify my thesis statement or central argument?
- What textual evidence—including details, examples, and interesting quotations in each body paragraph—supports the thesis statement?
- How well have I described the events I am discussing? Have I clearly established their relevance and significance in the context of my thesis statement?
- How effective are my references to two of the texts from the unit? Do they support my explanation and validate my response?
- How do my ideas interact and build upon one another to demonstrate how these events relate to the theme of America's early identity?
- What final thought do I want to leave with my readers?

Before you submit your draft, read it over carefully. You want to be sure that you've responded to all aspects of the prompt.

SKILL: STYLE

 DEFINE

An author's **style** refers to the overall manner or way in which he or she uses language throughout a particular piece of writing. Most informative/explanatory text establishes and maintains a formal writing style. This means that the writer follows standard conventions of grammar and syntax, relies on a third-person point of view, chooses precise and concrete words over vague or conversational language, avoids contractions and abbreviations, and incorporates academic or domain-specific language relevant to the topic being discussed or analyzed.

Tone is related to style in that both are expressed through choices in language. Tone, however, reflects an author's attitude or feelings toward a subject. Since expressing opinions and judgments is not the purpose of informative/explanatory text, writers of informational texts rely on an objective or neutral tone to convey information about the subject matter.

 IDENTIFICATION AND APPLICATION

- Point of view and word choice provide two excellent starting points for evaluating the style of a text.
  - › In informative/explanatory texts, the writer stays somewhat hidden and relies on a third-person point of view in order to present his or her information.
  - › The language is clear and precise, tending toward academic or technical rather than regional or conversational language.

- Tone often reflects a sense of the writer's feelings. An informative/explanatory writer typically uses an objective tone.
  - › An objective tone remains neutral and rarely expresses judgment or opinions.
  - › Writers can achieve an objective tone by relying on facts and explicit evidence rather than opinions or feelings.

Copyright © BookheadEd Learning, LLC

> Informative/explanatory writers should avoid slang words and colloquialisms in their work.

 MODEL

In "Education as a Survival Tactic in Early America," the author establishes a **formal writing style** right away in the introduction. The writer uses the **third-person point of view** to describe the arrival of the Pilgrims in North America:

> When some of the first European settlers arrived in North America, they were unprepared for the challenges that lay ahead of them. The **competent** crew of the *Mayflower* **could transport the Pilgrims** across the stormy Atlantic **with only one fatality**, but neither they nor their passengers were equipped to handle the lack of food and deadly New England winter that awaited them at their destination.

The **tone** of the introduction is mostly **objective;** when the author uses a word that seems to convey a subjective judgment such as "competent" to describe the crew of the Mayflower, he or she immediately supports the claim with evidence from the text: "[the crew] could transport the Pilgrims. . . with only one fatality."

Later, the use of a word such as "clearly" intends to offset any doubts or questions on the reader's part: "Clearly, if they were going to survive in the New World and lay down the building blocks of the America we know today, they would have to learn new skills and strategies." This authoritative tone is typical of an academic style of writing, and the rest of the textual analysis adheres to these conventions quite closely.

 PRACTICE

Review the draft of your essay. Look for any examples in which you use the first or second person or include slang. Identify opportunities to vary the sentence structure to create a more formal style. Find words for which you could substitute a more precise academic or domain-specific word to create a more formal tone. Provide corrections and revisions in the margins of your essay. Exchange your work with a partner and offer each other feedback.

Please note that excerpts and passages in the StudySync® library and this workbook are intended as touchstones to generate interest in an author's work. The excerpts and passages do not substitute for the reading of entire texts, and StudySync® strongly recommends that students seek out and purchase the whole literary or informational work in order to experience it as the author intended. Links to online resellers are available in our digital library. In addition, complete works may be ordered through an authorized reseller by filling out and returning to StudySync® the order form enclosed in this workbook.

Reading & Writing Companion   **115**

Copyright © BookheadEd Learning, LLC

SKILL: CONCLUSIONS

 DEFINE

A strong and effective **conclusion** should follow from and support the information or explanation that was presented in the preceding text. It should **restate the central or main idea** in some way and articulate the significance of the topic, noting any interesting or important implications the analysis or explanation may have for the reader. Perhaps most importantly, it should provide the reader with a sense of closure, the satisfying feeling that the central idea has been thoroughly addressed.

 IDENTIFICATION AND APPLICATION

- Conclusions normally restate the central or main idea of the text in a new way, often pointing out how the previous paragraphs of the analysis have built upon one another to arrive at this final paragraph.

- The conclusion may also revisit the author's original purpose for writing, perhaps acknowledging once more what prompted or inspired the writing and reaffirming its significance.

- The conclusion may establish itself as the final or end point of the text's overall structure. For example, the conclusion of a chronological structure might include words such as *lastly* or *finally*. The conclusion of a cause-and-effect structure might include words such as *as a result* or *therefore, it follows*. The conclusion of a compare-and-contrast structure might include words such as *both* and *together* that re-establish the connection between the two things being compared.

- A conclusion may offer a summary of the points already discussed or analyzed in order to restate them in a more concise manner.

- A conclusion based on events in the past may nonetheless relate them in some way to the present or future in order to demonstrate the significance of the analysis or explanation to the reader.

- A conclusion may include a new interesting fact or a slightly different perspective on the topic, but it should not introduce any major new evidence or any new themes or ideas that might need development and support.

MODEL

In the conclusion to the essay "Education as a Survival Tactic in Early America," the student writer brings together the two texts that have been compared and contrasted in the preceding paragraphs. The writer offers one last brief summary of the two texts, linking Bradford and Parris together with the term "the early Americans" as a means of acknowledging their similarities before going on to reaffirm their differences:

> *Whether they were confronting the unknown in the untamed landscape around them or the hearts and suspicious minds of their own community members, the early Americans knew that they didn't know enough to survive. Bradford's Pilgrims had to learn how to live off the land, and Parris's Puritan townspeople had to learn, perhaps the hard way, to replace their fears and suspicions with a more rational approach to the world.*

Following this, the writer immediately restates the central or main idea of the informative/explanatory writing:

> *There was, and would always be, much more to learn about life on the continent they now called their home. Education would prove to be an essential cornerstone in the foundation of this new country, and would thus establish itself as a crucial part of any subsequent American identity.*

With this shift toward a slightly different perspective on the analysis, the writer suggests that the implications of a connection between education and identity remain relevant throughout history. This adds further weight and significance to the author's original purpose for writing.

PRACTICE

Write a conclusion for your informative essay. When you are finished, trade with a partner and offer each other feedback. How effectively did the writer restate the main points of the essay in the conclusion? What final thought did the writer leave you with? Offer each other suggestions, and remember that they are most helpful when they are constructive.

Please note that excerpts and passages in the StudySync® library and this workbook are intended as touchstones to generate interest in an author's work. The excerpts and passages do not substitute for the reading of entire texts, and StudySync® strongly recommends that students seek out and purchase the whole literary or informational work in order to experience it as the author intended. Links to online resellers are available in our digital library. In addition, complete works may be ordered through an authorized reseller by filling out and returning to StudySync® the order form enclosed in this workbook.

Reading & Writing Companion   **117**

REVISE

WRITING PROMPT

How do the events depicted in both the literature and historical documents you have read introduce and develop a theme related to colonial America's identity? Select two of these texts to help explain your analysis and provide evidence for your response.

Your essay should include:

- an introduction with a clear thesis
- body paragraphs with relevant evidence to support your thesis
- a conclusion paragraph that effectively wraps up your essay

Think about the writing process steps and skills lessons you have completed on informative/explanatory writing. Combine all of this knowledge with the feedback you received on your initial draft. Reread the draft of your informative/explanatory essay in order to begin your revision. Here are some recommendations to help you revise:

- Reread your thesis statement for clarity.
- Focus on maintaining a formal yet engaging style.
- Evaluate the strength and relevance of your textual evidence.
- Improve the transitions between paragraphs.
- Add variety to your word choice, syntax, and sentence structures:
  › Substitute more precise words for any that are ambiguous or dull.
  › Make sure that the reader can understand what your pronouns and modifiers refer to.
- Check to see that you have properly cited all of your sources.
- Review your notes and resources to make sure that you have included all of your best ideas and supporting materials.

EDIT, PROOFREAD, AND PUBLISH

WRITING PROMPT

How do the events depicted in both the literature and historical documents you have read introduce and develop a theme related to colonial America's identity? Select two of these texts to help explain your analysis and provide evidence for your response.

Your essay should include:

- an introduction with a clear thesis
- body paragraphs with relevant evidence to support your thesis
- a conclusion paragraph that effectively wraps up your essay

Think about the process steps and lessons you have learned about informative/explanatory writing. Also review the feedback you have received from your peers. Reread your revised informative/explanatory essay and note any edits you would like to make. Ask yourself:

- Have I fully developed my thesis statement and main ideas with relevant research and strong textual evidence?
- Have I accurately cited my sources?
- Has my paper been formatted in a way that makes it easy to read?
- What more can I do to improve my essay's information, organization, and use of rhetorical strategies?

Just before you feel you are ready to publish your essay, read through it one more time with a focus on proofreading for grammar and spelling mistakes, punctuation errors, or word usage problems. When you are finished, publish

NOTES

your informative/explanatory essay. You can also send copies of your writing to family and friends, post it on a bulletin board, or upload it to your blog. If you publish online, create links to your sources and citations if they are available. That way, readers can follow up on ideas they've learned from your essay and continue to explore the topic further on their own.

studysync®

Reading & Writing Companion

How does one person find his or her place in society?

The Individual

UNIT 2   How does one person find his or her place in society?

The Individual

TEXTS

TEXTS

EXTENDED WRITING PROJECT

431

Text Fulfillment
through
StudySync

Please note that excerpts and passages in the StudySync® library and this workbook are intended as touchstones to generate interest in an author's work. The excerpts and passages do not substitute for the reading of entire texts, and StudySync® strongly recommends that students seek out and purchase the whole literary or informational work in order to experience it as the author intended. Links to online resellers are available in our digital library. In addition, complete works may be ordered through an authorized reseller by filling out and returning to StudySync® the order form enclosed in this workbook.

Reading & Writing Companion **123**

SONG OF MYSELF

POETRY
Walt Whitman
1860

INTRODUCTION

The opening lines of "Song of Myself" establish the fresh and optimistic tone for Walt Whitman's groundbreaking work, part of his collection of poems titled Leaves of Grass. Often said to represent the core of Whitman's poetic vision, "Song of Myself" was ultimately divided into 52 sections and covered a multitude of topics. Written in an informal, freewheeling style, with himself as the central character—the "*I*,"—Whitman urges the reader to join with him in the celebration of self.

"Not I, not any one else, can travel that road for you..."

 ## FIRST READ

 NOTES

1

1 I celebrate myself, and sing myself,
2 And what I assume you shall assume,
3 For every atom belonging to me as good belongs to you.

4 I loafe and invite my soul,
5 I lean and loafe at my ease observing a spear of summer grass.

6 My tongue, every atom of my blood, form'd from this soil, this air,
7 Born here of parents born here from parents the same, and their parents the same,
8 I, now thirty-seven years old in perfect health begin,
9 Hoping to cease not till death.

10 Creeds and schools in **abeyance,**
11 Retiring back a while sufficed at what they are, but never forgotten,
12 I harbor for good or bad, I permit to speak at every hazard,
13 Nature without check with original energy.

6

14 A child said, *What is the grass?* fetching it to me with full hands;
15 How could I answer the child? I do not know what it is any more than he.

16 I guess it must be the flag of my **disposition,** out of hopeful green stuff woven.

17 Or I guess it is the handkerchief of the Lord,
18 A scented gift and remembrancer designedly dropt,
19 Bearing the owner's name someway in the corners, that we may see and remark, and say, *Whose?*

Please note that excerpts and passages in the StudySync® library and this workbook are intended as touchstones to generate interest in an author's work. The excerpts and passages do not substitute for the reading of entire texts, and StudySync® strongly recommends that students seek out and purchase the whole literary or informational work in order to experience it as the author intended. Links to online resellers are available in our digital library. In addition, complete works may be ordered through an authorized reseller by filling out and returning to StudySync® the order form enclosed in this workbook.

Reading & Writing Companion **125**

20   Or I guess the grass is itself a child, the produced babe of the vegetation.

21   Or I guess it is a uniform hieroglyphic,
22   And it means, Sprouting alike in broad zones and narrow zones,
23   Growing among black folks as among white;
24   Kanuck, Tuckahoe, Congressman, Cuff, I give them the same, I receive them the same.

25   And now it seems to me the beautiful uncut hair of graves.

26   Tenderly will I use you curling grass,
27   It may be you **transpire** from the breasts of young men,
28   It may be if I had known them I would have loved them,
29   It may be you are from old people, or from offspring taken soon out of their mothers' laps,
30   And here you are the mothers' laps.

31   This grass is very dark to be from the white heads of old mothers,
32   Darker than the colorless beards of old men,
33   Dark to come from under the faint red roofs of mouths.

34   O I perceive after all so many uttering tongues,
35   And I perceive they do not come from the roofs of mouths for nothing.

36   I wish I could translate the hints about the dead young men and women,
37   And the hints about old men and mothers, and the offspring taken soon out of their laps.

38   What do you think has become of the young and old men?
39   And what do you think has become of the women and children?

40   They are alive and well somewhere,
41   The smallest sprout shows there is really no death,
42   And if ever there was it led forward life, and does not wait at the end to arrest it,
43   And ceas'd the moment life appear'd.

44   All goes onward and outward, nothing collapses,
45   And to die is different from what any one supposed, and luckier.

16

46   I am of old and young, of the foolish as much as the wise,
47   Regardless of others, ever regardful of others,
48   Maternal as well as paternal, a child as well as a man,
49   Stuff'd with the stuff that is coarse and stuff'd with the stuff that is fine,

50 One of the Nation of many nations, the smallest the same and the largest the same,
51 A Southerner soon as a Northerner, a planter nonchalant and hospitable down by the Oconee I live,
52 A Yankee bound my own way ready for trade, my joints the limberest joints on earth and the sternest joints on earth,
53 A Kentuckian, walking the vale of the Elkhorn in my deer-skin leggings, a Louisianian or Georgian,
54 A boatman over lakes or bays or along coasts, a Hoosier, Badger, Buckeye;
55 At home on Kanadian snow-shoes or up in the bush, or with fishermen off Newfoundland,
56 At home in the fleet of ice-boats, sailing with the rest and tacking,
57 At home on the hills of Vermont or in the woods of Maine, or the Texan ranch,
58 Comrade of Californians, comrade of free North-Westerners, (loving their big proportions,)
59 Comrade of raftsmen and coalmen, comrade of all who shake hands and welcome to drink and meat,
60 A learner with the simplest, a teacher of the thoughtfullest,
61 A novice beginning yet experient of **myriads** of seasons,
62 Of every hue and caste am I, of every rank and religion,
63 A farmer, mechanic, artist, gentleman, sailor, quaker,
64 Prisoner, fancy-man, rowdy, lawyer, physician, priest.

65 I resist any thing better than my own diversity,
66 Breathe the air but leave plenty after me,
67 And am not stuck up, and am in my place.

68 (The moth and the fish-eggs are in their place,
69 The bright suns I see and the dark suns I cannot see are in their place,
70 The palpable is in its place and the impalpable is in its place.)

46

71 I know I have the best of time and space, and was never measured and never will be measured.

72 I tramp a perpetual journey, (come listen all!)
73 My signs are a rain-proof coat, good shoes, and a staff cut from the woods,
74 No friend of mine takes his ease in my chair,
75 I have no chair, no church, no philosophy,
76 I lead no man to a dinner-table, library, exchange,
77 But each man and each woman of you I lead upon a knoll,
78 My left hand hooking you round the waist,
79 My right hand pointing to landscapes of continents, and the public road.

80   Not I, not any one else, can travel that road for you,
81   You must travel it for yourself.

82   It is not far, it is within reach,
83   Perhaps you have been on it since you were born and did not know,
84   Perhaps it is everywhere on water and on land.

85   Shoulder your duds dear son, and I will mine, and let us hasten forth,
86   Wonderful cities and free nations we shall fetch as we go.

87   If you tire, give me both burdens, and rest the chuff of your hand on my hip,
88   And in due time you shall repay the same service to me,
89   For after we start we never lie by again.

90   This day before dawn I ascended a hill, and look'd at the crowded heaven,
91   And I said to my spirit *When we become the enfolders of those orbs, and the pleasure and knowledge of every thing in them, shall we be fill'd and satisfied then?*
92   And my spirit said *No, we but level that lift to pass and continue beyond.*

93   You are also asking me questions and I hear you,
94   I answer that I cannot answer, you must find out for yourself.

95   Sit a while dear son,
96   Here are biscuits to eat and here is milk to drink,
97   But as soon as you sleep and renew yourself in sweet clothes, I kiss you with a good-by kiss and open the gate for your egress hence.

98   Long enough have you dream'd **contemptible** dreams,
99   Now I wash the gum from your eyes,
100   You must habit yourself to the dazzle of the light and of every moment of your life.

101   Long have you timidly waded holding a plank by the shore,
102   Now I will you to be a bold swimmer,
103   To jump off in the midst of the sea, rise again, nod to me, shout, and laughingly dash with your hair.

52

104   The spotted hawk swoops by and accuses me, he complains of my gab and my loitering.

105   I too am not a bit tamed, I too am untranslatable.
106   I sound my barbaric yawp over the roofs of the world.

NOTES

107 The last scud of day holds back for me,

108 It flings my likeness after the rest and true as any on the shadow'd wilds,

109 It coaxes me to the vapor and the dusk.

110 I depart as air, I shake my white locks at the runaway sun,

111 I effuse my flesh in eddies, and drift it in lacy jags.

112 I bequeath myself to the dirt to grow from the grass I love,

113 If you want me again look for me under your boot-soles.

114 You will hardly know who I am or what I mean,

115 But I shall be good health to you nevertheless,

116 And filter and fibre your blood.

117 Failing to fetch me at first keep encouraged,

118 Missing me one place search another,

119 I stop somewhere waiting for you.

THINK QUESTIONS

1. What do you learn about the speaker of the poem? How would you describe the speaker? Cite evidence from the text to support your response.

2. In Section 6, how does the image of grass represent the cycle of life and death? Cite evidence from the text to support your response.

3. Many critics believe that Whitman's poetry celebrates the democratic spirit and human equality. What evidence in Section 16 do you find to support this interpretation?

4. The word **hieroglyphic** refers to writing in hieroglyphs, which are the symbols used in the ancient Egyptian writing system. In addition, the word *hieroglyph* means sacred writing in Greek. Why do you think grass is described in the poem as a "hieroglyphic"?

5. How does knowing the root word and suffix of **contemptible** help you to understand the word's meaning? How does the word *contemptible* contrast with what the speaker advises his "son" to do in the same stanza?

Please note that excerpts and passages in the StudySync® library and this workbook are intended as touchstones to generate interest in an author's work. The excerpts and passages do not substitute for the reading of entire texts, and StudySync® strongly recommends that students seek out and purchase the whole literary or informational work in order to experience it as the author intended. Links to online resellers are available in our digital library. In addition, complete works may be ordered through an authorized reseller by filling out and returning to StudySync® the order form enclosed in this workbook.

Reading & Writing Companion **129**

CLOSE READ

Reread the poem "Song of Myself." As you reread, complete the Focus Questions below. Then use your answers and annotations from the questions to help you complete the Writing Prompt.

 FOCUS QUESTIONS

1. Recall that the poem "Song of Myself" is part of an even larger collection of poetry called *Leaves of Grass.* The title of the collection suggests that the symbolism of grass is of central importance. Reread Section 6. What metaphor is used to connect grass to life and death? What feelings does the speaker of the poem express toward the dead? What theme emerges from this section about the cycle of life and death?

2. A paradox is a seemingly contradictory statement. Highlight examples of paradox in the first four lines of Section 16. What theme emerges through these paradoxes?

3. Anaphora is a poetic technique that involves repeating a word or a phrase at the beginnings of lines. This is one of the world's oldest poetic techniques, and it appears frequently in religious texts. Highlight an example of anaphora in Section 16. Why do you think Whitman uses anaphora here? What theme does the repetition help to express?

4. What do you think the phrase "One of the Nation of many nations" in Section 16 means? Given that Whitman wrote the first version of this poem before the Civil War, what message about individuals and American society do you think he may have been trying to communicate in this section?

5. Reread Section 46. How does the speaker feel toward his "son"? What advice does he offer his son? What swimming metaphor does the speaker use to reinforce this advice to his son?

WRITING PROMPT

Whitman's purpose in writing "Song of Myself" was to explore a range of themes related to both himself and to his country. Imagine that you were to write your own "Song of Myself." What would your themes be and what advice would you give your readers? How would the content of your poem compare with Whitman's? Explore these questions in a short reflective essay.

WALDEN

NON-FICTION
Henry David Thoreau
1854

INTRODUCTION

studysync tv

Henry David Thoreau spent two years in solitude on Walden Pond in attempt to escape the chaos and distractions of civilization and his busy life. He observed nature and called himself an "inspector of snow-storms and rainstorms." Thoreau's goal was to live simply and self-sufficiently. In the excerpt below, from the second chapter of *Walden*, Thoreau explains "Where I Lived and What I Lived For."

"I did not wish to live what was not life..."

FIRST READ

1 I went to the woods because I wished to live deliberately, to front only the essential facts of life, and see if I could not learn what it had to teach, and not, when I came to die, discover that I had not lived. I did not wish to live what was not life, living is so dear; nor did I wish to practise **resignation,** unless it was quite necessary. I wanted to live deep and suck out all the marrow of life, to live so sturdily and Spartan-like as to put to rout all that was not life, to cut a broad swath and shave close, to drive life into a corner, and reduce it to its lowest terms, and, if it proved to be mean, why then to get the whole and genuine meanness of it, and publish its meanness to the world; or if it were **sublime,** to know it by experience, and be able to give a true account of it in my next excursion. For most men, it appears to me, are in a strange uncertainty about it, whether it is of the devil or of God, and have somewhat hastily concluded that it is the chief end of man here to "glorify God and enjoy him forever."

2 Still we live meanly, like ants; though the fable tells us that we were long ago changed into men; like pygmies we fight with cranes; it is error upon error, and clout upon clout, and our best virtue has for its occasion a **superfluous** and evitable wretchedness. Our life is frittered away by detail. An honest man has hardly need to count more than his ten fingers, or in extreme cases he may add his ten toes, and lump the rest. Simplicity, simplicity, simplicity! I say, let your affairs be as two or three, and not a hundred or a thousand; instead of a million count half a dozen, and keep your accounts on your thumb-nail. In the midst of this chopping sea of civilized life, such are the clouds and storms and quicksands and thousand-and-one items to be allowed for, that a man has to live, if he would not **founder** and go to the bottom and not make his port at all, by dead reckoning, and he must be a great calculator indeed who succeeds. Simplify, simplify. Instead of three meals a day, if it be necessary eat but one; instead of a hundred dishes, five; and reduce other things in proportion. Our life is like a German Confederacy, made up of petty states, with its boundary forever fluctuating, so that even a German cannot tell you

how it is bounded at any moment. The nation itself, with all its so-called internal improvements, which, by the way are all external and superficial, is just such an unwieldy and overgrown establishment, cluttered with furniture and tripped up by its own traps, ruined by luxury and heedless expense, by want of calculation and a worthy aim, as the million households in the land; and the only cure for it, as for them, is in a rigid economy, a stern and more than Spartan simplicity of life and elevation of purpose. It lives too fast. Men think that it is essential that the Nation have commerce, and export ice, and talk through a telegraph, and ride thirty miles an hour, without a doubt, whether they do or not; but whether we should live like baboons or like men, is a little uncertain. If we do not get out sleepers, and forge rails, and devote days and nights to the work, but go to tinkering upon our lives to improve them, who will build railroads? And if railroads are not built, how shall we get to heaven in season? But if we stay at home and mind our business, who will want railroads? We do not ride on the railroad; it rides upon us. Did you ever think what those sleepers are that underlie the railroad? Each one is a man, an Irishman, or a Yankee man. The rails are laid on them, and they are covered with sand, and the cars run smoothly over them. They are sound sleepers, I assure you. And every few years a new lot is laid down and run over; so that, if some have the pleasure of riding on a rail, others have the misfortune to be ridden upon. And when they run over a man that is walking in his sleep, a supernumerary sleeper in the wrong position, and wake him up, they suddenly stop the cars, and make a hue and cry about it, as if this were an exception. I am glad to know that it takes a gang of men for every five miles to keep the sleepers down and level in their beds as it is, for this is a sign that they may sometime get up again.

3   Why should we live with such hurry and waste of life? We are determined to be starved before we are hungry. Men say that a stitch in time saves nine, and so they take a thousand stitches today to save nine tomorrow. As for work, we haven't any of any consequence. We have the Saint Vitus' dance, and cannot possibly keep our heads still. If I should only give a few pulls at the parish bell-rope, as for a fire, that is, without setting the bell, there is hardly a man on his farm in the outskirts of Concord, notwithstanding that press of engagements which was his excuse so many times this morning, nor a boy, nor a woman, I might almost say, but would forsake all and follow that sound, not mainly to save property from the flames, but, if we will confess the truth, much more to see it burn, since burn it must, and we, be it known, did not set it on fire--or to see it put out, and have a hand in it, if that is done as handsomely; yes, even if it were the parish church itself. Hardly a man takes a half-hour's nap after dinner, but when he wakes he holds up his head and asks, "What's the news?" as if the rest of mankind had stood his sentinels. Some give directions to be waked every half-hour, doubtless for no other purpose; and then, to pay for it, they tell what they have dreamed. After a night's sleep the news is as **indispensable** as the breakfast. "Pray tell me anything new that

Please note that excerpts and passages in the StudySync® library and this workbook are intended as touchstones to generate interest in an author's work. The excerpts and passages do not substitute for the reading of entire texts, and StudySync® strongly recommends that students seek out and purchase the whole literary or informational work in order to experience it as the author intended. Links to online resellers are available in our digital library. In addition, complete works may be ordered through an authorized reseller by filling out and returning to StudySync® the order form enclosed in this workbook.

has happened to a man anywhere on this globe"—and he reads it over his coffee and rolls, that a man has had his eyes gouged out this morning on the Wachito River; never dreaming the while that he lives in the dark unfathomed mammoth cave of this world, and has but the **rudiment** of an eye himself.

 THINK QUESTIONS

1. In the first paragraph, what reasons does Thoreau provide for moving to the woods? What kind of life does he want to live? Cite evidence from the text to support your response.

2. In the second paragraph, what advice does Thoreau offer? Why do you think he gives this advice? Cite evidence from the text to support your response.

3. In the third paragraph, what view of the news does Thoreau express? Cite evidence from the text to support your response.

4. Locate the word **sublime** in the first paragraph. What word in the same sentence is a possible antonym, or has the opposite meaning, of *sublime?* How can you tell? Use this and other context clues to write a possible meaning for *sublime.* Check that meaning in the context of the original sentence.

5. Locate the word **indispensable** in the last paragraph. How can you use word parts to determine the part of speech and meaning of the word? How can you use context clues to check your predicted meaning?

CLOSE READ

Reread the excerpt from *Walden.* As you reread, complete the Focus Questions below. Then use your answers and annotations from the questions to help you complete the Writing Prompt.

FOCUS QUESTIONS

1. Reread the first paragraph. At the end of the first paragraph, Thoreau includes a direct quotation from religious instruction that was popular during his day. What does Thoreau mean by this last sentence? What does this sentence reveal about what Thoreau values?

2. Reread the second paragraph. Highlight the sentence that describes a "chopping sea." Explain this metaphor. What central idea is suggested by this metaphor?

3. The building of railroads was very important to commerce during the time that Thoreau was writing. In the second paragraph, what does Thoreau think about the railroads? What does this suggest about how Thoreau viewed technological and economic development in general?

4. Reread the last paragraph. Identify one thing that Thoreau believes is unimportant. Why does he think this is unimportant?

5. Highlight one or two phrases or sentences in each paragraph that you think convey the main idea of each paragraph. Then write a brief summary that describes Thoreau's ideas about the benefits of an individual removing him/herself from society. Make sure that your summary is objective and does not contain any of your opinions.

WRITING PROMPT

Identify two central ideas in the excerpt from *Walden* and explain how they develop and interact over the course of the text. Then explain your reactions to these ideas. Do you agree or disagree with them? Do you think that Thoreau's ideas are still relevant to life today?

Please note that excerpts and passages in the StudySync® library and this workbook are intended as touchstones to generate interest in an author's work. The excerpts and passages do not substitute for the reading of entire texts, and StudySync® strongly recommends that students seek out and purchase the whole literary or informational work in order to experience it as the author intended. Links to online resellers are available in our digital library. In addition, complete works may be ordered through an authorized reseller by filling out and returning to StudySync® the order form enclosed in this workbook.

Reading & Writing Companion | **135**

SOCIETY
AND
SOLITUDE

NON-FICTION
Ralph Waldo Emerson
1857

INTRODUCTION

R alph Waldo Emerson's essay "Society and Solitude" contemplates the nature of solitude and self-reliance in the real world, embracing independent thought and championing the individual, exploring our effect on society and society's on us. Emerson states that a sound mind will derive its principles from personal insight and interact with society accordingly.

"Solitude is impracticable, and society fatal."

FIRST READ

1   'Tis hard to **mesmerize** ourselves, to whip our own top; but through sympathy we are capable of energy and endurance. Concert fires people to a certain fury of performance they can rarely reach alone. Here is the use of society: it is so easy with the great to be great; so easy to come up to an existing standard;—as easy as it is to the lover to swim to his maiden through waves so grim before. The benefits of affection are immense; and the one event which never loses its romance, is the encounter with superior persons on terms allowing the happiest intercourse.

2   It by no means follows that we are not fit for society, because soirées are **tedious,** and because the soirée finds us tedious. A backwoodsman, who had been sent to the university, told me that, when he heard the best-bred young men at the law school talk together, he reckoned himself a boor; but whenever he caught them apart, and had one to himself alone, then they were the boors, and he the better man. And if we recall the rare hours when we encountered the best persons, we then found ourselves, and then first society seemed to exist. That was society, though in the transom of a brig, or on the Florida Keys.

3   A cold, sluggish blood thinks it has not facts enough to the purpose, and must decline its turn in the conversation. But they who speak have no more—have less. 'Tis not new facts that avail, but the heat to dissolve everybody's facts.

4   The capital defect of cold, arid natures is the want of animal spirits. They seem a power incredible, as if God should raise the dead. The **recluse** witnesses what others perform by their aid, with a kind of fear. It is as much out of his possibility as the prowess of Coeur-de-Lion, or an Irishman's day's-work on the railroad. 'Tis said, the present and the future are always rivals. Animal spirits constitute the power of the present, and their feats are like the structure of a pyramid. Their result is a lord, a general, or a boon companion. Before these, what a base mendicant is Memory with his leathern badge! But

Copyright © BookheadEd Learning, LLC

this **genial** heat is latent in all constitutions, and is disengaged only by the friction of society. As Bacon said of manners, "To obtain them, it only needs not to despise them," so we say of animal spirits, that they are the spontaneous product of health and of a social habit. "For behavior, men learn it, as they take diseases, one of another."

5   But the people are to be taken in very small doses. If solitude is proud, so is society vulgar. In society, high advantages are set down to the individual as disqualifications. We sink as easily as we rise, through sympathy. So many men whom I know are degraded by their sympathies, their native aims being high enough, but their relation all too tender to the gross people about them. Men cannot afford to live together by their merits, and they adjust themselves by their demerits,—by their love of gossip, or by sheer tolerance and animal good-nature. They untune and dissipate the brave aspirant.

6   The remedy is, to reinforce each of these moods from the other. Conversation will not corrupt us, if we come to the assembly in our own garb and speech, and with the energy of health to select what is ours and reject what is not.

7   Society we must have; but let it be society, and not exchanging news, or eating from the same dish. Is it society to sit in one of your chairs? I cannot go into the houses of my nearest relatives, because I do not wish to be alone. Society exists by chemical **affinity,** and not otherwise.

8   Put any company of people together with freedom for conversation, and a rapid self-distribution takes place, into sets and pairs. The best are accused of exclusiveness. It would be more true to say, they separate as oil from water, as children from old people, without love or hatred in the matter, each seeking his like; and any interference with the affinities would produce constraint and suffocation. All conversation is a magnetic experiment. I know that my friend can talk eloquently; you know that he cannot articulate a sentence: we have seen him in different company. Assort your party, or invite none. Put Stubbs and Coleridge, Quintilian and Aunt Miriam, into pairs, and you make them all wretched. 'Tis an extempore Sing-Sing built in a parlor. Leave them to seek their own mates, and they will be as merry as sparrows.

9   A higher civility will re-establish in our customs a certain reverence which we have lost. What to do with these brisk young men who break through all fences, and make themselves at home in every house? I find out in an instant if my companion does not want me, and ropes cannot hold me when my welcome is gone. One would think that the affinities would pronounce themselves with a surer reciprocity.

10 Here again, as so often, Nature delights to put us between extreme antagonisms, and our safety is in the skill with which we keep the diagonal line. Solitude is impracticable, and society fatal. We must keep our head in

NOTES

the one and our hands in the other. The conditions are met, if we keep our independence, yet do not lose our sympathy. These wonderful horses need to be driven by fine hands. We require such a solitude as shall hold us to its revelations when we are in the street and in palaces; for most men are cowed in society, and say good things to you in private, but will not stand to them in public. But let us not be the victims of words. Society and solitude are deceptive names. It is not the circumstance of seeing more or fewer people, but the readiness of sympathy, that imports; and a sound mind will derive its principles from insight, with ever a purer ascent to the sufficient and absolute right, and will accept society as the natural element in which they are to be applied.

THINK QUESTIONS

1. In the first paragraph, what does Emerson state is a benefit of society, or socializing with others? Cite textual evidence to support your response.

2. In the fifth paragraph, what does Emerson point out as a negative aspect of society? Cite textual evidence to support your response.

3. In the eighth paragraph, what advice does Emerson offer to party planners? Cite textual evidence to support your response.

4. The word **sympathy** appears four times in the excerpt. *Sympathy* is a multiple-meaning word. Look up the word in a dictionary and select the meaning that you think is the intended meaning in text. Explain your reasoning.

5. Locate the word **genial** in the fourth paragraph. This word shares the same root with the words *congenial* and *congeniality*. Given this information, what do you think *genial* means? Do you think this meaning makes sense in the sentence in which it appears?

Please note that excerpts and passages in the StudySync® library and this workbook are intended as touchstones to generate interest in an author's work. The excerpts and passages do not substitute for the reading of entire texts, and StudySync® strongly recommends that students seek out and purchase the whole literary or informational work in order to experience it as the author intended. Links to online resellers are available in our digital library. In addition, complete works may be ordered through an authorized reseller by filling out and returning to StudySync® the order form enclosed in this workbook.

Reading & Writing Companion

139

CLOSE READ

Reread the essay "Society and Solitude." As you reread, complete the Focus Questions below. Then use your answers and annotations from the questions to help you complete the Writing Prompt.

FOCUS QUESTIONS

1. In this excerpt, the word *society* appears 15 times. Over the course of the text, Emerson provides information at various points to clarify what he means by "society." Reread the second paragraph. How does this paragraph help clarify Emerson's definition of "society"?

2. Reread the fourth paragraph. According to this essay, what are "animal spirits"? How does a person tap into the power of animal spirits? What does Emerson suggest about the "recluse" and animal spirits?

3. Reread the fifth and sixth paragraphs. According to Emerson, what is the problem with society? What is the remedy to this problem?

4. Reread the seventh and eighth paragraphs. How does Emerson further develop his definition of "society" in these paragraphs?

5. Reread the last paragraph. What do you think Emerson favors—society, solitude, or neither? Which sentences or phrases reveal this preference? What advice does Emerson offer the reader in terms of finding his or her own place in society? Is it consistent with his ideas in the previous paragraphs?

WRITING PROMPT

Emerson expresses the idea that one must have both solitude and society in life. How does this relate to your own personal life? In what ways do you thrive in solitude and in what ways do you thrive in the company of others? Write a 300-word reflection about the role of solitude and the role of companionship in your own life, responding to specific quotations from the excerpt from Emerson's essay "Society and Solitude."

THE ADVENTURES OF HUCKLEBERRY FINN
(CHAPTER 1)

FICTION
Mark Twain
1885

INTRODUCTION

Ernest Hemingway claimed that Mark Twain's *The Adventures of Huckleberry Finn* is the one book from which all modern American literature springs. While capturing cultural changes of the times, Twain weaves a memorable tale as told by the spirited Huck. In Chapter 1, Huck considers settling into a respectable life with the decent Widow Douglas.

"I got so down-hearted and scared I did wish I had some company."

 FIRST READ

CHAPTER 1

1   You don't know about me without you have read a book by the name of The Adventures of Tom Sawyer; but that ain't no matter. That book was made by Mr. Mark Twain, and he told the truth, mainly. There was things which he stretched, but mainly he told the truth. That is nothing. I never seen anybody but lied one time or another, without it was Aunt Polly, or the widow, or maybe Mary. Aunt Polly—Tom's Aunt Polly, she is—and Mary, and the Widow Douglas is all told about in that book, which is mostly a true book, with some stretchers, as I said before.

2   Now the way that the book winds up is this: Tom and me found the money that the robbers hid in the cave, and it made us rich. We got six thousand dollars apiece—all gold. It was an awful sight of money when it was piled up. Well, Judge Thatcher he took it and put it out at interest, and it fetched us a dollar a day apiece all the year round—more than a body could tell what to do with. The Widow Douglas she took me for her son, and allowed she would sivilize me; but it was rough living in the house all the time, considering how **dismal** regular and decent the widow was in all her ways; and so when I couldn't stand it no longer I lit out. I got into my old rags and my sugar-hogshead again, and was free and satisfied. But Tom Sawyer he hunted me up and said he was going to start a band of robbers, and I might join if I would go back to the widow and be respectable. So I went back.

3   The widow she cried over me, and called me a poor lost lamb, and she called me a lot of other names, too, but she never meant no harm by it. She put me in them new clothes again, and I couldn't do nothing but sweat and sweat, and feel all cramped up. Well, then, the old thing **commenced** again. The widow rung a bell for supper, and you had to come to time. When you got to the table you couldn't go right to eating, but you had to wait for the widow to tuck down her head and **grumble** a little over the victuals, though there warn't

really anything the matter with them,—that is, nothing only everything was cooked by itself. In a barrel of odds and ends it is different; things get mixed up, and the juice kind of swaps around, and the things go better.

4   After supper she got out her book and learned me about Moses and the Bulrushers, and I was in a sweat to find out all about him; but by and by she let it out that Moses had been dead a **considerable** long time; so then I didn't care no more about him, because I don't take no stock in dead people.

5   Pretty soon I wanted to smoke, and asked the widow to let me. But she wouldn't. She said it was a mean practice and wasn't clean, and I must try to not do it any more. That is just the way with some people. They get down on a thing when they don't know nothing about it. Here she was a-bothering about Moses, which was no kin to her, and no use to anybody, being gone, you see, yet finding a power of fault with me for doing a thing that had some good in it. And she took snuff, too; of course that was all right, because she done it herself.

6   Her sister, Miss Watson, a tolerable slim old maid, with goggles on, had just come to live with her, and took a set at me now with a spelling-book. She worked me middling hard for about an hour, and then the widow made her ease up. I couldn't stood it much longer. Then for an hour it was deadly dull, and I was fidgety. Miss Watson would say, "Don't put your feet up there, Huckleberry;" and "Don't scrunch up like that, Huckleberry—set up straight;" and pretty soon she would say, "Don't gap and stretch like that, Huckleberry— why don't you try to behave?" Then she told me all about the bad place, and I said I wished I was there. She got mad then, but I didn't mean no harm. All I wanted was to go somewheres; all I wanted was a change, I warn't particular. She said it was wicked to say what I said; said she wouldn't say it for the whole world; she was going to live so as to go to the good place. Well, I couldn't see no advantage in going where she was going, so I made up my mind I wouldn't try for it. But I never said so, because it would only make trouble, and wouldn't do no good.

7   Now she had got a start, and she went on and told me all about the good place. She said all a body would have to do there was to go around all day long with a harp and sing, forever and ever. So I didn't think much of it. But I never said so. I asked her if she reckoned Tom Sawyer would go there, and she said not by a considerable sight. I was glad about that, because I wanted him and me to be together.

8   Miss Watson she kept pecking at me, and it got tiresome and lonesome. By and by they fetched the n------ in and had prayers, and then everybody was off to bed. I went up to my room with a piece of candle, and put it on the table. Then I set down in a chair by the window and tried to think of something

cheerful, but it warn't no use. I felt so lonesome I most wished I was dead. The stars were shining, and the leaves rustled in the woods ever so mournful; and I heard an owl, away off, who-whooing about somebody that was dead, and a whippowill and a dog crying about somebody that was going to die; and the wind was trying to whisper something to me, and I couldn't make out what it was, and so it made the cold shivers run over me. Then away out in the woods I heard that kind of a sound that a ghost makes when it wants to tell about something that's on its mind and can't make itself understood, and so can't rest easy in its grave, and has to go about that way every night grieving. I got so down-hearted and scared I did wish I had some company. Pretty soon a spider went crawling up my shoulder, and I flipped it off and it lit in the candle; and before I could budge it was all shriveled up. I didn't need anybody to tell me that that was an awful bad sign and would fetch me some bad luck, so I was scared and most shook the clothes off of me. I got up and turned around in my tracks three times and crossed my breast every time; and then I tied up a little lock of my hair with a thread to keep witches away. But I hadn't no confidence. You do that when you've lost a horseshoe that you've found, instead of nailing it up over the door, but I hadn't ever heard anybody say it was any way to keep off bad luck when you'd killed a spider.

9   I set down again, a-shaking all over, and got out my pipe for a smoke; for the house was all as still as death now, and so the widow wouldn't know. Well, after a long time I heard the clock away off in the town go boom—boom—boom—twelve licks; and all still again—stiller than ever. Pretty soon I heard a twig snap down in the dark amongst the trees—something was a stirring. I set still and listened. Directly I could just barely hear a "me-yow! me-yow!" down there. That was good! Says I, "me-yow! me-yow!" as soft as I could, and then I put out the light and **scrambled** out of the window on to the shed. Then I slipped down to the ground and crawled in among the trees, and, sure enough, there was Tom Sawyer waiting for me.

THINK QUESTIONS

1. How does Huck describe living with the Widow Douglas? What does Huck's view of the widow reveal about himself? Cite evidence from the text to support your response.

2. What is the conflict between Huck Finn and Miss Watson? How does this conflict reveal that the two characters do not fully understand each other? Cite evidence from the text to support your response.

3. In the eighth paragraph, how does Huck feel? How does Huck's description of the evening reflect his own mood? Cite evidence from the text to support your response.

4. In the second paragraph, do you think the word **dismal** has a negative or positive connotation? How can you tell from the context clues in the sentence in which it appears?

5. Look up the word **scramble** in a dictionary and notice that it has multiple meanings. Explain how context clues help you determine which is the intended meaning in the last paragraph.

Please note that excerpts and passages in the StudySync® library and this workbook are intended as touchstones to generate interest in an author's work. The excerpts and passages do not substitute for the reading of entire texts, and StudySync® strongly recommends that students seek out and purchase the whole literary or informational work in order to experience it as the author intended. Links to online resellers are available in our digital library. In addition, complete works may be ordered through an authorized reseller by filling out and returning to StudySync® the order form enclosed in this workbook.

Reading & Writing Companion   **145**

CLOSE READ

Reread the excerpt from *The Adventures of Huckleberry Finn*. As you reread, complete the Focus Questions below. Then use your answers and annotations from the questions to help you complete the Writing Prompt.

FOCUS QUESTIONS

1. Many literary critics have identified Huck as an unreliable narrator. An **unreliable narrator** is one who does not understand the full significance of the characters and events that he or she is describing and commenting on. Huck is not intentionally unreliable. His narration is unreliable because Huck is a teenager who lacks formal education and experience. In fact, much of the humor in the first chapters comes from Huck's incomplete understanding of the adults around him and their "sivilized" ways. Reread the first paragraph. Highlight text that you find humorous, and explain how that text begins to establish Huck as an unreliable narrator.

2. Reread paragraphs 2 and 3. What does Huck value? What does the Widow Douglas value?

3. Reread paragraphs 6 and 7. How do these paragraphs establish Huck as an unreliable narrator? How do they create humor in the narrative?

4. Huck says that he wants to join "a band of robbers" and go to "the bad place." Despite these statements, what evidence can you find of Huck's goodness?

5. Reread paragraph 8. How does this paragraph demonstrate Huck's connection to nature? How would you describe his connection to nature?

6. Reread the final paragraph. What decision does Huck make? How does the stillness of the house and the stirring of trees outside relate to Huck's decision? What does this decision reveal about Huck's sense of belonging in relation to "civilized society"?

WRITING PROMPT

What do you think freedom means to the speaker of Walt Whitman's "Song of Myself" and to Huck Finn in Mark Twain's *The Adventures of Huckleberry Finn*? Write a response in which you compare and contrast how the two literary works from the 19th century treat the concept of freedom. Cite evidence from the text to support your response.

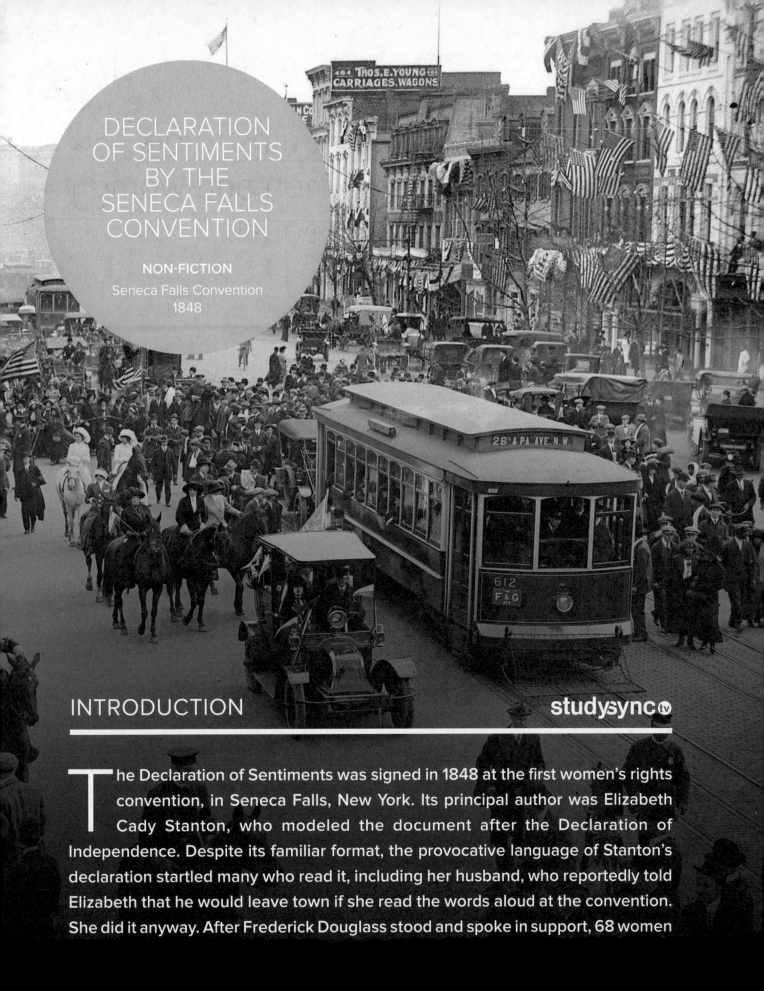

DECLARATION OF SENTIMENTS BY THE SENECA FALLS CONVENTION

NON-FICTION
Seneca Falls Convention
1848

INTRODUCTION

studysync tv

The Declaration of Sentiments was signed in 1848 at the first women's rights convention, in Seneca Falls, New York. Its principal author was Elizabeth Cady Stanton, who modeled the document after the Declaration of Independence. Despite its familiar format, the provocative language of Stanton's declaration startled many who read it, including her husband, who reportedly told Elizabeth that he would leave town if she read the words aloud at the convention. She did it anyway. After Frederick Douglass stood and spoke in support, 68 women

"We hold these truths to be self-evident: that all men and women are created equal..."

 FIRST READ

 NOTES

1   When, in the course of human events, it becomes necessary for one portion of the family of man to assume among the people of the earth a position different from that which they have hitherto occupied, but one to which the laws of nature and of nature's God entitle them, a decent respect to the opinions of mankind requires that they should declare the causes that impel them to such a course.

2   We hold these truths to be self-evident: that all men and women are created equal; that they are endowed by their Creator with certain inalienable rights; that among these are life, liberty, and the pursuit of happiness; that to secure these rights governments are instituted, deriving their just powers from the consent of the governed. Whenever any form of government becomes destructive of these ends, it is the right of those who suffer from it to refuse allegiance to it, and to insist upon the institution of a new government, laying its foundation on such principles, and organizing its powers in such form, as to them shall seem most likely to effect their safety and happiness. Prudence, indeed, will dictate that governments long established should not be changed for light and transient causes; and accordingly all experience hath shown that mankind are more disposed to suffer while evils are sufferable, than to right themselves by abolishing the forms to which they are accustomed. But when a long train of abuses and usurpations, pursuing invariably the same object, evinces a design to reduce them under absolute despotism, it is their duty to throw off such government, and to provide new guards for their future security. Such has been the patient **sufferance** of the women under this government, and such is now the necessity which constrains them to demand the equal station to which they are entitled. The history of mankind is a history of repeated injuries and usurpations on the part of man toward woman, having in direct object the establishment of an absolute tyranny over her. To prove this, let facts be submitted to a candid world.

3   He has never permitted her to exercise her inalienable right to the elective **franchise.**

4   He has compelled her to submit to laws, in the formation of which she had no voice.

5   He has withheld from her rights which are given to the most ignorant and **degraded** men—both natives and foreigners.

6   Having deprived her of this first right of a citizen, the elective franchise, thereby leaving her without representation in the halls of legislation, he has oppressed her on all sides.

7   He has made her, if married, in the eye of the law, civilly dead.

8   He has taken from her all right in property, even to the wages she earns.

9   He has made her, morally, an irresponsible being, as she can commit many crimes with impunity, provided they be done in the presence of her husband. In the covenant of marriage, she is compelled to promise obedience to her husband, he becoming, to all intents and purposes, her master—the law giving him power to deprive her of her liberty, and to administer **chastisement.**

10 He has so framed the laws of divorce, as to what shall be the proper causes, and in case of separation, to whom the guardianship of the children shall be given, as to be wholly regardless of the happiness of women—the law, in all cases, going upon a false supposition of the supremacy of man, and giving all power into his hands.

11 After depriving her of all rights as a married woman, if single, and the owner of property, he has taxed her to support a government which recognizes her only when her property can be made profitable to it.

12 He has **monopolized** nearly all the profitable employments, and from those she is permitted to follow, she receives but a scanty remuneration. He closes against her all the avenues to wealth and distinction which he considers most honorable to himself. As a teacher of theology, medicine, or law, she is not known.

13 He has denied her the facilities for obtaining a thorough education, all colleges being closed against her.

14 He allows her in church, as well as state, but a subordinate position, claiming apostolic authority for her exclusion from the ministry, and, with some exceptions, from any public participation in the affairs of the church.

15   He has created a false public sentiment by giving to the world a different code of morals for men and women, by which moral **delinquencies** which exclude women from society are not only tolerated, but deemed of little account in man.

16   He has usurped the **prerogative** of Jehovah himself, claiming it as his right to assign for her a sphere of action, when that belongs to her conscience and to her God.

17   He has endeavored, in every way that he could, to destroy her confidence in her own powers, to lessen her self-respect, and to make her willing to lead a dependent and abject life.

18   Now, in view of this entire disfranchisement of one-half the people of this country, their social and religious degradation—in view of the unjust laws above mentioned, and because women do feel themselves aggrieved, oppressed, and fraudulently deprived of their most sacred rights, we insist that they have immediate admission to all the rights and privileges which belong to them as citizens of the United States.

 THINK QUESTIONS

1.   Write a one- to two-sentence summary of the Declaration of Sentiments. In your summary, state the purpose of the speech and describe the structure of the text.

2.   In the Declaration of Independence, the pronoun "he" refers to King George III of Great Britain. To whom does the pronoun "he" refer in the Declaration of Sentiments? What comparison is being made between King George and the "he" being referred to in the Declaration of Sentiments? Cite evidence from the text to support your response.

3.   What effect did reading the Declaration of Sentiments have on you? What were your thoughts and feelings as you read or listened to the speech? Explain what caused your response, using specific examples from the text.

4.   The word **franchise** has the root *franchir,* which means "to free." How does this knowledge and other clues in the sentence help you guess at the definition of "franchise"?

5.   Using knowledge of how word parts can change the part of speech or meaning of a word, what do you think the word **disfranchisement** in the last paragraph means?

CLOSE READ

Reread the text "Declaration of Sentiments by the Seneca Falls Convention." As you reread, complete the Focus Questions below. Then use your answers and annotations from the questions to help you complete the Writing Prompt.

FOCUS QUESTIONS

1. Reread the second paragraph. Highlight a word or a group of words intended to elicit a strong emotional response. What do you think was the intended effect of that word or group of words? Imagine substituting a different word or group of words with a similar meaning. How would a different word or group of words change the speech?

2. In the second paragraph, the Declaration of Sentiments repeats the words "life, liberty, and the pursuit of happiness" from the Declaration of Independence. How does the list of grievances that follows connect to these ideas?

3. Highlight two grievances. How do these grievances demonstrate that lacking political, economic, or educational power can affect a woman's personal life?

4. Reread the last paragraph. Highlight a word or a group of words with strong emotional connotations. Imagine substituting a different word or group of words with similar denotations. How would a different word or group of words change the speech?

5. Select one of the grievances listed in the body of the Declaration. Relate this to the conclusion of the document in order to explain how the resolution of the grievance could help women find a better place in society.

WRITING PROMPT

During its time, the Declaration of Sentiments was extremely controversial. Only 100 out of the 300 attendees at the convention signed the document. Men and women of conventional mindsets found it shocking. Even some women who supported women's rights were concerned that it would cause the movement to lose public support. What made it so controversial? Write a response in which you describe how text structure (modeled on the Declaration of Independence) and word connotations may have contributed to the controversy. Cite evidence from the text to support your response.

Please note that excerpts and passages in the StudySync® library and this workbook are intended as touchstones to generate interest in an author's work. The excerpts and passages do not substitute for the reading of entire texts, and StudySync® strongly recommends that students seek out and purchase the whole literary or informational work in order to experience it as the author intended. Links to online resellers are available in our digital library. In addition, complete works may be ordered through an authorized reseller by filling out and returning to StudySync® the order form enclosed in this workbook.

Reading & Writing Companion   **151**

THE STORY OF AN HOUR

FICTION

Kate Chopin
1894

INTRODUCTION

American author Kate Chopin set most of her stories in Louisiana, boldly addressing subjects that most other writers of the late-19th century avoided. Her best-known work focused on the lives of strong, intelligent women, often liberated to a degree that made many people at the time uncomfortable. Considered to be a piece of early feminism, "The Story of an Hour"—first published in *Vogue* magazine in 1894—is a prime example. Here, we follow the main plot line—a wife learning that her husband is dead, and her

"She wept at once, with sudden, wild abandonment..."

FIRST READ

NOTES

1 Knowing that Mrs. Mallard was **afflicted** with heart trouble, great care was taken to break to her as gently as possible the news of her husband's death. It was her sister Josephine who told her, in broken sentences; veiled hints that revealed in half concealing. Her husband's friend Richards was there, too, near her. It was he who had been in the newspaper office when **intelligence** of the railroad disaster was received, with Brently Mallard's name leading the list of "killed." He had only taken the time to assure himself of its truth by a second telegram, and had hastened to forestall any less careful, less tender friend in bearing the sad message.

2 She did not hear the story as many women have heard the same, with a paralyzed inability to accept its significance. She wept at once, with sudden, wild **abandonment,** in her sister's arms. When the storm of grief had spent itself she went away to her room alone. She would have no one follow her.

3 There stood, facing the open window, a comfortable, roomy armchair. Into this she sank, pressed down by a physical exhaustion that haunted her body and seemed to reach into her soul.

4 She could see in the open square before her house the tops of trees that were all aquiver with the new spring life. The delicious breath of rain was in the air. In the street below a peddler was crying his wares. The notes of a distant song which some one was singing reached her faintly, and countless sparrows were twittering in the eaves.

5 There were patches of blue sky showing here and there through the clouds that had met and piled one above the other in the west facing her window.

6 She sat with her head thrown back upon the cushion of the chair, quite motionless, except when a sob came up into her throat and shook her, as a child who has cried itself to sleep continues to sob in its dreams.

7   She was young, with a fair, calm face, whose lines bespoke repression and even a certain strength. But now there was a dull stare in her eyes, whose gaze was fixed away off yonder on one of those patches of blue sky. It was not a glance of reflection, but rather indicated a suspension of intelligent thought.

8   There was something coming to her and she was waiting for it, fearfully. What was it? She did not know; it was too subtle and **elusive** to name. But she felt it, creeping out of the sky, reaching toward her through the sounds, the scents, the color that filled the air.

9   Now her bosom rose and fell tumultuously. She was beginning to recognize this thing that was approaching to possess her, and she was striving to beat it back with her will—as powerless as her two white slender hands would have been.

10 When she abandoned herself a little whispered word escaped her slightly parted lips. She said it over and over under her breath: "free, free, free!" The vacant stare and the look of terror that had followed it went from her eyes. They stayed keen and bright. Her pulses beat fast, and the coursing blood warmed and relaxed every inch of her body.

11 She did not stop to ask if it were or were not a monstrous joy that held her. A clear and exalted perception enabled her to dismiss the suggestion as trivial.

12 She knew that she would weep again when she saw the kind, tender hands folded in death; the face that had never looked save with love upon her, fixed and gray and dead. But she saw beyond that bitter moment a long procession of years to come that would belong to her absolutely. And she opened and spread her arms out to them in welcome.

13 There would be no one to live for during those coming years; she would live for herself. There would be no powerful will bending hers in that blind persistence with which men and women believe they have a right to impose a private will upon a fellow-creature. A kind intention or a cruel intention made the act seem no less a crime as she looked upon it in that brief moment of **illumination.**

14 And yet she had loved him—sometimes. Often she had not. What did it matter! What could love, the unsolved mystery, count for in face of this possession of self-assertion which she suddenly recognized as the strongest impulse of her being!

15 "Free! Body and soul free!" she kept whispering.

16 Josephine was kneeling before the closed door with her lips to the keyhole, **imploring** for admission. "Louise, open the door! I beg, open the door—you will make yourself ill. What are you doing Louise? For heaven's sake open the door."

17 "Go away. I am not making myself ill." No; she was drinking in a very **elixir** of life through that open window.

18 Her fancy was running riot along those days ahead of her. Spring days, and summer days, and all sorts of days that would be her own. She breathed a quick prayer that life might be long. It was only yesterday she had thought with a shudder that life might be long.

19 She arose at length and opened the door to her sister's **importunities.** There was a feverish triumph in her eyes, and she carried herself unwittingly like a goddess of Victory. She clasped her sister's waist, and together they descended the stairs. Richards stood waiting for them at the bottom.

20 Some one was opening the front door with a latchkey. It was Brently Mallard who entered, a little travel-stained, composedly carrying his grip-sack and umbrella. He had been far from the scene of accident, and did not even know there had been one. He stood amazed at Josephine's piercing cry; at Richards' quick motion to screen him from the view of his wife.

21 But Richards was too late.

22 When the doctors came they said she had died of heart disease—of joy that kills.

 THINK QUESTIONS

1. At the beginning of the 8th paragraph, Mrs. Mallard senses "something coming to her." What is it? What effect physically does it have on her?

2. In paragraphs 4 through 8, how do the details about the natural setting outside of Mrs. Mallard's room relate to her emotional state?

3. At the end of the story, why would the doctors think that Mrs. Mallard died of "joy that kills"? Do you think their diagnosis is accurate? Why or why not?

4. The word **abandonment** has multiple meanings. Which meaning do you think is intended by the sentence in which the word appears?

5. Locate the word **imploring** in the text. Which context clues in the surrounding text help you arrive at a possible definition for the word? Which nearby word might be a synonym of the base verb "implore"? If you replace "imploring" with that synonym, would it change the meaning of the sentence?

Please note that excerpts and passages in the StudySync® library and this workbook are intended as touchstones to generate interest in an author's work. The excerpts and passages do not substitute for the reading of entire texts, and StudySync® strongly recommends that students seek out and purchase the whole literary or informational work in order to experience it as the author intended. Links to online resellers are available in our digital library. In addition, complete works may be ordered through an authorized reseller by filling out and returning to StudySync® the order form enclosed in this workbook.

Reading & Writing Companion

155

CLOSE READ

Reread the short story "The Story of an Hour." As you reread, complete the Focus Questions below. Then use your answers and annotations from the questions to help you complete the Writing Prompt.

FOCUS QUESTIONS

1. Reread paragraphs 4 and 5. Highlight examples of imagery used to describe the world outside Mrs. Mallard's bedroom window. What do you think the outside world might **symbolize** in Mrs. Mallard's life?

2. Reread paragraphs 8 through 11. A **paradox** is a statement that seems contradictory but conveys a deeper truth. What do you think the paradox "monstrous joy" in paragraph 11 refers to? Explain the meaning of "monstrous joy."

3. Reread paragraphs 12 through 14. What kind of relationship do you think the Mallards had? Was it the kind of relationship that would justify Mrs. Mallard's response? If not, what reasons might Mrs. Mallard have to respond the way she did?

4. Reread paragraphs 17 and 18. Explain the **metaphor** of the "elixir of life" in this passage. How does this passage help set up the **situational irony** of the ending?

5. How is the last line of the story an example of **dramatic irony**? How does Mrs. Mallard's response to the news of her husband's death differ from the perceptions of her response by the people around her? What does this difference reflect about the attitudes regarding a woman's place in society at the time the story was written?

WRITING PROMPT

Think about the SyncTV students' overarching argument in the episode. In a persuasive response, argue whether this is a story about a cold, emotionally disturbed woman or a story about the secret, repressed desires of women for individuality and freedom. You might also argue in favor of a different perspective, if your view of the story differs from the two interpretations offered. Provide at least two supporting examples, using quotes and passages from the text.

WHAT TO THE SLAVE IS THE FOURTH OF JULY?

NON-FICTION
Frederick Douglass
1852

INTRODUCTION

A former slave who escaped to freedom in 1838, Frederick Douglass went on to become a leading abolitionist and social reformer. Acclaimed for his brilliant oratory skills and incisive writing, Douglass was invited by leading citizens of Rochester, NY to speak at an Independence Day celebration in 1852. With his characteristic eloquence and even-handed logic, Douglass answers the question posed in the title of his speech.

"The blessings in which you, this day, rejoice, are not enjoyed in common."

FIRST READ

NOTES

1   Fellow Citizens, I am not wanting in respect for the fathers of this republic. The signers of the Declaration of Independence were brave men. They were great men, too great enough to give frame to a great age. It does not often happen to a nation to raise, at one time, such a number of truly great men. The point from which I am compelled to view them is not, certainly, the most favorable; and yet I cannot contemplate their great deeds with less than admiration. They were statesmen, patriots and heroes, and for the good they did, and the principles they contended for, I will unite with you to honor their memory....

2   ...Fellow-citizens, pardon me, allow me to ask, why am I called upon to speak here to-day? What have I, or those I represent, to do with your national independence? Are the great principles of political freedom and of natural justice, embodied in that Declaration of Independence, extended to us? And am I, therefore, called upon to bring our humble offering to the national altar, and to confess the benefits and express devout gratitude for the blessings resulting from your independence to us?

3   Would to God, both for your sakes and ours, that an affirmative answer could be truthfully returned to these questions! Then would my task be light, and my burden easy and delightful. For who is there so cold, that a nation's sympathy could not warm him? Who so **obdurate** and dead to the claims of gratitude, that would not thankfully acknowledge such priceless benefits? Who so stolid and selfish, that would not give his voice to swell the hallelujahs of a nation's jubilee, when the chains of servitude had been torn from his limbs? I am not that man. In a case like that, the dumb might eloquently speak, and the "lame man leap as an hart."

4   But such is not the state of the case. I say it with a sad sense of the **disparity** between us. I am not included within the pale of glorious anniversary! Your high independence only reveals the immeasurable distance between us.

NOTES

The blessings in which you, this day, rejoice, are not enjoyed in common. The rich inheritance of justice, liberty, prosperity and independence, bequeathed by your fathers, is shared by you, not by me. The sunlight that brought light and healing to you, has brought stripes and death to me. This Fourth July is yours, not mine. You may rejoice, I must mourn. To drag a man in fetters into the grand illuminated temple of liberty, and call upon him to join you in joyous anthems, were inhuman mockery and sacrilegious irony. Do you mean, citizens, to mock me, by asking me to speak to-day? If so, there is a parallel to your conduct. And let me warn you that it is dangerous to copy the example of a nation whose crimes, towering up to heaven, were thrown down by the breath of the Almighty, burying that nation in **irrevocable** ruin! I can to-day take up the plaintive lament of a peeled and woe-smitten people!

5   "By the rivers of Babylon, there we sat down. Yea! We wept when we remembered Zion. We hanged our harps upon the willows in the midst thereof. For there, they that carried us away captive, required of us a song; and they who wasted us required of us mirth, saying, Sing us one of the songs of Zion. How can we sing the Lord's song in a strange land? If I forget thee, O Jerusalem, let my right hand forget her cunning. If I do not remember thee, let my tongue cleave to the roof of my mouth."

6   Fellow-citizens, above your national, tumultuous joy, I hear the mournful wail of millions! whose chains, heavy and grievous yesterday, are, to-day, rendered more intolerable by the jubilee shouts that reach them. If I do forget, if I do not faithfully remember those bleeding children of sorrow this day, "may my right hand forget her cunning, and may my tongue cleave to the roof of my mouth!" To forget them, to pass lightly over their wrongs, and to chime in with the popular theme, would be treason most scandalous and shocking, and would make me a **reproach** before God and the world. My subject, then, fellow-citizens, is American slavery. I shall see this day and its popular characteristics from the slave's point of view. Standing there identified with the American bondman, making his wrongs mine, I do not hesitate to declare, with all my soul, that the character and conduct of this nation never looked blacker to me than on this 4th of July! Whether we turn to the declarations of the past, or to the professions of the present, the conduct of the nation seems equally hideous and revolting. America is false to the past, false to the present, and solemnly binds herself to be false to the future. Standing with God and the crushed and bleeding slave on this occasion, I will, in the name of humanity which is outraged, in the name of liberty which is fettered, in the name of the constitution and the Bible which are disregarded and trampled upon, dare to call in question and to denounce, with all the emphasis I can command, everything that serves to perpetuate slavery the great sin and shame of America! "I will not equivocate; I will not excuse"; I will use the severest language I can command; and yet not one word shall escape me that any

Please note that excerpts and passages in the StudySync® library and this workbook are intended as touchstones to generate interest in an author's work. The excerpts and passages do not substitute for the reading of entire texts, and StudySync® strongly recommends that students seek out and purchase the whole literary or informational work in order to experience it as the author intended. Links to online resellers are available in our digital library. In addition, complete works may be ordered through an authorized reseller by filling out and returning to StudySync® the order form enclosed in this workbook.

Reading & Writing Companion   **159**

man, whose judgment is not blinded by prejudice, or who is not at heart a slaveholder, shall not confess to be right and just.

7   But I fancy I hear some one of my audience say, "It is just in this circumstance that you and your brother abolitionists fail to make a favorable impression on the public mind. Would you argue more, and denounce less; would you persuade more, and rebuke less; your cause would be much more likely to succeed." But, I submit, where all is plain there is nothing to be argued. What point in the anti-slavery creed would you have me argue? On what branch of the subject do the people of this country need light? Must I undertake to prove that the slave is a man? That point is **conceded** already. Nobody doubts it. The slaveholders themselves acknowledge it in the enactment of laws for their government. They acknowledge it when they punish disobedience on the part of the slave. There are seventy-two crimes in the State of Virginia which, if committed by a black man (no matter how ignorant he be), subject him to the punishment of death; while only two of the same crimes will subject a white man to the like punishment. What is this but the acknowledgment that the slave is a moral, intellectual, and responsible being? The manhood of the slave is conceded. It is admitted in the fact that Southern statute books are covered with enactments forbidding, under severe fines and penalties, the teaching of the slave to read or to write. When you can point to any such laws in reference to the beasts of the field, then I may consent to argue the manhood of the slave. When the dogs in your streets, when the fowls of the air, when the cattle on your hills, when the fish of the sea, and the reptiles that crawl, shall be unable to distinguish the slave from a brute, then will I argue with you that the slave is a man!

8   For the present, it is enough to affirm the equal manhood of the Negro race. Is it not astonishing that, while we are ploughing, planting, and reaping, using all kinds of mechanical tools, erecting houses, constructing bridges, building ships, working in metals of brass, iron, copper, silver and gold; that, while we are reading, writing and ciphering, acting as clerks, merchants and secretaries, having among us lawyers, doctors, ministers, poets, authors, editors, orators and teachers; that, while we are engaged in all manner of enterprises common to other men, digging gold in California, capturing the whale in the Pacific, feeding sheep and cattle on the hill-side, living, moving, acting, thinking, planning, living in families as husbands, wives and children, and, above all, confessing and worshipping the Christian's God, and looking hopefully for life and immortality beyond the grave, we are called upon to prove that we are men!

9   Would you have me argue that man is entitled to liberty? That he is the rightful owner of his own body? You have already declared it. Must I argue the wrongfulness of slavery? Is that a question for Republicans? Is it to be settled by the rules of logic and argumentation, as a matter beset with great difficulty,

involving a doubtful application of the principle of justice, hard to be understood? How should I look to-day, in the presence of Americans, dividing, and subdividing a discourse, to show that men have a natural right to freedom? Speaking of it relatively and positively, negatively and affirmatively. To do so, would be to make myself ridiculous, and to offer an insult to your understanding. There is not a man beneath the canopy of heaven that does not know that slavery is wrong for him.

10 What, am I to argue that it is wrong to make men brutes, to rob them of their liberty, to work them without wages, to keep them ignorant of their relations to their fellow men, to beat them with sticks, to flay their flesh with the lash, to load their limbs with irons, to hunt them with dogs, to sell them at auction, to sunder their families, to knock out their teeth, to burn their flesh, to starve them into obedience and submission to their masters? Must I argue that a system thus marked with blood, and stained with pollution, is wrong? No! I will not. I have better employment for my time and strength than such arguments would imply.

11 What, then, remains to be argued? Is it that slavery is not divine; that God did not establish it; that our doctors of divinity are mistaken? There is blasphemy in the thought. That which is inhuman, cannot be divine! Who can reason on such a proposition? They that can, may; I cannot. The time for such argument is passed.

12 At a time like this, scorching irony, not convincing argument, is needed. O! Had I the ability, and could reach the nation's ear, I would, to-day, pour out a fiery stream of biting ridicule, blasting reproach, withering sarcasm, and stern **rebuke.** For it is not light that is needed, but fire; it is not the gentle shower, but thunder. We need the storm, the whirlwind, and the earthquake. The feeling of the nation must be quickened; the conscience of the nation must be roused; the propriety of the nation must be startled; the **hypocrisy** of the nation must be exposed; and its crimes against God and man must be proclaimed and denounced.

13 What, to the American slave, is your 4th of July? I answer; a day that reveals to him, more than all other days in the year, the gross injustice and cruelty to which he is the constant victim. To him, your celebration is a sham; your boasted liberty, an unholy license; your national greatness, swelling vanity; your sounds of rejoicing are empty and heartless; your denunciation of tyrants, brass fronted impudence; your shouts of liberty and equality, hollow mockery; your prayers and hymns, your sermons and thanksgivings, with all your religious parade and solemnity, are, to Him, mere **bombast,** fraud, deception, impiety, and hypocrisy — a thin veil to cover up crimes which would disgrace a nation of savages. There is not a nation on the earth guilty

NOTES

Please note that excerpts and passages in the StudySync® library and this workbook are intended as touchstones to generate interest in an author's work. The excerpts and passages do not substitute for the reading of entire texts, and StudySync® strongly recommends that students seek out and purchase the whole literary or informational work in order to experience it as the author intended. Links to online resellers are available in our digital library. In addition, complete works may be ordered through an authorized reseller by filling out and returning to StudySync® the order form enclosed in this workbook.

Reading & Writing Companion **161**

NOTES

of practices more shocking and bloody than are the people of the United States, at this very hour.

14   Go where you may, search where you will, roam through all the monarchies and despotisms of the Old World, travel through South America, search out every abuse, and when you have found the last, lay your facts by the side of the everyday practices of this nation, and you will say with me, that, for revolting barbarity and shameless hypocrisy, America reigns without a rival.

THINK QUESTIONS

1. What is Frederick Douglass's opinion of the Founding Fathers and the Declaration of Independence? Why does he feel that he cannot celebrate the Fourth of July? Cite evidence from the text to support your response.

2. In the sixth paragraph, what does Douglass reveal as is his purpose and point of view? What explanation does he give for his purpose? Cite evidence from the text to support your response.

3. In the third to last paragraph, Douglass describes the type of rhetoric, or use of language, that he believes is fitting for this occasion. What type of rhetoric does Douglass say is appropriate? Why does he believe this type of rhetoric is appropriate? Cite evidence from the text to support your response.

4. The Latin root "par" means equal. Use this knowledge and your familiarity with affixes to arrive at a definition of **disparity**. How is this definition confirmed by context clues in the fourth paragraph?

5. The Greek word "hypokrisis" refers to an actor playing a role on stage. How does this relate to your understanding of the denotation of **hypocrisy** in the third-from-last paragraph? Are the connotations of the words the same or different? What other words in the text help to support the connotation of the word "hypocrisy"?

CLOSE READ

Reread the speech "What to the Slave Is the Fourth of July?" As you reread, complete the Focus Questions below. Then use your answers and annotations from the questions to help you complete the Writing Prompt.

FOCUS QUESTIONS

1. Reread the second paragraph. What **rhetorical device** does Douglass use in this paragraph? Highlight one example of this rhetorical device. Explain how Douglass uses this rhetorical device to strengthen his argument.

2. Reread paragraphs 4–6. Paragraph 5 consists of a lengthy quotation from Psalm 137 in the Christian Bible, which expresses the sorrow of the Jewish people held as captives in Babylon. How do paragraphs 4 and 6 relate to this quotation? How does this **Biblical allusion** support Douglass' argument?

3. Reread paragraphs 9–11. Highlight an example of a **rhetorical appeal.** Explain how it appeals to logic (logos), emotions (pathos), ethics (ethos), or some combination and how it helps strengthen Douglass' argument.

4. In the third-to-last paragraph, what **figurative language** does Douglass use? Identify the type of figurative language. What point do you think Douglass was trying to make? Do you find his use of figurative language powerful and persuasive?

5. The complete version of Douglass's speech follows a standard **text structure** for argumentative writing. The speech begins with an introduction, presents body paragraphs with arguments and counterarguments, and ends with a conclusion. However, within the speech, Douglass uses a **compare-contrast text structure.** Reread the last two paragraphs. Highlight at least one example of comparison and contrast. Explain how that text structure helps to strengthen his argument.

6. What does Douglass directly express about his point of view and purpose for speaking? Do these differ from the expectations of his audience? How do his point of view and purpose reflect the role in society that Douglass envisions for himself?

WRITING PROMPT

Select an example of text from "What to the Slave Is the Fourth of July?" that is particularly powerful, persuasive, and/or beautiful. How does the style and content of this passage, particularly Douglass's choice of effective rhetorical strategies and/or devices, contribute to one or more of those qualities? Provide strong and relevant details from the text that help you develop and support your analysis.

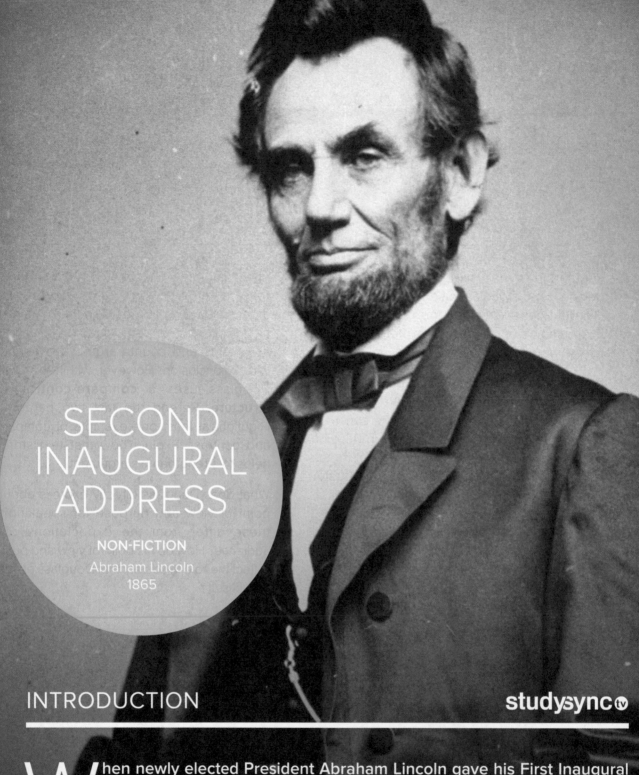

SECOND INAUGURAL ADDRESS

NON-FICTION
Abraham Lincoln
1865

INTRODUCTION

When newly elected President Abraham Lincoln gave his First Inaugural Address, he promised to uphold the Union, even though Northern and Southern states were already tearing apart over the issue of slavery. Four years later, on March 4th, 1865, nearing the end of a bitter Civil War, Lincoln stood again on the steps of the Capitol, and delivered his Second Inaugural Address. He used this opportunity to reflect upon the war, urge healing, and express hope for the future of the country.

studysync tv

"Fondly do we hope, fervently do we pray, that this mighty scourge of war may speedily pass away."

 FIRST READ

 NOTES

1   Fellow-Countrymen:

2   At this second appearing to take the oath of the Presidential office there is less occasion for an extended address than there was at the first. Then a statement somewhat in detail of a course to be pursued seemed fitting and proper. Now, at the expiration of four years, during which public declarations have been constantly called forth on every point and phase of the great contest which still absorbs the attention and **engrosses** the energies of the nation, little that is new could be presented. The progress of our arms, upon which all else chiefly depends, is as well known to the public as to myself, and it is, I trust, reasonably satisfactory and encouraging to all. With high hope for the future, no prediction in regard to it is ventured.

3   On the occasion corresponding to this four years ago all thoughts were anxiously directed to an impending civil war. All dreaded it, all sought to avert it. While the inaugural address was being delivered from this place, devoted altogether to saving the Union without war, **insurgent** agents were in the city seeking to destroy it without war—seeking to dissolve the Union and divide effects by negotiation. Both parties deprecated war, but one of them would make war rather than let the nation survive, and the other would accept war rather than let it perish, and the war came.

4   One-eighth of the whole population were colored slaves, not distributed generally over the Union, but localized in the southern part of it. These slaves constituted a peculiar and powerful interest. All knew that this interest was somehow the cause of the war. To strengthen, **perpetuate,** and extend this interest was the object for which the insurgents would rend the Union even by war, while the Government claimed no right to do more than to restrict the territorial enlargement of it. Neither party expected for the war the **magnitude** or the duration which it has already attained. Neither anticipated that the cause of the conflict might cease with or even before the conflict itself should

cease. Each looked for an easier triumph, and a result less fundamental and astounding. Both read the same Bible and pray to the same God, and each invokes His aid against the other. It may seem strange that any men should dare to ask a just God's assistance in wringing their bread from the sweat of other men's faces, but let us judge not, that we be not judged. The prayers of both could not be answered. That of neither has been answered fully. The Almighty has His own purposes. "Woe unto the world because of offenses; for it must needs be that offenses come, but woe to that man by whom the offense cometh." If we shall suppose that American slavery is one of those offenses which, in the providence of God, must needs come, but which, having continued through His appointed time, He now wills to remove, and that He gives to both North and South this terrible war as the woe due to those by whom the offense came, shall we **discern** therein any departure from those divine attributes which the believers in a living God always ascribe to Him? Fondly do we hope, **fervently** do we pray, that this mighty scourge of war may speedily pass away. Yet, if God wills that it continue until all the wealth piled by the bondsman's two hundred and fifty years of **unrequited** toil shall be sunk, and until every drop of blood drawn with the lash shall be paid by another drawn with the sword, as was said three thousand years ago, so still it must be said "the judgments of the Lord are true and righteous altogether."

5   With malice toward none, with charity for all, with firmness in the right as God gives us to see the right, let us strive on to finish the work we are in, to bind up the nation's wounds, to care for him who shall have borne the battle and for his widow and his orphan, to do all which may achieve and cherish a just and lasting peace among ourselves and with all nations.

THINK QUESTIONS

1. What do you think was Lincoln's main purpose in this inaugural address? Cite evidence from the text to support your response.

2. In the third paragraph, the word "interest" appears three times. What does "interest" refer to? Cite evidence from the text to support your response.

3. Lincoln mentions God and the Almighty a great deal toward the end of his speech. Does he believe that God is on the side of the North, the South, both, or neither? Cite evidence from the text to support your response.

4. The word "perpetual" is an adjective that means continuing for a very long time. Locate the word **perpetuate** in the third paragraph. Explain how you can determine its part of speech and describe what you think "perpetuate" means. Then explain whether your inferred meaning makes sense in the context of the sentence.

5. You might recall that the Latin word "magna" means "great or large." How does this knowledge help you arrive at a preliminary definition of the word **magnitude?** What other words can you think of that share the same root "magna"? How are the words related? Then explain if your predicted meaning makes sense in the context of the sentence.

Please note that excerpts and passages in the StudySync® library and this workbook are intended as touchstones to generate interest in an author's work. The excerpts and passages do not substitute for the reading of entire texts, and StudySync® strongly recommends that students seek out and purchase the whole literary or informational work in order to experience it as the author intended. Links to online resellers are available in our digital library. In addition, complete works may be ordered through an authorized reseller by filling out and returning to StudySync® the order form enclosed in this workbook.

Reading & Writing Companion 167

CLOSE READ

Reread the speech "Second Inaugural Address." As you reread, complete the Focus Questions below. Then use your answers and annotations from the questions to help you complete the Writing Prompt.

FOCUS QUESTIONS

1. What do you think was the purpose of the first paragraph?

2. Reread the second paragraph. How did Lincoln compare and contrast the South and the North? How did Lincoln use the connotation of the word "insurgent" to reveal his view of the South? Why didn't he, for example, use a synonym such as "revolutionary"?

3. Reread the third paragraph. Why do you think Lincoln used the word "interest" to describe slavery instead of the term "slavery" itself? Make sure that your response considers the connotation of the word "interest."

4. In the third paragraph, what ideas did Lincoln express about God and the events of the civil war? How do the references to God and the Bible relate to Lincoln's main message about peace and healing?

5. Reread the last paragraph. Describe the rhetorical appeals (such as, appeals to logic, emotion, or ethics) and rhetorical devices (for instance, parallelism and figurative language) that Lincoln used in his concluding remarks. How did his use of rhetoric help him describe and express the roles he expected citizens to play in rebuilding society after the war?

WRITING PROMPT

Pretend you work for a newspaper of the time and are tasked with writing an account of Lincoln's speech, which you just witnessed live. Prepare a 300-word article that summarizes the speech and explains Lincoln's message to the American people. Your article should incorporate quotes from the speech and evaluate how well Lincoln used rhetoric to get his points across. You may include any imaginary details about the speaker, setting, and crowd that you wish.

LEE SURRENDERS TO GRANT, APRIL 9TH 1865

NON-FICTION
Horace Porter
1865

INTRODUCTION

Richmond, the capital of the Confederacy, fell to the Union on April 3, 1865. After a few more days of battle, Ulysses S. Grant wrote to Robert E. Lee and suggested that further fighting could only result in more senseless deaths. With his army overwhelmed and out of resources, Lee reluctantly agreed. Horace Porter, a Union officer, was present when the great generals met to discuss the surrender, and the excerpt below comes from his first-hand account.

"His face showed plainly that he was quite anxious to have this concession made..."

FIRST READ

1 When Lee came to the sentence about the officers' side-arms, private horses, and baggage, he showed for the first time during the reading of the letter a slight change of **countenance,** and was evidently touched by this act of generosity. It was doubtless the condition mentioned to which he particularly alluded when he looked toward General Grant as he finished reading and said with some degree of warmth in his manner: "This will have a very happy effect upon my army."

2 General Grant then said: "Unless you have some suggestions to make in regard to the form in which I have stated the terms, I will have a copy of the letter made in ink and sign it."

3 "There is one thing I would like to mention," Lee replied after a short pause. "The cavalrymen and artillerists own their own horses in our army. Its organization in this respect differs from that of the United States." This expression attracted the notice of our officers present, as showing how firmly the **conviction** was grounded in his mind that we were two distinct countries. He continued: "I would like to understand whether these men will be permitted to retain their horses?"

4 "You will find that the terms as written do not allow this," General Grant replied; "only the officers are permitted to take their private property."

5 Lee read over the second page of the letter again, and then said: "No, I see the terms do not allow it; that is clear."

6 His face showed plainly that he was quite anxious to have this **concession** made, and Grant said very promptly and without giving Lee time to make a direct request.

Copyright © BookheadEd Learning, LLC

7   "Well, the subject is quite new to me. Of course I did not know that any private soldiers owned their animals, but I think this will be the last battle of the war—I sincerely hope so—and that the surrender of this army will be followed soon by that of all the others, and I take it that most of the men in the ranks are small farmers, and as the country has been so raided by the two armies, it is doubtful whether they will be able to put in a crop to carry themselves and their families through the next winter without the aid of the horses they are now riding, and I will arrange it in this way: I will not change the terms as now written, but I will instruct the officers I shall appoint to receive the paroles to let all the men who claim to own a horse or mule take the animals home with them to work their little farms."

8   Lee now looked greatly relieved, and though anything but a **demonstrative** man, he gave every evidence of his appreciation of this concession, and said, "This will have the best possible effect upon the men. It will be very gratifying and will do much toward **conciliating** our people."

THINK QUESTIONS

1. If General Lee feels at first that the terms of surrender "will have a very happy effect upon my army," why does he suggest a change? Support your answer with evidence from the text.

2. In paragraph 3, what observation did the Union officers make about General Lee? What led them to this observation?

3. In the second to last paragraph, what modification does Grant make to the way the surrender will be carried out? Why does he make this change? Support your answer with evidence from the text.

4. The word **concession** is related to the word "concede." Use this knowledge along with the meaning of the suffix "-ion" to determine a possible meaning for the word "concession." Next, review the surrounding text to identify an example of a concession. Does the context support your predicted meaning?

5. According to the dictionary, the origin of the word **conciliate** is the Latin word "conciliare," which means "to assemble, unite, win over." Given this information, what do you think the word "conciliating" means in the final sentence? Does the context support your inferred definition?

Please note that excerpts and passages in the StudySync® library and this workbook are intended as touchstones to generate interest in an author's work. The excerpts and passages do not substitute for the reading of entire texts, and StudySync® strongly recommends that students seek out and purchase the whole literary or informational work in order to experience it as the author intended. Links to online resellers are available in our digital library. In addition, complete works may be ordered through an authorized reseller by filling out and returning to StudySync® the order form enclosed in this workbook.

Reading & Writing Companion   **171**

CLOSE READ

Reread the excerpt from the text "Lee Surrenders to Grant, April 9th, 1865." As you reread, complete the Focus Questions below. Then use your answers and annotations from the questions to help you complete the Writing Prompt.

FOCUS QUESTIONS

1. Reread the first two paragraphs. How would you describe the feelings that Generals Grant and Lee show toward each other?

2. Reread paragraph 3. How does the narrator Horace Porter make his presence known in this passage? What is the effect of his commentary here?

3. Reread paragraphs 6 and 7. What can you infer about Grant's leadership qualities as they relate to conflict resolution?

4. Reread the last paragraph. What do you think was one of the goals of this meeting? Do you think the generals achieved this goal?

5. Consider the effects that Grant's decisions will have on the defeated troops. In his point of view, what is the best way for these men to find their new places in the post-war society?

WRITING PROMPT

What admirable qualities of leadership do the two generals demonstrate? How do these qualities help the generals resolve conflict and broker a deal that is considerate to both sides? Provide strong and thorough evidence from the text to support your inferences.

WHAT THEY FOUGHT FOR 1861-1865

NON-FICTION

James M. McPherson
1994

INTRODUCTION

Diaries and letters leave a first-hand account long after their writers are gone. Author James McPherson used the accounts of nearly a thousand Union and Confederate soldiers to describe the motivations of those who fought in the Civil War. In this passage, we hear from Union soldiers.

"I will fight till I die if necessary for the liberties which you have so long enjoyed."

FIRST READ

NOTES

Excerpt From Chapter 2: "The Best Government on God's Footstool"

1   One of the questions often asked a Civil War historian is, "Why did the North fight?" Southern motives seem easier to understand. Confederates fought for independence, for their own property and way of life, for their very survival as a nation. But what did the Yankees fight for? Why did they persist through four years of the bloodiest conflict in American history, costing 360,000 northern lives—not to mention 260,000 southern lives and untold destruction of resources? Puzzling over this question in 1863, Confederate War Department clerk John Jones wrote in his diary: "Our men must prevail in combat, or lose their property, country, freedom, everything.... On the other hand the enemy, in yielding the contest, may retire into their own country, and possess everything they enjoyed before the war began."

2   If that was true, why did the Yankees keep fighting? We can find much of the answer in Abraham Lincoln's notable speeches: the Gettysburg Address, his first and second inaugural addresses, the **peroration** of his message to Congress on December 1, 1862. But we can find even more of the answer in the wartime letters and diaries of the men who did the fighting. Confederates who said that they fought for the same goals as their forebears of 1776 would have been surprised by the intense conviction of the northern soldiers that they were upholding the legacy of the American Revolution.

3   "We fight for the blessings bought by the blood and treasure of our Fathers," wrote an enlisted man from Missouri to his parents in 1861. "I will fight till I die if necessary for the liberties which you have so long enjoyed." A Michigan soldier told his younger brother that he fought against "Traitors who sought to tear down and break into fragments the glorious temple that our forefathers reared with blood and tears." A New Jersey officer declared that "the man who doesn't give hearty support to our bleeding country in this day of our country's trial is not worthy to be a descendant of our forefathers. . . . We will

Copyright © BookheadEd Learning, LLC

NOTES

be held responsible before God if we don't do our part in helping to transmit this boon of civil and religious liberty down to succeeding generations." An Illinois farm boy whose parents had opposed his enlistment asked them tartly: "Should We the youngest and brightest nation of all the earth bow to traters and forsake the graves of our Fathers?" He answered his own question: "No no never."

4   The theme of parallel sacrifice with the patriots of 1776 punctuated the letters of many Union soldiers. An officer in the 101st Ohio wrote in December, 1862, that "our fathers in coldest winter, half clad marked the road they trod with crimson streams from their bleeding feet that we might enjoy the blessings of a free government." Likewise, "our business in being here [is] to lay down our lives if need be for our country's cause." Two weeks later he was killed in the battle of Stones River. A young Michigan private was also killed in action not long after he wrote a letter to his uncle describing the hardships of a soldier's life. But "did the revolutionary patriots in valley forge," he asked rhetorically, "complain [when] they had to march in the snow with there bare feet and to stand the cold twenty degrees below zero without blankets? . . . We will show our fathers and mothers wifes sisters brothers and sweethearts that we are" worthy of that heritage.

5   Some of those wives, however, told their soldier husbands that they had a greater responsibility to their present families than to the founding fathers. In response to such letters from wives, a good many Union soldiers wrote as did an Ohio lieutenant: "Our Fathers made this country, we, their children are to save it . . . and you should . . . experience a **laudable** pride in the part your [husband and brothers] are now taking to suppress the greatest rebellion the history of the world has ever witnessed . . . Why **denounce** the war when the interest at stake is so vital? . . . Without Union & peace our freedom is worthless . . . our children would have no warrant of liberty. . . . [If] our Country be numbered among the things that were but are not, of what value will be house, family, and friends?" Another Ohio soldier, whose wife complained repeatedly of the burdens of raising three children while worrying about his fate, asked her to "bear your trouble with good cheer. . . . It only gives another trouble on my mind to know that you are so discontented. . . . If you **esteem** me with a true woman's love you will not ask me to disgrace myself by deserting the flag of our Union a flag that is as dear as life to me. . . . No it will never do, cheer up and . . . remember that thousands went forth and poured out their lifs blood in the Revolution to establish this government; and twould be a disgrace to the whole American people if she had not noble sons enough who had the spirit of seventy six in their hearts." Justifying to *his* wife a decision to stay in the army after more than a year's fighting instead of accepting a medical discharge, a thirty-three-year-old Minnesota sergeant, father of three children, wrote home from an army hospital where he was recovering from exhaustion: "My grandfather fought and risked his life to

bequeath to his posterity . . . the glorious Institutions" now threatened by "this infernal rebellion. . . . It is not for you and I, or us & our dear little ones, alone, that I was and am willing to risk the fortunes of the battlefield, but also for the sake of the country's millions who are to come after us."

6   But why did these soldiers think that the "infernal rebellion" jeopardized the survival of the glorious republic? Why could they not, as Confederate Ward Department clerk John Jones suggested, merely return home to a northern nation and leave the South alone so that the two republics could live in peace as dual heirs of the Revolution? Because, said northern soldiers, almost as if in echo of Abraham Lincoln, once admit that a state can secede at will, and republican government by majority rule will come to an end. The dis-United States would fragment into several petty, squabbling autocracies, proving the contention of European monarchists and reactionaries that this harebrained experiment in democracy could not last. Government of the people, by the people, for the people would perish from the earth. Many Union soldiers voiced with extraordinary passion the conviction that preservation of the *United* States as "the beacon light of liberty & freedom to the human race," in the words of a thirty-five-year-old Indiana sergeant, was indeed the last, best hope for the survival of republican liberties in the Western world.

Excerpted from *What They Fought For 1861–1865* by James M. McPherson, published by Anchor Books.

 THINK QUESTIONS

1.   Based on the first paragraph, how would you describe McPherson's purpose for writing? Do you think he presents his purpose in a clear way that engages the reader's interest? Cite evidence from the text to support your response.

2.   Why did Union soldiers consider Confederate soldiers to be traitors? Provide details from the text, including direct quotes from the soldiers themselves, to support your response.

3.   According to the text, what did Europe think about American democracy and how would that view be affected by the outcome of the U.S. Civil War? Cite evidence from the text to support your response.

4.   Reread the sentence that contains the vocabulary word **esteem.** Explain how context clues can help you determine a possible meaning for this word.

5.   How do context clues help you understand the meaning of the word **bequeath?** Write the possible meaning of the word and cite textual evidence that supports your prediction. Then check whether your definition makes sense in the original sentence.

CLOSE READ

Reread the excerpt from *What They Fought For 1861–1865*. As you reread, complete the Focus Questions below. Then use your answers and annotations from the questions to help you complete the Writing Prompt.

 FOCUS QUESTIONS

1. In the first paragraph, McPherson tells us that he is "a Civil War historian." What details in the second paragraph support and expand upon this description? What do these details suggest about the purpose of this chapter?

2. Reread the first three paragraphs. In the second paragraph, what surprising similarity does McPherson describe between Northern and Southern soldiers? How does the first paragraph help explain the Southern viewpoint and the third paragraph the Northern viewpoint?

3. What is the main idea of the fourth paragraph? Highlight a supporting detail and explain how it relates to the main idea? Do you think the structure of this paragraph helps to express the main idea in a convincing and engaging way?

4. In the fifth paragraph, what new idea is introduced? How does that idea relate to and build upon another central idea expressed in a previous paragraph?

5. Reread the last paragraph. How does that paragraph function as a conclusion? What does this paragraph suggest about the writer's point of view, or thoughts and feelings, about the role that individual northern soldiers played in the Civil War?

WRITING PROMPT

Did you find McPherson's presentation of historical information engaging? Did you think he was persuasive in convincing readers to accept his claims about the Civil War? Write a short essay explaining whether you found the text engaging and persuasive. In your essay, support your response by analyzing examples from the text of McPherson's writing style and the content he chose to include.

Please note that excerpts and passages in the StudySync® library and this workbook are intended as touchstones to generate interest in an author's work. The excerpts and passages do not substitute for the reading of entire texts, and StudySync® strongly recommends that students seek out and purchase the whole literary or informational work in order to experience it as the author intended. Links to online resellers are available in our digital library. In addition, complete works may be ordered through an authorized reseller by filling out and returning to StudySync® the order form enclosed in this workbook.

Reading & Writing Companion   **177**

THE CASK OF AMONTILLADO

FICTION
Edgar Allan Poe
1846

INTRODUCTION

In his final short story, Poe's distinctive style and characteristic themes of murder and revenge find their appropriate setting in a dark, damp, Italian catacomb. Claiming he needs his opinion on a rare vintage, Montresor lures an acquaintance, Fortunato, into the depths of an underground wine cellar. Once inside, it's more than a taste of sherry that awaits the unsuspecting visitor.

"At length I would be avenged..."

FIRST READ

NOTES

1 The thousand injuries of Fortunato I had borne as I best could; but when he ventured upon insult, I vowed revenge. You, who so well know the nature of my soul, will not suppose, however, that I gave **utterance** to a threat. At length I would be avenged; this was a point definitively settled—but the very definitiveness with which it was resolved, precluded the idea of risk. I must not only punish, but punish with **impunity.** A wrong is unredressed when **retribution** overtakes its redresser. It is equally unredressed when the avenger fails to make himself felt as such to him who has done the wrong.

2 It must be understood, that neither by word nor deed had I given Fortunato cause to doubt my good will. I continued, as was my wont, to smile in his face, and he did not perceive that my smile now was at the thought of his immolation.

3 He had a weak point—this Fortunato—although in other regards he was a man to be respected and even feared. He prided himself on his **connoisseurship** in wine. Few Italians have the true virtuoso spirit. For the most part their enthusiasm is adopted to suit the time and opportunity—to practise imposture upon the British and Austrian millionaires. In painting and gemmary, Fortunato, like his countrymen, was a quack—but in the matter of old wines he was sincere. In this respect I did not differ from him materially: I was skilful in the Italian vintages myself, and bought largely whenever I could.

4 It was about dusk, one evening during the supreme madness of the carnival season, that I encountered my friend. He **accosted** me with excessive warmth, for he had been drinking much. The man wore motley. He had on a tight-fitting parti-striped dress, and his head was surmounted by the conical cap and bells. I was so pleased to see him, that I thought I should never have done wringing his hand.

Please note that excerpts and passages in the StudySync® library and this workbook are intended as touchstones to generate interest in an author's work. The excerpts and passages do not substitute for the reading of entire texts, and StudySync® strongly recommends that students seek out and purchase the whole literary or informational work in order to experience it as the author intended. Links to online resellers are available in our digital library. In addition, complete works may be ordered through an authorized reseller by filling out and returning to StudySync® the order form enclosed in this workbook.

Reading & Writing Companion   **179**

5   I said to him—"My dear Fortunato, you are luckily met. How remarkably well you are looking to-day! But I have received a pipe of what passes for Amontillado, and I have my doubts."

6   "How?" said he. "Amontillado? A pipe? Impossible! And in the middle of the carnival!"

7   "I have my doubts," I replied; "and I was silly enough to pay the full Amontillado price without consulting you in the matter. You were not to be found, and I was fearful of losing a bargain."

8   "Amontillado!"

9   "I have my doubts."

10   "Amontillado!"

11   "And I must satisfy them."

12   "Amontillado!"

13   "As you are engaged, I am on my way to Luchesi. If any one has a critical turn, it is he. He will tell me—"

14   "Luchesi cannot tell Amontillado from Sherry."

15   "And yet some fools will have it that his taste is a match for your own."

16   "Come, let us go."

17   "Whither?"

18   "To your vaults."

19   "My friend, no; I will not impose upon your good nature. I perceive you have an engagement. Luchesi—"

20   "I have no engagement;—come."

21   "My friend, no. It is not the engagement, but the severe cold with which I perceive you are afflicted. The vaults are insufferably damp. They are encrusted with nitre."

22   "Let us go, nevertheless. The cold is merely nothing. Amontillado! You have been imposed upon. And as for Luchesi, he cannot distinguish Sherry from Amontillado."

23   Thus speaking, Fortunato possessed himself of my arm. Putting on a mask of black silk, and drawing a roquelaire closely about my person, I suffered him to hurry me to my palazzo.

24   There were no attendants at home; they had absconded to make merry in honor of the time. I had told them that I should not return until the morning, and had given them explicit orders not to stir from the house. These orders were sufficient, I well knew, to insure their immediate disappearance, one and all, as soon as my back was turned.

25   I took from their sconces two flambeaux, and giving one to Fortunato, bowed him through several suites of rooms to the archway that led into the vaults. I passed down a long and winding staircase, requesting him to be cautious as he followed. We came at length to the foot of the descent, and stood together on the damp ground of the catacombs of the Montresors.

26   The gait of my friend was unsteady, and the bells upon his cap jingled as he strode.

27   "The pipe," said he.

28   "It is farther on," said I; "but observe the white web-work which gleams from these cavern walls."

29   He turned towards me, and looked into my eyes with two filmy orbs that distilled the rheum of intoxication.

30   "Nitre?" he asked, at length.

31   "Nitre," I replied. "How long have you had that cough?"

32   "Ugh! ugh! ugh!—ugh! ugh! ugh!—ugh! ugh! ugh!—ugh! ugh! ugh!—ugh! ugh! ugh!"

33   My poor friend found it impossible to reply for many minutes.

34   "It is nothing," he said, at last.

35   "Come," I said, with decision, "we will go back; your health is precious. You are rich, respected, admired, beloved; you are happy, as once I was. You are a man to be missed. For me it is no matter. We will go back; you will be ill, and I cannot be responsible. Besides, there is Luchesi—"

36   "Enough," he said; "the cough is a mere nothing; it will not kill me. I shall not die of a cough."

Please note that excerpts and passages in the StudySync® library and this workbook are intended as touchstones to generate interest in an author's work. The excerpts and passages do not substitute for the reading of entire texts, and StudySync® strongly recommends that students seek out and purchase the whole literary or informational work in order to experience it as the author intended. Links to online resellers are available in our digital library. In addition, complete works may be ordered through an authorized reseller by filling out and returning to StudySync® the order form enclosed in this workbook.

Reading & Writing Companion   **181**

Copyright © BookheadEd Learning, LLC

37 "True—true," I replied; "and, indeed, I had no intention of alarming you unnecessarily—but you should use all proper caution. A draught of this Medoc will defend us from the damps."

38 Here I knocked off the neck of a bottle which I drew from a long row of its fellows that lay upon the mould.

39 "Drink," I said, presenting him the wine.

40 He raised it to his lips with a leer. He paused and nodded to me familiarly, while his bells jingled.

41 "I drink," he said, "to the buried that repose around us."

42 "And I to your long life."

43 He again took my arm, and we proceeded.

44 "These vaults," he said, "are extensive."

45 "The Montresors," I replied, "were a great and numerous family."

46 "I forget your arms."

47 "A huge human foot d'or, in a field azure; the foot crushes a serpent rampant whose fangs are imbedded in the heel."

48 "And the motto?"

49 "Nemo me impune lacessit."

50 "Good!" he said.

51 The wine sparkled in his eyes and the bells jingled. My own fancy grew warm with the Medoc. We had passed through walls of piled bones, with casks and puncheons intermingling, into the inmost recesses of the catacombs. I paused again, and this time I made bold to seize Fortunato by an arm above the elbow.

52 "The nitre!" I said: "see, it increases. It hangs like moss upon the vaults. We are below the river's bed. The drops of moisture trickle among the bones. Come, we will go back ere it is too late. Your cough—"

53 "It is nothing," he said; "let us go on. But first, another draught of the Medoc."

54   I broke and reached him a flagon of De Grave. He emptied it at a breath. His eyes flashed with a fierce light. He laughed and threw the bottle upwards with a **gesticulation** I did not understand.

55   I looked at him in surprise. He repeated the movement—a grotesque one.

56   "You do not comprehend?" he said.

57   "Not I," I replied.

58   "Then you are not of the brotherhood."

59   "How?"

60   "You are not of the masons."

61   "Yes, yes," I said, "yes, yes."

62   "You? Impossible! A mason?"

63   "A mason," I replied.

64   "A sign," he said.

65   "It is this," I answered, producing a trowel from beneath the folds of my roquelaire.

66   "You jest," he exclaimed, recoiling a few paces. "But let us proceed to the Amontillado."

67   "Be it so," I said, replacing the tool beneath the cloak, and again offering him my arm. He leaned upon it heavily. We continued our route in search of the Amontillado. We passed through a range of low arches, descended, passed on, and descending again, arrived at a deep crypt, in which the foulness of the air caused our flambeaux rather to glow than flame.

68   At the most remote end of the crypt there appeared another less spacious. Its walls had been lined with human remains, piled to the vault overhead, in the fashion of the great catacombs of Paris. Three sides of this interior crypt were still ornamented in this manner. From the fourth the bones had been thrown down, and lay promiscuously upon the earth, forming at one point a mound of some size. Within the wall thus exposed by the displacing of the bones, we perceived a still interior recess, in depth about four feet, in width three, in height six or seven. It seemed to have been constructed for no especial use in itself, but formed merely the interval between two of the colossal supports of the roof of the catacombs, and was backed by one of their circumscribing walls of solid granite.

69   It was in vain that Fortunato, uplifting his dull torch, endeavored to pry into the depths of the recess. Its termination the feeble light did not enable us to see.

70   "Proceed," I said; "herein is the Amontillado. As for Luchesi—"

71   "He is an ignoramus," interrupted my friend, as he stepped unsteadily forward, while I followed immediately at his heels. In an instant he had reached the extremity of the niche, and finding his progress arrested by the rock, stood stupidly bewildered. A moment more and I had fettered him to the granite. In its surface were two iron staples, distant from each other about two feet, horizontally. From one of these depended a short chain, from the other a padlock. Throwing the links about his waist, it was but the work of a few seconds to secure it. He was too much astounded to resist. Withdrawing the key I stepped back from the recess.

72   "Pass your hand," I said, "over the wall; you cannot help feeling the nitre. Indeed it is very damp. Once more let me implore you to return. No? Then I must positively leave you. But I must first render you all the little attentions in my power."

73   "The Amontillado!" ejaculated my friend, not yet recovered from his astonishment.

74   "True," I replied; "the Amontillado."

75   As I said these words I busied myself among the pile of bones of which I have before spoken. Throwing them aside, I soon uncovered a quantity of building stone and mortar. With these materials and with the aid of my trowel, I began vigorously to wall up the entrance of the niche.

76   I had scarcely laid the first tier of my masonry when I discovered that the intoxication of Fortunato had in a great measure worn off. The earliest indication I had of this was a low moaning cry from the depth of the recess. It was not the cry of a drunken man. There was then a long and obstinate silence. I laid the second tier, and the third, and the fourth; and then I heard the furious vibrations of the chain. The noise lasted for several minutes, during which, that I might hearken to it with the more satisfaction, I ceased my labors and sat down upon the bones. When at last the clanking subsided, I resumed the trowel, and finished without interruption the fifth, the sixth, and the seventh tier. The wall was now nearly upon a level with my breast. I again paused, and holding the flambeaux over the mason-work, threw a few feeble rays upon the figure within.

77   A succession of loud and shrill screams, bursting suddenly from the throat of the chained form, seemed to thrust me violently back. For a brief moment I hesitated—I trembled. Unsheathing my rapier, I began to grope with it about

Copyright © BookheadEd Learning, LLC

the recess: but the thought of an instant reassured me. I placed my hand upon the solid fabric of the catacombs, and felt satisfied. I reapproached the wall. I replied to the yells of him who clamored. I re-echoed—I aided—I surpassed them in volume and in strength. I did this, and the clamorer grew still.

78 It was now midnight, and my task was drawing to a close. I had completed the eighth, the ninth, and the tenth tier. I had finished a portion of the last and the eleventh; there remained but a single stone to be fitted and plastered in. I struggled with its weight; I placed it partially in its destined position. But now there came from out the niche a low laugh that erected the hairs upon my head. It was succeeded by a sad voice, which I had difficulty in recognising as that of the noble Fortunato. The voice said—

79 "Ha! ha! ha!—he! he!—a very good joke indeed—an excellent jest. We will have many a rich laugh about it at the palazzo—he! he! he!—over our wine—he! he! he!"

80 "The Amontillado!" I said.

81 "He! he! he!—he! he! he!—yes, the Amontillado. But is it not getting late? Will not they be awaiting us at the palazzo, the Lady Fortunato and the rest? Let us be gone."

82 "Yes," I said, "let us be gone."

83 "For the love of God, Montressor!"

84 "Yes," I said, "for the love of God!" But to these words I hearkened in vain for a reply. I grew impatient. I called aloud—

85 "Fortunato!"

86 No answer. I called again—

87 "Fortunato!"

88 No answer still. I thrust a torch through the remaining aperture and let it fall within. There came forth in return only a jingling of the bells. My heart grew sick—on account of the dampness of the catacombs. I hastened to make an end of my labor. I forced the last stone into its position; I plastered it up. Against the new masonry I re-erected the old rampart of bones. For the half of a century no mortal has disturbed them. *In pace requiescat!*

THINK QUESTIONS

1. How would you describe the narrator of this story? Cite evidence from the text to support your response.

2. How do the narrator's spoken remarks to Fortunato compare with his internal feelings for the man? Cite evidence from the text to support your response.

3. Montresor tells Fortunato that his family motto is *Nemo me impune lacessit*, which is Latin for "No one attacks me with impunity." How does that motto, along with image of a foot crushing a serpent in the Montresor's family coat of arms, symbolize the events of the story?

4. In the first paragraph, notice that the two words **punish** and **impunity** share the same root word. How do the prefix "im-" and the suffix "-ity" provide clues about the meaning of "impunity"? Use that information to explain what the narrator means by the sentence, "I must not only punish, but punish with impunity."

5. Locate the vocabulary word **gesticulation** in the text. What paragraph clues help you determine the possible meaning of the word? What synonym clue shows up in the next paragraph?

CLOSE READ

Reread the short story "The Cask of Amontillado." As you reread, complete the Focus Questions below. Then use your answers and annotations from the questions to help you complete the Writing Prompt.

FOCUS QUESTIONS

1. Reread the first paragraph. Why does Montresor vow revenge against Fortunato? Why do you think Poe chooses to leave matters uncertain by not specifying what Fortunato did?

2. Reread paragraphs 3 and 4. How does Poe introduce the character of Fortunato? What do you think Fortunato's costume might symbolize? What might be ironic about his costume?

3. What ploy does Montresor use on his staff to make sure that no one else will be home when he takes Fortunato there? How is this an example of verbal irony? How does Montresor use the same type of ploy on Fortunato?

4. Poe's story is filled with irony. Identify at least one example of irony in the story and explain how it is ironic. Then describe the effect of this irony.

5. In the middle of the story, Montresor and Fortunato discuss the "brotherhood" of the masons. How does this exchange and the dual meaning of the word "mason" relate to the rest of the story, particularly the climax?

6. Reread the description of the setting following the "mason" dialogue. What is the mood, or overall atmosphere, of the scene? How does Poe use setting details to create this mood? What might the setting symbolize?

7. Reread the part of the story where Montresor builds a brick wall to trap Fortunato in the crypt. Why do you think Montresor begins to refer to Fortunato by terms such as "the figure," "the chained form," and "the clamorer"?

8. Reread the beginning and resolution of the story. How do these paragraphs relate to Montresor's sense of his place in society? Do you think he sees himself in a positive or negative light? Explain.

WRITING PROMPT

What insights about the dark side of human nature does "The Cask of Amontillado" offer its readers? What themes emerge regarding pride and revenge? Consider the symbolism in the story, including the overall story structure of a journey into the underworld. Explain your response using strong and thorough evidence from the text.

Please note that excerpts and passages in the StudySync® library and this workbook are intended as touchstones to generate interest in an author's work. The excerpts and passages do not substitute for the reading of entire texts, and StudySync® strongly recommends that students seek out and purchase the whole literary or informational work in order to experience it as the author intended. Links to online resellers are available in our digital library. In addition, complete works may be ordered through an authorized reseller by filling out and returning to StudySync® the order form enclosed in this workbook.

Reading & Writing Companion   **187**

BECAUSE I COULD NOT STOP FOR DEATH

POETRY
Emily Dickinson
1890

INTRODUCTION

Beloved American poet Emily Dickinson composed nearly 1,800 poems, but less than a dozen were published during her lifetime. The famously private Dickinson lived an untraditional lifestyle, but held a deep understanding of the human condition. It shines through in "Because I could not stop for Death," her flawlessly written lyrical poem about death and what might follow.

"Because I could not stop for Death—He kindly stopped for me..."

FIRST READ

NOTES

1 Because I could not stop for Death—
2 He kindly stopped for me—
3 The Carriage held but just Ourselves—
4 And **Immortality.**

5 We slowly drove—He knew no haste
6 And I had put away
7 My labor and my leisure too,
8 For His **Civility—**

9 We passed the School, where Children strove
10 At Recess—in the Ring—
11 We passed the Fields of Gazing Grain—
12 We passed the Setting Sun—

13 Or rather—He passed us—
14 The Dews drew quivering and chill—
15 For only **Gossamer,** my Gown—
16 My Tippet—only Tulle—

17 We paused before a House that seemed
18 A Swelling of the Ground—
19 The Roof was scarcely visible—
20 The Cornice—in the Ground—

21 Since then—'tis Centuries—and yet
22 Feels shorter than the Day
23 I first **surmised** the Horses' Heads
24 Were toward **Eternity—**

Reading & Writing
Companion

THINK QUESTIONS

1. Based on the first two stanzas of the poem, what inferences can you make about the speaker? Provide textual evidence that supports your response.

2. Look at the third stanza of the poem. Explain how the poet uses repetition for effect in this stanza, both in terms of style and meaning. Cite direct quotations to help develop your explanation.

3. In what different ways is time referenced and represented in the poem? What might this treatment suggest about a possible theme for the poem? Provide details from the text to develop and support your ideas.

4. Consider the Latin root of "civility," civis," which means "citizen." How does this information, combined with your knowledge of suffixes, help you to determine the meaning of the word **civility** in the poem? Which word from the previous stanza supports your prediction? What other words do you know that build from the same root? Check that the meaning you determine makes sense in the context of the poem.

5. What context clues throughout the poem help you determine the meaning of the word "Eternity" in the final line? Explain how you arrived at your answer.

CLOSE READ

Reread the poem "Because I could not stop for Death." As you reread, complete the Focus Questions below. Then use your answers and annotations from the questions to help you complete the Writing Prompt.

FOCUS QUESTIONS

1. Analyze the structure of the poem's first and second stanzas in terms of stanza length and meter. What effect does this structure have on the tone at the start of the poem?

2. Locate Dickinson's description of the children in the third stanza. How does their activity relate to the overall theme of the poem? Locate and highlight the word "Ring." How does the word "Ring" link these two lines to the rest of the poem in meaning?

3. Locate and highlight the word "house" in the next-to-last stanza of the poem. How do the figurative and connotative meanings of this specific word influence the tone of the poem? Explore the poet's possible intentions for using this word at this particular point in the poem.

4. Highlight the words "Immortality" at the start of the poem and "Eternity" at the end. What effect

does their placement have on the overall tone of the poem? How does Dickinson's use of these words reflect a primary theme in the poem and suggest her personal views about the nature of life and death?

5. Review your annotations of the poem and select an example of a line that you considered to be "light" in tone. Next, select an example of a line that you considered to be "dark" in tone. Annotate to compare and contrast these two lines of text as evidence to support your own interpretation and summary of the poem's overall theme.

6. After reviewing your annotations, how would you describe the relationship between the speaker of the poem and society in general? What impact does this have on the overall meaning or tone of the poem?

WRITING PROMPT

Locate, read, and closely examine another of Dickinson's poems about death, such as "I felt a Funeral, in my Brain" or "It was not Death, for I stood up." Then write an analysis in which you compare and contrast the tone Dickinson takes toward death in this poem and "Because I could not stop for Death." What do Dickinson's characterizations of death suggest about how she viewed life? How does her use of figurative language help set the tone and develop the theme(s)? Provide strong and thorough textual evidence from both poems to support your analysis.

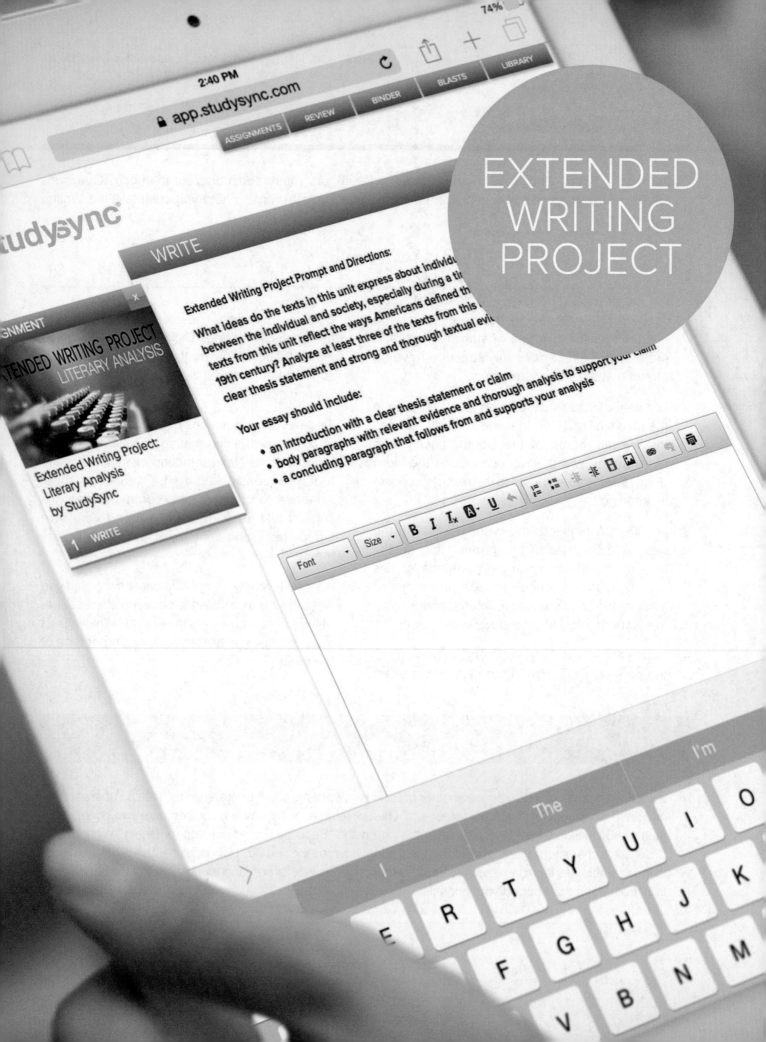

EXTENDED WRITING PROJECT

WRITE

Extended Writing Project Prompt and Directions:

What ideas do the texts in this unit express about individual... between the individual and society, especially during a ti... texts from this unit reflect the ways Americans defined th... 19th century? Analyze at least three of the texts from this... clear thesis statement and strong and thorough textual evi...

Your essay should include:

- an introduction with a clear thesis statement or claim
- body paragraphs with relevant evidence and thorough analysis to support your claim
- a concluding paragraph that follows from and supports your analysis

Extended Writing Project: Literary Analysis by StudySync

1   WRITE

LITERARY ANALYSIS

WRITING PROMPT

What ideas do the texts in this unit express about individualism and the relationship between the individual and society, especially during a time of cultural turmoil? How do the texts from this unit reflect the ways Americans defined themselves as individuals in the 19th century? Analyze at least three of the texts from this unit in an essay that provides a clear thesis statement and strong and thorough textual evidence.

Your essay should include:

- an introduction with a clear thesis statement or claim
- body paragraphs with relevant evidence and thorough analysis to support your claim
- a concluding paragraph that follows from and supports your analysis

Literary analysis is a form of **argumentative writing.** There are different purposes for argumentative writing. For example, an argument might aim to change the readers' perspective, inspire readers to take action, or convince readers to accept the writer's ideas, beliefs, or analysis. In a literary analysis essay, a writer makes claims about the meaning or the value of a literary work and defends his or her interpretations with evidence from the text.

Strong argumentative writing introduces a main idea, often in the form of a central claim, and establishes the significance of that claim with strong and thorough evidence. The writing should stay focused on the central claim and create an organizational structure that logically sequences the supporting details and textual evidence. Though analysis and argumentative writing may express strong opinions based on textual evidence, the writing should maintain a formal style and an objective tone.

The features of literary analysis and argumentative writing include:

- an engaging introduction with a clear thesis statement or central claim
- a clear organizational structure
- body paragraphs that present supporting details
- transitions between paragraphs and ideas
- a formal style and an objective tone
- a strong and memorable conclusion

As you continue with this extended writing project, you'll receive more instructions and practice to help you craft a literary analysis essay.

 ## STUDENT MODEL

Before you get started on your own literary analysis essay, consider this model that one student wrote in response to the writing prompt. As you read, highlight and annotate the features of argumentative writing that the student included in her essay.

Making the Personal Political

One isn't always the loneliest number. While it may be true that there is strength in numbers, there's no denying the social power of the individual. According to the *Encyclopedia Britannica,* the term "individualism" emerged in the 19th century and means a *"political and social philosophy that emphasized the moral worth of the individual (Lukes)."* Many American writers of that period adopted that philosophy and used it to push for changes in society. Sometimes the individual set a new course for his or her own life. At other times, the individual rallied the masses to action. As demonstrated by the works of Henry David Thoreau, Elizabeth Cady Stanton, and Frederick Douglass, some of the most influential social movements relied on significant contributions by individual writers.

Thoreau immediately springs to mind in any discussion of 19th century intellectuals with new ideas about the individual. Alone in his cabin on Walden Pond, Thoreau set out to "front only the essential facts of life, and see if I could not learn what it had to teach." In other words, Thoreau opened himself up to discovering new truths and ideas about the individual and his role in society. As a white man, he probably had more personal freedom than other writers of the time did. The primary goal of his time alone on Walden Pond was self-discovery, but he did not want to keep his epiphanies to himself. Thoreau understood that he could write about his personal experiences and influence the outside world and hope to change things for the better. If life "proved to be mean," Thoreau said, then he would "get the whole and genuine meanness of it, and publish its meanness to the world." At the conclusion of that investigation, Thoreau published *Walden*, a philosophical autobiography that showed readers the value of individual insight and observation.

Thoreau's belief in the power of each individual's personal experience led him to urge his readers to not so readily accept any established belief system but to draw their own conclusions about life based on their direct experiences. He states, "For most men, it appears to me, are in a strange uncertainty about it, whether it is of the devil or of God, and have somewhat hastily concluded that it is the chief end of man here to 'glorify God and enjoy him forever.'" Thoreau himself did not want to arrive at any "hasty conclusions" about the nature and the meaning of life. Instead, he wanted "to know it by experience, and be able to give a true account of it." Thoreau states that he launched into this project of discovery making no assumptions. If life "proved to be mean" or "sublime," whatever he observed, he would write about honestly. Thoreau's observations included criticisms of society, which is perhaps one of the roles that he saw for himself as a writer. For instance, Thoreau believed in nature and simplicity and thought that the country in pursuing economic and technological improvements was becoming "an unwieldy and overgrown establishment."

"The Declaration of Sentiments" by the Seneca Falls Convention described a lot of "mean" things about life in the 19th century, primarily the social, political, and educational inequalities between men and women. One of its main authors, Elizabeth Cady Stanton, intentionally alluded to the Declaration of Independence to make a clear connection between the personal and the political. Unlike Thoreau, she wanted to unite individuals in society, not wander off alone in search of truth and insights in nature. She didn't feel that women shared in the same personal freedoms as men. When it came to moral truths, she and her friends added to what the Founding Fathers claimed was "self-evident," clarifying "that all men and women are created equal." When the suffragists listed their grievances, they didn't use plural nouns like "women" and "men." Instead, they wrote "he" and "she" and described their complaints in the singular person to point out society's injustices against individuals. This final claim shows how angry they were: "He has endeavored, in every way that he could, to destroy her confidence in her own powers, to lessen her self-respect, and to make her willing to lead a dependent and abject life." Stanton and the other writers of the "Declaration of Sentiments" hoped to convince the conference attendees that only full freedom and independence for every individual, man or woman, mattered.

Frederick Douglass also looked to the Declaration of Independence as an opportunity to demonstrate that full freedom and independence for all remained an illusion for many individuals in 19th century America. Born into slavery, Douglass later escaped and became one of the nation's most famous speakers of the abolitionist movement. As the country headed closer and closer to an all-out civil war, Douglass' forceful rhetoric was matched by an equally strong sense of self, both of which he used to empower others. Quiet meditations like Henry David Thoreau's *Walden* musings would not suffice. As the convention members at Seneca Falls realized, louder voices were needed to respond to the surrounding political turmoil. Whenever Douglass told his own individual story, he recognized that he had to speak for others in society who still had little or no political voice. For example, when asked to speak at a Fourth of July event, he asked his audience, "What have I, or those I represent, to do with your national independence?" Douglass repeated this strong need to represent the many people still in bondage when he said, "I shall see this day and its popular characteristics from the slave's point of view." In this instance, the controversial politics of the situation made Douglass' personal situation and insights even more compelling. He helped to rally the masses and inspire others to continue their work toward freedom not just for himself but for all enslaved people.

Like Thoreau, Douglass challenged individuals in society to take a critical look at themselves and their beliefs. To emphasize his points, Douglass used sarcasm in his rhetoric. "Would you have me argue that man is entitled to liberty?" he asked, knowing that the answer, at least to his audience, was self-evident. "Must I argue the wrongfulness of slavery?" The idea of answering the question seemed ridiculous to him. Rhetorical questions like these were meant to show individuals that if they just stopped to think about such issues, they would find the obvious answer themselves. "What, then, remains to be argued?" he asked near the end of his speech. If his role in society was to continue arguing about something that seemed self-evident, he would accept invitations to speak on the subject. However, that didn't mean he would leave people's ideas about things such as freedom and slavery unchallenged.

NOTES

Each of the authors mentioned above expanded upon ideas about the roles individuals played in society. They pushed for changes that would improve the world around them and empower more and more individuals. Their words would inspire future leaders such as Gandhi and Martin Luther King, Jr., who both wrote about how Thoreau's ideas and writings influenced their own contributions to society. Such personal calls for political change continue today. Whether in cabins, convention halls, courtrooms, or classrooms, individuals continue to speak out on behalf of others in order to make this a better world for all.

Works Cited

Lukes, Steven M. "Individualism: Politics and Philosophy"; Encyclopaedia Brittanica

 Online. Encyclopædia Britannica Inc., 2014. Web. Jul 17 2015

Douglass, Frederick. "What to the Slave Is the Fourth of July?"

 StudySync. BookheadEd Learning, LLC., 2015. Web. 4 June 2015.

Stanton, Elizabeth Cady. "Declaration of Sentiments by the Seneca Falls

 Convention." StudySync. BookheadEd Learning, LLC., 2015. Web. 4 June 2015.

Thoreau, Henry David. Walden. StudySync. BookheadEd Learning, LLC., 2015.

 Web. 4 June 2015.

 THINK QUESTIONS

1. Which sentence from the first paragraph states the main idea of the essay?

2. How is the text in "Making the Personal Political" organized?

3. Do you think the writer addressed all aspects of the prompt in the essay? Were there any points that could have been better developed or supported more strongly?

4. Which selections, Blasts, or other resources do you think would best address the writing prompt in a literary analysis essay? Why do these particular texts appeal to you? What are some ideas or claims that you may want to develop in your analysis?

5. Based on what you have read, listened to, and researched, what ideas do you have about how particular individuals in the 19th century viewed the relationship between the individual and society?

PREWRITE

WRITING PROMPT

What ideas do the texts in this unit express about individualism and the relationship between the individual and society, especially during a time of cultural turmoil? How do the texts from this unit reflect the ways Americans defined themselves as individuals in the 19th century? Analyze at least three of the texts from this unit in an essay that provides a clear thesis statement and strong and thorough textual evidence.

Your essay should include:

- an introduction with a clear thesis statement or claim
- body paragraphs with relevant evidence and thorough analysis to support your claim
- a concluding paragraph that follows from and supports your analysis

In addition to studying techniques authors use to convey information, you have been reading and learning about how individuals define themselves in relation to society. Now you will use those argumentative writing techniques to compose your own literary analysis essay.

As you reread and reflect upon the writing prompt for your literary analysis essay, think about the key words "individual" and "society." How do the writers you've read so far portray or depict each one in their works? Do they suggest a relationship between the two? How might you describe that relationship? As you brainstorm ideas, think about how these questions and your answers relate back to the context of the United States in the 19th century.

The prompt also asks you to select at least three works for discussion in your essay. Based on the questions above, which ones come to mind first? Use a concept map or three-column chart to record your choices and list reasons why you think they relate to the prompt. For example, how did these three writers define "society"? Did they view it in a positive or negative way? Did they believe that society helped individuals achieve their goals or did it present obstacles toward that achievement? What role(s) did they believe the individual could play to change or sustain society? How did their own writing fulfill those roles?

As you write down your ideas, look for similarities or relationships between the texts. Do you notice ideas that are repeated? Looking for patterns such as these may help you clarify the claims you want to propose in your essay. Use the observations and details from your concept map or chart to write down any claims that you think might be interesting to develop and explore in a literary analysis of the selected texts.

Use this model to give you ideas or guidance for your own prewriting:

Text: "What to the Slave Is the Fourth of July?"

Author: Frederick Douglass

Ideas about the individual: Believes all people should be free with equal rights. Douglass escaped to freedom from slavery.

Ideas about society: Government promises freedom for all, but Douglass sees hypocrisy in that. Not all people are free in 19th-century society in the U.S.

Douglass's role in society: Speaks of his own individual experiences. Also represents those who aren't free to speak out. Believes that telling his story can help to change society.

Please note that excerpts and passages in the StudySync® library and this workbook are intended as touchstones to generate interest in an author's work. The excerpts and passages do not substitute for the reading of entire texts, and StudySync® strongly recommends that students seek out and purchase the whole literary or informational work in order to experience it as the author intended. Links to online resellers are available in our digital library. In addition, complete works may be ordered through an authorized reseller by filling out and returning to StudySync® the order form enclosed in this workbook.

Reading & Writing Companion   **199**

NOTES

SKILL:
THESIS
STATEMENT

 DEFINE

The **thesis statement** is the most important sentence in an essay because it introduces the topic that the writer will explore and develop in the body paragraphs. The thesis statement expresses the writer's **central argument or claim** about a topic. The thesis statement usually appears in the essay's introductory paragraph and is often the introduction's last sentence. The body paragraphs in a literary analysis all develop and support the thesis statement with evidence drawn from the texts being analyzed. Quite often, the writer will restate the thesis statement for added emphasis in the concluding paragraph.

 IDENTIFICATION AND APPLICATION

A thesis statement:

- appears in the introductory paragraph
- makes a clear statement about the writer's central idea or argument
- lets the reader know what to expect in the body of the essay
- may be restated in the concluding paragraph
- responds fully and completely to an essay prompt

 MODEL

Consider the introductory paragraph from the student model essay "Making the Personal Political":

> One isn't always the loneliest number. While it may be true that there is strength in numbers, there's no denying the social power of the individual. According to the *Encyclopedia Britannica*, the term "individualism" emerged

in the 19th century and means a "political and social philosophy that emphasized the moral worth of the individual (Lukes)." Many American writers of that period adopted that philosophy and used it to push for changes in society. Sometimes the individual set a new course for his or her own life. At other times, the individual rallied the masses to action. **As demonstrated by the works of Henry David Thoreau, Elizabeth Cady Stanton, and Frederick Douglass, some of the most influential social movements relied on significant contributions by individual writers.**

Notice the boldfaced thesis statement. This student's thesis statement clearly responds to the prompt. It includes two of the key words from the prompt, "social" and "individual", and states an objective claim rather than simply restating the prompt. Without being too specific, the writers leads the reader to understand that the essay will include information about "influential social movements" and "contributions by individual writers." This might engage the reader's interest and provide a hint at how the essay might be structured.

 PRACTICE

Review the essay prompt for the extended writing project. Next, write a rough draft of your thesis statement. Refer back to your prewriting activity to guide your writing and include the main point[s] you generated during the prewriting activity in their thesis statements. Once you have completed your rough draft, exchange papers or request a peer's thesis statement online. Provide each other with courteous and constructive feedback on the thesis statements.

SKILL:
SUPPORTING
DETAILS

 DEFINE

In literary analysis and argumentative writing, writers develop their main ideas and central claims with relevant information called **supporting details.** Supporting details can be any facts, definitions, details, quotations, or textual evidence that are important to the reader's understanding of the topic and closely relate to the thesis statement of the essay. For the purposes of literary analysis, most of the supporting details should come from the texts being analyzed.

Strong and relevant supporting details include:

- Facts, definitions, and details important to understanding the topic
- Quoted passages from and descriptions about the texts being analyzed
- Accurate summaries of texts and/or significant scenes
- Research related to the thesis statement or the texts
- Pertinent quotations from experts, such as scholars and critics

Writers can choose supporting details from many sources. Encyclopedias, research papers, newspaper articles, memoirs, biographies, book reviews and criticism, documentaries, and online resources can all provide relevant information to develop and support claims and arguments. Though information is plentiful, the writer must be careful to evaluate the quality of information to determine what information is most important and most closely related to the thesis. If the information doesn't support the topic or if the information doesn't strengthen the writer's point, it is not relevant. For the purposes of a literary analysis essay, the best and most important resources are the texts themselves.

IDENTIFICATION AND APPLICATION

Copyright © BookheadEd Learning, LLC

Step 1:

Review your thesis statement. To identify relevant supporting details, ask yourself, "What is my main idea or central claim about this topic?" For example, a writer might be making a claim about the influence of oratory, or the art of formal public speaking, in 19th-century America:

> **The political speeches of 19th-century America were more powerful and influential than today's speeches.**

Step 2:

Ask what a reader needs to know about the topic (such as the definition of the word "oratory" above) in order to understand the main idea. In addition to definitions of key words and phrases, examples may help a reader better understand the author's argument.

> **Both Abraham Lincoln and Frederick Douglass provide strong examples of how convincing one person can be when speaking to a crowd.**

A writer might add another detail to develop and strengthen the claim further in the continued hopes of convincing the reader:

> **For example, many school children today still memorize "The Gettysburg Address," which has become a foundational U.S. document with historical significance.**

Finally, an excerpt from the text can drive the point home:

> **Most Americans instantly recognize the memorable and meaningful opening words in their recollection of the "Gettysburg Address": "Four score and seven years ago our fathers brought forth on this continent, a new nation, conceived in Liberty, and dedicated to the proposition that all men are created equal."**

Step 3:

Look for other related facts, quotations, details, and data. These will strengthen your thesis statement. Keep in mind that identifying and gathering supporting details is a building process. In an essay, one sentence often builds on another and guides the reader forward. Unrelated details, however, can stop readers in their tracks and leave them confused. Ask yourself:

- Is this information necessary to the reader's understanding?
- Does this information help to develop and prove my point?

- Does this information relate closely to my thesis statement?
- Can I find stronger evidence to support my argument?

 MODEL

In response to the writing prompt about the individual's role in society, the writer of the student essay determined that a reader might want to know the meaning of the term "individualism," especially as its definition has changed over time. For that reason, the introduction contains a bit of research that places the central term in the proper context of the literary analysis:

> According to the Encyclopedia Britannica, the term "individualism" emerged in the 19th century and means a **"political and social philosophy** that emphasized the **moral worth of the individual"** (Lukes). Many American writers of that period adopted that philosophy and used it to push for **changes in society.**

The writer knew that this definition would support the thesis statement because it contains other key words related to the prompt. The writer's purpose is to convince the reader that the "personal" and the "political" are linked. The idea of a "political and social philosophy" that also considers the "moral worth of the individual" provides direct support for this central argument from a respected and authoritative source. The writer then links this philosophy to "changes in society," which will be addressed in further detail in subsequent paragraphs.

First however, the student writer directly connects the term "individualism" to the first text under consideration in the essay, Henry David Thoreau's *Walden:*

> Thoreau immediately springs to mind in any discussion of 19th century intellectuals with **new ideas about the individual.** Alone in his cabin on Walden Pond, Thoreau set out to **"front only the essential facts of life, and see if I could not learn what it had to teach." In other words,** Thoreau opened himself up to discovering new truths and ideas about **the individual and his role in society.**

With Thoreau, the writer has provided an example of a 19th-century writer who has "new ideas about the individual." In order to demonstrate this further, the writer provides a relevant quotation from the text, noting Thoreau's intention to "front only the essential facts of life, and see if I could not learn what it had to teach." A reader might not be able to make a direct connection back to the thesis statement, and so the writer provides a restatement—"in other words"—of Thoreau's purpose in going to Walden Pond. By mentioning both "the individual and his role in society," the writer repeats key words from the prompt and demonstrates how this piece of textual evidence relates to the thesis.

 PRACTICE

Look at the draft of the Thesis Statement you have developed over previous lessons. List out all the possible relevant textual evidence you might use to support your thesis statement. Then form pairs to review each other's thesis statement and list of evidence and to provide feedback and suggestions for improvement. When providing feedback, consider the following questions:

1. How well does the textual evidence support the thesis statement?

2. Is some textual evidence better than other evidence? How would you rank the evidence in terms of relevance to the thesis?

3. Is any of the textual evidence off topic?

4. Do you think the thesis statement needs to be revised in light of the textual evidence?

NOTES

SKILL: ORGANIZE ARGUMENTATIVE WRITING

DEFINE

The purpose of writing a literary analysis is to convince readers of a particular claim about one or more texts. To do this effectively, writers need to organize and present their ideas, supporting details, and textual evidence in a logical sequence that's easy for a reader to follow.

Experienced writers carefully evaluate and select an **organizational structure** that best suits their material. They often use an outline or other graphic organizer to determine which organizational structure will help them express their ideas effectively.

For example, writers seeking to convince readers of an argument or claim often use logical reasoning as the basis of their structure. They seek to show how evidence relates to and supports the claims. Literary analysis papers might focus on a single text or multiple texts. The general structure of a literary analysis paper consists of an introduction, body paragraphs, and a conclusion. The body paragraphs might appear in order of importance of the points being made, in chronological order reflecting the order in which the texts were published, or in an alternating sequence that compares and contrasts the texts being discussed.

IDENTIFICATION AND APPLICATION

- When selecting an organizational structure, writers must be clear about their purpose for writing. They often ask themselves questions about the kind of information they are writing about. They might consider:
  › What is the central claim I would like to make about the topic?
  › What kinds of evidence will help me develop and support my claim?
  › Which texts most directly address the ideas or themes I am writing about?
  › Do any of the texts provide examples of themes or ideas in the other texts?

Copyright © BookheadEd Learning, LLC

> Would it make sense to discuss the texts in the order in which they were published?
> Do any of the texts address the same or related issues?
> Does information in one text lead to or result in ideas or information in another text?
> Do the ideas in the texts progress in a logical sequence that can be mapped or outlined?

- Writers often use word choice to create connections between texts and hint at the organizational structure being used. For example:
  > Logical reasoning: if...then, therefore, it follows that, however
  > Sequential or chronological order: first, next, then, initially, in the beginning, ultimately, at the conclusion, finally, last
  > Cause and effect: because, accordingly, as a result, effect, so
  > Compare and contrast: like, unlike, also, both, similarly, although, while, but, however
  > Definition or example: in other words, for example, for instance

- Sometimes writers may find it necessary to organize individual paragraphs using other structures — a definition paragraph within an overall chronological structure, for instance.

 MODEL

The writer of the student model literary analysis essay "Making the Personal Political" crafted a thesis statement that linked individual American writers of the 19th century to social movements of the time. In the introduction, the writer also suggested two categories into which the texts might be grouped:

> Many American writers of that period adopted that philosophy and used it to push for **changes in society. Sometimes** the individual set a new course for his or her own life. **At other times,** the individual **rallied the masses to action.**

These sentences suggest two different approaches that an author might take when addressing the common topic of individualism and how it led to "changes in society." At first glance, it might seem that the writer might follows a chronological structure in the essay, though words such as "sometimes" and "at other times" don't make the time order as clear as it might could be. A look at a graphic organizer that the writer used to plan his or her essay might tell us why.

The writer chose three texts to develop and support his or her central argument and used a three-column chart to organize ideas and evidence during the prewriting process. Color-coding made clear what either two or all three of the texts had in common. Items that were not color-coded demonstrated differences or contrasts among the texts. For example, both the Declaration of Sentiments and Douglass's speech were presented to audiences at political rallies, which places them in the second category mentioned above: "(rallying) the masses to action."

WALDEN	DECLARATION OF SENTIMENTS BY THE SENECA FALLS CONVENTION	"WHAT TO THE SLAVE IS THE FOURTH OF JULY?"
published in 1854	written in 1848	delivered in 1852
nonfiction	nonfiction	nonfiction
personal memoir	presented at political rally	presented at political rally
philosophical	addresses women's voting rights	addresses freedom from slavery
recounts personal observations	refers to the Declaration of Independence	recounts personal observations
		refers to the Declaration of Independence

From the chart, you can see that the publication dates are rather close together. The writer probably decided that they were too close to prove any substantive chronological or cause-and-effect relationships among all three texts. However, the chart shows a number of links between the Declaration of Sentiments by the Seneca Falls Convention and Frederick Douglass's speech. These similarities and connections no doubt led the writer to consider those two texts in adjacent paragraphs within the main essay.

Copyright © BookheadEd Learning, LLC

PRACTICE

Using an Organize Evidence Three Column Chart like the one you have just studied, fill in the information you gathered in the Prewrite stage of writing your essay. You can then use color-coding or draw lines between entries to identify and develop possible organizational strategies for your own literary analysis essay.

Please note that excerpts and passages in the StudySync® library and this workbook are intended as touchstones to generate interest in an author's work. The excerpts and passages do not substitute for the reading of entire texts, and StudySync® strongly recommends that students seek out and purchase the whole literary or informational work in order to experience it as the author intended. Links to online resellers are available in our digital library. In addition, complete works may be ordered through an authorized reseller by filling out and returning to StudySync® the order form enclosed in this workbook.

Reading & Writing Companion

209

NOTES

PLAN

WRITING PROMPT

What ideas do the texts in this unit express about individualism and the relationship between the individual and society, especially during a time of cultural turmoil? How do the texts from this unit reflect the ways Americans defined themselves as individuals in the 19th century? Analyze at least three of the texts from this unit in an essay that provides a clear thesis statement and strong and thorough textual evidence.

Your essay should include:

- an introduction with a clear thesis statement or claim
- body paragraphs with relevant evidence and thorough analysis to support your claim
- a concluding paragraph that follows from and supports your analysis

In addition to studying techniques authors use to convey information, you have been reading and learning about how individuals define themselves in relation to society. Now you will use those argumentative writing techniques to compose your own literary analysis essay.

Plan Prompt:

Review the information you listed in your graphic organizer during the prewriting lesson and skills activities. This organized information and your completed thesis statement will help you fill in and finalize a road map to use as you write your literary analysis essay.

Consider the following questions as you develop your main paragraph topics and consider related supporting details in the road map:

- Which text provides the strongest and most direct support for my thesis statement?

- Which text might be most familiar to my readers or audience? Would placing it first engage them more quickly with my essay?

- Do any of the texts I have selected deal with the same topic or idea? Which one would provide the best introduction or explanation of the idea?

- Does any of my evidence require additional explanation or development?

- Will I need to build a bridge as part of my road map in order to link two seemingly unrelated texts?

- For each selection, can my evidence be presented in the same order in which it appears in the text?

- Which text provides the most interesting treatment or development of my thesis statement? Would that be more effective coming first or last?

You can use this model or the Literary Analysis Outline graphic organizer to get started with your road map:

Literary Analysis Road Map

Thesis statement:

Introductory Paragraph:
Body Paragraph 1 Text or Topic:
    Supporting Detail #1:
    Supporting Detail #2:
Body Paragraph 2 Text or Topic:
    Supporting Detail #1:
    Supporting Detail #2:
Body Paragraph 3 Text or Topic:
    Supporting Detail #1:
    Supporting Detail #2:
Concluding Paragraph:

Note: You should have a minimum of three body paragraphs. You may find, however, that you need more body paragraphs to fully develop your thesis statement.

Please note that excerpts and passages in the StudySync® library and this workbook are intended as touchstones to generate interest in an author's work. The excerpts and passages do not substitute for the reading of entire texts, and StudySync® strongly recommends that students seek out and purchase the whole literary or informational work in order to experience it as the author intended. Links to online resellers are available in our digital library. In addition, complete works may be ordered through an authorized reseller by filling out and returning to StudySync® the order form enclosed in this workbook.

Reading & Writing Companion   **211**

SKILL: INTRODUCTIONS

 ## DEFINE

The **introduction** is the opening paragraph or section of a nonfiction text. In a literary analysis essay, the introduction sets forth a precise and knowledgeable **claim** by introducing the **topic** and stating the **thesis** that will be developed and supported in the body of the text. The introduction of some argumentative texts may also acknowledge an **alternate or opposing claim** that the writer may disprove over the course of the essay. A strong introduction also generates interest in the topic by inserting a **"hook"** that engages readers in an interesting or unexpected way.

 ## IDENTIFICATION AND APPLICATION

- In argumentative writing, the introduction identifies the topic or central claim of the essay by explicitly stating what the text will be about. The writer may also use the introduction to provide some necessary background information about the topic to help the reader understand the argument that he or she is about the make.

- In addition to the topic, the introduction includes the main, or most important, claim that the writer will include in the text. This main idea is the thesis. A strong thesis serves as a roadmap for the remainder of the work. It should indicate the point the writer will make and the source materials he or she will discuss. Note that a thesis is not always stated explicitly within the text. A writer might instead hint at the thesis through details and ideas in the introduction.

- The writer may also distinguish his or her argument from opposing views by establishing its relative importance or significance in the introduction.

- It is customary to build interest in the topic by beginning the introduction with a "hook," or a way to grab the reader's attention. This awakens the reader's natural curiosity and encourages him or her to read on. Hooks can ask open-ended questions, make connections to the reader or to life, or introduce a surprising fact.

MODEL

The title of the student essay, "Making the Personal Political," almost serves as an introduction in and of itself by establishing two of the main topics that the text will address. The reader's easy prediction about the content is immediately confirmed by the opening sentences:

> **One isn't always the loneliest number.** While it may be true that there is strength in numbers, there's no denying the **social power of the individual.** According to the *Encyclopedia Britannica,* the term **"individualism" emerged in the 19th century** and means a "political and social philosophy that emphasized the moral worth of the individual."

The student writer starts things off with a hook, playing off of the familiar saying that "one is the loneliest number." From there, the author moves quickly to restate the topics found in the title, though this time the term "social power of the individual" borrows key ideas from the writing prompt itself. Sensing that the reader may be unfamiliar with the academic meaning of "individualism," the writer includes a definition from a reliable source. This definition also firmly places the term in the context of the topic by stating that the idea "emerged in the 19th century."

After developing some of these topics in the subsequent sentences, the writer provides a precise and comprehensive thesis statement in the last sentence:

> As demonstrated by the works of Henry David Thoreau, Elizabeth Cady Stanton, and Frederick Douglass, some of the most **influential social movements relied on significant contributions by individual writers.**

Once again, the ideas of the individual and society, the personal and the political, return. On the topic of society, the writer will address "influential social movements" of the period. To show the individual's role in society, he or she will present examples of "significant contributions by individual writers." The writer will establish a link between the two and provide evidence that the former "relied on" on the latter.

 PRACTICE

Write an introduction for your essay that includes the thesis statement you have already worked on and a hook to capture your readers' interest. Trade with a peer review partner when you are finished and offer feedback on each other's introductions.

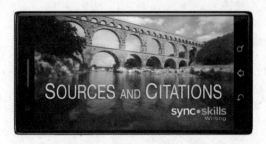

SKILL:
SOURCES AND
CITATIONS

 DEFINE

When writing a literary analysis essay, writers cannot simply make up information or rely on their own subjective experiences or opinions. To thoroughly support the treatment and analysis of their topics, writers need to include information from relevant, accurate, and reliable sources and cite, or acknowledge, them properly.

Sources are the documents and information that an author uses to research his or her writing. Some sources are **primary sources.** A primary source is a first-hand account of thoughts or events by the individual who experienced them. Other sources are **secondary sources.** A secondary source analyzes and interprets primary sources. **Citations** are notes that give information about the sources an author used in his or her writing. Citations are required whenever authors quote others' words or refer to others' ideas in their writing. Citations let readers know who originally came up with those words and ideas.

Writers should keep track of all their sources as they research and plan their work. When it comes time to write, they can use this information to acknowledge the sources they've used within the text. Failure to acknowledge those sources is **plagiarism,** or stealing someone else's words and ideas. In some academic texts, writers may be asked to provide sources and citations in **footnotes** or **endnotes,** which link specific references within the essay to the correlating pages or chapters in an outside source. In addition to **internal citations,** such as those noted within parentheses, writers may also need to provide a full list of sources in a **Works Cited** section or standard **bibliography.**

 IDENTIFICATION AND APPLICATION

- When gathering sources and information for an literary analysis essay, writers should take note of as much of the following information as possible:

Copyright © BookheadEd Learning, LLC

> Title of the work or website
> Author(s) or editor(s) of the work
> Pages referenced, if available (relate this to specific quotations or information)
> Date of publication
> Publisher name and address (city, state, and/or country)
> Medium of publication (web or print)
> Version numbers (revisions, issue numbers, volumes, editions)
> Date of access

- Always avoid plagiarism by either quoting the original text directly or paraphrasing the original and crediting the author.

- Citations are also necessary when a writer borrows ideas from another source, even if the writer paraphrases, or puts those ideas in his or her own words. Citations demonstrate that the writer did credible work, but they also help readers discover where they can learn more.

- Different organizations and references, such as the Modern Language Association (MLA), the American Psychological Association (APA), and the *Chicago Manual of Style,* recommend different ways of handling the proper formatting of citations and sources. When you receive an assignment, always check for and follow the proper formatting requirements.

 ## MODEL

When writing any essay that draws information from outside sources, a writer must give credit to any ideas or words he or she borrows from another person. Modern Language Association (MLA) guidelines for citing research sources is one method for doing so, and it is the style mostly used in English classes. MLA citation can sometimes seem confusing, especially if writers don't pay close attention to the sources they use. But if a writer keeps track of his or her sources and carefully follows the instructions here and in other source guides, MLA citation can be very straightforward. For detailed guidelines, refer to the *MLA Handbook for Writers of Research Papers* or a reliable online source such as the Purdue Online Writing Lab (OWL).

MLA style for citing sources takes a two-pronged approach. Writers following MLA style provide both a Works Cited page and in-text citations. The Works Cited page appears at the end of the essay and lists all the sources cited in the paper. The in-text citations, which appear at the end of sentences that contain researched information, link to the entries on the Works Cited page. These citations correspond to the first word or first few words of the related entry on the Works Cited page and are typically the author's last name or the first few words of the title.

Please note that excerpts and passages in the StudySync® library and this workbook are intended as touchstones to generate interest in an author's work. The excerpts and passages do not substitute for the reading of entire texts, and StudySync® strongly recommends that students seek out and purchase the whole literary or informational work in order to experience it as the author intended. Links to online resellers are available in our digital library. In addition, complete works may be ordered through an authorized reseller by filling out and returning to StudySync® the order form enclosed in this workbook.

Reading & Writing Companion

215

These are the rules for in-text citations:

- After a quotation or a paraphrase of researched information, insert in parentheses the author's last name and the page number where the information was found. For instance:

  > According to the *Encyclopedia Britannica,* the term "individualism" emerged in the 19th century and means a "political and social philosophy that emphasized the moral worth of the individual" (Lukes).

- If you mention the author's name in the sentence, you do not need to include it again in the parentheses:

  > According to Steven Lukes, the term "individualism" emerged in the 19th century and means a "political and social philosophy that emphasized the moral worth of the individual."

- If the source does not indicate the author, use the first few words of the title or if it is short title, the entire title to identify the piece:

  > The term "individualism" emerged in the 19th century and means a "political and social philosophy that emphasized the moral worth of the individual" ("Individualism: Politics").

For the Works Cited page, follow these general formatting guidelines:

- The title Works Cited should be centered at the top of the page and appear in regular font. (It should not be bold or underlined, nor should it be in a font larger than that of the surrounding text.)
- Arrange the entries alphabetically by author's last name or by the first word in the title, if no author is mentioned.
- Long entries, that is, entries that take up more than one line, should be indented half an inch every line after the first.
- The entire list should be double spaced. Some writers mistakenly use single spacing for long entries and then use double spacing between entries. That is not correct. Double spacing should be used between all lines of text.

The format for each entry in the Works Cited list depends on the type of source. Here are two of the most commonly used formats:

Book
Structure:
Last, First M., and First M. Last (for additional author or editor). *Book Title*. City,

State: Publisher, Year Published. Medium.

Example:

Thoreau, Henry David. *Walden, Civil Disobedience, and Other Writings*. New

York, New York: Classic Books International, 2010. Print.

Website
Structure:

Last, First M. "Article or Page Title." *Website Title*. Website Publisher. Date

Month Year Published (if available). Web. Date Month Year Accessed.

Example:

Douglass, Frederick. "What to the Slave is the Fourth of July" *StudySync*.

BookheadEd Learning, LLC., 2014. Web. 21 July 2014.

The Purdue OWL site can serve as a quick reference for examples for many different types of formats, including <u>books</u>, <u>periodicals</u>, <u>electronic sources</u>, and <u>other common sources</u>.

 PRACTICE

Use the information you have learned about sources and citations to apply to your own literary analysis. Find two examples of places where you need to cite a source, and then follow the correct format to write the citations within the text of your essay. Next, write a complete entry for each resource in a Works Cited section to place at the end of your essay. Exchange citations and Works Cited entries with a partner to see if your have formatted them correctly. Offer each other suggestions, and remember that suggestions are most helpful when they are constructive.

Please note that excerpts and passages in the StudySync® library and this workbook are intended as touchstones to generate interest in an author's work. The excerpts and passages do not substitute for the reading of entire texts, and StudySync® strongly recommends that students seek out and purchase the whole literary or informational work in order to experience it as the author intended. Links to online resellers are available in our digital library. In addition, complete works may be ordered through an authorized reseller by filling out and returning to StudySync® the order form enclosed in this workbook.

Reading & Writing
Companion

217

SKILL: BODY
PARAGRAPHS
AND TRANSITIONS

 DEFINE

Body paragraphs are the paragraphs that appear between the introduction and the conclusion. The body of the essay is where you support your thesis statement by developing your main points with evidence from the text and analysis. Typically, each body paragraph will focus on one main point or idea. The main point of each body paragraph must support the thesis statement.

It's important to structure your body paragraphs clearly. One strategy for structuring a body paragraph for an argumentative essay is the following:

1. **Topic sentence:** The topic sentence is the first substantive sentence of your body paragraph and clearly states the main idea or claim in that paragraph. It's important that this also relates back to your thesis statement from the introduction.

   a. **Evidence #1:** It's important to support your topic sentence with evidence. In a literary essay, most of your evidence will consist of quoted material or descriptions of textual elements from the selections being analyzed.

      i. **Analysis/Explanation #1:** After presenting evidence to support your topic sentence, you may need to analyze that evidence and explain how it supports your topic sentence and, in effect, your overall thesis.

   b. **Evidence #2:** Continue to develop your topic sentence with a second piece of evidence.

      i. **Analysis/Explanation #2:** Analyze this second piece of evidence and explain how it supports your topic sentence and, in effect, your thesis.

2. **Concluding sentence:** After presenting your evidence you need to wrap up your main idea and establish a transition to the next paragraph in your concluding sentence.

Transitions are connecting words and phrases that clarify the relationships among ideas in a text. Transitions work at three different levels: within a sentence, between paragraphs, and to indicate organizational structure.

Copyright © BookheadEd Learning, LLC

Authors of literary analyses and other argumentative texts use transitions to help readers recognize and follow the overall organizational structure. Transitions also help readers make connections between and among the texts being discussed in a literary analysis. By providing transitional words or phrases at the beginnings or endings of paragraphs, authors guide readers smoothly through the text.

In addition, transition words and phrases help authors make connections between words and ideas within a sentence. Conjunctions such as *and, or,* and *but* and prepositions such as *with, beyond, inside,* can clarify and develop these relationships. Transitions help readers understand how words fit together to make meaning.

••• IDENTIFICATION AND APPLICATION

- In a literary analysis paper, the body paragraphs provide the textual evidence and the analysis/explanation of that evidence to support the thesis statement. Typically, writers develop one main idea per body paragraph.

- Transition words and phrases are necessary elements of effective writing. They help readers understand the text structure and organizational strategy of an argumentative text. Here are some transition words commonly associated with three different text structures:
  › Cause-effect: *because, accordingly, as a result, effect, so, for, since*
  › Compare-contrast: *like, unlike, also, both, similarly, although, while, but, however, whereas, conversely, meanwhile, on the contrary, and yet, still*
  › Chronological order: *first, next, then, finally, last, initially, ultimately*

- Transition words help readers understand the flow of ideas and concepts in a text. Some of the most useful transitions are words that indicate that the ideas in one paragraph are building on or adding to those in another. Examples include: *furthermore, therefore, in addition, moreover, by extension, in order to,* etc.

MODEL

At the start of the third body paragraph of the student model essay, "Making the Personal Political," the writer makes a direct reference to the previous paragraph, which dealt with the Declaration of Sentiments by the Seneca Falls Convention:

*Frederick Douglass **also** looked to **the Declaration of Independence** as an opportunity to demonstrate that full freedom and independence for all remained an illusion for many **individuals in 19th century America**. Born into slavery, Douglass later escaped and **became one of the nation's most famous speakers of the abolitionist movement**.*

The transitional word "also" makes the link clear to the reader, as does the repeated reference to the Declaration of Independence. The topic sentence for this body paragraph follows, telling the reader that Douglass "became one of the nation's most famous speakers of the abolitionist movement." Together with the earlier reference to "individuals in 19th century America," this ties in directly with the thesis statement of the essay as a whole and repeats key words from the writing prompt itself.

As the body paragraph continues, the writer makes an effort to acknowledge both of the texts that have already been discussed. In doing so, he or she provides additional context for Douglass's speech, "What to the Slave Is the Fourth of July?"

> *__Quiet meditations__ like Henry David Thoreau's* Walden *musings would not suffice. __As__ the convention members at Seneca Falls realized, __louder voices__ were needed to __respond to the surrounding political turmoil__.*

The writer develops a progression of sorts here that might speak to an underlying structure to the essay as a whole. A discussion of Thoreau's "quiet meditations" gives way to the "louder voices" of the Seneca Falls Convention, which sets the stage for textual evidence of Douglass's strong rhetoric and oratory. The transitional word "as" provides a short but effective comparison between the convention members and Douglass, both of whom were asked to "respond to the surrounding political turmoil." The latter half of the sentence once again connects back to the thesis statement for the essay as a whole. This helps to unify the analysis even as the writer prepares to make new and unique claims about Douglass's remarks.

 ## PRACTICE

Use a Venn diagram to identify transitional details, key words, and statements from the student model and place them in the proper overlapping areas on the diagram. Then identify two or three details and statements that are specific or unique to each body paragraph and place them in the non-overlapping areas of the diagram. Next, look at the plan you worked on in a previous lesson. Use a fresh diagram to help you map out the body paragraphs and transitions in your own literary analysis essay. Draft a body paragraph that includes transition words and phrases that show how your essay will be structured and how your ideas are connected.

SKILL:
CONCLUSIONS

⭐ DEFINE

The **conclusion** is the final paragraph or section of a nonfiction text. In an argumentative text, the conclusion brings the analysis of the texts or claims to a close. It follows directly from the introduction and body of the text by referring back to the main ideas presented there. A conclusion should reiterate the thesis statement and summarize the main ideas covered in the body of the text. Depending on the type of text, a conclusion might also include a recommendation or solution, a call to action, or an insightful statement. Many conclusions try to engage and connect with readers by encouraging them to apply what they have learned from the text to their own lives.

••• IDENTIFICATION AND APPLICATION

- If the essay as a whole has been structured around a logical and effective "road map," the conclusion should clearly feel like "the destination."
- An effective literary analysis conclusion will draw together all the texts or authors who have been discussed in the body of the essay in a substantive and meaningful way.
- An effective literary analysis or argumentative conclusion reinforces the thesis statement or central claim and reiterates why it is significant or worth considering.
- An effective literary analysis or argumentative conclusion briefly mentions or reviews the strongest supporting details or evidence. This reminds readers of the most relevant information and evidence in the essay.
- The conclusion leaves the reader with a final thought. In literary analysis or argumentative writing, this final thought may:
  › Answer a question posed by the introduction
  › Ask a question on which the reader can reflect
  › Present a last, compelling example
  › Convey a memorable or inspiring message

Please note that excerpts and passages in the StudySync® library and this workbook are intended as touchstones to generate interest in an author's work. The excerpts and passages do not substitute for the reading of entire texts, and StudySync® strongly recommends that students seek out and purchase the whole literary or informational work in order to experience it as the author intended. Links to online resellers are available in our digital library. In addition, complete works may be ordered through an authorized reseller by filling out and returning to StudySync® the order form enclosed in this workbook.

Reading & Writing
Companion

221

NOTES

› Recommend other authors or texts that extend the argument
› Spark curiosity and encourage readers to learn more

 MODEL

In the concluding paragraph of the student model, "Making the Personal Political," the writer reinforces the thesis statement and reiterates how all the texts and authors discussed helped to support the central claim:

> **Each of the authors** mentioned above **expanded upon ideas about the roles individuals played in society.** They pushed for **changes that would improve the world around them** and empower more and more individuals.

Since this was an essay written to a prompt, the student writer is also careful to include language that had appeared in the initial assignment as a kind of "double-check" before closing. In the first two sentences, the writer brings together all the texts discussed by referring to "each of the authors." The writer restates the thesis statement, claiming that these writers "expanded upon ideas about the role individuals played in society." Further, the student writer repeats the claim that these writers inspired "changes that would improve the world around them."

This opens up an avenue for the writer to leave the reader with a final thought. In doing so, he or she can draw a connection between the 19th-century texts being analyzed to more contemporary writers and historical figures:

> Their words would inspire future leaders such as **Gandhi and Martin Luther King, Jr.,** who both wrote about how Thoreau's ideas and writings influenced their own contributions to society. Such personal calls for political change continue today. Whether in cabins, convention halls, courtrooms, or classrooms, individuals continue to speak out on behalf of others in order to **make this a better world for all.**

The writer's final remarks are meant to encourage and give hope to the reader that individuals can "make this a better world for all." The reader may be inspired to seek out more information about Gandhi and King in order to make his or her own judgments and comparisons back to writers like Thoreau. The language of the final sentence also establishes a tone of closure. The central thesis statement is restated in a way that gives the reader more to think about even after the final word.

PRACTICE

Write a conclusion for your essay. Your concluding paragraph should include reinforcement or a restatement of the thesis you have already worked on and a final thought that you want readers to ponder or consider once they have finished the essay. Trade with a peer review partner when you are finished and offer feedback on each other's conclusion.

Please note that excerpts and passages in the StudySync® library and this workbook are intended as touchstones to generate interest in an author's work. The excerpts and passages do not substitute for the reading of entire texts, and StudySync® strongly recommends that students seek out and purchase the whole literary or informational work in order to experience it as the author intended. Links to online resellers are available in our digital library. In addition, complete works may be ordered through an authorized reseller by filling out and returning to StudySync® the order form enclosed in this workbook.

Reading & Writing Companion **223**

DRAFT

WRITING PROMPT

What ideas do the texts in this unit express about individualism and the relationship between the individual and society, especially during a time of cultural turmoil? How do the texts from this unit reflect the ways Americans defined themselves as individuals in the 19th century? Analyze at least three of the texts from this unit in an essay that provides a clear thesis statement and strong and thorough textual evidence.

Your essay should include:

- an introduction with a clear thesis statement or claim
- body paragraphs with relevant evidence and thorough analysis to support your claim
- a concluding paragraph that follows from and supports your analysis

In addition to studying techniques authors use to convey information, you have been reading and learning about how individuals defined themselves in relation to society. Now you will use argumentative writing techniques to draft your own literary analysis essay.

You've already made progress toward writing your own literary analysis essay. You've thought about the topic and selected three relevant texts for evidence. You've identified what you want to say about the relationship between the individual and society. You've decided how to organize information and sequence supporting details in a logical way. Now it's time to write a draft.

NOTES

When drafting, ask yourself these questions:

- How can I improve the hook in my introduction to make it more engaging to the audience I have identified?

- What can I do to clarify and establish the significance of my thesis statement?

- What transitional words and organizational structures can I use to link the major sections of my essay and clarify the relationships between claims, textual evidence, and my analysis or explanation of that evidence?

- Which relevant facts, strong details, and interesting quotations in each body paragraph clearly support the thesis statement?

- Would more precise or objective language make my claim more powerful and convincing?

- What final thought do I want to leave with my readers?

Using your essay road map and your other prewriting materials, write a draft of your essay. Remember that argumentative writing begins with an introduction and presents a claim. Body paragraphs provide supporting evidence and relevant information. A concluding paragraph restates or reinforces your claim to leave a lasting impression on your readers. Before you submit your draft, read it over carefully. You want to be sure that you've responded to all aspects of the prompt.

Please note that excerpts and passages in the StudySync® library and this workbook are intended as touchstones to generate interest in an author's work. The excerpts and passages do not substitute for the reading of entire texts, and StudySync® strongly recommends that students seek out and purchase the whole literary or informational work in order to experience it as the author intended. Links to online resellers are available in our digital library. In addition, complete works may be ordered through an authorized reseller by filling out and returning to StudySync® the order form enclosed in this workbook.

Reading & Writing
Companion

225

REVISE

WRITING PROMPT

What ideas do the texts in this unit express about individualism and the relationship between the individual and society, especially during a time of cultural turmoil? How do the texts from this unit reflect the ways Americans defined themselves as individuals in the 19th century? Analyze at least three of the texts from this unit in an essay that provides a clear thesis statement and strong and thorough textual evidence.

Your essay should include:

- an introduction with a clear thesis statement or claim
- body paragraphs with relevant evidence and thorough analysis to support your claim
- a concluding paragraph that follows from and supports your analysis

You have written the first draft of your literary analysis essay and received input from your peers about how to improve it. Now you are ready to reread and revise the draft of your literary analysis.

Here are some recommendations to help you revise:

- Reread the prompt one more time to refresh your memory and ensure that your essay addresses all aspects of the purpose for writing.
- Review the suggestions made by your peers.
- Focus on maintaining a formal style and objective tone. A formal style establishes a sense of authority and confidence as you write about your claim. It also respects your audience—the students, teachers, and other readers who are interested in considering and evaluating your ideas.

> As you revise, eliminate any slang or jargon.
> Remove first-person pronouns such as "I," "me," or "mine" or instances of addressing readers as "you" unless you are using them for valid rhetorical purposes. These are more suitable for the expression of opinions rather than claims made within a literary analysis.
> Substitute more precise words for any that are general or dull.

- Think about whether there is anything else you can do to improve your essay's organization or expression of ideas.

  > Are there any claims that still require further explanation or support?
  > Did you properly acknowledge and cite your sources?
  > Do the paragraphs seem like they're in the proper order?
  > Would your essay flow better if you strengthened the transitions between paragraphs?

- As you add new details or change information, check for any issues or problems with spelling, grammar, syntax, usage, or punctuation.

Please note that excerpts and passages in the StudySync® library and this workbook are intended as touchstones to generate interest in an author's work. The excerpts and passages do not substitute for the reading of entire texts, and StudySync® strongly recommends that students seek out and purchase the whole literary or informational work in order to experience it as the author intended. Links to online resellers are available in our digital library. In addition, complete works may be ordered through an authorized reseller by filling out and returning to StudySync® the order form enclosed in this workbook.

Reading & Writing Companion **227**

EDIT, PROOFREAD, AND PUBLISH

WRITING PROMPT

What ideas do the texts in this unit express about individualism and the relationship between the individual and society, especially during a time of cultural turmoil? How do the texts from this unit reflect the ways Americans defined themselves as individuals in the 19th century? Analyze at least three of the texts from this unit in an essay that provides a clear thesis statement and strong and thorough textual evidence.

Your essay should include:

- an introduction with a clear thesis statement or claim
- body paragraphs with relevant evidence and thorough analysis to support your claim
- a concluding paragraph that follows from and supports your analysis

You have revised your literary analysis essay and received suggestions and advice from your peers on that revision. Now it's time to edit and proofread your essay to produce a final version. Have you considered all the valuable suggestions from your peers and incorporated those that improved your essay? Ask yourself: What more can I do to improve my essay's information and organization?

When you are satisfied with the content and substance of your work, proofread it for errors. For example, check that you have used correct punctuation, resolved all remaining issues with syntax and usage, and corrected any misspelled words.

As you are proofreading, make sure that your writing reflects standard usage. Usage refers to the rules that govern the correct way to use words and phrases. In order to maintain a formal tone in your essay, make sure to correct any errors in word usage. For example, do you know when to use "than" versus "then," "who" versus "whom," or "its" versus "it's"? To determine the correct usage, you can look up words in resources, such as the Usage Glossary on pages 10-13 in the *Grammar & Language Handbook* available on the StudySync site.

Once you have made all your corrections, you are ready to publish your work. You can distribute your writing to family and friends, hang it on a bulletin board, or post it on your blog. If you publish online, create links to your sources and citations when possible. That way, interested readers can follow up on what they've learned from your essay and read more on their own.

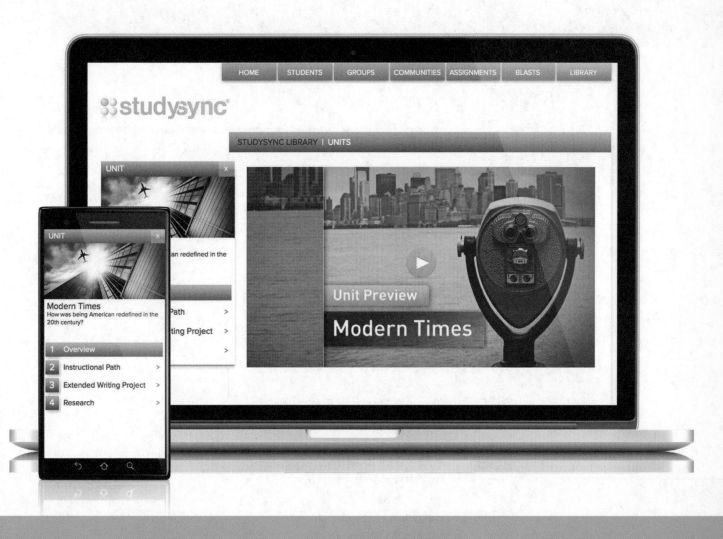

studysync®

Reading & Writing Companion

How was being American redefined in the 20th century?

Modern Times

UNIT 3   How was being American redefined in the 20th century?

Modern Times

TEXTS

TEXTS

EXTENDED WRITING PROJECT

431

Text Fulfillment
through
StudySync

THE GREAT GATSBY

FICTION

F. Scott Fitzgerald
1925

INTRODUCTION

F. Scott Fitzgerald was a key member of the "Lost Generation" of authors who served in World War I and later wrote about the war and the post-war world. The following passages are from Fitzgerald's most famous work, *The Great Gatsby,* a novel depicting America's extravagant and roaring 1920s. These excerpts explore the relationship between Nick Carraway, the narrator, and Jay Gatsby, a mysterious millionaire whose lavish parties embody the spirit and spectacle that led Fitzgerald to dub the 1920s "The Jazz Age." As Nick delves into the mystery of Gatsby's past, he finds that the legend of the Great Gatsby is as much a tale of one

"Gatsby...represented everything for which I have an unaffected scorn."

FIRST READ

From Chapter 1

1 In my younger and more **vulnerable** years my father gave me some advice that I've been turning over in my mind ever since.

2 "Whenever you feel like criticizing any one," he told me, "just remember that all the people in this world haven't had the advantages that you've had."

3 He didn't say any more but we've always been unusually communicative in a reserved way, and I understood that he meant a great deal more than that. In consequence I'm inclined to reserve all judgments, a habit that has opened up many curious natures to me and also made me the victim of not a few veteran bores. The abnormal mind is quick to detect and attach itself to this quality when it appears in a normal person, and so it came about that in college I was unjustly accused of being a politician, because I was privy to the secret griefs of wild, unknown men. Most of the confidences were unsought—frequently I have feigned sleep, **preoccupation,** or a hostile levity when I realized by some unmistakable sign that an intimate revelation was quivering on the horizon—for the intimate revelations of young men or at least the terms in which they express them are usually plagiaristic and marred by obvious suppressions. Reserving judgments is a matter of infinite hope. I am still a little afraid of missing something if I forget that, as my father snobbishly suggested, and I snobbishly repeat, a sense of the fundamental decencies is parceled out unequally at birth.

4 And, after boasting this way of my tolerance, I come to the admission that it has a limit. Conduct may be founded on the hard rock or the wet marshes but after a certain point I don't care what it's founded on. When I came back from the East last autumn I felt that I wanted the world to be in uniform and at a sort of moral attention forever; I wanted no more riotous excursions with privileged glimpses into the human heart. Only Gatsby, the man who gives his name to

Please note that excerpts and passages in the StudySync® library and this workbook are intended as touchstones to generate interest in an author's work. The excerpts and passages do not substitute for the reading of entire texts, and StudySync® strongly recommends that students seek out and purchase the whole literary or informational work in order to experience it as the author intended. Links to online resellers are available in our digital library. In addition, complete works may be ordered through an authorized reseller by filling out and returning to StudySync® the order form enclosed in this workbook.

Reading & Writing Companion   **235**

NOTES

this book, was exempt from my reaction—Gatsby who represented everything for which I have an unaffected scorn. If personality is an unbroken series of successful gestures, then there was something gorgeous about him, some heightened sensitivity to the promises of life, as if he were related to one of those intricate machines that register earthquakes ten thousand miles away. This responsiveness had nothing to do with that flabby **impressionability** which is dignified under the name of the "creative temperament"—it was an extraordinary gift for hope, a romantic readiness such as I have never found in any other person and which it is not likely I shall ever find again. No— Gatsby turned out all right at the end; it is what preyed on Gatsby, what foul dust floated in the wake of his dreams that temporarily closed out my interest in the abortive sorrows and short-winded elations of men.

From Chapter 3

5 By midnight the hilarity had increased. A celebrated tenor had sung in Italian, and a notorious contralto had sung in jazz, and between the numbers people were doing "stunts" all over the garden, while happy, **vacuous** bursts of laughter rose toward the summer sky. A pair of stage twins, who turned out to be the girls in yellow, did a baby act in costume, and champagne was served in glasses bigger than finger-bowls. The moon had risen higher, and floating in the Sound was a triangle of silver scales, trembling a little to the stiff, tinny drip of the banjoes on the lawn.

6 I was still with Jordan Baker. We were sitting at a table with a man of about my age and a rowdy little girl, who gave way upon the slightest **provocation** to uncontrollable laughter. I was enjoying myself now. I had taken two finger-bowls of champagne, and the scene had changed before my eyes into something significant, elemental, and profound.

7 At a lull in the entertainment the man looked at me and smiled.

8 "Your face is familiar," he said, politely. "Weren't you in the Third Division during the war?"

9 "Why, yes. I was in the ninth machine-gun battalion."

10 "I was in the Seventh Infantry until June nineteen-eighteen. I knew I'd seen you somewhere before."

11 We talked for a moment about some wet, gray little villages in France. Evidently he lived in this vicinity, for he told me that he had just bought a hydroplane, and was going to try it out in the morning.

12 "Want to go with me, old sport? Just near the shore along the Sound."

13 "What time?"

NOTES

14   "Any time that suits you best."

15   It was on the tip of my tongue to ask his name when Jordan looked around and smiled.

16   "Having a gay time now?" she inquired.

17   "Much better." I turned again to my new acquaintance. "This is an unusual party for me. I haven't even seen the host. I live over there—" I waved my hand at the invisible hedge in the distance, "and this man Gatsby sent over his chauffeur with an invitation." For a moment he looked at me as if he failed to understand.

18   "I'm Gatsby," he said suddenly.

19   "What!" I exclaimed. "Oh, I beg your pardon."

20   "I thought you knew, old sport. I'm afraid I'm not a very good host."

21   He smiled understandingly—much more than understandingly. It was one of those rare smiles with a quality of eternal reassurance in it, that you may come across four or five times in life. It faced—or seemed to face—the whole external world for an instant, and then concentrated on you with an irresistible prejudice in your favor. It understood you just so far as you wanted to be understood, believed in you as you would like to believe in yourself, and assured you that it had precisely the impression of you that, at your best, you hoped to convey. Precisely at that point it vanished—and I was looking at an elegant young rough-neck, a year or two over thirty, whose elaborate formality of speech just missed being absurd. Some time before he introduced himself I'd got a strong impression that he was picking his words with care.

22   Almost at the moment when Mr. Gatsby identified himself, a butler hurried toward him with the information that Chicago was calling him on the wire. He excused himself with a small bow that included each of us in turn.

23   "If you want anything just ask for it, old sport," he urged me. "Excuse me. I will rejoin you later."

24   When he was gone I turned immediately to Jordan—constrained to assure her of my surprise. I had expected that Mr. Gatsby would be a florid and **corpulent** person in his middle years.

25   "Who is he?" I demanded. "Do you know?"

26   "He's just a man named Gatsby."

27   "Where is he from, I mean? And what does he do?"

28 "Now *you're* started on the subject," she answered with a wan smile. "Well, he told me once he was an Oxford man."

29 A dim background started to take shape behind him, but at her next remark it faded away.

30 "However, I don't believe it."

31 "Why not?"

32 "I don't know," she insisted, "I just don't think he went there."

33 Something in her tone reminded me of the other girl's "I think he killed a man," and had the effect of stimulating my curiosity. I would have accepted without question the information that Gatsby sprang from the swamps of Louisiana or from the lower East Side of New York. That was comprehensible. But young men didn't—at least in my **provincial** inexperience I believed they didn't—drift coolly out of nowhere and buy a palace on Long Island Sound.

34 "Anyhow, he gives large parties," said Jordan, changing the subject with an **urbane** distaste for the concrete. "And I like large parties. They're so intimate. At small parties there isn't any privacy."

Excerpted from The Great Gatsby *by F. Scott Fitzgerald, published by Scribner.*

 THINK QUESTIONS

1. What was the advice Nick's father gave him as a youth, and what has been the result of Nick's following this advice? Use details from the text to support your answer.

2. Based on what Nick tells the reader in Chapter 1, what seems to be his attitude toward Gatsby? Provide details from the text that support your response.

3. How did Nick's first impression on meeting Gatsby compare to his prior expectations of the man? Support your answer with textual evidence.

4. Use context and your knowledge of word parts to determine the meaning of the word **impressionability.** Write your definition of "impressionability" here and explain the reasoning that led to that definition.

5. Analyze the word **provocation** to provide a possible meaning based on its base word and affix(es). Tell how the context clues in the sentence help you confirm or revise your predicted definition.

CLOSE READ

Reread the excerpt from *The Great Gatsby*. As you reread, complete the Focus Questions below. Then use your answers and annotations from the questions to help you complete the Writing Prompt.

FOCUS QUESTIONS

1. Reread the third paragraph of Chapter 1. What is Nick explaining about himself?

2. Reread the fourth paragraph of Chapter 1. What seems to be Nick's attitude toward Gatsby?

3. Reread the first paragraphs of Chapter 3. What does the party setting of this chapter reveal or suggest about Gatsby?

4. Reread the paragraph in which Nick describes Gatsby's smile. What more do you learn about Gatsby from this paragraph, and are these qualities positive or negative?

5. Reread Nick's dialogue with Jordan at the end of the excerpt. Do you think that Nick trusts Jordan's ideas about Gatsby? What makes you think so?

6. If the character Gatsby represents new values and possibilities taking shape in early 20th-century America, what might these values and possibilities be? Look again at the description of his party and at the dialogue Nick and Jordan have about him.

WRITING PROMPT

Think about the choices F. Scott Fitzgerald makes as he introduces and develops characters in *The Great Gatsby*. Identify the main source of information you get about Gatsby, and tell what you learn from this source. Include relevant textual evidence to support your claims. Then identify other sources of information about Gatsby and tell what you learn from them. Considering all the sources together, what general impression of Gatsby are you left with, and how clear is this picture?

Please note that excerpts and passages in the StudySync® library and this workbook are intended as touchstones to generate interest in an author's work. The excerpts and passages do not substitute for the reading of entire texts, and StudySync® strongly recommends that students seek out and purchase the whole literary or informational work in order to experience it as the author intended. Links to online resellers are available in our digital library. In addition, complete works may be ordered through an authorized reseller by filling out and returning to StudySync® the order form enclosed in this workbook.

Reading & Writing Companion

239

THEME FOR ENGLISH B

POETRY
Langston Hughes
1949

INTRODUCTION

The writing of Langston Hughes captured African-American experiences and explored ideas that have resonated with generations of readers. Born and raised in the Midwest, Hughes relocated to New York in 1921 to attend Columbia University. Once there he was introduced to Harlem, the place that would define his career as a writer. Mingling with groundbreaking African-American writers, musicians, and painters in the clubs and homes of Harlem, by the end of the decade Hughes had established himself as one of the leaders of the cultural movement known as the Harlem Renaissance.

"I guess you learn from me— although you're older—and white— and somewhat more free."

 FIRST READ

 NOTES

1 The instructor said,
2 Go home and write
3 a page tonight.
4 And let that page come out of you—
5 Then, it will be true.

6 I wonder if it's that simple?
7 I am twenty-two, colored, born in Winston-Salem.
8 I went to school there, then Durham, then here
9 to this college on the hill above Harlem.
10 I am the only colored student in my class.
11 The steps from the hill lead down into Harlem,
12 through a park, then I cross St. Nicholas,
13 Eighth Avenue, Seventh, and I come to the Y,
14 the Harlem Branch Y, where I take the elevator
15 up to my room, sit down, and write this page:

16 It's not easy to know what is true for you or me
17 at twenty-two, my age. But I guess I'm what
18 I feel and see and hear, Harlem, I hear you:
19 hear you, hear me—we two—you, me, talk on this page.
20 (I hear New York, too.) Me—who?
21 Well, I like to eat, sleep, drink, and be in love.
22 I like to work, read, learn, and understand life.
23 I like a pipe for a Christmas present,
24 or records—Bessie, bop, or Bach.
25 I guess being colored doesn't make me not like
26 the same things other folks like who are other races.
27 So will my page be colored that I write?
28 Being me, it will not be white.
29 But it will be

NOTES

30　a part of you, instructor.

31　You are white—

32　yet a part of me, as I am a part of you.

33　That's American.

34　Sometimes perhaps you don't want to be a part of me.

35　Nor do I often want to be a part of you.

36　But we are, that's true!

37　As I learn from you,

38　I guess you learn from me—

39　although you're older—and white—

40　and somewhat more free.

41　This is my page for English B.

"Theme for English B" from THE COLLECTED POEMS OF LANGSTON HUGHES by Langston Hughes, edited by Arnold Rampersad with David Roessel, Associate Editor, copyright © 1994 by the Estate of Langston Hughes. Used by permission of Alfred A. Knopf, an imprint of the Knopf Doubleday Publishing Group, a division of Random House LLC. All rights reserved.

 ## THINK QUESTIONS

1. Use two or more details from the text to describe the speaker of the poem. What detail distinguishes him from other people mentioned in the poem?

2. Who is the "you" in line one of stanza three? Who is the "you" in line three of that stanza? Use specific examples from the text to explain how the poet makes this difference clear.

3. Which lines from the poem make up the actual "page" that the speaker writes for his instructor? How do they differ from the rest of the poem? Provide details from the text that support your response.

4. The word "theme" is sometimes used to mean an assignment or an essay; however, it can also refer to the central idea or message in a work. What is the impact of using the word "theme" in the poem's title? What other words and phrases in the text are clues to a possible second meaning for the title?

5. How do the meanings and nuances of the word "true" change and shift throughout the poem? Support your explanations with evidence drawn from the text.

CLOSE READ

Reread the poem "Theme for English B." As you reread, complete the Focus Questions below. Then use your answers and annotations from the questions to help you complete the Writing Prompt.

FOCUS QUESTIONS

1. Reread the first stanza. Based on the description of the instructor's writing prompt, what kind of class do you think "English B" is? Use clues from the rest of the poem to infer what the speaker's attitude toward the class might be. Highlight evidence from the text to support your inferences.

2. The second stanza begins with the speaker asking himself a question. Based on the second and third stanzas, what do you think his answer to that question would be? Highlight evidence from the text that explains your inference.

3. In the first part of the third stanza, the speaker addresses Harlem. What can you infer about his feelings toward the neighborhood? Use the annotation tool to record your inferences, and highlight evidence from the text to support those inferences.

4. In the second half of the third stanza, the speaker lists several things he likes. Based on what you know about him, what might he want this list to express? Use the annotation tool to make inferences about the stanza, and support your inferences with evidence from the text.

5. In the fourth stanza, the speaker says, "That's American." Highlight the words and phrases from the text that the speaker includes under being "American." Explain how rereading the stanza can help you make inferences about what being American means to the speaker.

WRITING PROMPT

Based on what you can infer about him, why might the speaker of "Theme for English B" have wanted to emphasize the statement, "That's American"? What might he want his instructor to learn from him? Be sure to explain how textual evidence supports any inferences you make.

ANY HUMAN TO ANOTHER

POETRY
Countee Cullen
1934

INTRODUCTION

Countee Cullen grew up during the Harlem Renaissance, a movement led by the African-American community in Harlem that cultivated a new black urban consciousness and produced large amounts of socially-conscious art and literature. As a Harlem Renaissance poet, Cullen's works successfully reached both African-American and white audiences and eloquently addressed the issues of racism and injustice. In his poem "Any Human to Another," the speaker points out that no person stands completely alone and that sorrow is often shared

"My sorrow must be laid on your head like a crown."

FIRST READ

1 The ills I sorrow at
2 Not me alone
3 Like an arrow,
4 Pierce to the **marrow,**
5 Through the fat
6 And past the bone.

7 Your grief and mine
8 Must **intertwine**
9 Like sea and river,
10 Be fused and mingle,
11 Diverse yet single,
12 Forever and forever.

13 Let no man be so proud
14 And confident,
15 To think he is allowed
16 A little tent
17 Pitched in a meadow
18 Of sun and shadow
19 All his little own.

20 Joy may be shy, unique,
21 Friendly to a few,
22 Sorrow never **scorned** to speak
23 To any who
24 Were false or true.

25 Your every grief
26 Like a blade
27 Shining and unsheathed

28 Must strike me down.
29 Of bitter aloes wreathed,
30 My sorrow must be laid
31 On your head like a crown.

Copyrights held by The Amistad Research Center, Tulane University Administered by Thompson and Thompson, Brooklyn, NY.

THINK QUESTIONS

1. Whom does the speaker in this poem address? Refer to one or more details from the text to support your answer.

2. How would you summarize or restate the main idea in the third stanza of the poem? What textual evidence supports your response?

3. Use details from the text to write two or three sentences exploring the significance of grief and sorrow according to the speaker of the poem. Support your answer with textual evidence.

4. Use context to determine the meaning of the word **intertwine** as it is used in the poem. Write your definition here and tell how you found it.

5. Use the context clues and your knowledge of affixes to determine the meaning of **unsheathed.** Write your definition of "unsheathed" here and tell how you got it.

CLOSE READ

Reread the poem "Any Human to Another." As you reread, complete the Focus Questions below. Then use your answers and annotations from the questions to help you complete the Writing Prompt.

FOCUS QUESTIONS

1. Consider the first stanza of the poem. What comparison does the speaker make in this stanza? What theme is suggested by the comparison? Highlight evidence from the text and make annotations to explain your choices.

2. The second stanza makes a connection between the speaker's grief and the reader's grief. How are the two related? What does this relation imply about the human condition? Support your answer with textual evidence and make annotations to explain your answer choices.

3. How does the image in the third stanza differ from other images in the poem? What point does it help the author to make? Highlight textual evidence from the third stanza and make annotations to support your answer.

4. Consider the fourth stanza of the poem. According to the speaker, what is the main difference between joy and sorrow? Highlight evidence from the text and make annotations to explain your choices.

5. Analyze the final stanza. How do the similes and formal, elevated language of the stanza help to reinforce the message of the poem? Highlight textual evidence and make annotations to support your explanation.

6. In what sense might this poem be Countee Cullen's contribution to a redefinition of American identity during the 20th century? Highlight textual evidence and make annotations to support your answer.

WRITING PROMPT

The poems "Any Human to Another" and "Theme for English B" treat similar topics: the nature of human connection. How is Countee Cullen's treatment of this topic similar to Langston Hughes's treatment? How is it different? What similarities and differences do you see in the themes of the poems? How is the influence of the Harlem Renaissance reflected in the themes? Support your response with evidence drawn from both poems.

Please note that excerpts and passages in the StudySync® library and this workbook are intended as touchstones to generate interest in an author's work. The excerpts and passages do not substitute for the reading of entire texts, and StudySync® strongly recommends that students seek out and purchase the whole literary or informational work in order to experience it as the author intended. Links to online resellers are available in our digital library. In addition, complete works may be ordered through an authorized reseller by filling out and returning to StudySync® the order form enclosed in this workbook.

Reading & Writing Companion   **247**

PLESSY V. FERGUSON

NON-FICTION
U.S. Supreme Court
1896

INTRODUCTION

P*lessy v. Ferguson* was an 1896 U.S. Supreme Court case that allowed segregation of public facilities under the doctrine of "separate but equal." The underlying case was orchestrated by a committee of concerned citizens who opposed a Louisiana law that required separate railroad cars for blacks and whites. Plaintiff Homer Plessy, a man with one-eighth African blood, challenged that law when he attempted to ride as a passenger on a whites-only car on the East Louisiana Railroad and refused requests to leave. He was found guilty by Judge John Howard Ferguson, who ruled that Louisiana had the right to regulate railroad companies that operated within the state. The Supreme Court's ruling that "separate but equal" was not in violation of the constitution was eventually invalidated by *Brown v. Board of Education* in 1954.

"It was said in argument that the statute of Louisiana does not discriminate against either race..."

FIRST READ

NOTES

From the majority opinion of the Court, delivered by Justice Henry Billings Brown:

1   The constitutionality of this act is attacked upon the ground that it conflicts both with the thirteenth amendment of the constitution, abolishing slavery, and the fourteenth amendment, which prohibits certain restrictive legislation on the part of the states.

2   1.   That it does not conflict with the thirteenth amendment, which abolished slavery and involuntary servitude, except as a punishment for crime, is too clear for argument. Slavery implies involuntary servitude,—a state of bondage; the ownership of mankind as a chattel, or, at least, the control of the labor and services of one man for the benefit of another, and the absence of a legal right to the disposal of his own person, property, and services. This amendment was said in the Slaughter-House Cases to have been intended primarily to abolish slavery, as it had been previously known in this country and that it equally forbade Mexican peonage or the Chinese coolie trade, when they amounted to slavery or involuntary servitude, and that the use of the word "servitude" was intended to prohibit the use of all forms of involuntary slavery, of whatever class or name. It was **intimated,** however, in that case, that this amendment was regarded by the statesmen of that day as insufficient to protect the colored race from certain laws which had been enacted in the Southern states, imposing upon the colored race **onerous** disabilities and burdens, and curtailing their rights in the pursuit of life, liberty, and property to such an extent that their freedom was of little value; and that the fourteenth amendment was devised to meet this **exigency.**

. . . .

Copyright © BookheadEd Learning, LLC

NOTES

3 2. By the fourteenth amendment, all persons born or naturalized in the United States, and subject to the jurisdiction thereof, are made citizens of the United States and of the state wherein they reside; and the states are forbidden from making or enforcing any law which shall abridge the privileges or immunities of citizens of the United States, or shall deprive any person of life, liberty, or property without due process of law, or deny to any person within their jurisdiction the equal protection of the laws.

. . . .

4 The object of the amendment was undoubtedly to enforce the absolute equality of the two races before the law, but, in the nature of things, it could not have been intended to abolish distinctions based upon color, or to enforce social, as distinguished from political, equality, or a commingling of the two races upon terms unsatisfactory to either. Laws permitting, and even requiring, their separation, in places where they are liable to be brought into contact, do not necessarily imply the inferiority of either race to the other, and have been generally, if not universally, recognized as within the competency of the state legislatures in the exercise of their police power. The most common instance of this is connected with the establishment of separate schools for white and colored children, which have been held to be a valid exercise of the legislative power even by courts of states where the political rights of the colored race have been longest and most earnestly enforced.

. . . .

5 We consider the underlying **fallacy** of the plaintiff's argument to consist in the assumption that the enforced separation of the two races stamps the colored race with a badge of inferiority. If this be so, it is not by reason of anything found in the act, but solely because the colored race chooses to put that construction upon it. The argument necessarily assumes that if, as has been more than once the case, and is not unlikely to be so again, the colored race should become the dominant power in the state legislature, and should enact a law in precisely similar terms, it would thereby **relegate** the white race to an inferior position. We imagine that the white race, at least, would not **acquiesce** in this assumption. The argument also assumes that social prejudices may be overcome by legislation, and that equal rights cannot be secured to the negro except by an enforced commingling of the two races. We cannot accept this proposition. If the two races are to meet upon terms of social equality, it must be the result of natural affinities, a mutual appreciation of each other's merits, and a voluntary consent of individuals. As was said by the court of appeals of New York in People v. Gallagher: 'This end can neither be accomplished nor promoted by laws which conflict with the general sentiment of the community upon whom they are designed to operate. When the government, therefore, has secured to each of its citizens equal rights before

the law, and equal opportunities for improvement and progress, it has accomplished the end for which it was organized, and performed all of the functions respecting social advantages with which it is endowed.' Legislation is powerless to **eradicate** racial instincts, or to abolish distinctions based upon physical differences, and the attempt to do so can only result in accentuating the difficulties of the present situation. If the civil and political rights of both races be equal, one cannot be inferior to the other civilly or politically. If one race be inferior to the other socially, the constitution of the United States cannot put them upon the same plane.

6   It is true that the question of the proportion of colored blood necessary to constitute a colored person, as distinguished from a white person, is one upon which there is a difference of opinion in the different states; some holding that any visible admixture of black blood stamps the person as belonging to the colored race; others, that it depends upon the preponderance of blood; and still others, that the predominance of white blood must only be in the proportion of three-fourths. But these are questions to be determined under the laws of each state, and are not properly put in issue in this case. Under the allegations of his petition, it may undoubtedly become a question of importance whether, under the laws of Louisiana, the petitioner belongs to the white or colored race.

7   The judgment of the court below is therefore affirmed.

From Justice John Marshall Harlan's dissenting opinion:

8   The thirteenth amendment does not permit the withholding or the deprivation of any right necessarily inhering in freedom. It not only struck down the institution of slavery as previously existing in the United States, but it prevents the imposition of any burdens or disabilities that constitute badges of slavery or servitude. It decreed universal civil freedom in this country. This court has so adjudged. But, that amendment having been found inadequate to the protection of the rights of those who had been in slavery, it was followed by the fourteenth amendment, which added greatly to the dignity and glory of American citizenship, and to the security of personal liberty, by declaring that 'all persons born or naturalized in the United States, and subject to the jurisdiction thereof, are citizens of the United States and of the state wherein they reside,' and that 'no state shall make or enforce any law which shall abridge the privileges or immunities of citizens of the United States; nor shall any state deprive any person of life, liberty or property without due process of law, nor deny to any person within its jurisdiction the equal protection of the laws.' These two amendments, if enforced according to their true intent and meaning, will protect all the civil rights that pertain to freedom and citizenship. Finally, and to the end that no citizen should be denied, on account of his race, the privilege of participating in the political control of his

Please note that excerpts and passages in the StudySync® library and this workbook are intended as touchstones to generate interest in an author's work. The excerpts and passages do not substitute for the reading of entire texts, and StudySync® strongly recommends that students seek out and purchase the whole literary or informational work in order to experience it as the author intended. Links to online resellers are available in our digital library. In addition, complete works may be ordered through an authorized reseller by filling out and returning to StudySync® the order form enclosed in this workbook.

Reading & Writing Companion   **251**

country, it was declared by the fifteenth amendment that 'the right of citizens of the United States to vote shall not be denied or abridged by the United States or by any state on account of race, color or previous condition of servitude.'

9   These notable additions to the fundamental law were welcomed by the friends of liberty throughout the world. They removed the race line from our governmental systems. They had, as this court has said, a common purpose, namely, to secure 'to a race recently emancipated, a race that through many generations have been held in slavery, all the civil rights that the superior race enjoy.' They declared, in legal effect, this court has further said, 'that the law in the states shall be the same for the black as for the white; that all persons, whether colored or white, shall stand equal before the laws of the states; and in regard to the colored race, for whose protection the amendment was primarily designed, that no discrimination shall be made against them by law because of their color.' We also said: 'The words of the amendment, it is true, are prohibitory, but they contain a necessary implication of a positive immunity or right, most valuable to the colored race,—the right to exemption from unfriendly legislation against them distinctively as colored; exemption from legal discriminations, implying inferiority in civil society, lessening the security of their enjoyment of the rights which others enjoy; and discriminations which are steps towards reducing them to the condition of a subject race.' It was, consequently, adjudged that a state law that excluded citizens of the colored race from juries, because of their race, however well qualified in other respects to discharge the duties of jurymen, was **repugnant** to the fourteenth amendment. At the present term, referring to the previous adjudications, this court declared that 'underlying all of those decisions is the principle that the constitution of the United States, in its present form, forbids, so far as civil and political rights are concerned, discrimination by the general government or the states against any citizen because of his race. All citizens are equal before the law.'

10   The decisions referred to show the scope of the recent amendments of the constitution. They also show that it is not within the power of a state to prohibit colored citizens, because of their race, from participating as jurors in the administration of justice.

11   It was said in argument that the statute of Louisiana does not discriminate against either race, but prescribes a rule applicable alike to white and colored citizens. But this argument does not meet the difficulty. Every one knows that the statute in question had its origin in the purpose, not so much to exclude white persons from railroad cars occupied by blacks, as to exclude colored people from coaches occupied by or assigned to white persons. Railroad corporations of Louisiana did not make discrimination among whites in the matter of commodation for travelers. The thing to accomplish was, under the

NOTES

guise of giving equal accommodation for whites and blacks, to compel the latter to keep to themselves while traveling in railroad passenger coaches. No one would be so wanting in **candor** as to assert the contrary. The fundamental objection, therefore, to the statute, is that it interferes with the personal freedom of citizens. 'Personal liberty,' it has been well said, 'consists in the power of locomotion, of changing situation, or removing one's person to whatsoever places one's own inclination may direct, without imprisonment or restraint, unless by due course of law.' If a white man and a black man choose to occupy the same public conveyance on a public highway, it is their right to do so; and no government, proceeding alone on grounds of race, can prevent it without infringing the personal liberty of each.

. . . .

12   The sure guaranty of the peace and security of each race is the clear, distinct, unconditional recognition by our governments, national and state, of every right that inheres in civil freedom, and of the equality before the law of all citizens of the United States, without regard to race. State enactments regulating the enjoyment of civil rights upon the basis of race, and cunningly devised to defeat legitimate results of the war, under the pretense of recognizing equality of rights, can have no other result than to render permanent peace impossible, and to keep alive a conflict of races, the continuance of which must do harm to all concerned.

THINK QUESTIONS

1.   Refer to one or more details from the text to explain what Justice Brown believes to be the limitations of the Supreme Court's power. What words and phrases hint at why he feels the Court has this limit?

2.   According to Justice Brown, who is at fault if one group of people feels inferior to another? How do you think he would suggest Plessy deal with the segregation laws? Support your answer with textual evidence.

3.   According to Justice Harlan, what did the railroad claim was its motivation for the decision to separate passengers? How does Harlan feel about that claim, and what does he think the real motivation was? Use details from the text to describe Justice Harlan's response to the railroad's actions and the arguments made in court.

4.   Use sentence clues, such as contextual definitions or restatements, to determine the meaning of the word **relegate**. Verify that your determined meaning makes sense by checking it in the context of the sentence or paragraph. Write your definition here and explain how you determined and verified it.

5.   Use contextual clues to determine the meaning of the word **eradicate**. Write your definition here and tell how you found it. Then, consult a reference work, such as a dictionary, to check your definition and trace the etymology of "eradicate." Explain how knowing the word's Latin roots helps you to understand its full meaning.

CLOSE READ

Reread the ruling in *Plessy v. Ferguson*. As you reread, complete the Focus Questions below. Then use your answers and annotations from the questions to help you complete the Writing Prompt.

FOCUS QUESTIONS

1. Look closely at the first part of the third paragraph in section 2 of Justice Brown's majority opinion. What legal reasoning does Justice Brown use to challenge what he claims is an "assumption" on the part of the plaintiff? Use the annotation tool to highlight Brown's claims and reasoning.

2. Reread section 1 of the majority opinion and the first half of the first paragraph of the dissenting opinion. Do Justices Brown and Harlan agree or disagree with each other on how the thirteenth amendment relates to the case at hand? Highlight details that express their interpretations and their similarities or differences.

3. Reread section 2 of the majority opinion and the second half of the first paragraph of the dissenting opinion. Do Justices Brown and Harlan agree or disagree with each other on how the fourteenth amendment relates to the case at hand? Highlight text in each opinion that supports your answer.

4. Explain why Justice Harlan, in the first two paragraphs of the dissenting opinion, also mentions the fifteenth amendment. How does this relate to the case of *Plessy v. Ferguson*? Use the annotation tool to highlight details from the text that helped you form your explanation.

5. Reread the last paragraph of the reading selection. Summarize Justice Harlan's argument here and explain what kind of rhetorical strategy he uses to discredit the Louisiana railroad's statute and the claims of Justice Brown's majority opinion. Highlight details from the text that support your explanation. In what way might Harlan's position reflect changing attitudes toward American citizenship and American values?

WRITING PROMPT

Compare and contrast the arguments in Justice Brown's majority opinion with Justice Harlan's dissenting opinion in *Plessy v. Ferguson*. Which rhetorical strategies does each use most effectively in their arguments? Which arguments or instances of legal reasoning don't seem to have withstood the test of time? Explain your response using thorough and relevant evidence from each part of the text.

BROWN V. BOARD OF EDUCATION

NON-FICTION

U.S. Supreme Court
1954

INTRODUCTION

B *rown v. Board of Education*, a class action suit filed by 13 Topeka, Kansas parents on behalf of their children, was a landmark 1954 U.S. Supreme Court case that declared unanimously, with no dissenting opinions, that separate public schools for African-American students was unconstitutional. The ruling overturned the previous *Plessy v. Ferguson* decision from 1896, which sanctioned segregation in public institutions.

"Does segregation...deprive the children of the minority group of equal educational opportunities?"

FIRST READ

From the unanimous decision of the Court, delivered by Chief Justice Earl Warren:

1   In approaching this problem, we cannot turn the clock back to 1868, when the [Fourteenth] Amendment was adopted, or even to 1896, when *Plessy v. Ferguson* was written. We must consider public education in the light of its full development and its present place in American life throughout the Nation. Only in this way can it be determined if segregation in public schools deprives these plaintiffs of the equal protection of the laws.

2   Today, education is perhaps the most important function of state and local governments. **Compulsory** school attendance laws and the great expenditures for education both demonstrate our recognition of the importance of education to our democratic society. It is required in the performance of our most basic public responsibilities, even service in the armed forces. It is the very foundation of good citizenship. Today it is a principal instrument in awakening the child to cultural values, in preparing him for later professional training, and in helping him to adjust normally to his environment. In these days, it is doubtful that any child may reasonably be expected to succeed in life if he is denied the opportunity of an education. Such an opportunity, where the state has undertaken to provide it, is a right which must be made available to all on equal terms.

3   We come then to the question presented: Does segregation of children in public schools solely on the basis of race, even though the physical facilities and other **"tangible"** factors may be equal, deprive the children of the minority group of equal educational opportunities? We believe that it does.

4   In *Sweatt* v. *Painter,* in finding that a segregated law school for Negroes could not provide them equal educational opportunities, this Court relied in large part on "those qualities which are incapable of objective measurement but which make for greatness in a law school." In *McLaurin* v. *Oklahoma State Regents,* the Court, in requiring that a Negro admitted to a white graduate

NOTES

school be treated like all other students, again resorted to intangible considerations: "... his ability to study, to engage in discussions and exchange views with other students, and, in general, to learn his profession." Such considerations apply with added force to children in grade and high schools. To separate them from others of similar age and qualifications solely because of their race generates a feeling of inferiority as to their status in the community that may affect their hearts and minds in a way unlikely ever to be undone. The effect of this separation on their educational opportunities was well stated by a finding in the Kansas case by a court which nevertheless felt compelled to rule against the Negro plaintiffs: Segregation of white and colored children in public schools has a **detrimental** effect upon the colored children. The impact is greater when it has the **sanction** of the law, for the policy of separating the races is usually interpreted as denoting the inferiority of the negro group. A sense of inferiority affects the motivation of a child to learn. Segregation with the sanction of law, therefore, has a tendency to [retard] the educational and mental development of negro children and to deprive them of some of the benefits they would receive in a racial[ly] integrated school system. Whatever may have been the extent of psychological knowledge at the time of *Plessy* v. *Ferguson*, this finding is amply supported by modern authority. Any language in *Plessy* v. *Ferguson* contrary to this finding is rejected.

5 We conclude that, in the field of public education, the doctrine of "separate but equal" has no place. Separate educational facilities are **inherently** unequal. Therefore, we hold that the plaintiffs and others similarly situated for whom the actions have been brought are, by reason of the segregation complained of, deprived of the equal protection of the laws guaranteed by the Fourteenth Amendment.

THINK QUESTIONS

1. Why might the Supreme Court have thought that this ruling, overturning *Plessy v. Ferguson,* was important for the country? Refer to one or more details from the text to support your explanation.

2. According to Chief Justice Warren, what effect did a court ruling such as *Plessy v. Ferguson* have on educational opportunities for non-white students? Support your answer with textual evidence.

3. Use details and evidence provided in the text to explain what Chief Justice Warren means by the phrase "modern authority" at the end of the next-to-last paragraph.

4. Use contextual clues to determine the meaning of the word **tangible** in the reading selection. Write your definition here. Explain how this knowledge, and your knowledge of affixes, helps you define the word "intangible" in the next paragraph.

5. What kinds of contextual clues help you determine the meaning of **detrimental** in the next-to-last paragraph? Write your definition of "detrimental" here and explain how you verified it. Then, use a dictionary or other reference work to clarify its precise meaning.

CLOSE READ

Reread the court ruling in *Brown* v. *Board of Education*. As you reread, complete the Focus Questions below. Then use your answers and annotations from the questions to help you complete the Writing Prompt.

FOCUS QUESTIONS

1. Look at the opening paragraph of the selection. How does the language reveal Chief Justice Warren's perspective on decisions such as *Plessy v. Ferguson*? Highlight words and phrases in the text that support your inference.

2. Reread the second paragraph. What can you infer about the changes in the educational system between 1896 and 1954 based on Chief Justice Warren's descriptions? What is the purpose of the last sentence in the paragraph? Highlight textual evidence and make annotations to explain how you made your inferences.

3. Reread the first half of the fourth paragraph. How does the Chief Justice relate the cases of *Sweatt v. Painter* and *McLaurin v. Oklahoma State Regents* to students in grade or high schools? What might be the author's purpose in focusing on "intangibles"? Highlight textual evidence and make annotations to support your response.

4. Examine and summarize the logical argument Warren makes in the second half of the fourth paragraph. How does this section address the question of "intangible" qualities mentioned in the precedent cases? Highlight evidence from the text that supports your response.

5. Consider the end of the fourth paragraph and how it relates back to the rest of the text. What do you think is the purpose of Warren's references to *Plessy v. Ferguson* in these sentences? How does this reflect on how America itself had changed in the years between the court rulings?

WRITING PROMPT

At the conclusion of its 1954 decision in *Brown v. Board of Education*, the U.S. Supreme Court ruled that "the doctrine of 'separate but equal' has no place" in public education. Do you think the justices realized that this decision might have an impact beyond the public school system? Would they have agreed or disagreed with such an application? Combine textual evidence from *Brown v. Board of Education* with your background knowledge of the judicial system and legal reasoning to support your claim.

A FAREWELL TO ARMS

FICTION
Ernest Hemingway
1929

INTRODUCTION

Known for a life of adventure, American author Ernest Hemingway based his semi-autobiographical novel, *A Farewell to Arms*, on his experiences as an ambulance driver in Italy during World War I. The story revolves around the exploits of Lieutenant ("Tenente") Frederic Henry—also an ambulance driver with the Italian Army—and his doomed romance with a British nurse. In the excerpt here, Henry engages the drivers under his command in a philosophical debate about war.

"There is nothing worse than war."

FIRST READ

From Chapter 9

1 "Were you there, Tenente, when they wouldn't attack and they shot every tenth man?"

2 "No."

3 "It is true. They lined them up afterward and took every tenth man. Carabinieri shot them."

4 "Carabinieri," said Passini and spat on the floor. "But those grenadiers; all over six feet. They wouldn't attack."

5 "If everybody would not attack the war would be over," Manera said.

6 "It wasn't that way with the granatieri. They were afraid. The officers all came from such good families."

7 "Some of the officers went alone."

8 "A sergeant shot two officers who would not get out."

9 "Some troops went out."

10 "Those that went out were not lined up when they took the tenth man."

11 "One of those shot by the carabinieri is from my town," Passini said. "He was a big smart tall boy to be in the granatieri. Always in Rome. Always with the girls. Always with the carabinieri." He laughed. "Now they have a guard outside his house with a bayonet and nobody can come to see his mother and father and sisters and his father loses his civil rights and cannot even vote. They are all without law to protect them. Anybody can take their property."

Copyright © BookheadEd Learning, LLC

12 "If it wasn't that that happens to their families nobody would go to the attack."

13 "Yes. Alpini would. These V. E. soldiers would. Some bersaglieri."

14 "Bersaglieri have run too. Now they try to forget it."

15 "You should not let us talk this way, Tenente. Evviva l'esercito," Passini said sarcastically.

16 "I know how you talk," I said. "But as long as you drive the cars and behave—"

17 "—and don't talk so other officers can hear," Manera finished.

18 "I believe we should get the war over," I said. "It would not finish it if one side stopped fighting. It would only be worse if we stopped fighting."

19 "It could not be worse," Passini said respectfully. "There is nothing worse than war."

20 "Defeat is worse."

21 "I do not believe it," Passini said still respectfully. "What is defeat? You go home."

22 "They come after you. They take your home. They take your sisters."

23 "I don't believe it," Passini said. "They can't do that to everybody. Let everybody defend his home. Let them keep their sisters in the house."

24 "They hang you. They come and make you be a soldier again. Not in the auto-ambulance, in the **infantry**."

25 "They can't hang every one."

26 "An outside nation can't make you be a soldier," Manera said. "At the first battle you all run."

27 "Like the Tchecos."

28 "I think you do not know anything about being conquered and so you think it is not bad."

29 "Tenente," Passini said. "We understand you let us talk. Listen. There is nothing as bad as war. We in the auto-ambulance cannot realize at all how bad it is. When people realize how bad it is they cannot do anything to stop it because they go crazy. There are some people who never realize. There are people who are afraid of their officers. It is with them the war is made."

30 "I know it is bad but we must finish it."

31 "It doesn't finish. There is no finish to a war."

Copyright © BookheadEd Learning, LLC

32 "Yes there is."

33 Passini shook his head.

34 "War is not won by victory. What if we take San Gabriele? What if we take the Carso and Monfalcone and Trieste? Where are we then? Did you see all the far mountains to-day? Do you think we could take all them too? Only if the Austrians stop fighting. One side must stop fighting. Why don't we stop fighting? If they come down into Italy they will get tired and go away. They have their own country. But no, instead there is a war."

35 "You're an **orator.**"

36 "We think. We read. We are not peasants. We are mechanics. But even the peasants know better than to believe in a war. Everybody hates this war."

37 "There is a class that controls a country that is stupid and does not realize anything and never can. That is why we have this war."

38 "Also they make money out of it."

39 "Most of them don't," said Passini. "They are too stupid. They do it for nothing. For stupidity."

40 "We must shut up," said Manera. "We talk too much even for the Tenente."

41 "He likes it," said Passini. "We will convert him."

42 "But now we will shut up," Manera said.

From Chapter 27

43 "I am a patriot," Gino said. "But I cannot love Brindisi or Taranto."

44 "Do you love the Bainsizza?" I asked.

45 "The soil is sacred," he said. "But I wish it grew more potatoes. You know when we came here we found fields of potatoes the Austrians had planted."

46 "Has the food really been short?"

47 "I myself have never had enough to eat but I am a big eater and I have not starved. The mess is average. The regiments in the line get pretty good food but those in support don't get so much. Something is wrong somewhere. There should be plenty of food."

48 "The dogfish are selling it somewhere else."

49 "Yes, they give the battalions in the front line as much as they can but the ones in back are very short. They have eaten all the Austrians' potatoes and chestnuts from the woods. They ought to feed them better. We are big eaters.

NOTES

I am sure there is plenty of food. It is very bad for the soldiers to be short of food. Have you ever noticed the difference it makes in the way you can think?"

50 "Yes," I said. "It can't win a war but it can lose one."

51 "We won't talk about losing. There is enough talk about losing. What has been done this summer cannot have been done in vain."

52 I did not say anything. I was always embarrassed by the words sacred, glorious, and sacrifice and the expression in vain. We had heard them, sometimes standing in the rain almost out of earshot, so that only the shouted words came through, and had read them, on **proclamations** that were slapped up by billposters over other proclamations, now for a long time, and I had seen nothing sacred, and the things that were glorious had no glory and the sacrifices were like the stockyards at Chicago if nothing was done with the meat except to bury it. There were many words that you could not stand to hear and finally only the names of places had dignity. Certain numbers were the same way and certain dates and these with the names of the places were all you could say and have them mean anything. Abstract words such as glory, honor, courage, or **hallow** were **obscene** beside the concrete names of villages, the numbers of roads, the names of rivers, the numbers of regiments and the dates. Gino was a patriot, so he said things that separated us sometimes, but he was also a fine boy and I understood his being a patriot. He was born one.

Excerpted from *A Farewell to Arms* by Ernest Hemingway, published by Scribner.

 THINK QUESTIONS

1. Based on what you read in the introduction and the excerpt from Chapter 9, compare and contrast the characters of Tenente, Passini, and Manera. Consider details about their ranks and personalities in your response.

2. Frederic Henry, whom Passini and Manera refer to as "Tenente" in Chapter 9, refers to Gino as a "fine boy" in Chapter 27. How might details in Gino's conversation with Henry about the shortage of food suggest that he is indeed a young, perhaps naive boy?

3. Gino is a "patriot," according to his own and Henry's descriptions. Does Henry share Gino's patriotism? Support your answer with textual evidence.

4. Use context and your knowledge of word roots and affixes to determine the meaning of the word **proclamations.** Write your definition of the word here and explain how you found and verified it.

5. Use context to determine the meaning of the word **infantry.** Write your definition of the word here and explain how you arrived at it and checked it in its original context.

Please note that excerpts and passages in the StudySync® library and this workbook are intended as touchstones to generate interest in an author's work. The excerpts and passages do not substitute for the reading of entire texts, and StudySync® strongly recommends that students seek out and purchase the whole literary or informational work in order to experience it as the author intended. Links to online resellers are available in our digital library. In addition, complete works may be ordered through an authorized reseller by filling out and returning to StudySync® the order form enclosed in this workbook.

Reading & Writing Companion **263**

CLOSE READ

Reread the excerpt from *A Farewell to Arms*. As you reread, complete the Focus Questions below. Then use your answers and annotations from the questions to help you complete the Writing Prompt.

FOCUS QUESTIONS

1. Consider the central section of the men's dialogue in the Chapter 9 passage. How do Tenente's views on war differ from Manera's and Passini's?

2. Review the latter third of the passage from Chapter 9. What does Passini hope to achieve by voicing his opinions? How does his message relate to a theme explored in the excerpt?

3. Compare the character of Gino in Chapter 27 with Passini and Manera in Chapter 9. How are their views on war similar or different?

4. Does Henry's point of view about the war appear to have changed or remained the same between the conversations in Chapter 9 and Chapter 27?

5. Consider Henry's final words in Chapter 27 about Gino's being a patriot: "He was born one." What concepts does Henry associate with the traditional definition of a patriot, of which Gino is the perfect example? How have Henry's experiences as an American ambulance driver for the Italian army during World War I led him to reject the validity of such concepts? In what ways might Hemingway's novel suggest the need to redefine the term *patriot*?

WRITING PROMPT

Now that you have analyzed the two excerpts from *A Farewell to Arms* in depth, what theme or message about life do you believe is most central to both? Briefly summarize your interpretation of this theme. Then, explain how Hemingway's choices regarding story elements such as setting, character, plot, and conflict allow him to approach and develop this theme from multiple angles. Provide examples and other textual evidence to support your ideas.

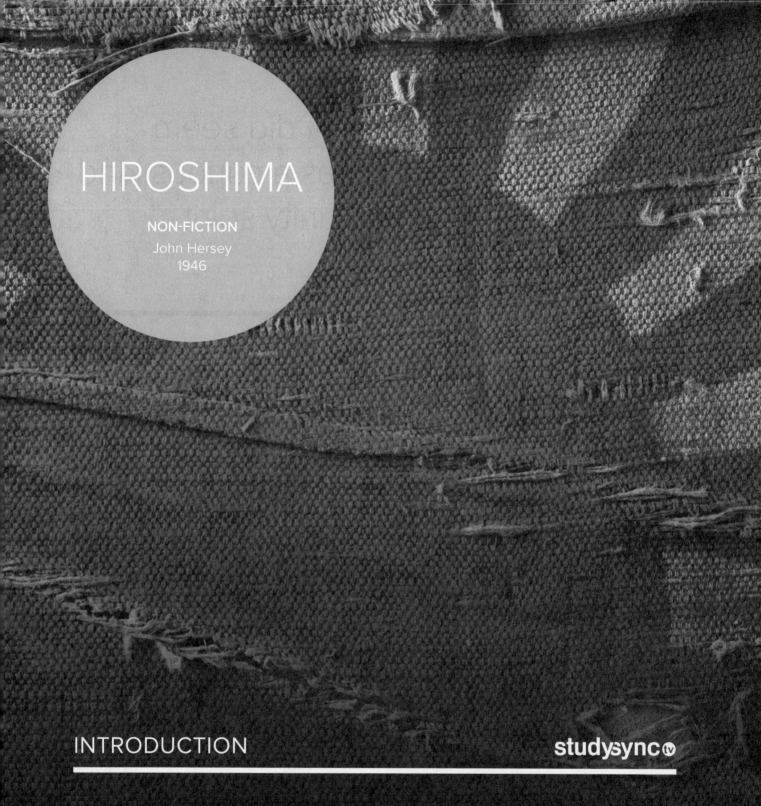

HIROSHIMA

NON-FICTION
John Hersey
1946

INTRODUCTION

John Hersey's eyewitness account of life in Hiroshima after the bomb was meant to be published in serial form in *The New Yorker* magazine, but the editors made a last minute decision to devote the whole issue to it. The article was an immediate sensation, giving Americans their first real understanding of the impact of a nuclear weapon. In this excerpt, Hersey describes some of the

"One feeling they did seem to share, however, was a curious kind of elated community spirit..."

NOTES

FIRST READ

Excerpt from Chapter Four: Panic Grass and Feverfew

1 The hospitals and aid stations around Hiroshima were so crowded in the first weeks after the bombing and staffs were so variable, depending on their health and on the unpredictable arrival of outside help, that patients had to be constantly shifted from place to place. Miss Sasaki, who had already been moved three times, twice by ship, was taken at the end of August to an engineering school, also at Hatsukaichi. Because her leg did not improve but swelled more and more, the doctors at the school bound it with crude splints and took her by car, on September 9th, to the Red Cross Hospital in Hiroshima. This was the first chance she had had to look at the ruins of Hiroshima; the last time she had been carried through the city's streets, she had been hovering on the edge of **unconsciousness**. Even though the wreckage had been described to her, and though she was still in pain, the sight horrified and amazed her, and there was something she noticed about it that particularly gave her the creeps. Over everything—up through the wreckage of the city, in gutters, along the riverbanks, tangled among tiles and tin roofing, climbing on charred tree trunks—was a blanket of fresh, vivid, lush, optimistic green; the **verdancy** rose even from the foundations of ruined houses. Weeds already hid the ashes, and wild flowers were in bloom among the city's bones. The bomb had not only left the underground organs of plants intact; it had stimulated them. Everywhere were bluets and Spanish bayonets, goosefoot, morning glories and day lilies, the hairy-fruited bean, purslane and clotbur and sesame and panic grass and feverfew. Especially in a circle at the center, sickle senna grew in extraordinary **regeneration**, not only standing among the charred remnants of the same plant but pushing up in new places, among bricks and through cracks in the asphalt. It actually seemed as if a load of sickle-senna seed had been dropped along with the bomb. ...

2   A year after the bomb was dropped, Miss Sasaki was a cripple; Mrs. Nakamura was **destitute**; Father Kleinsorge was back in the hospital; Dr. Sasaki was not capable of the work he once could do; Dr. Fujii had lost the thirty-room hospital it took him many years to acquire, and had no prospects of rebuilding it; Mr. Tanimoto's church had been ruined and he no longer had his exceptional **vitality**. The lives of these six people, among the luckiest in Hiroshima, would never be the same. What they thought of their experiences and of the use of the atomic bomb was, of course, not unanimous. One feeling they did seem to share, however, was a curious kind of elated community spirit, something like that of the Londoners after their blitz—a pride in the way they and their fellow survivors had stood up to a dreadful ordeal. Just before the anniversary, Mr. Tanimoto wrote in a letter to an American some words which expressed this feeling: "What a heartbreaking scene this was the first night! About midnight I landed on the riverbank. So many injured people lied on the ground that I made my way by striding over them. Repeating 'Excuse me,' I forwarded and carried a tub of water with me and gave a cup of water to each of them. They raised their upper bodies slowly and accepted a cup of water with a bow and drunk quietly and, spilling any remnants gave back a cup with hearty expression of their thankfulness, and said, 'I couldn't help my sister, who was buried under the house, because I had to take care of my mother who got a deep wound on her eye and our house soon set fire and we hardly escaped. Look, I lost my home, my family, and at last myself bitterly injured. But now I have gotten my mind to dedicate what I have and to complete the war for our country's sake.' Thus they pledged to me, even women and children did the same. Being entirely tired I lied down on the ground among them, but couldn't sleep at all. Next morning I found many men and women dead, whom I gave water last night. But to my great surprise, I never heard any one cried in disorder, even though they suffered in great agony. They died in silence, with no grudge, setting their teeth to bear it. All for the country."...

3   It would be impossible to say what horrors were **embedded** in the minds of the children who lived through the day of the bombing in Hiroshima. On the surface their recollections, months after the disasters, were of an exhilarating adventure. Toshio Nakamura, who was ten at the time of the bombing, was soon able to talk freely, even gaily, about the experience, and a few weeks before the anniversary he wrote the following matter-of-fact essay for his teacher at No-bori-cho Primary School: "The day before the bomb, I went for a swim. In the morning, I was eating peanuts. I saw a light. I was knocked to little sister's sleeping place. When we were saved, I could only see as far as the tram. My mother and I started to pack our things. The neighbors were walking around burned and bleeding. Hataya-*san* told me to run away with her. I said I wanted to wait for my mother. We went to the park. A whirlwind came. At night a gas tank burned and I saw the reflection in the river. We stayed in the park one night. Next day I went to Taiko Bridge and met my girl

NOTES

friends Kikuki and Murakami. They were looking for their mothers. But Kikuki's mother was wounded and Murakami's mother, alas, was dead."

Excerpted from *Hiroshima* by John Hersey, published by Ishi Press.

☁ THINK QUESTIONS

1. How much time has elapsed between the atomic bomb explosion and Miss Sasaki's observation of Hiroshima in the first paragraph? How does this relate to the description of the plant life at the end of the paragraph?

2. Use details from the text to write two or three sentences describing Mr. Tanimoto. What important aspects of his character can the reader infer from the letter he wrote?

3. How does Toshio Nakamura's school essay relate to the central or main idea of the final paragraph? Provide textual evidence that supports your response.

4. Use context to determine the meaning of the word **verdancy.** Write your definition here and explain how you inferred its meaning.

5. Given that the Latin root "genus" means "origin or birth," use the context clues and your knowledge of affixes to determine the meaning of **regeneration.** Write your definition of "regeneration" here and tell how you got it.

CLOSE READ

Reread the excerpt from "Hiroshima." As you reread, complete the Focus Questions below. Then use your answers and annotations from the questions to help you complete the Writing Prompt.

FOCUS QUESTIONS

1. Look at the middle of the first paragraph. In terms of word choice and syntax, explain how and why Hersey uses the phrase "gave her the creeps" in the sentence about Miss Sasaki. How does the multiple-meaning word "creeps" relate to the author's purpose in the rest of the paragraph?

2. Reread the last half of the first paragraph. Would you describe Hersey's description of the vegetation as "photographic" or "cinematic"? Explain how the text suggests one or the other of these visual treatments.

3. Reread Mr. Tanimoto's description of the bombing in the second paragraph. How does Mr. Tanimoto's syntax and grammar differ from Hersey's? How might you explain these differences?

4. Refer to one or more details from the text to explain why the author has chosen the title "Panic Grass and Feverfew" for this chapter.

5. Remember that *Hiroshima* was originally published in 1946 and that the Preview video and SyncTV discussion were created recently. How does comparing and contrasting the book with the contemporary Preview video and SyncTV discussion reflect changes in the country's attitude toward the bombing of Hiroshima over the last half of the 20th century?

WRITING PROMPT

Imagine that you're a media designer who has been assigned to create a video advertisement for a new edition of John Hersey's book *Hiroshima*. Create a written description of the images, music, and spoken text that you will use to promote this new version of the book effectively for a contemporary audience. Explain how you would select and organize your choices and relate these decisions back to details and information in the reading selection.

Please note that excerpts and passages in the StudySync® library and this workbook are intended as touchstones to generate interest in an author's work. The excerpts and passages do not substitute for the reading of entire texts, and StudySync® strongly recommends that students seek out and purchase the whole literary or informational work in order to experience it as the author intended. Links to online resellers are available in our digital library. In addition, complete works may be ordered through an authorized reseller by filling out and returning to StudySync® the order form enclosed in this workbook.

Reading & Writing Companion **269**

THE ROAD

FICTION
Cormac McCarthy
2006

INTRODUCTION

American novelist, playwright and screenwriter Cormac McCarthy has received numerous accolades for his work, which spans across multiple genres. His novel *The Road* won the 2007 Pulitzer Prize for Fiction, and tells the story of a father and son trying to survive in a lawless and nearly lifeless environment after an unspecified apocalyptic event wipes out most civilization. In the excerpt below, from the beginning of the novel, the father and son journey down the road to an abandoned gas station and eventually spy a ruined city in the distance.

"This was not a safe place."

FIRST READ

NOTES

1   They left the cart in a gully covered with the tarp and made their way up the slope through the dark poles of the standing trees to where he'd seen a running ledge of rock and they sat under the rock overhang and watched the gray sheets of rain blow across the valley. It was very cold. They sat huddled together wrapped each in a blanket over their coats and after a while the rain stopped and there was just the dripping in the woods.

2   When it had cleared they went down to the cart and pulled away the tarp and got their blankets and the things they would need for the night. They went back up the hill and made their camp in the dry dirt under the rocks and the man sat with his arms around the boy trying to warm him. Wrapped in the blankets, watching the nameless dark come to **enshroud** them. The gray shape of the city vanished in the night's onset like an **apparition** and he lit the little lamp and set it back out of the wind. Then they walked out to the road and he took the boy's hand and they went to the top of the hill where the road crested and where they could see out over the darkening country to the south, standing there in the wind, wrapped in their blankets, watching for any sign of a fire or a lamp. There was nothing. The lamp in the rocks on the side of the hill was little more than a mote of light and after a while they walked back. Everything too wet to make a fire. They ate their poor meal cold and lay down in their bedding with the lamp between them. He'd brought the boy's book but the boy was too tired for reading. Can we leave the lamp on till I'm asleep? he said. Yes. Of course we can.

. . .

3   On the outskirts of the city they came to a supermarket. A few old cars in the trash strewn parking lot. They left the cart in the lot and walked the littered aisles. In the produce section in the bottom of the bins they found a few ancient runner beans and what looked to have once been apricots, longdried to wrinkled effigies of themselves. The boy followed behind. They pushed

out through the rear door. In the alleyway behind the store a few shopping carts, all badly rusted. They went back through the store again looking for another cart but there were none. By the door were two soft drink machines that had been tilted over into the floor and opened with a prybar. Coins everywhere in the ash. He sat and ran his hand around in the works of the gutted machines and in the second one it closed over a cold metal cylinder. He withdrew his hand slowly and sat looking at a Coca Cola.

4   What is it, Papa?

5   It's a treat. For you.

6   What is it?

7   Here. Sit down.

8   He slipped the boy's knapsack straps loose and set the pack on the floor behind him and he put his thumbnail under the aluminum clip on the top of the can and opened it. He leaned his nose to the slight fizz coming from the can and then handed it to the boy. Go ahead, he said.

9   The boy took the can. It's bubbly, he said.

10 Go ahead.

11 He looked at his father and then tilted the can and drank. He sat there thinking about it. It's really good, he said.

12 Yes. It is.

13 You have some, Papa.

14 I want you to drink it.

15 You have some.

16 He took the can and sipped it and handed it back. You drink it, he said. Let's just sit here.

17 It's because I wont ever get to drink another one, isnt it?

18 Ever's a long time.

19 Okay, the boy said.

20 By dusk of the day following they were at the city. The long concrete sweeps of the interstate exchanges like the ruins of a vast funhouse against the

distant murk. He carried the revolver in his belt at the front and wore his parka unzipped. The mummied dead everywhere. The flesh cloven along the bones, the ligaments dried to tug and taut as wires. Shriveled and drawn like latterday bogfolk, their faces of boiled sheeting, the yellowed palings of their teeth. They were discalced to a man like pilgrims of some common order for all their shoes were long since stolen.

21 They went on. He kept constant watch behind him in the mirror. The only thing that moved in the streets was the blowing ash. They crossed the high concrete bridge over the rivers. A dock below. Small pleasure boats half sunken in the gray water. Tall stacks downriver dim in the soot.

22 The day following some few miles south of the city at a bend in the road and half lost in the dead brambles they came upon an old frame house with chimneys and gables and a stone wall. The man stopped. Then he pushed the cart up the drive.

23 What is this place, Papa?

24 It's the house where I grew up.

25 The boy stood looking at it. The peeling wooden clapboards were largely gone from the lower walls for firewood leaving the studs and the insulation exposed. The rotted screening from the back porch lay on the concrete terrace.

26 Are we going in?

27 Why not?

28 I'm scared.

29 Dont you want to see where I used to live?

30 No.

31 It'll be okay.

32 There could be somebody here.

33 I dont think so.

34 But suppose there is?

35 He stood looking up at the gable to his old room. He looked at the boy. Do you want to wait here?

36 No. You always say that.

37 I'm sorry.

38 I know. But you do.

39 They slipped out of their backpacks and left them on the terrace and kicked their way through the trash on the porch and pushed into the kitchen. The boy held on to his hand. All much as he'd remembered it. The rooms empty. In the small room off the dining room there was a bare iron cot, a metal folding table. The same cast iron coal grate in the small fireplace. The pine paneling was gone from the walls leaving just the furring strips. He stood there. He felt with his thumb in the painted wood of the mantle the pinholes from tacks that had held stockings forty years ago. This is where we used to have Christmas when I was a boy. He turned and looked out at the waste of the yard. A tangle of dead lilac. The shape of a hedge. On cold winter nights when the electricity was out in a storm we would sit at the fire here, me and my sisters, doing our homework. The boy watched him. Watched shapes claiming him he could not see. We should go, Papa, he said. Yes, the man said. But he didn't.

40 They walked through the diningroom where the firebrick in the hearth was as yellow as the day it was laid because his mother could not bear to see it blackened. The floor buckled from the rainwater. In the livingroom the bones of a small animal **dismembered** and placed in a pile. Possibly a cat. A glass tumbler by the door. The boy gripped his hand. They went up the stairs and turned and went down the hallway. Small cones of damp plaster standing in the floor. The wooden lathes of the ceiling exposed. He stood in the doorway to his room. A small space under the eaves. This is where I used to sleep. My cot was against this wall. In the nights in their thousands to dream the dreams of a child's imaginings, worlds rich or fearful such as might offer themselves but never the one to be. He pushed open the closet door half expecting to find his childhood things. Raw cold daylight fell through from the roof. Gray as his heart.

41 We should go, Papa. Can we go?

42 Yes. We can go.

43 I'm scared.

44 I know. I'm sorry.

45 I'm really scared.

46 It's all right. We shouldnt have come.

Excerpted from *The Road* by Cormac McCarthy, published by Vintage Books.

 THINK QUESTIONS

1. What is the mood (that is, the atmosphere or emotional quality) of the first paragraph of this excerpt? Cite details from the text to support your response.

2. What does the incident with the can of soda tell us about the father and the son? Use details from the text to develop and support your answer.

3. Why do you think the boy is "really scared" at the end of the excerpt? Explain your response using inferences drawn from the text.

4. How does the use of the word **apparition** in a simile help you determine its meaning? Write your definition of the word and explain how you arrived at it.

5. Knowing that the Latin word "calceus" means "shoe," how can you determine the meaning and part of speech of **discalced**? Write your definition here and explain how context clues in the passage can help verify your predicted meaning.

Please note that excerpts and passages in the StudySync® library and this workbook are intended as touchstones to generate interest in an author's work. The excerpts and passages do not substitute for the reading of entire texts, and StudySync® strongly recommends that students seek out and purchase the whole literary or informational work in order to experience it as the author intended. Links to online resellers are available in our digital library. In addition, complete works may be ordered through an authorized reseller by filling out and returning to StudySync® the order form enclosed in this workbook.

Reading & Writing Companion   **275**

CLOSE READ

Reread the excerpt from *The Road*. As you reread, complete the Focus Questions below. Then use your answers and annotations from the questions to help you complete the Writing Prompt.

FOCUS QUESTIONS

1. What do you think the little lamp in the second paragraph of the story might represent? How does it relate to the setting of this scene?

2. Reread the scene in which the father gives his son a can of soda. Why is this can of soda so significant? What do you learn about the characters from this scene?

3. Reread the description of the city. Based on details and clues in the two paragraphs that describe the city, what do you think happened there in the past? What questions remain unanswered?

4. Reread the scene in which the father and son enter and explore the house. What do you learn about the two characters from this scene?

5. Reread the last full paragraph and the dialogue at the end of the excerpt. Why might the father have said "We shouldnt have come"?

WRITING PROMPT

Consider how the author describes the setting and the interactions between the father and the son in this setting. How do the author's choices in describing setting and characters impact your thoughts about the father and son and their chance of survival? Provide evidence from the text to support your response.

THE WOMAN WARRIOR:

MEMOIRS OF A GIRLHOOD AMONG GHOSTS

NON-FICTION
Maxine Hong Kingston
1975

INTRODUCTION

Maxine Hong Kingston has written extensively about the experiences of Chinese immigrants living in the United States. Born in America, she was long fascinated by the beliefs that Chinese immigrants of her parents' generation seemed to have about women. In talking with her parents, Kingston discovered that cherished myths about powerful warrior women existed side by side with what Kingston perceived as sexist ideas. These conflicting views are reflected in the writing of Kingston's autobiographical work, *The Woman Warrior: Memoirs of a Girlhood Among Ghosts*. In this excerpt, Kingston's mother Brave Orchid waits at the airport for her sister Moon Orchid, whom she has not seen for

"Their hands reached out as if to touch the other's face, then returned to their own..."

NOTES

FIRST READ

From Chapter Four: At the Western Palace

1   When she was about sixty-eight years old, Brave Orchid took a day off to wait at San Francisco International Airport for the plane that was bringing her sister to the United States. She had not seen Moon Orchid for thirty years. She had begun this waiting at home, getting up a half-hour before Moon Orchid's plane took off in Hong Kong. Brave Orchid would add her will power to the forces that keep an airplane up. Her head hurt with the concentration. The plane had to be light, so no matter how tired she felt, she dared not rest her spirit on a wing but continuously and gently pushed up on the plane's belly. She had already been waiting at the airport for nine hours. She was wakeful.

2   Next to Brave Orchid sat Moon Orchid's only daughter, who was helping her aunt wait. Brave Orchid had made two of her own children come too because they could drive, but they had been lured away by the magazine racks and the gift shops and coffee shops. Her American children could not sit for very long. They did not understand sitting; they had wandering feet. She hoped they would get back from the pay TV's or the pay toilets or wherever they were spending their money before the plane arrived. If they did not come back soon, she would go look for them. If her son thought he could hide in the men's room, he was wrong.

3   "Are you all right, Aunt?" asked her niece.

4   "No, this chair hurts me. Help me pull some chairs together so I can put my feet up."

5   She unbundled a blanket and spread it out to make a bed for herself. On the floor she had two shopping bags full of canned peaches, real peaches, beans wrapped in taro leaves, cookies, Thermos bottles, enough food for everybody, though only her niece would eat with her. Her bad boy and bad girl were probably sneaking hamburgers, wasting their money. She would scold them.

6   Many soldiers and sailors sat about, oddly calm, like little boys in cowboy uniforms. (She thought "cowboy" was what you would call a Boy Scout.) They should have been crying hysterically on their way to Vietnam. "If I see one that looks Chinese," she thought, "I'll go over and give him some advice." She sat up suddenly; she had forgotten about her own son, who was even now in Vietnam. Carefully she split her attention, beaming half of it to the ocean, into the water to keep him afloat. He was on a ship. He was in Vietnamese waters. She was sure of it. He and the other children were lying to her. They had said he was in Japan, and then they said he was in the Philippines. But when she sent him her help, she could feel that he was on a ship in Da Nang. Also she had seen the children hide the envelopes that his letters came in.

7   "Do you think my son is in Vietnam?" she asked her niece, who was dutifully eating.

8   "No. Didn't your children say he was in the Philippines?"

9   "Have you ever seen any of his letters with Philippine stamps on them?"

10 "Oh, yes. Your children showed me one."

11 "I wouldn't put it past them to send the letters to some Filipino they know. He puts Manila postmarks on them to fool me."

12 "Yes, I can imagine them doing that. But don't worry. Your son can take care of himself. All your children can take care of themselves."

13 "Not him. He's not like other people. Not normal at all. He sticks erasers in his ears, and the erasers are still attached to the pencil stubs. The captain will say, 'Abandon ship,' or 'Watch out for bombs,' and he won't hear. He doesn't listen to orders. I told him to flee to Canada, but he wouldn't go."

14 She closed her eyes. After a short while, plane and ship under control, she looked again at the children in uniforms. Some of the blond ones looked like baby chicks, their crew cuts like the downy yellow on baby chicks. You had to feel sorry for them even though they were Army and Navy Ghosts.

15 Suddenly her son and daughter came running. "Come, Mother. The plane's landed early. She's here already." They hurried, folding up their mother's **encampment**. She was glad her children were not useless. They must have

Please note that excerpts and passages in the StudySync® library and this workbook are intended as touchstones to generate interest in an author's work. The excerpts and passages do not substitute for the reading of entire texts, and StudySync® strongly recommends that students seek out and purchase the whole literary or informational work in order to experience it as the author intended. Links to online resellers are available in our digital library. In addition, complete works may be ordered through an authorized reseller by filling out and returning to StudySync® the order form enclosed in this workbook.

Reading & Writing
Companion

279

known what this trip to San Francisco was about then. "It's a good thing I made you come early," she said.

16   . . . .

17   She was a tiny, tiny lady, very thin, with little fluttering hands, and her hair was in a gray knot. She was dressed in a gray wool suit; she wore pearls around her neck and in her earlobes. Moon Orchid *would* travel with her jewels showing. Brave Orchid momentarily saw, like a larger, younger outline around this old woman, the sister she had been waiting for. The familiar dim halo faded, leaving the woman so old, so gray. So old. Brave Orchid pressed against the glass. *That* old lady? Yes, that old lady facing the ghost who stamped her papers without questioning her was her sister. Then, without noticing her family, Moon Orchid walked smiling over to the Suitcase Inspector Ghost, who took her boxes apart, pulling out puffs of tissue. From where she was, Brave Orchid could not see what her sister had chosen to carry across the ocean. She wished her sister would look her way. Brave Orchid thought that if she were entering a new country, she would be at the windows. Instead Moon Orchid hovered over the unwrapping, surprised at each reappearance as if she were opening presents after a birthday party.

18   "Mama!" Moon Orchid's daughter kept calling. Brave Orchid said to her children, "Why don't you call your aunt too? Maybe she'll hear us if all of you call out together." But her children slunk away. Maybe that shame-fame they so often wore was American politeness.

19   "Mama!" Moon Orchid's daughter called again, and this time her mother looked right at her. She left her bundles in a heap and came running. "Hey!" the Customs Ghost yelled at her. She went back to clear up her mess, talking **inaudibly** to her daughter all the while. Her daughter pointed toward Brave Orchid. And at last Moon Orchid looked at her—two old women with faces like mirrors.

20   Their hands reached out as if to touch the other's face, then returned to their own, the fingers checking the grooves in the forehead and along the sides of the mouth. Moon Orchid, who never understood the **gravity** of things, started smiling and laughing, pointing at Brave Orchid. Finally Moon Orchid gathered up her stuff, strings hanging and papers loose, and met her sister at the door, where they shook hands, **oblivious** to blocking the way.

21   "You're an old woman," said Brave Orchid.

22   "Aiaa. *You're* an old woman."

23   "But you are really old. Surely, you can't say that about me. I'm not old the way you're old."

NOTES

24   "But *you* really are old. You're one year older than I am."

25   "Your hair is white and your face all wrinkled."

26   "You're so skinny."

27   "You're so fat."

28   "Fat women are more beautiful than skinny women."

29   The children pulled them out of the doorway. One of Brave Orchid's children brought the car from the parking lot, and the other heaved the luggage into the trunk. They put the two old ladies and the niece in the back seat. All the way home—across the Bay Bridge, over the Diablo hills, across the San Joaquin River to the valley, the valley moon so white at dusk—all the way home, the two sisters exclaimed every time they turned to look at each other, "Aiaa! How old!"

30   Brave Orchid forgot that she got sick in cars, that all vehicles but palanquins made her dizzy. "You're so old," she kept saying. "How did you get so old?"

31   Brave Orchid had tears in her eyes. But Moon Orchid said, "You look older than I. You are older than I," and again she'd laugh. "You're wearing an old mask to tease me." It surprised Brave Orchid that after thirty years she could still get annoyed at her sister's silliness.

Excerpted from The Woman Warrior: Memoirs of a Girlhood Among Ghosts *by Maxine Hong Kingston, published by Random House.*

 ## THINK QUESTIONS

1. Refer to one or more details from the text to describe and support your understanding of Brave Orchid's personality.

2. Use details from the text to write two or three sentences summarizing what Brave Orchid thinks and feels about her children. For example, do you think she trusts them?

3. How would you characterize the relationship between the two sisters after they meet in the airport? Support your answer with textual evidence.

4. Use your knowledge of word parts to arrive at a definition for the word **inaudibly.** Does your definition make sense in the sentence? Explain.

5. Knowing that the word **gravity** has multiple meanings, use context clues to determine which meaning applies in the reading selection. Write that definition of "gravity" here and explain how you determined it was the intended meaning.

Please note that excerpts and passages in the StudySync® library and this workbook are intended as touchstones to generate interest in an author's work. The excerpts and passages do not substitute for the reading of entire texts, and StudySync® strongly recommends that students seek out and purchase the whole literary or informational work in order to experience it as the author intended. Links to online resellers are available in our digital library. In addition, complete works may be ordered through an authorized reseller by filling out and returning to StudySync® the order form enclosed in this workbook.

Reading & Writing Companion   **281**

CLOSE READ

Reread the excerpt from *The Woman Warrior*. As you reread, complete the Focus Questions below. Then use your answers and annotations from the questions to help you complete the Writing Prompt.

FOCUS QUESTIONS

1. Reread the first paragraph of the reading selection. How does the author express Brave Orchid's emotions about her sister's upcoming visit?

2. Reread the description of the soldiers and sailors in the waiting area. How does seeing them affect Brave Orchid? How does her own background influence her perception of them?

3. Reread the initial description of Moon Orchid. Use the annotation tool to differentiate between factual details and subjective impressions about Moon Orchid's appearance. Explain how these descriptions help to develop the character of Brave Orchid.

4. Highlight the author's use of the word "ghost" over the course of the text. What meaning does this word have in the context of the reading selection? What does this word and its connotations tell you about how Brave Orchid interacts with the world? Why do you think the author uses this word in the title?

5. Highlight and annotate details and examples in the reading selection that depict the differences between Chinese and American cultures. How does Brave Orchid feel about the way in which these differences have influenced her children?

WRITING PROMPT

Consider the interactions between Brave Orchid and one or more of the other individuals in this excerpt. What do you learn about Brave Orchid's background based on the way she interacts with others? How does this influence the people she interacts with? Provide examples from the selection to support your response.

TAKE THE TORTILLAS OUT OF YOUR POETRY

NON-FICTION

Rudolfo Anaya
1995

INTRODUCTION

Born and raised in New Mexico, author Rudulfo Anaya is a leading figure in contemporary Chicano literature. Best known for his novel *Bless Me Ultima*, Anaya has also published works in a variety of other genres, including short stories, essays, drama and poetry. Here, in "Take the Tortillas Out of Your Poetry," he celebrates the importance of books—describing reading as "a path toward liberation and fulfillment"—but warns that a bias against bilingual literature has prevented some writers from telling their stories.

"The national norm simply does not want to bother reading us."

 FIRST READ

1 In a recent lecture, "Is Nothing Sacred?," Salman Rushdie, one of the most censored authors of our time, talked about the importance of books. He grew up in a household in India where books were as sacred as bread. If anyone in the household dropped a piece of bread or a book, the person not only picked it up, but also kissed the object by way of apologizing for clumsy disrespect.

2 He goes on to say that he had kissed many books before he had kissed a girl. Bread and books were for his household, and for many like his, food for the body and the soul. This image of the kissing of the book one had accidentally dropped made an impression on me. It speaks to the love and respect many people have for them.

3 I grew up in a small town in New Mexico, and we had very few books in our household. The first one I remember reading was my **catechism** book. Before I went to school to learn English, my mother taught me catechism in Spanish. I remember the questions and answers I had to learn, and I remember the well-thumbed, well-frayed book that was sacred to me.

4 Growing up with few books in the house created in me a desire and a need for them. When I started school, I remember visiting the one room library of our town and standing in front of the dusty shelves. In reality there were only a few shelves and not over a thousand books, but I wanted to read them all. There was food for my soul in the books, that much I realized.

5 As a child I listened to the stories of the people, the cuentos the old ones told. Those stories were my first contact with the magic of storytelling. These stories fed my imagination, and later, when I wrote books, I found the same sense of magic and mystery in writing.

6   In *Bless Me, Ultima,* my first novel, Antonio, my main character, who has just started to school, sees in books the power of the written word. He calls books the "magic of words."

7   For me, reading has always been a path toward liberation and fulfillment. To learn to read is to start down the road to liberation. It is a road that should be accessible to everyone. No one has the right to keep you from reading, and yet that is what is happening in many areas in this country today. There are those who think they know best what we should read. These **censors** are at work in all areas of our daily lives.

8   Censorship has affected me directly, and I have formed some ideas on this **insidious** activity, but first, I want to give an example of censorship which recently affected a friend of mine. My friend is a Chicano poet and scholar, one of the finest I know. For some time I have been encouraging Chicano writers to apply for literary **fellowships** from the National Endowment for the Arts. A number of poets who use Spanish and English in their poetry applied but did not receive fellowships; they were so discouraged they did not reapply. This happened to my friend. He is an excellent poet—mature, intelligent—and he had an impressive academic background. He knew that when you apply for a fellowship you take your chances, so he did not give up after being turned down twice. He also knew—we all knew—that many of the panels that judged the **manuscripts** did not have readers who could read Spanish or bilingual manuscripts. In other words, the judges could not read the poetic language that expresses our reality. My friend rightfully deduced that his poetry was not receiving a fair reading.

9   "You know," he told me, "If they can't read my bilingual poetry, next time I apply I'm sending them only poems I write in English. My best poetry is bilingual, it reflects our reality, it's the way we speak, the way we are. But if I stand a better chance at getting a fellowship in English, I'll send that. But the poems I write in English are really not my best work. It's just not me."

10   I was dismayed by my friend's conclusion. How he coped with the problem has tremendous cultural **implications**. It has implications that we may call self-imposed censorship. My friend was censoring his creativity in order to fit the imposed criteria. He sent in his poorer work because that was the work the panelists could read and, therefore, consider for reward.

11   My friend had concluded that if he took his language and culture out of his poetry, he stood a better chance of receiving a fellowship. He took out his native language, the poetic **patois** of our reality, the rich mixture of Spanish, English, pachuco, and street talk that we know so well. In other words, he took the tortillas out of his poetry, which is to say he took the soul out of his poetry. He still has not received a fellowship, and many of those other poets

NOTES

and writers I have encouraged to apply for the fellowships have quit trying. The national norm simply does not want to bother reading us.

12 I do not believe we should have to leave out the crucial elements of our language and culture to contribute to American literature but, unfortunately, this is a conclusion I am forced to reach. I have been writing for a quarter century and have been a published author for eighteen years. As a writer, I was part of the Chicano Movement, which created a new literature in this country. We struggled to change the way the world looks at Mexican Americans by reflecting our reality in literature, and many eagerly sought our works, but the iron curtain of censorship was still there.

Excerpted from The Anaya Reader by Rudolfo Anaya, published by Grand Central Publishing.

THINK QUESTIONS

1. Refer to one or more details from the text to support your understanding of how Salman Rushdie influenced Rudolfo Anaya.

2. Based on the information provided in the text, where does Anaya find inspiration for his own creative work? Cite textual evidence that supports your inference.

3. Summarize how Anaya feels about his friend's decision regarding his applications for fellowships. Does he blame his friend for this decision? Support your answer with textual evidence.

4. Use paragraph clues to identify the definition of the word **censors.** Restate the definition in your own words here. Tell how knowing the meaning of this word helps you to understand and verify the meaning and use of the word "censorship" in the next paragraph.

5. The Latin word "manus" means "hand," and the Latin word "scriptum" means "something written." Use that information to determine the meaning of the word **manuscript.** Then verify your definition in the context of the sentence. What does the context suggest about how the meaning of the word may have changed over time?

CLOSE READ

Reread the essay, "Take the Tortillas Out of Your Poetry." As you reread, complete the Focus Questions below. Then use your answers and annotations from the questions to help you complete the Writing Prompt

FOCUS QUESTIONS

1. Reread the first four paragraphs. Explain how the mention of Salman Rushdie relates to the central or main ideas that Rudolfo Anaya will develop in his essay. Highlight evidence from the text and make annotations to support your explanation.

2. Review the fourth through seventh paragraphs. What central or main ideas connect these paragraphs? How does Anaya build upon them to provide a complex analysis of reading and storytelling? Highlight evidence from the text and make annotations to support your explanation.

3. Reread Paragraph 8, which starts with the word "censorship." How does Anaya state and develop the central idea of this paragraph? Do you think that he has provided thorough evidence to support his claims? Highlight evidence from the

text and make annotations to support your explanation.

4. In Paragraph 11, the author concludes that his friend, the Chicano poet, "took the tortillas out of his poetry." What does it mean to take the tortillas out of one's poetry? Does Anaya think this is a good idea or not? How does this statement connect to a central idea of the selection? Highlight evidence from the text and make annotations to support your explanation.

5. Consider the final paragraph of the essay. How has Anaya been redefining what it means to be American? Does he feel hopeful or discouraged about his efforts? Highlight evidence from the text and make annotations to support your explanation.

WRITING PROMPT

Analyze the main ideas in "Take the Tortillas Out of Your Poetry" in order to write an objective summary of the text. What is Anaya's central or main idea? Does he state it explicitly? How does he develop his arguments throughout the essay? Provide thorough and relevant textual evidence to support your own analysis of his central or main ideas.

Please note that excerpts and passages in the StudySync® library and this workbook are intended as touchstones to generate interest in an author's work. The excerpts and passages do not substitute for the reading of entire texts, and StudySync® strongly recommends that students seek out and purchase the whole literary or informational work in order to experience it as the author intended. Links to online resellers are available in our digital library. In addition, complete works may be ordered through an authorized reseller by filling out and returning to StudySync® the order form enclosed in this workbook.

Reading & Writing Companion **287**

THE LATIN DELI: AN ARS POETICA

POETRY
Judith Cofer Ortiz
1993

INTRODUCTION

Acclaimed author Judith Ortiz Cofer was born in Puerto Rico, but spent most of her childhood in Patterson, New Jersey before moving to Georgia as a teenager. Writing in a variety of literary genres including poetry, short stories, essays and autobiography, Ortiz Cofer draws from personal experience to explore cultural conflicts, women's issues and the American South. As is often true in her work, "The Latin Deli" captures the intimate, poignant struggles of

"...she is the Patroness of Exiles, a woman of no-age who was never pretty..."

 FIRST READ

 NOTES

1. Presiding over a formica counter,
2. Plastic Mother and Child magnetized
3. to the top of an ancient register,
4. the heady mix of smells from the open bins
5. of dried codfish, the green plantains
6. hanging in stalks like **votive** offerings,
7. she is the **Patroness** of **Exiles**,
8. a woman of no-age who was never pretty,
9. who spends her days selling canned memories
10. while listening to the Puerto Ricans complain
11. that it would be cheaper to fly to San Juan
12. than to buy a pound of Bustelo coffee here,
13. and to the Cubans perfecting their speech
14. of a "glorious return" to Havana—where no one
15. has been allowed to die and nothing to change until then;
16. to Mexicans who pass through, talking **lyrically**
17. of dólares to be made in El Norte—

18. all wanting the comfort
19. of spoken Spanish, to gaze upon the family portrait
20. of her plain wide face, her ample bosom
21. resting on her plump arms, her look of **maternal** interest
22. as they speak to her and each other
23. of their dreams and their **disillusions**—
24. how she smiles understanding,
25. when they walk down the narrow aisles of her store
26. reading the labels of the packages aloud, as if
27. they were the names of lost lovers: Suspiros,
28. Merengues, the stale candy of everyone's childhood.

29 She spends her days
30 Slicing jamón y queso and wrapping it in wax paper
31 tied with string: plain ham and cheese
32 that would cost less at the A&P, but it would not satisfy
33 the hunger of the fragile old man lost in the folds
34 of his winter coat, who brings her lists of items
35 that he reads to her like poetry, or the others,
36 whose needs she must **divine,** conjuring up products
37 from places that now exist only in their hearts—
38 closed ports she must trade with.

"The Latin Deli: An Ars Poetica" is reprinted with permission from the publisher of "America's Review" by Judith Ortiz Cofer (©1992 Arte Publico Press—University of Houston).

THINK QUESTIONS

1. Refer to one or more details from the text to describe the physical setting of this poem in both objective and subjective terms. Which of the five senses does the poet write about in her description?

2. Use details from the text to write two or three sentences that explore the poet's frequent references to speech and language in the poem. From these, what inferences can you make about the shopkeeper's attitude toward her clients?

3. Why do you think the Latin deli attracts so many customers despite its high prices? Support your response with textual evidence.

4. Use context to determine the meaning and part of speech of the word **lyrically**. Write your definition of the word here. Briefly explain how the multiple meanings of the base word, "lyric," might have influenced Ortiz Cofer's decision to include this particular word in her poem.

5. Remembering that the Latin word "mater" means "mother," use the context clues provided in the passage to determine the meaning of **maternal**. Write your definition of "maternal" here and explain how other context clues in the poem help you verify that definition.

CLOSE READ

Reread the poem "The Latin Deli: An Ars Poetica." As you reread, complete the Focus Questions below. Then use your answers and annotations from the questions to help you complete the Writing Prompt.

FOCUS QUESTIONS

1. Consider the first full sentence of the poem. How does its structure contribute to the overall tone that the poet creates in relation to the setting?

2. Reread the lines in the middle of the first stanza. How does the connotation of the words the poet has chosen to describe the shopkeeper's physical appearance contribute to the tone of the poem? How might this, in turn, relate to one of the poem's themes?

3. Analyze the last four lines of the second stanza. How do the figurative and connotative meanings of specific key words in these lines develop the themes of the poem?

4. Consider the final stanza of the poem. What impact does the poet's use of figurative language have on the overall tone and theme of the poem? How does it relate back to the title of the poem itself?

5. What does this poem say about how cultures are defined and redefined? How does the poet use tone to express different possible responses to this question?

WRITING PROMPT

Analyze the impact that Judith Ortiz Cofer's specific word choices have on the meaning and tone in her poem. What kind of relationship does this establish between the shopkeeper and her customers in the poem? How might each of them describe their attitudes toward one another? Include textual evidence to support your response.

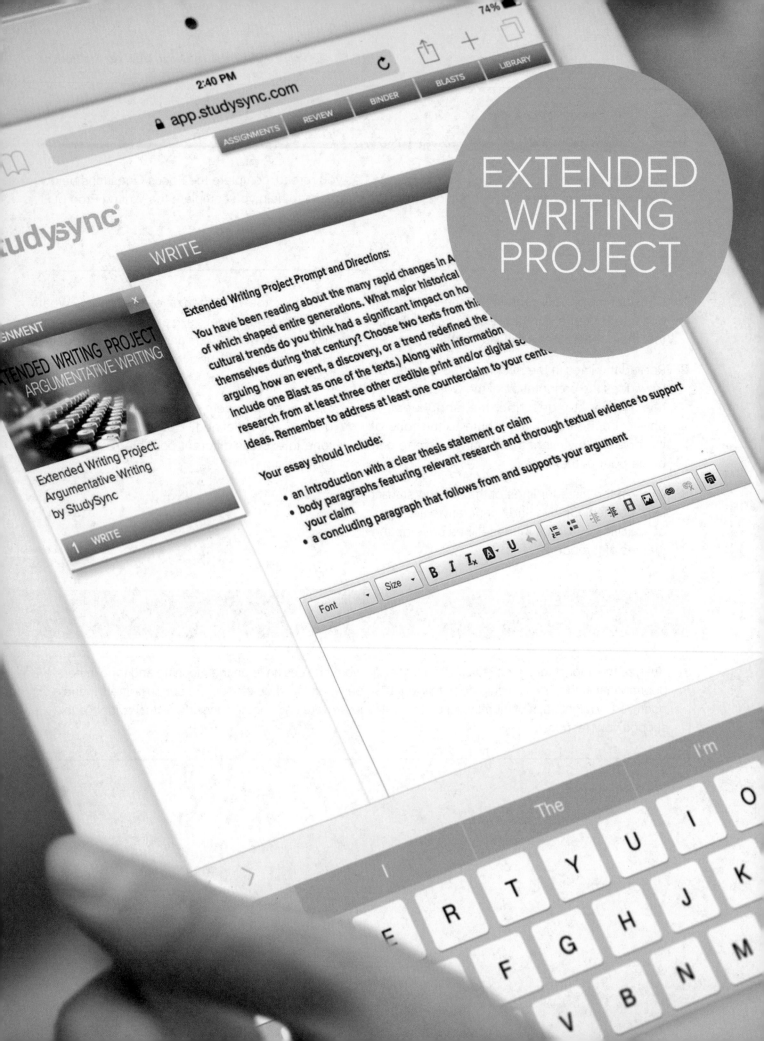

EXTENDED
WRITING
PROJECT

studysync®

WRITE

EXTENDED WRITING PROJECT
ARGUMENTATIVE WRITING

Extended Writing Project:
Argumentative Writing
by StudySync

1   WRITE

Extended Writing Project Prompt and Directions:

You have been reading about the many rapid changes in A___
of which shaped entire generations. What major historical ___
cultural trends do you think had a significant impact on ho___
themselves during that century? Choose two texts from thi___
arguing how an event, a discovery, or a trend redefined the ___
Include one Blast as one of the texts.) Along with information ___
research from at least three other credible print and/or digital so___
ideas. Remember to address at least one counterclaim to your cent___

Your essay should include:

- an introduction with a clear thesis statement or claim
- body paragraphs featuring relevant research and thorough textual evidence to support your claim
- a concluding paragraph that follows from and supports your argument

ARGUMENTATIVE WRITING

WRITING PROMPT

You have been reading about the many rapid changes in America in the 20th century, some of which shaped entire generations. What major historical events, scientific discoveries, or cultural trends do you think had a significant impact on how Americans redefined themselves during that century? Choose two texts from this unit and write an essay arguing how an event, a discovery, or a trend redefined the American identity. (You may include one Blast as one of the texts.) Along with information from the selections, include research from at least three other credible print and/or digital sources to support your ideas. Remember to address at least one counterclaim to your central argument.

Your essay should include:

- an introduction with a clear thesis statement or claim
- body paragraphs featuring relevant research and thorough textual evidence to support your claim
- a concluding paragraph that follows from and supports your argument

Argumentative writing asks you to make a claim or take a position on a topic and then to identify, evaluate, and provide evidence that offers thorough and relevant support for the claim. This evidence can come from texts that you have read or from additional research you do on the topic. Strong argumentative writing begins with an introductory paragraph that provides a thesis statement and general context for the topic, includes body paragraphs that support the main idea, and ends with a conclusion that revisits the main point and synthesizes the evidence that has been provided. The writing in an argumentative essay is clear, coherent, formal in tone, and appropriate to its task, purpose, and intended audience.

Argumentative essays often contain direct quotations, or citations, from the texts being analyzed. Writers of argumentative essays often perform outside research using sources such as academic articles or news stories. By smoothly integrating this research into their essays, writers provide greater context, legitimacy and refinement to their arguments.

The features of argumentative writing include:

- an introduction with a clear thesis statement
- a clear and logical organizational structure
- body paragraphs that offer supporting details and evidence
- precise and compelling language and rhetoric
- proper citations of reference and research sources
- a concluding paragraph that summarizes the central argument

As you continue with this extended writing project, you'll receive more instructions and practice to help you craft each of the elements of argumentative writing in your own essay. You will also learn techniques for performing outside research and including your findings in your essay.

 ## STUDENT MODEL

Before you begin developing your own argumentative essay, consider this essay that one student wrote in response to the writing prompt. As you read, highlight and annotate the features of argumentative writing that the student addressed in the essay. This essay uses one specific method for citing sources, but you will learn about other methods as well in a later lesson.

Building Bridges in Harlem

Major shifts in population during the 20th century, particularly into urban areas, led to huge cultural changes that continue to redefine what is "American" even today. Imagine more than six million people moving from south to north as part of the Great Migration, building new communities and creating a rich cultural scene like the Harlem Renaissance in New York City ("Great Migration"). Writers such as Langston Hughes understood that such a movement provided an opportunity to build a bridge between communities while preserving the differences of each. Others, such as Countee Cullen, would insist on a more integrated artistic approach that might erase cultural boundaries. In striving to shape and define the urban African American experience, both writers would influence not only Harlem, but also the nation as a whole.

NOTES

What attracted African Americans to urban neighborhoods such as Harlem in the first place? Some sought better work opportunities. Others fled racial violence that troubled the South in the early 20th century. Maryemma Graham, a professor at the University of Kansas, notes that even though their reasons for moving varied, "none could escape the race consciousness that bound together a people sharing a history of oppression" (Graham). Between 1910 and 1920, the African American population in New York City grew by 66 percent ("Great Migration"). By the time it was over in 1970, the Great Migration would represent the largest movement of people from one place to another in U.S. history.

The early life of the poet Langston Hughes is an example of a typical Great Migration story. Born in 1902 in Joplin, Missouri, and raised there by his grandmother, he later moved north to Illinois to live with his mother. The family eventually settled in Cleveland, Ohio, though Hughes's travels didn't stop there. Like the speaker in his poem "Theme for English B," he enrolled in college in New York City:

> I am twenty-two, colored, born in Winston-Salem.
> I went to school there, then Durham, then here
> to this college on the hill above Harlem. (Hughes 409-410)

In writing a college essay about himself, the speaker starts off with his own migration northward. The mentions of "school" and "college" establish a central theme: the importance of education in his life. Hughes worked a number of jobs to pay his tuition and completed his education in 1929. By that time, he had already written and published his first book of poetry, *The Weary Blues*.

For Hughes, blues music was a bridge between cultures, between African and American, past and present, south and north, rural and urban. It connected the beginning and ending points of the Great Migration. In his essay "Jazz as Communication," he writes,

> Life is as hard on Broadway as it is in Blues-originating-land. The Brill Building Blues is just as hungry as the Mississippi Levee Blues. One communicates to the other, brother! (Hughes, "Jazz as Communication")

Hughes believed that this ability to communicate and connect could build bridges between races as well. In responding to his white instructor in "Theme for English B," the speaker writes,

You are white—
yet a part of me, as I am a part of you.
That's American.
Sometimes perhaps you don't want to be a part of me.
Nor do I often want to be a part of you.
But we are, that's true! (Hughes 409-410)

In these lines, Hughes acknowledges that there might be tension and resistance, especially as the poem's speaker addresses the theme of what it means to be American. This tension is a two-way street, traveling in both directions. Still, his positive excitement over this blend of cultures is evident in that final exclamation mark: "But we are, that's true!"

As another poet of the Harlem Renaissance, Countee Cullen also wanted to blend cultures. Unlike Hughes, Cullen grew up in New York City during the heyday of the Harlem Renaissance. Like Hughes, he placed a high value on education. Cullen attended mostly white schools and college. As Cullen's biography on the Poetry Foundation Web site states:

Because of Cullen's success in both black and white cultures . . . he formulated an aesthetic that embraced both cultures. He came to believe that art transcended race and that it could be used as a vehicle to minimize the distance between black and white peoples. ("Countee Cullen")

Whereas Hughes shows distinct black and white people being "a part" of each other, the characters in Cullen's poem "Any Human to Another" move beyond race to become almost universal:

Your grief and mine
Must intertwine
Like sea and river,
Be fused and mingle,
Diverse yet single,
Forever and ever. (Cullen)

In Cullen's poem, there is no distinct black or white, so there's no need to build a bridge from one culture to the other. Both cultures "intertwine" in the same space, "diverse yet single." He makes integration sound almost effortless. The title suggests an almost generic ideal, with "any human" and "another" existing apart from racial or cultural backgrounds. This may have worked well in poems on paper, but the "history of oppression" that Graham mentioned earlier could not be so easily overlooked.

This more idealistic, integrated view caused some tensions between Cullen and Hughes. In a review of *The Weary Blues*, Cullen criticized Hughes for being a "racial poet" and suggested that he leave out the jazz-like sounds and rhythms in his work because these aspects of black culture might alienate some readers ("Countee Cullen"). Unlike Cullen, Hughes wanted to preserve and protect all aspects of black culture. His official biography with the Academy of American Poets states, "He wanted to tell the stories of his people in ways that reflected their actual culture, including both their suffering and their love of music, laughter, and language itself" ("Langston Hughes"). This is evident in "Theme for English B":

> But I guess I'm what
> I feel and see and hear. Harlem, I hear you:
> hear you, hear me—we two—you, me, talk on this page. (Hughes 409-410)

Hughes didn't want to leave the past behind. It had to be part of that conversation between person and place, between Harlem and Hughes himself. That's what made poetry, like jazz and the blues, such an important part of cultural identity. Diversity couldn't be overlooked or taken out of culture. It had to play a vital role in the constant evolution and redefinition of culture. Because he represented this view so fully, Hughes became known as "the bard of Harlem" (Schmidt 707).

Despite their differing views, both Cullen and Hughes contributed a great deal to the culture of the Harlem Renaissance. Both understood that the Great Migration had brought African Americans together in a new and diverse urban environment. Their poetry, together with the music of jazz and the blues, helped people blend their African pasts with an American present to define what it meant to be African American. As the tensions between Cullen and Hughes show, it wasn't always easy. Some of those same cultural conflicts continue even today in largely urban communities. Even so, the Great Migration and its effect on the Harlem Renaissance added a transformative chapter in our country's history and helped to redefine what it meant to be American.

Works Cited

Cullen, Countee. "Any Human to Another" from *Countee Cullen: Collected Poems.*

The Library of America, American Poets Project. 2013. Print.

"Countee Cullen." Poetry Foundation. Poetry Foundation, n.d. Web. 20 Oct. 2014.

Graham, Maryemma. "The New Negro Renaissance." *The New Negro Renaissance.* N.p., n.d. Web. 18 Oct. 2014.

"Great Migration." History.com. A&E Television Networks, n.d. Web. 19 Oct. 2014.

Hughes, Langston. "Jazz as Communication (1956)." Poetry Foundation. 13 Oct. 2009. Web. 18 Oct. 2014.

—. "Theme for English B" from *The Collected Poems of Langston Hughes.* New York: Vintage Books, a division of Random House. 1995. Print.

"Langston Hughes." *Poets.org.* Academy of American Poets, n.d. Web. 18 Oct. 2014.

Schmidt, Michael. *Lives of the Poets.* New York, New York: Knopf, 1998. Print.

THINK QUESTIONS

1. What is the main point in this essay? Where has the writer most clearly expressed it?

2. Which two reading selections has the author chosen to discuss? How do they relate to the main idea?

3. What additional research did the writer include in the essay? How is it related to the main idea?

4. Reflect on what you have read, listened to, and researched throughout the unit and the entire school year. Combine this with your own personal experience and background knowledge to answer this question: What kinds of events might have caused an entire nation to reflect on its identity and redefine itself during the 20th century?

5. Which selections, Blasts, or other resources seem most relevant to the argumentative writing prompt? What are some ideas that you may want to explore in more detail during the writing process? What resources might be most helpful to you as you research these ideas?

PREWRITE

Copyright © BookheadEd Learning, LLC

WRITING PROMPT

You have been reading about the many rapid changes in America in the 20th century, some of which shaped entire generations. What major historical events, scientific discoveries, or cultural trends do you think had a significant impact on how Americans redefined themselves during that century? Choose two texts from this unit and write an essay arguing how an event, a discovery, or a trend redefined the American identity. (You may include one Blast as one of the texts.) Along with information from the selections, include research from at least three other credible print and/or digital sources to support your ideas. Remember to address at least one counterclaim to your central argument.

Your essay should include:

- an introduction with a clear thesis statement or claim
- body paragraphs featuring relevant research and thorough textual evidence to support your claim
- a concluding paragraph that follows from and supports your argument

In addition to studying the techniques that authors use to convey information, you have been reading and learning about various challenges and responses to life in 20th century America. In the extended writing project, you will use various writing techniques and rhetorical strategies to compose an argumentative essay that addresses this topic.

First you'll want to explore possible texts and ideas that relate directly to the writing prompt itself. To do this, think back on prewriting strategies that you've used in the past, such as list making, brainstorming, concept mapping, and free-writing. Keep in mind that different strategies might help you with specific parts of the prompt. For example, list making might help you

Please note that excerpts and passages in the StudySync® library and this workbook are intended as touchstones to generate interest in an author's work. The excerpts and passages do not substitute for the reading of entire texts, and StudySync® strongly recommends that students seek out and purchase the whole literary or informational work in order to experience it as the author intended. Links to online resellers are available in our digital library. In addition, complete works may be ordered through an authorized reseller by filling out and returning to StudySync® the order form enclosed in this workbook.

Reading & Writing Companion   **299**

NOTES

determine the texts you'd like to focus on, whereas concept mapping might be the best way to determine what you need to research in order to find the information you need.

Since your argumentative essay will explore how Americans have redefined themselves, you'll want to think about how the lives of the people you've read about have been influenced and affected by major changes in America during the 20th century. What were some of those events? Make a list of these to provide yourself with plenty of options. Where might you find out more about these events? What questions would like to answer as you research? Keep in mind, these lists are a great starting point, but will not be conclusive.

As you consider your list of events, note which specific texts from the unit might match up with the events. For example, the court cases on *Plessy v. Ferguson* and *Brown v. Board of Education* deal with the trend toward civil rights in America, as does the Blast on the media's influence on that movement. *A Farewell to Arms* and *Hiroshima* deal with different aspects of war, as does the Blast on the Greatest Generation.

Next, think about the key word "redefined" in the prompt. What does it mean or suggest to you? How might the word lead you to consider a "before and after" relationship in your essay? How might it lead you to consider a "cause and effect" connection? Use these questions to help you generate additional ideas, topics, or questions that you can list or map out.

Always keep in mind the various parts of the prompt. You may want to break the requirements down into a helpful list of questions, such as the sample below. It may seem complex at first, but once you begin to answer questions and make connections between events and texts, you'll find your ideas developing and suggesting new paths and avenues for consideration in your essay. Use this model to help you get started with your own prewriting:

What major event, discovery, or trend will I address? *The Great Migration*

How did it redefine American identity? *African Americans moved from the plantations of the South to the cities of the North and developed strong, well-defined communities in the urban settings.*

What counterclaim suggests an alternate response? *African Americans risked losing their sense of identity and definition by moving north to a new setting.*

Which two texts will I focus on in my essay?
1. *"Theme for English B"*
2. *"Any Human to Another"*

Where might I look to find three other credible sources?

1. *History textbooks*
2. *Biographies of Langston Hughes and Countee Cullen*
3. *Museum Web sites or online exhibits*

What questions would I liked answered as I research this topic?

1. *How did the Great Migration impact Langston Hughes?*
2. *How did the Great Migration impact Countee Cullen?*
3. *What were the similarities and differences between how Langston Hughes and Countee Cullen redefined themselves?*

Please note that excerpts and passages in the StudySync® library and this workbook are intended as touchstones to generate interest in an author's work. The excerpts and passages do not substitute for the reading of entire texts, and StudySync® strongly recommends that students seek out and purchase the whole literary or informational work in order to experience it as the author intended. Links to online resellers are available in our digital library. In addition, complete works may be ordered through an authorized reseller by filling out and returning to StudySync® the order form enclosed in this workbook.

Reading & Writing
Companion

301

SKILL:
RESEARCH AND
NOTE-TAKING

 DEFINE

Some people think of **research** and imagine stacks of musty books crowding a tiny desk in the cramped stacks of a college library. Others envision paying a quick visit to Wikipedia online and they're done for the day. Neither one is entirely accurate.

Simply put, research is finding out or verifying something that you do not know for sure. This might mean looking up an unfamiliar word in the dictionary, visiting an online encyclopedia for information about a foreign country, talking to someone who is an expert in a particular field, or trying out something for yourself, such as skydiving, in order to have firsthand knowledge of the experience.

Whatever form of research you undertake, **note-taking** is an essential skill to learn. First and foremost, you should always record information about your **source**, whether it's a book, an article, a Web site, or an authority on the subject. Titles and authors are most important to note so that readers can follow up on your resources if they are interested in learning more. Dates of publication will establish how current your resources are, which may be an issue if different or more accurate information has been published more recently. You'll need all of this information in order to prepare footnotes, endnotes, or a bibliography of works cited.

 IDENTIFICATION AND APPLICATION

- You've probably already undertaken research for various projects and activities throughout the school year. Remember that the most productive research takes place when you have a clear idea of what you're looking for.

- You will need to broaden or narrow your search inquiry depending on your needs. A broad search inquiry may turn up some general articles about your topic that can suggest paths to follow in your research. If you already have a good general idea about your topic, you may want to narrow your search or drill down to find out more specific information about a particular aspect of that topic.

- Advanced searches can help you target information more quickly by looking for specific phrases, selecting only the most recent information, and scanning inside digitized books for key concepts or terms. This can save you time in the long run.

- You should always evaluate the accuracy and reliability of your sources, especially when searching online. Look for well-known and trusted outlets, such as fact-based newspaper, magazines, and scholarly journals, or educational and governmental websites (ending in .edu and .gov instead of .com or .org). When possible, try to determine the author's credentials and any biases he or she might have.

- When taking notes, stay focused on your topic in order to save time and avoid including any irrelevant details in your essay. Be sure that the material you intend to reference matches the task, purpose, and audience you have identified for your essay.

- You might choose to use a physical note card system for recording, evaluating, and organizing your information. Many writers now use online documents and folders to track their research as well as a variety of software programs and apps.

- You can avoid plagiarism by quoting sources directly or paraphrasing in your essay, but always remember to provide proper credit or citation. To do this, you will need to take careful, accurate notes, including where each piece of information you use came from.

 MODEL

Consider the following paragraph from the student model essay "Building Bridges in Harlem":

> This more idealistic, integrated view caused some tensions between Cullen and Hughes. In **a review of _The Weary Blues_,** Cullen criticized Hughes for being a **"racial poet"** and suggested that he leave out the jazz-like sounds and rhythms in his work because these **aspects of black culture might alienate some readers ("Countee Cullen")** Unlike Cullen, Hughes wanted to preserve and protect all aspects of black culture. His **official biography** with the **Academy of American Poets** states, "He wanted to tell the stories of his people in ways that reflected their actual culture, including both their suffering and their love of music, laughter, and language itself" (**"Langston Hughes")** This is evident in **"Theme for English B":**

Please note that excerpts and passages in the StudySync® library and this workbook are intended as touchstones to generate interest in an author's work. The excerpts and passages do not substitute for the reading of entire texts, and StudySync® strongly recommends that students seek out and purchase the whole literary or informational work in order to experience it as the author intended. Links to online resellers are available in our digital library. In addition, complete works may be ordered through an authorized reseller by filling out and returning to StudySync® the order form enclosed in this workbook.

Reading & Writing Companion

303

But I guess I'm what

I feel and see and hear. Harlem, I hear you:

hear you, hear me—we two—you, me, talk on this page.
(Hughes 409-410)

These sentences show a number of different ways to incorporate research into an essay. For example, the writer identifies the source of the first quoted term, "racial poet," as a remark made by Cullen in "a review of *The Weary Blues*." Though this review itself is not cited, the writer provides a source ("Countee Cullen") that relates to a reliable and accurate Web site (poetryfoundation.org) for information related to poets and poetry. The writer highlights the key phrase "racial poet" by quoting it directly. However, the writer chooses to paraphrase some of the other material from the source. For example, the idea that Cullen felt that "aspects of black culture might alienate some readers" is a restated opinion and not necessarily the writer's own assessment of Cullen's outlook. For that reason as well, the source "Langston Hughes" (poetry.com) needs to be clearly cited.

The paragraph goes on to talk about the poet Langston Hughes. The writer might have searched for an "official biography" online, finding one at the trustworthy site of "the Academy of American Poets." Once again, the student writer uses a direct quote and, in the Works Cited section, lists "poets.org" as the source. The writer then connects this research to the textual evidence from the reading selection and introduces the specific poem, "Theme for English B," before providing a quoted excerpt. Because this quote is lengthy and in the form of a poem, the writer indents it rather than quoting it within a sentence. The writer may have consulted a style guide or asked the teacher for instructions on how to format a longer quote such as this one in the essay.

 PRACTICE

Search for a definition, more information, or factual statistics related to a key person, event, or idea you will be writing about in your essay. Find and record a strong, relevant quote that you might include to support one of your claims or arguments. Beneath that, paraphrase or restate the quote in your own words, providing context if needed so that a reader will understand how this relates to your own original ideas and arguments. Be sure to take down as much information as you can about the title, author, date, and place of publication of the source.

SKILL:
THESIS
STATEMENT

 DEFINE

The thesis statement is the most important sentence in an argumentative essay because it introduces what the writer is going to say about the essay's topic. The thesis statement expresses the writer's central or main claim about that topic, an argument the writer will develop in the body of the essay. The thesis statement usually appears in the essay's introductory paragraph. The rest of the paragraphs in the essay all support the thesis statement with facts, research, quotes, evidence, and/or examples.

 IDENTIFICATION AND APPLICATION

A thesis statement:

- clearly states the writer's main idea or central claim
- lets the reader know what to expect in the body of the essay
- responds fully and completely to an essay prompt
- is presented in the introductory paragraph

 MODEL

The following is the introductory paragraph from the student model essay, "Building Bridges in Harlem":

> **Major shifts in population during the 20th century, particularly into urban areas, led to huge cultural changes that continue to redefine what is "American" even today.** Imagine more than six million people moving from south to north as part of the Great Migration, building new communities and creating a rich cultural scene like the Harlem Renaissance in New York City ("Great Migration"). Writers such as Langston Hughes understood that such a movement provided an opportunity to build a bridge between

Please note that excerpts and passages in the StudySync® library and this workbook are intended as touchstones to generate interest in an author's work. The excerpts and passages do not substitute for the reading of entire texts, and StudySync® strongly recommends that students seek out and purchase the whole literary or informational work in order to experience it as the author intended. Links to online resellers are available in our digital library. In addition, complete works may be ordered through an authorized reseller by filling out and returning to StudySync® the order form enclosed in this workbook.

Reading & Writing
Companion

305

communities while preserving the differences of each. Others, such as Countee Cullen, would insist on a more integrated artistic approach that might erase cultural boundaries. In striving to shape and define the urban African American experience, both writers would influence not only Harlem, but also the nation as a whole.

Notice the bold-faced thesis statement. This student's thesis statement responds to the prompt, which asks about a particular event, discovery or trend from the 20th century that redefined what it meant to be an "American." In particular, the writer will address "major shifts in population," which he or she later relates to the Great Migration in American history. The writer will address "huge cultural changes" by looking at the Harlem Renaissance as an example. In turn, he or she will focus on two writers, Langston Hughes and Countee Cullen, for textual evidence. Finally, the writer establishes the significance of his or her claim by arguing that these changes in culture and definition "continue... today."

The thesis statement contains all of the most vital information for the student's essay without overwhelming the reader. It does this clearly and effectively while addressing the key aspects of the original writing prompt.

 PRACTICE

Now that you have brainstormed and researched your topic, write a thesis statement for your argumentative essay that sets forth your central idea or claim in relation to the essay prompt. When you are finished, trade with a partner and offer each other constructive suggestions for improvement. Remember that feedback is most helpful when it is offered in a respectful and supportive spirit.

SKILL:
ORGANIZE
ARGUMENTATIVE
WRITING

 DEFINE

Argumentative essays intend to convince readers of an author's position or point of view on a subject. To build an argument, authors introduce **claims,** or arguments, they will support with valid reasoning and relevant and sufficient evidence from reliable sources. The author's claim is stated in an **argumentative thesis statement.** In order to make a convincing argument, authors must distinguish their claims from **alternate or opposing claims,** also called **counterclaims.** Authors then organize the claims, reasons, supporting evidence, and counterclaims into the logical sequence that most effectively and persuasively communicates their argument.

Experienced writers carefully choose an **organizational structure** that best suits their material. They often use an outline or other graphic organizer to determine which organizational structure will help them express their ideas most effectively over the course of the essay.

For example, writers seeking to convince readers of an argument or claim often use **logical reasoning** as a basis for their structure. They seek to show how evidence relates to and supports the claims, sometimes by demonstrating that alternate or opposing claims are invalid. Other commonly used organizational structures in argumentative essays include **cause and effect** and **definition and example.**

Keep in mind that many writers combine different kinds of writing within a single essay, such as a narrative case study that provides an example of a claim within an argumentative essay. Even so, these paragraph-level strategies should fit logically into the overall organizational structure of the essay as a whole.

 IDENTIFICATION AND APPLICATION

- When considering and deciding between organizational structures, writers must clarify their purpose for writing. They should ask themselves:

Copyright © BookheadEd Learning, LLC

NOTES

› What is the central claim I would like to make about the topic?

› What kinds of evidence will help me develop and support my claim?

› How will my research relate to the argument I am developing?

› Which texts most directly address the ideas or themes I am writing about?

› Do any of the texts provide examples of themes or ideas in the other texts?

› Would it make sense to discuss the texts in the order in which they were published?

› Do any of the texts address the same or related issues?

› Does information in one text lead to or result in ideas or information in another text?

› Do the ideas in the texts progress in a logical sequence that can be mapped or outlined?

• Writers often use word choice to create connections and transitions between texts and hint at the organizational structure being used. For example:

› Cause and effect: *because, accordingly, as a result, effect, so*

› Compare and contrast: *like, unlike, also, both, similarly, although, while, but, whereas*

› Definition or example: *in other words, for example, for instance*

› Logical reasoning: *if... then, therefore, it follows that, however*

› Sequential or chronological order: *first, next, then, initially, in the beginning, ultimately, at the conclusion, finally, lastly*

• Sometimes writers may find it effective or necessary to organize individual paragraphs using other structures—a chronological narrative paragraph within an overall compare-and-contrast structure, for instance.

 ## MODEL

Before beginning to draft his or her essay, the writer of "Building Bridges in Harlem" most likely studied the assigned prompt and determined the major elements that he or she would discuss. During this prewriting phase, the writer kept track of various details in a three-column chart such as the one below. You can see from the first entry that the writer chose to associate Langston Hughes and Countee Cullen with the Great Migration based on a significant commonality. The writer also included some of his or her research in the chart and noted other similarities with color-coded highlighting.

In addition to noticing similarities, the writer also noted differences that could be useful in a compare-and-contrast structure. He or she jotted down some other organization possibilities for individual paragraphs related to specific content within the essay. The writer could then select the appropriate graphic organizer to help order the ideas and evidence within each paragraph.

EVENT, DISCOVERY, OR TREND	TEXT ONE	TEXT TWO
The Great Migration	Langston Hughes	Countee Cullen
African Americans	African Americans	African Americans
Research: People moved from south to north - *chronology?* - *causes and effects?* Carried cultural history with them - *chronology?*	"Theme for English B" Poet of the Harlem Renaissance - *definition?* Moved from south to north - *spatial movement?* - *chronological narrative?* Believed in preserving cultural history Research: Saw value in blues, jazz, and other musical traditions	"Any Human to Another" Poet of the Harlem Renaissance Grew up and educated in north - *chronology?* Wanted greater integration between cultures Research: Criticized Hughes for being a "racial poet" - *compare and contrast?*

PRACTICE

Use a three-column chart like the one you have just studied to record the information you have gathered during the prewriting stage of writing your essay. Use color-coding to indicate related ideas and evidence. Use other codes and symbols to indicate the kinds of relationships you see between the entries, such as "cause-and-effect" and "definition/example." You can also add numbers to group ideas into paragraphs and show how they might lead into or naturally follow from other paragraphs.

SKILL:
SUPPORTING
DETAILS

DEFINE

In argumentative writing, writers develop their main ideas and central claims with thorough and relevant **supporting details.** Supporting details can be any fact, definition, concrete detail, example, or quotation that is important to the reader's understanding of the topic and closely related to the thesis, or main idea. Supporting details can be found in a variety of places, but they must provide substance for the thesis to be necessary:

- Facts, definitions, and details important to understanding the central argument
- Quoted passages from and descriptions about the texts being examined
- Research related to the thesis statement or the claims
- Pertinent quotations from experts, such as scholars and critics

Writers can choose supporting details from many sources. Encyclopedias, research papers, newspaper articles, graphs, memoirs, biographies, criticism, documentaries, and online references can all provide relevant information for source material. Though information is plentiful and the source material varied, the writer must be careful to evaluate the quality of information to determine what is most important and most closely related to the thesis or central argument. If the information doesn't support the topic or if the information doesn't strengthen the writer's point, it is not relevant.

IDENTIFICATION AND APPLICATION

Step 1:

To identify relevant supporting details, review your thesis statement and ask: What is my main argument in this essay? A writer might be making a claim about weapons of mass destruction, for example:

The looming threat of nuclear apocalypse forced Americans to confront deep-rooted fears.

Copyright © BookheadEd Learning, LLC

Step 2:

Ask what a reader needs to know about the topic in order to understand the main idea. In order to establish the significance of the threat of nuclear apocalypse, for example, the writer might include examples that describe such a threat. When might such a threat have been on the minds of Americans? In a sentence following, the writer provides a related historical fact:

> **The bombing of Hiroshima during World War II provided a first look at such devastation.**

The writer then links this to one of the reading selections under discussion and establishes its authority with a short description:

> **John Hersey's landmark book *Hiroshima* offered eyewitness accounts of the blast.**

How might the writer link this to the idea of "deep-rooted fears" of Americans? The writer identifies and includes a relevant quote (with citation) from the text to establish a vivid connection:

> **When a Japanese boy described in plain language how "the neighbors were walking around burned and bleeding" (Hersey), American readers could easily imagine their own friends and neighbors staggering about after a blast.**

Step 3:

Look for additional facts, quotations, and research that will strengthen your central claims. In an argumentative essay, one sentence or idea often builds on another to guide the reader forward in a powerful and persuasive manner. Unrelated details, however, can stop readers in their tracks and leave them confused. Ask yourself:

- Does this information enhance the reader's understanding in a vital way?
- Does this information help to develop and validate my claim?
- Does this information relate closely to my thesis statement?
- Can I find more compelling or persuasive evidence to support my central argument?

 MODEL

The student writer of "Building Bridges in Harlem" identifies the Great Migration as one of the major events that influenced the culture of America in the 20th century. Since some readers may not be familiar with the term, the writer did some research to define it as "more than six million people ("Great

Please note that excerpts and passages in the StudySync® library and this workbook are intended as touchstones to generate interest in an author's work. The excerpts and passages do not substitute for the reading of entire texts, and StudySync® strongly recommends that students seek out and purchase the whole literary or informational work in order to experience it as the author intended. Links to online resellers are available in our digital library. In addition, complete works may be ordered through an authorized reseller by filling out and returning to StudySync® the order form enclosed in this workbook.

Reading & Writing Companion

311

NOTES

Migration") moving from south to north." This concrete definition provides an essential supporting detail. Without it, the reader may not have understood the writer's main idea or central argument.

In order to build upon the concept of the Great Migration, the writer introduces the first author under consideration in this manner:

> The early life of the poet Langston Hughes is **an example of a typical Great Migration story.** Born in 1902 in Joplin, Missouri, and raised there by his grandmother, he later moved north to Illinois to live with his mother. The family eventually settled in Cleveland, Ohio, though Hughes's travels didn't stop there. **Like the speaker in his poem** "Theme for English B," he enrolled in college in New York City.

By regarding Hughes's background to be "an example of a typical Great Migration story," the writer provides thorough and relevant support that links Langston Hughes to the historical event under discussion. They also confirm his role as a leading figure in the Harlem Renaissance. The writer is then able to describe Hughes as being "like the speaker in his poem." This strengthens the relevance and persuasiveness of the textual evidence that will follow.

The writer mentions that Hughes had entitled his first book of poetry *The Weary Blues*. Though this detail may seem irrelevant at first, the essay builds upon this mention of the blues in an important way in the very next paragraph:

> For Hughes, blues music **was a bridge** between cultures, between African and American, past and present, south and north, rural and urban. It **connected** the beginning and ending points of the Great Migration.

With the use of the metaphor "was a bridge" in this sentence, the writer echoes and reinforces the title of the essay, "Building Bridges in Harlem." These descriptive details are "connected" to the cultural aspects of the Great Migration. By subsequently quoting Hughes's essay "Jazz as Communication," the writer provides primary textual evidence that further supports this connection. All of these details interact and build upon one another to provide a compelling and complex analysis of this influential event in American history.

 PRACTICE

Look at the information you have already gathered for your argumentative essays. Ask yourself, is this relevant to the main argument of my essay? Will readers need to know about this to understand my main idea? You may wish to remove information that seemed interesting while researching, but does not fit into your essay as it develops. Next, ask what additional facts, quotations, and research will strengthen your central claims. Use the Concept Map graphic organizer to identify and record additional ideas and information along with the strongest relevant details you have already gathered for your argumentative essay. You can use separate organizers for each paragraph based on decisions you have made for organizing and structuring your essay.

Please note that excerpts and passages in the StudySync® library and this workbook are intended as touchstones to generate interest in an author's work. The excerpts and passages do not substitute for the reading of entire texts, and StudySync® strongly recommends that students seek out and purchase the whole literary or informational work in order to experience it as the author intended. Links to online resellers are available in our digital library. In addition, complete works may be ordered through an authorized reseller by filling out and returning to StudySync® the order form enclosed in this workbook.

Reading & Writing
Companion **313**

PLAN

WRITING PROMPT

You have been reading about the many rapid changes in America in the 20th century, some of which shaped entire generations. What major historical events, scientific discoveries, or cultural trends do you think had a significant impact on how Americans redefined themselves during that century? Choose two texts from this unit and write an essay arguing how an event, a discovery, or a trend redefined the American identity. (You may include one Blast as one of the texts.) Along with information from the selections, include research from at least three other credible print and/or digital sources to support your ideas. Remember to address at least one counterclaim to your central argument.

Your essay should include:

- an introduction with a clear thesis statement or claim
- body paragraphs featuring relevant research and thorough textual evidence to support your claim
- a concluding paragraph that follows from and supports your argument

Review the information and ideas you identified and developed over the past writing and skills lessons. Check them against the original writing prompt to make sure that you've addressed all of the requirements for this assignment. Then use this organized information and your thesis to generate the main ideas and topics for individual paragraphs. You can also note specific places to include your researched information along with relevant textual evidence. This detailed road map or outline will help you write the first draft of your essay.

Consider the following questions as you develop your main paragraph topics and organizational strategies in the road map:

NOTES

- How are the component parts of your essay related? Does this suggest any overall organizational strategy, such as a chronology or a compareand-contrast structure?

- What organizational strategies would work best in each of your paragraphs? For example, will you define a term and provide examples in one paragraph before exploring a cause-and-effect relationship related to that term in the next paragraph?

- Where will you be including most of your research for the essay? Is it related to the reading selections or to the event, discovery, or trend you are discussing?

- Does the reader need to know any information before he or she can fully understand your central argument or any counterclaims?

- Are there any special words or terms that may need to be defined or explained for the reader?

Use the model below to get started with your road map. Depending on your central argument and supporting materials, you may need to include additional information or evidence in each paragraph or map out additional paragraphs.

ARGUMENTATIVE ESSAY ROAD MAP

Thesis statement:

    Counterclaim:

Paragraph 1 Topic:

Organizational Strategy:

    Research Information or Textual Evidence #1:

    Research Information or Textual Evidence #2:

Paragraph 2 Topic:

Organizational Strategy:

    Research Information or Textual Evidence #1:

    Research Information or Textual Evidence #2:

Paragraph 3 Topic:

Organizational Strategy:

    Research Information or Textual Evidence #1:

    Research Information or Textual Evidence #2:

NOTES

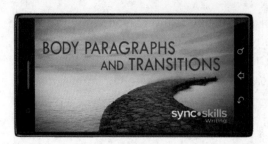

SKILL: BODY PARAGRAPHS AND TRANSITIONS

 DEFINE

Body paragraphs are the sections of the essay between the introduction and conclusion paragraphs. This is where you support your thesis statement by developing your main points with evidence from the text, relevant information from research, and analysis. Typically, each body paragraph will focus on one main point or idea to avoid confusing their reader. The main point of each body paragraph must support the thesis statement.

It's important to structure your body paragraph clearly. One strategy for structuring the body paragraph for an argumentative essay is the following:

Topic sentence: The topic sentence is the first sentence of your body paragraph and clearly states the main point or claim of the paragraph. It's important that your topic sentence relates to or develops the central argument you made in your thesis statement.

Evidence #1: Support your topic sentence with evidence. Evidence can be relevant facts, research, definitions, concrete details, quotations, or other information and examples.

Analysis/Explanation #1: After presenting evidence to support your topic sentence, you will need to analyze that evidence and explain how it supports your topic sentence and, in effect, your overall thesis or central argument.

Evidence #2: Continue to develop your topic sentence with a second piece of evidence.

Analysis/Explanation #2: Analyze this second piece of evidence and explain how it supports your topic sentence and overall thesis.

Concluding sentence: After presenting your evidence, you need to wrap up your main idea and transition to the next paragraph in your conclusion sentence.

Transitions are connecting words and phrases that clarify the relationships among ideas in a text. Transitions work at three different levels: within a sentence, between paragraphs, and to indicate organizational structure.

The types of transitions authors use can help readers recognize the overall organizational structure or rhetorical strategies in the essay. Transitions also help readers make connections among ideas within and across sentences and paragraphs. Conjunctions such as *and*, *or*, and *but* and prepositions such as *with*, *beyond*, *inside*, show the relationships between words in a sentence. Also, by adding transition words or phrases to the beginning or end of a paragraph, authors guide readers smoothly through the text.

 ## IDENTIFICATION AND APPLICATION

- In an argumentative essay, the body paragraphs provide the research information and textual evidence that support the thesis statement or central argument. Typically, writers develop one main idea per body paragraph.

- Transition words and phrases are necessary elements of effective writing. They help readers understand the text structure and organizational strategy of an argumentative text. Here are some transition words commonly associated with four different text structures:

  › Cause-effect: *because, accordingly, as a result, effect, so, for, since*
  › Compare-contrast: *like, unlike, also, both, similarly, although, while, but, however, whereas, conversely, meanwhile, on the contrary, and yet, still*
  › Chronological order: *first, next, then, finally, last, initially, ultimately*
  › Definition and example: *in other words, for example, to illustrate, as you can see*

- Transition words help readers understand the flow of ideas and concepts in a text. Some of the most useful transitions are words that indicate that the ideas in one paragraph are logically building on or adding to those in another. Examples include: *if... then, furthermore, therefore, in addition, moreover, by extension, in order to*, etc.

 ## MODEL

In the introduction to the student essay, the writer establishes the main idea or central argument that he or she will develop in the subsequent **body paragraphs.** The writer uses **transitions** to help the reader understand the relationship between ideas within each paragraph and between the paragraphs themselves.

Consider the first sentences in the first body paragraph:

*What attracted African Americans to urban neighborhoods such as Harlem in the first place? Some sought **better work opportunities**. Others fled **racial violence** that troubled the South in the early 20th century. **Maryemma Graham**, a professor at the University of Kansas, notes that even though their reasons for moving varied, "none could escape the race consciousness that bound together a people sharing a history of oppression" (Graham). Between 1910 and 1920, the African American population in New York City grew by **66 percent** ("Great Migration"). By the time it was over in 1970, the Great Migration would represent **the largest movement of people from one place to another in U.S. history.***

In the introductory paragraph, the writer had established that the essay would explore the Great Migration as one of the important events of 20th century America. Knowing that some readers might not be familiar with the term, the writer chooses to describe and explain it in more detail in the first body paragraph.

Right away, however, the reader encounters a bit of a twist. The writer of the student essay asks a rhetorical question in place of stating a traditional **topic sentence.** This grabs the reader's attention while doing what a good topic sentence should: telling what the paragraph will be about and providing the reader with an idea about the organizational **text structure** that will follow. By asking "what attracted African Americans to urban neighborhoods," the writer suggests that the Great Migration to cities was an effect of other causes. From this, the reader can infer that the paragraph will most likely follow a cause-and-effect text structure. It also provides a transition, or link, back to the introductory paragraph with the phrase "such as Harlem."

To answer the topic sentence's question, the writer mentions "better work opportunities" and "racial violence" as contributing factors. These **supporting details** develop and strengthen the central idea of this paragraph. In addition, this body paragraph provides **evidence** from research that further supports the central claims. The writer includes a direct quote from a professor, Maryemma Graham, that provides a deeper **analysis** of the topic and relates it to culture and shared history. The writer also provides a second piece of evidence in the form of statistical data, the figure "66 percent" from "Great Migration" at History.com. This allows the writer to strengthen the claim that the Great Migration was a significant historical event by calling it "the largest movement of people from one place to another in U.S. history."

The essay then moves on from the Great Migration to discuss Langston Hughes and his work in the next body paragraph. This might seem like an abrupt shift from one body paragraph to the next, but notice how the writer has managed the transition by linking ideas:

> The **early life** of the poet Langston Hughes is **an example of a typical Great Migration story.**

This topic sentence tells the reader that the paragraph will address the "early life" of Langston Hughes, which suggests a chronological text structure. It also establishes a link to the previous paragraph by explaining that this is "an example of a typical Great Migration story." The reader therefore has a sense of how this paragraph fits strategically into the overall context of the larger essay and relates back to the main idea or central argument.

 PRACTICE

Use your notes and graphic organizers to compose one body paragraph for your argumentative essay. If possible, follow the suggested format above. When you are finished, trade with a partner. As you offer each other advice, remember that suggestions are most helpful when they are constructive.

DRAFT

WRITING PROMPT

You have been reading about the many rapid changes in America in the 20th century, some of which shaped entire generations. What major historical events, scientific discoveries, or cultural trends do you think had a significant impact on how Americans redefined themselves during that century? Choose two texts from this unit and write an essay arguing how an event, a discovery, or a trend redefined the American identity. (You may include one Blast as one of the texts.) Along with information from the selections, include research from at least three other credible print and/or digital sources to support your ideas. Remember to address at least one counterclaim to your central argument.

Your essay should include:

- an introduction with a clear thesis statement or claim
- body paragraphs featuring relevant research and thorough textual evidence to support your claim
- a concluding paragraph that follows from and supports your argument

You've already made substantial progress toward writing your own argumentative text. You've thought about your purpose, audience, and topic. You've carefully examined the unit's texts and consulted relevant research materials for background information. Based on your analysis of these resources, you've developed a central argument about an event, a discovery, or a trend that redefined the American identity. You've decided how to organize information and gathered supporting details. Now it's time to write a draft of your essay.

Use your outline and your other prewriting materials to help you as you write. Remember that argumentative writing begins with an introduction and

NOTES

presents a thesis statement or central argument. Body paragraphs develop and justify your claim with supporting ideas, details, quotations, research, and other relevant information and explanations drawn from your selected resources. Strong rhetoric adds power and persuasiveness to your writing. Transitions help readers understand the logical relationships among your ideas and follow the flow of information. A concluding paragraph restates or reinforces your thesis statement. An effective conclusion can also leave a lasting impression on your readers.

When drafting, ask yourself these questions:

- What can I do to further clarify my thesis statement or central argument?
- How can I improve my own claim to distinguish it further from possible counterclaims?
- What textual evidence—including researched facts, strong details, case studies, and interesting quotations in each body paragraph—supports the thesis statement?
- What kinds of rhetorical strategies or devices would make the text more powerful and persuasive?
- How well have I communicated why my chosen event, discovery, or trend is significant?
- How do my ideas interact and build upon one another to demonstrate one way in which American identity was redefined in the 20th century?
- What final thought do I want to leave with my readers?

Before you submit your draft, read it over carefully. You want to be sure that you've responded to all aspects of the prompt.

SKILL: SOURCES AND CITATIONS

⭐ DEFINE

Sources are the documents and information that an author uses to research his or her writing. Some sources are **primary sources.** A primary source is a first-hand account of thoughts or events by the individual who experienced them. Other sources are **secondary sources.** A secondary source analyzes and interprets primary sources. **Citations** are notes that give information about the sources an author used in his or her writing. Citations are required whenever authors quote others' words or refer to others' ideas in their writing. Citations let readers know who originally came up with those words and ideas.

Writers should keep track of all their sources as they research and plan their work. When it comes time to write, they can use this information to acknowledge the sources they've used within the text. Failure to acknowledge those sources is **plagiarism,** or stealing someone else's words and ideas. In some academic texts, writers may be asked to provide sources and citations in **footnotes** or **endnotes,** which link specific references within the essay to the correlating pages or chapters in an outside source. In addition to **internal citations,** such as those noted within parentheses, writers may also need to provide a full list of sources in a **"Works Cited"** section or standard **bibliography.**

⬤⬤⬤ IDENTIFICATION AND APPLICATION

- Primary sources are first-hand accounts, artifacts, or other original materials. Examples of primary sources include: Letters or other correspondence, photographs, official documents, diaries or journals, autobiographies or memoirs, eyewitness accounts and interviews, audio recordings and radio broadcasts, works of art, and artifacts.

- Secondary sources are usually text. Secondary sources are the written interpretation and analysis of primary source materials. Some examples of secondary sources include: Encyclopedia articles, textbooks, commentary or criticism, histories and biographies, documentary films, and news analyses.

- As you identify possible sources for reference in your work, consider the accuracy and reliability of the material:

  › Is it published by a well-known and reliable person or company?

  › Is the material contemporary and current, or is it possible that the facts and data may have changed?

  › Would a reader be able to find this source easily if he or she were interested?

  › Does the Web site have a reliable extension (.edu and .gov, for example) or is more research needed to verify the truth and objectivity of the information?

  › Remember, some seemingly popular or reliable sources, such as Wikipedia, have been known to include misinformation. It's a good idea to have a backup source listed for any information that might attract an editor's or reader's doubts or concerns.

- When performing research online using a search engine, remember to use accurate keywords and online filters to narrow the results and limit the number of distracting and irrelevant results. Try a variety of words and specific phrases for different searches in order to come up with the widest range of options. Such advanced searches can very often weed out a great deal of distracting and useless information.

- When including outside sources and references in your work, think of them as additional pieces of relevant information. In other words, they should clearly fit the purpose and context of your explanation or analysis. If this is not obvious from the citation itself, you might need to add text that establishes this relevance or relationship.

- When gathering sources and information for an argumentative essay, writers should take note of as much of the following information as possible:

  › Title of the work or Web site

  › Author(s) or editor(s) of the work

  › Pages referenced, if available (relate this to specific quotations or information)

  › Date of publication

  › Publisher name and address (city, state, and/or country)

  › Medium of publication (Web or print)

  › Version numbers (revisions, issue numbers, volumes, editions)

  › Date of access

Please note that excerpts and passages in the StudySync® library and this workbook are intended as touchstones to generate interest in an author's work. The excerpts and passages do not substitute for the reading of entire texts, and StudySync® strongly recommends that students seek out and purchase the whole literary or informational work in order to experience it as the author intended. Links to online resellers are available in our digital library. In addition, complete works may be ordered through an authorized reseller by filling out and returning to StudySync® the order form enclosed in this workbook.

Reading & Writing Companion   **323**

- Always avoid plagiarism by either quoting the original text directly and crediting the author or paraphrasing the original ideas and crediting the author.

- Different organizations and agencies have different ways of handling the proper formatting of citations and sources. When you receive an assignment, always check for and follow the proper formatting requirements. A scholarly article may have stricter requirements than a newspaper article, for example, though both will expect your information to be factually accurate and supported by a secondary source if needed.

- Familiarize yourself with the footnote and citation features of your word processing software. These can often make the task of tracking sources much less challenging. They may also be able to assist you in creating a final bibliography once your document is complete.

 ## MODEL

Most English and language arts classes rely on the Modern Language Association (MLA) guidelines for citing research sources. For detailed guidelines, refer to the *MLA Handbook for Writers of Research Papers*. MLA style for citing sources takes a two-pronged approach. Writers provide in-text citations corresponding to entries in their Works Cited list, which appears as the final page of a research paper. At the end of each quotation, paraphrase, or summary of researched information, insert in parentheses the author's last name and the page number where the information was found (if available). If the source does not indicate the author, use the first word or two of the title to identify the piece. For example, consider these in-line citations from the student essay, "Building Bridges in Harlem":

> Because he represented this view so fully, Hughes became known as "the bard of Harlem" (Schmidt, 707).

> Between 1910 and 1920, the African American population in New York City grew by 66 percent ("Great Migration").

All the sources referred to in a research paper should appear on the last page in a **Works Cited page**. The title Works Cited should be centered at the top of the page. The entries should be arranged alphabetically by author's last name or by the first word in the title, if no author is mentioned. The list should be double-spaced. Long entries that take up more than one line, should be indented five spaces every line after the first. The format of each entry depends on the type of source. Here are two of the most commonly used formats:

Copyright © BookheadEd Learning, LLC

Book Structure:

Last, First M., and First M. Last (for additional author or editor), *Book Title*. City,

State: Publisher, Year Published. Medium (Print).

Example:

Schmidt, Michael. *Lives of the Poets*. New York, New York: Knopf, 1998. Print.

Web site Structure:

Last, First M. "Article Title." *Website Title*. Website Publisher. Date Month Year

Published (if available). Medium (Web). Date Month Year Accessed.

Example:

Hughes, Langston. "Jazz as Communication (1956)." Poetry Foundation. 13

Oct. 2009. Web. 18 Oct. 2014.

In order to properly format all your citations, follow the specific MLA guidelines for each type of source. There are very helpful online tools, such as EasyBib (www.easybib.com), that can automatically generate properly formatted citations when writers enter requested information such as the ISBN of a book or the Web site URL. However, EasyBib does sometimes make mistakes, so it's a good idea to cross-reference your results with a website like Purdue OWL (http://owl.english.purdue.edu).

 PRACTICE

Cite your sources for your draft of your argumentative essay wit in-text references and a Works Cited page. When you are finished, trade with a partner and offer each other feedback. How successful was the writer in citing sources for the essay? How well did the writer make use of varied sources? Offer each other suggestions, and remember that suggestions are most helpful when they are constructive.

Please note that excerpts and passages in the StudySync® library and this workbook are intended as touchstones to generate interest in an author's work. The excerpts and passages do not substitute for the reading of entire texts, and StudySync® strongly recommends that students seek out and purchase the whole literary or informational work in order to experience it as the author intended. Links to online resellers are available in our digital library. In addition, complete works may be ordered through an authorized reseller by filling out and returning to StudySync® the order form enclosed in this workbook.

Reading & Writing Companion **325**

REVISE

WRITING PROMPT

You have been reading about the many rapid changes in America in the 20th century, some of which shaped entire generations. What major historical events, scientific discoveries, or cultural trends do you think had a significant impact on how Americans redefined themselves during that century? Choose two texts from this unit and write an essay arguing how an event, a discovery, or a trend redefined the American identity. (You may include one Blast as one of the texts.) Along with information from the selections, include research from at least three other credible print and/or digital sources to support your ideas. Remember to address at least one counterclaim to your central argument.

Your essay should include:

- an introduction with a clear thesis statement or claim
- body paragraphs featuring relevant research and thorough textual evidence to support your claim
- a concluding paragraph that follows from and supports your argument

Congratulations! You've written the first draft of your informative/explanatory text. You have also received input from your peers about how to improve it. Now you are going to revise your draft. Here are some recommendations to help you revise:

- Review the suggestions made by your peers about your first draft.
- Reread your thesis statement for clarity.
- Focus on maintaining a formal yet engaging style.
- Evaluate the strength and relevance of your evidence.
- Enhance the effectiveness of your rhetorical strategies.

- Improve the transitions between paragraphs.
- Add variety to your word choice, syntax, and sentence structures:
  › Substitute more precise words for any that are ambiguous or dull.
  › Combine sentences to connect ideas and add variety.
- Check to see that you have properly cited all of your sources.
- Review your notes and resources to make sure that you have included all of your best ideas and supporting materials.

Please note that excerpts and passages in the StudySync® library and this workbook are intended as touchstones to generate interest in an author's work. The excerpts and passages do not substitute for the reading of entire texts, and StudySync® strongly recommends that students seek out and purchase the whole literary or informational work in order to experience it as the author intended. Links to online resellers are available in our digital library. In addition, complete works may be ordered through an authorized reseller by filling out and returning to StudySync® the order form enclosed in this workbook.

Reading & Writing
Companion

327

EDIT, PROOFREAD, AND PUBLISH

WRITING PROMPT

You have been reading about the many rapid changes in America in the 20th century, some of which shaped entire generations. What major historical events, scientific discoveries, or cultural trends do you think had a significant impact on how Americans redefined themselves during that century? Choose two texts from this unit and write an essay arguing how an event, a discovery, or a trend redefined the American identity. (You may include one Blast as one of the texts.) Along with information from the selections, include research from at least three other credible print and/or digital sources to support your ideas. Remember to address at least one counterclaim to your central argument.

Your essay should include:

- an introduction with a clear thesis statement or claim
- body paragraphs featuring relevant research and thorough textual evidence to support your claim
- a concluding paragraph that follows from and supports your argument

You have revised your argumentative essay and received input from your peers on that revision. Now it's time to edit and proofread your essay to produce a final version. Have you considered all of the valuable suggestions from your peers and acted on those that would improve your essay? Ask yourself:

- Have I fully developed my thesis statement and central argument with relevant research and strong textual evidence?
- Have I distinguished my claim from a counterclaim?

Copyright © BookheadEd Learning, LLC

- Have I accurately cited my sources?
- What more can I do to improve my essay's information, organization, and use of rhetorical strategies?

When you are satisfied with your work, move on to proofread it for errors. For example, check that you have used correct punctuation for quotations, citations, and restrictive/nonrestrictive phrases and clauses. Do all sentences have proper subject-verb agreement? Have you used all academic and technical words and phrases correctly? Be sure to correct any misspelled words.

Once you have made all your corrections, you are ready to submit and publish your work. You can distribute your writing to family and friends, hang it on a bulletin board, or post it on your blog. If you publish online, create links to your sources and citations when possible. That way, readers can follow up on what they've learned from your essay and read more on their own.

Please note that excerpts and passages in the StudySync® library and this workbook are intended as touchstones to generate interest in an author's work. The excerpts and passages do not substitute for the reading of entire texts, and StudySync® strongly recommends that students seek out and purchase the whole literary or informational work in order to experience it as the author intended. Links to online resellers are available in our digital library. In addition, complete works may be ordered through an authorized reseller by filling out and returning to StudySync® the order form enclosed in this workbook.

Reading & Writing
Companion
329

studysync®

Reading & Writing Companion

How can love inspire both folly and wisdom?

Seeking Romance

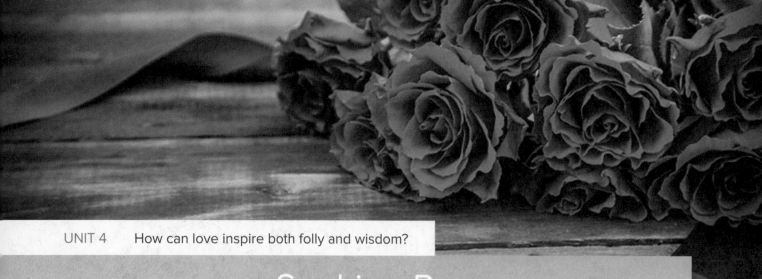

Seeking Romance

TEXTS

TEXTS

EXTENDED WRITING PROJECT

SONNET 116

POETRY
William Shakespeare
1609

INTRODUCTION

William Shakespeare is regarded as a literary genius and the father of modern Western literature, famous for both his plays and his poetry. Few extant sources comment on Shakespeare's personal life, leaving scholars to debate his origins, influences, and even the authorship of some of the works attributed to him. His sonnets were published in 1609 and generally explore themes of love, time, immortality, and beauty. One of the most well known, Sonnet 116 describes love in its most ideal form.

"Let me not to the marriage of true minds admit impediments."

 ## FIRST READ

 NOTES

1 Let me not to the marriage of true minds
2 Admit **impediments**. Love is not love
3 Which **alters** when it alteration finds,
4 Or bends with the remover to remove:
5 O no; it is an ever-fixed mark,
6 That looks on **tempests,** and is never shaken;
7 It is the star to every wandering **bark,**
8 Whose worth's unknown, although his height be taken.
9 Love's not Time's fool, though rosy lips and cheeks
10 Within his bending sickle's **compass** come;
11 Love alters not with his brief hours and weeks,
12 But bears it out even to the edge of doom.
13   If this be error and upon me proved,
14   I never writ, nor no man ever loved.

THINK QUESTIONS

1. Use details from the text to write two or three sentences describing the author's purpose in writing this poem.

2. Refer to one or more details from the text to support your understanding of the main quality or characteristic of love according to the speaker of the poem.

3. Use details from the text to explain the challenge the speaker makes in the final lines. Do you think this is a serious challenge? Why or why not?

4. Use context to determine the meaning of the word "alters." Write your definition here. Then use this information to determine the meaning of the word "alteration" in the same line. Explain how the words are related and how knowing the meaning of "alters" helps you to know the meaning of "alteration."

5. Use contextual clues to determine the meaning of the word "compass." Write your definition of "compass" here and tell how you were able to determine its meaning in this context. What other definitions of this word do you know?

Reading & Writing Companion

CLOSE READ

Reread the poem "Sonnet 116." As you reread, complete the Focus Questions below. Then use your answers and annotations from the questions to help you complete the Writing Prompt.

 ## FOCUS QUESTIONS

1. Reread the first four lines of the poem. Explain why the speaker of the poem uses the word "love" twice in the second line. How does the first use differ from the second use?

2. Highlight examples of figurative language in the second four lines of the poem. How does the speaker's use of connotative meanings and words with multiple meanings here differ from the first four lines? In your annotations, explain how this relates to the overall theme of love in the poem.

3. Reread lines 7 and 8 in the poem. To what or whom is the speaker referring with the clause "although his height be taken"? Explain how these words relate to other figurative language in the poem.

4. What does love "bear out" in the twelfth line of the poem? Highlight any figurative language that supports your response and explain your interpretation of it using the annotation tool.

5. Reflect on the major themes and language of the poem. How does love inspire the speaker of the poem? Highlight details from the text that support your answer and include an analysis of any relevant figurative language in your annotations.

WRITING PROMPT

Many people today include Shakespeare's "Sonnet 116" as part of their wedding ceremonies. Do you think this is a fitting context for the poem? Why or why not? Refer back to the central ideas and figurative language of the poem to develop and support your claim.

SONNET
18

POETRY
William Shakespeare
1609

INTRODUCTION

William Shakespeare is regarded as a literary genius and the father of modern Western literature, famous for both his plays and his poetry. Few extant sources comment on Shakespeare's personal life, leaving scholars to debate his origins, influences, and even the authorship of some of the works attributed to him. His sonnets were published in 1609 and generally explore themes of love, time, immortality, and beauty. Sonnet 18 is perhaps his most famous. Frequently recited at weddings, the beautifully written verse captures the

"Shall I compare thee to a summer's day?"

 FIRST READ

 NOTES

1 Shall I compare thee to a summer's day?
2 Thou art more lovely and more **temperate:**
3 Rough winds do shake the darling buds of May,
4 And summer's **lease** hath all too short a date:
5 Sometime too hot the eye of heaven shines,
6 And often is his gold **complexion** dimm'd;
7 And every fair from fair sometime **declines,**
8 By chance, or nature's changing course, **untrimm'd;**
9 But thy eternal summer shall not fade
10 Nor lose possession of that fair thou ow'st;
11 Nor shall Death brag thou wander'st in his shade,
12 When in eternal lines to time thou grow'st;
13   So long as men can breathe or eyes can see,
14   So long lives this, and this gives life to thee.

 THINK QUESTIONS

1. Using one or more details from the text, explain to whom the word "thee" refers in the poem.

2. Use details from the text to write two or three sentences summarizing the difference between the poem's intended recipient and the summer.

3. To what does the word "this" refer in the final line of the poem? Support your response with details and evidence from the text.

4. Use context to determine the meaning of the word "lease." Write the word's part of speech and definition here and tell how you found and verified it.

5. Use sentence clues to determine the meaning of the word "complexion." Write the definition here and explain how the word relates to the rest of the sentence.

Please note that excerpts and passages in the StudySync® library and this workbook are intended as touchstones to generate interest in an author's work. The excerpts and passages do not substitute for the reading of entire texts, and StudySync® strongly recommends that students seek out and purchase the whole literary or informational work in order to experience it as the author intended. Links to online resellers are available in our digital library. In addition, complete works may be ordered through an authorized reseller by filling out and returning to StudySync® the order form enclosed in this workbook.

Reading & Writing Companion | **339**

CLOSE READ

Reread the poem "Sonnet 18." As you reread, complete the Focus Questions below. Then use your answers and annotations from the questions to help you complete the Writing Prompt.

FOCUS QUESTIONS

1. Consider the first four lines of the poem. How would you describe the speaker's initial mood in this poem? How does the poet convey this feeling to the reader?

2. Reread lines 5–10. How does the use of fresh, beautiful language and imagery in these four lines explain the speaker's attitude toward summer? Which particular words or phrases best express the tone in these lines?

3. Reread lines 10–12. Highlight words and/or phrases that relate to Death in these lines. In your annotations, describe the tone or attitude of the speaker toward Death and explain how these words and/or phrases convey that feeling.

4. Reflect on the final two lines of the poem. How would you describe the speaker's tone in these lines? What effect does the poet hope to convey with this tone?

5. According to the speaker of the poem, what is one of the most important benefits of love? Locate where in the poem this idea is most clearly expressed. Then tell where in the poem you think the poet most effectively supports this idea.

WRITING PROMPT

In the traditional sonnet form, the poem contains a "volta," or a "turn" of thought. Where in "Sonnet 18" do you sense such a change? Explain how the poet uses language and tone to suggest a shift or development in the central theme of the poem. Remember to provide relevant and thorough textual evidence to support your response.

METAMORPHOSES

FICTION

Ovid
8 AD

INTRODUCTION

Phoebus, known as Apollo in Greek mythology, was the Roman god of the sun, poetry, music, medicine, and prophecy. He was as handsome as he was proud. The son of Jupiter, king of the gods, Phoebus was especially delighted with his own skill as an archer. Hadn't he slain the fearsome Python, the enormous serpent who guarded the center of the earth? But when Phoebus sneers at another god also proficient with the bow—Cupid, the son of Venus—he suffers the consequences. In this excerpt from a modern translation of Roman poet Ovid's *Metamorphoses*, Cupid's arrow has left Phoebus obsessed with love for Daphne, daughter of Peneus. Despite his prowess and charm, she will never return his affections, for Daphne also has fallen victim to Cupid's vengeful plot.

"But even the wood shrank from his kisses..."

FIRST READ

Excerpt from Book I

Bk I: 438–472 Phoebus kills the Python and sees Daphne

1 . . . Phoebus's first love was Daphne, daughter of Peneus, and not through chance but because of Cupid's fierce anger. Recently the Delian god, exulting at his victory over the serpent, had seen him bending his tightly strung bow and said **'Impudent** boy, what are you doing with a man's weapons? That one is suited to my shoulders, since I can hit wild beasts of a certainty, and wound my enemies, and not long ago destroyed with countless arrows the swollen Python that covered many acres with its plague-ridden belly. You should be intent on stirring the concealed fires of love with your burning brand, not laying claim to my glories!' Venus's son replied 'You may hit every other thing Phoebus, but my bow will strike you: to the degree that all living creatures are less than gods, by that degree is your glory less than mine.' He spoke, and striking the air fiercely with beating wings, he landed on the shady peak of Parnassus, and took two arrows with opposite effects from his full quiver: one **kindles** love, the other dispels it. The one that kindles is golden with a sharp glistening point, the one that dispels is blunt with lead beneath its shaft. With the second he transfixed Peneus's daughter, but with the first he wounded Apollo piercing him to the marrow of his bones.

Bk I: 473–503 Phoebus pursues Daphne

2 Now the one loved, and the other fled from love's name, taking delight in the depths of the woods, and the skins of the wild beasts she caught, **emulating** virgin Phoebe, a careless ribbon holding back her hair. Many courted her, but she, averse to being wooed, free from men and unable to endure them, roamed the pathless woods, careless of Hymen or Amor, or whatever marriage might be. Her father often said 'Girl you owe me a son-in-law', and again often 'Daughter, you owe me grandsons.' But, hating the wedding torch

as if it smacked of crime she would blush red with shame all over her beautiful face, and clinging to her father's neck with coaxing arms, she would say ' Dearest father, let me be a virgin for ever! Diana's father granted it to her.' He yields to that plea, but your beauty itself, Daphne, prevents your wish, and your loveliness opposes your prayer.

3   Phoebus loves her at first sight, and desires to wed her, and hopes for what he desires, but his own oracular powers fail him. As the light stubble of an empty cornfield blazes; as sparks fire a hedge when a traveller, by mischance, lets them get too close, or forgets them in the morning; so the god was altered by the flames, and all his heart burned, feeding his useless desire with hope. He sees her disordered hair hanging about her neck and sighs 'What if it were properly dressed?' He gazes at her eyes sparkling with the brightness of starlight. He gazes on her lips, where mere gazing does not satisfy. He praises her wrists and hands and fingers, and her arms bare to the shoulder: whatever is hidden, he imagines more beautiful. But she flees swifter than the lightest breath of air, and resists his words calling her back again.

Bk I: 504–524 Phoebus begs Daphne to yield to him

4   'Wait nymph, daughter of Peneus, I beg you! I who am chasing you am not your enemy. Nymph, Wait! This is the way a sheep runs from the wolf, a deer from the mountain lion, and a dove with fluttering wings flies from the eagle: everything flies from its foes, but it is love that is driving me to follow you! Pity me! I am afraid you might fall headlong or thorns undeservedly scar your legs and I be a cause of grief to you! These are rough places you run through. Slow down, I ask you, check your flight, and I too will slow. At least enquire whom it is you have charmed. I am no mountain man, no shepherd, no rough guardian of the herds and flocks. Rash girl, you do not know, you cannot realise, who you run from, and so you run. Delphi's lands are mine, Claros and Tenedos, and Patara acknowledges me king. Jupiter is my father. Through me what was, what is, and what will be, are revealed. Through me strings sound in harmony, to song. My aim is certain, but an arrow truer than mine, has wounded my free heart! The whole world calls me the bringer of aid; medicine is my invention; my power is in herbs. But love cannot be healed by any herb, nor can the arts that cure others cure their lord!'

Bk I: 525–552 Daphne becomes the laurel bough

5   He would have said more as timid Peneus ran, still lovely to see, leaving him with his words unfinished. The winds bared her body, the opposing breezes in her way fluttered her clothes, and the light airs threw her streaming hair behind her, her beauty **enhanced** by flight. But the young god could no longer waste time on further **blandishments,** urged on by Amor, he ran on at full speed. Like a hound of Gaul starting a hare in an empty field, that heads for

Please note that excerpts and passages in the StudySync® library and this workbook are intended as touchstones to generate interest in an author's work. The excerpts and passages do not substitute for the reading of entire texts, and StudySync® strongly recommends that students seek out and purchase the whole literary or informational work in order to experience it as the author intended. Links to online resellers are available in our digital library. In addition, complete works may be ordered through an authorized reseller by filling out and returning to StudySync® the order form enclosed in this workbook.

Reading & Writing Companion   **343**

its prey, she for safety: he, seeming about to clutch her, thinks now, or now, he has her fast, grazing her heels with his outstretched jaws, while she uncertain whether she is already caught, escaping his bite, spurts from the muzzle touching her. So the virgin and the god: he driven by desire, she by fear. He ran faster, Amor giving him wings, and allowed her no rest, hung on her fleeing shoulders, breathed on the hair flying round her neck. Her strength was gone, she grew pale, overcome by the effort of her rapid flight, and seeing Peneus's waters near cried out 'Help me father! If your streams have divine powers change me, destroy this beauty that pleases too well!' Her prayer was scarcely done when a heavy numbness seized her limbs, thin bark closed over her breast, her hair turned into leaves, her arms into branches, her feet so swift a moment ago stuck fast in slow-growing roots, her face was lost in the canopy. Only her shining beauty was left.

Bk I: 553–567 Phoebus honours Daphne

6 Even like this Phoebus loved her and, placing his hand against the trunk, he felt her heart still quivering under the new bark. He clasped the branches as if they were parts of human arms, and kissed the wood. But even the wood shrank from his kisses, and the god said 'Since you cannot be my bride, you must be my tree! Laurel, with you my hair will be wreathed, with you my lyre, with you my quiver. You will go with the Roman generals when joyful voices acclaim their triumph, and the Capitol witnesses their long processions. You will stand outside Augustus's doorposts, a faithful guardian, and keep watch over the crown of oak between them. And just as my head with its uncropped hair is always young, so you also will wear the beauty of undying leaves.' Paean had done: the laurel bowed her newly made branches, and seemed to shake her leafy crown like a head giving consent.

THINK QUESTIONS

1. Why does Cupid cast a love spell on Phoebus? What is the intended result of the two arrows that Cupid shoots? Cite evidence from the text to support your response.

2. In Book 1, lines 504–524, what does Phoebus say to Daphne to try to persuade her to stop running away from him? Cite evidence from the text to support your response.

3. How does Daphne finally escape Phoebus? How does Phoebus respond to what happens to Daphne? Cite evidence from the text to support your response.

4. Use context to determine the part of speech and the meaning of the word **kindles.** Write your definition of "kindles" and explain how you inferred the meaning. Also identify a word from the same sentence that is an antonym of "kindles."

5. Use the context clues in the passage to find examples of **blandishments** that help you define and understand the word. Write your definition here and tell how you verified it.

CLOSE READ

Reread the excerpt from *Metamorphoses*. As you reread, complete the Focus Questions below. Then use your answers and annotations from the questions to help you complete the Writing Prompt.

FOCUS QUESTIONS

1. Reread the second section of the text, 473–503. How does Daphne change after being hit by Cupid's arrow? How does her transformation affect her relationship with her father?

2. Reflect on the third section of text, 504–524. How has Phoebus changed after being hit by Cupid's arrow? Even after his transformation, does he continue to show any evidence of a prideful disposition?

3. Think back on the fourth section, 525–552. How does the metaphor of the "hound of Gaul" relate to the characters and plot in this scene? (In ancient times, Gaul was a part of Europe often in conflict with Rome.) How does this metaphor also relate to the theme of love and desire in the story?

4. Reread the fifth section of the text, 553–567. What new transformation has occurred in Phoebus? What do you think of this transformation?

5. Consider the final outcome of the story. In your opinion, what does this story suggest about the influence of romantic love in people's lives? Develop and support your position with textual evidence.

WRITING PROMPT

How does the conclusion of this story from *Metamorphoses* differ from Cupid's original expectations? Do you think he is pleased with the outcome? Why or why not? Remember to include strong textual evidence in your response to support your claims.

Please note that excerpts and passages in the StudySync® library and this workbook are intended as touchstones to generate interest in an author's work. The excerpts and passages do not substitute for the reading of entire texts, and StudySync® strongly recommends that students seek out and purchase the whole literary or informational work in order to experience it as the author intended. Links to online resellers are available in our digital library. In addition, complete works may be ordered through an authorized reseller by filling out and returning to StudySync® the order form enclosed in this workbook.

Reading & Writing Companion   **345**

A MIDSUMMER NIGHT'S DREAM

DRAMA
William Shakespeare
1596

INTRODUCTION

studysync tv

Set in an Athenian woodland shared by mortals and fairies on one enchanted night, Shakespeare's comedy explores the fickleness of love. As the excerpt begins, a troupe of amateur actors is preparing a play for the marriage of the Duke of Athens and the Queen of the Amazons. One actor, Bottom, has been given a donkey's head by the mischievous fairy Puck. Meanwhile, Puck sows further confusion with a magical potion that causes its victim to fall in love with the first being he or she sees upon waking. Falling into this trap are two young men, Lysander and Demetrius, as well as the Fairy Queen Titania.

"O monstrous! O strange! We are haunted."

 FIRST READ

From Act III, Scene i

1 *Oberon and Titania, the king and queen of the fairies, are fighting. Oberon has entrusted his assistant, the mischievous fairy Puck, with a magical flower whose juice will make anyone fall in love with the first person they see. Oberon hopes to teach Titania a lesson by making her appear ridiculous, and Puck finds the perfect object for her love amongst a band of amateur players practicing in the woods nearby. Not only is Bottom full of himself (and a very poor actor), but Puck affixes a donkey's head upon him so that Titania truly loves an ass.*

The Characters:
Fairies:
PUCK: Who's a Trickster, Assistant to King Oberon
TITANIA: Queen of the Fairies
PEASEBLOSSOM, COBWEB, MOTH, MUSTARDSEED

Peasants:
BOTTOM: A weaver, preparing to act the role of Pyramus in a presentation of Pyramus and Thisby
QUINCE, SNUG, FLUTE, SNOUT, STARVELING: Various tradesmen, preparing to present the playPyramus and Thisby

Location: *The wood.*

2 *[Enter PUCK, and BOTTOM with an ass's head.]*

3 BOTTOM: If I were fair, Thisby, I were only thine.

4 QUINCE: O monstrous! O strange! We are haunted. Pray, masters, fly, masters! Help!

NOTES

5   *[Exeunt QUINCE, SNUG, FLUTE, SNOUT, and STARVELING.]*

6   PUCK: I'll follow you, I'll lead you about a round,
7   Through bog, through bush, through brake, through brier:
8   Sometime a horse I'll be, sometime a hound,
9   A hog, a headless bear, sometime a fire;
10   And neigh, and bark, and grunt, and roar, and burn,
11   Like horse, hound, hog, bear, fire, at every turn.

12   *[Exit.]*

13   BOTTOM: Why do they run away? this is a **knavery** of them to make me afeard.

14   *[Re-enter SNOUT.]*

15   SNOUT: O Bottom, thou art changed! what do I see on thee?

16   BOTTOM: What do you see? you see an asshead of your own, do you?

17   *[Exit SNOUT.]*

18   *[Re-enter QUINCE.]*

19   QUINCE: Bless thee, Bottom! bless thee! thou art translated.

20   *[Exit.]*

21   BOTTOM: I see their knavery: this is to make an ass of me; to fright me, if they could. But I will not stir from this place, do what they can: I will walk up and down here, and I will sing, that they shall hear I am not afraid.

22   *[Sings.]*

23   The ousel cock so black of hue,
24   With orange-tawny bill,
25   The throstle with his note so true,
26   The wren with little quill,—

27   TITANIA *[awaking]*: What angel wakes me from my flowery bed?

28   BOTTOM *[sings]*:
29   The finch, the sparrow and the lark,
30   The plain-song cuckoo gray,
31   Whose note full many a man doth mark,
32   And dares not answer nay;—

33 for, indeed, who would set his wit to so foolish a bird? who would give a bird the lie, though he cry 'cuckoo' never so?

34 TITANIA: I pray thee, gentle mortal, sing again:
35 Mine ear is much enamour'd of thy note;
36 So is mine eye **enthralled** to thy shape;
37 And thy fair virtue's force perforce doth move me
38 On the first view to say, to swear, I love thee.

39 BOTTOM: Methinks, mistress, you should have little reason for that: and yet, to say the truth, reason and love keep little company together now-a-days; the more the pity that some honest neighbours will not make them friends. Nay, I can gleek upon occasion.

40 TITANIA: Thou art as wise as thou art beautiful.

41 BOTTOM: Not so, neither: but if I had wit enough to get out of this wood, I have enough to serve mine own turn.

42 TITANIA: Out of this wood do not desire to go:
43 Thou shalt remain here, whether thou wilt or no.
44 I am a spirit of no common rate;
45 The summer still doth tend upon my state;
46 And I do love thee: therefore, go with me;
47 I'll give thee fairies to attend on thee,
48 And they shall fetch thee jewels from the deep,
49 And sing while thou on pressed flowers dost sleep;
50 And I will purge thy mortal grossness so
51 That thou shalt like an airy spirit go.
52 Peaseblossom! Cobweb! Moth! and Mustardseed!

53 *[Enter four fairies, PEASEBLOSSOM, COBWEB, MOTH, and MUSTARDSEED.]*

54 PEASEBLOSSOM: Ready.

55 COBWEB: And I.

56 MOTH: And I.

57 MUSTARDSEED: Oh, And I.

58 ALL: Where shall we go?

59 TITANIA: Be kind and courteous to this gentleman;
60 Hop in his walks and gambol in his eyes;
61 Feed him with apricocks and dewberries,

NOTES

62 With purple grapes, green figs, and mulberries;
63 The honey-bags steal from the humble-bees,
64 And for night-tapers crop their waxen thighs
65 And light them at the fiery glow-worm's eyes,
66 To have my love to bed and to arise;
67 And pluck the wings from Painted butterflies
68 To fan the moonbeams from his sleeping eyes:
69 Nod to him, elves, and do him courtesies.

From Act III, Scene ii

70 *Helena loves Demetrius, but Demetrius loves Hermia. Hermia loves Lysander, who loves her in return, but Hermia's father does not approve of the match. To avoid her father's disapproval and the strict rules of Athens, Hermia and Lysander have run away together, with Demetrius and Helena following close behind. But their journey is long and first they must all spend the night in the woods, a place where fairies rule.*

71 *Oberon, having observed Helena's hopeless entreaties to Demetrius, takes pity on her and has ordered Puck to use the flower's love potion on the Athenian man (thinking there to be only one Athenian man in the woods). But Puck mistakenly comes across Lysander and uses the flower on him. When Lysander wakes, he immediately falls in love with Helena. Puck is then sent to find Helena so that Oberon may correct the mistake and make Demetrius fall in love with her. Though Oberon's intervention, then, the tables have turned, and Helena finds herself with two suitors while Hermia is left with none.*

Characters:

Fairies:

PUCK: *Trickster, Assistant to King Oberon*
OBERON: *King of the Fairies*

Nobles:
LYSANDER: *in love with Hermia*
DEMETRIUS: *in love with Hermia*
HELENA: *in love with Demetrius*
HERMIA: *in love with Lysander*

Location: A dark wood near Athens, at night.

72 *[Enter PUCK.]*

73 PUCK: Captain of our fairy band,
74 Helena is here at hand,

75 And the youth, mistook by me,
76 Pleading for a lover's fee.
77 Shall we their fond pageant see?
78 Lord, what fools these mortals be!

79 OBERON: Stand aside. The noise they make
80 Will cause Demetrius to awake.

81 PUCK: Then will two at once woo one;
82 That must needs be sport alone;
83 And those things do best please me
84 That befall prepost'rously.

85 *[Enter LYSANDER and HELENA.]*

86 LYSANDER: Why should you think that I should woo in **scorn?**
87 Scorn and derision never come in tears.
88 Look when I vow, I weep; and vows so born,
89 In their nativity all truth appears.
90 How can these things in me seem scorn to you,
91 Bearing the badge of faith, to prove them true?

92 HELENA: You do advance your cunning more and more;
93 When truth kills truth, O devilish-holy fray!
94 These vows are Hermia's. Will you give her o'er?
95 Weigh oath with oath, and you will nothing weigh.
96 Your vows to her and me, put in two scales,
97 Will even weigh; and both as light as tales.

98 LYSANDER: I had no judgment when to her I swore.

99 HELENA: Nor none, in my mind, now you give her o'er.

100 LYSANDER: Demetrius loves her; and he loves not you.

101 DEMETRIUS *[awaking]*: O Helen, goddess, nymph, perfect, divine!
102 To what, my love, shall I compare thine eyne?
103 Crystal is muddy. O, how ripe in show
104 Thy lips, those kissing cherries, tempting grow!
105 That pure congealed white, high Taurus' snow,
106 Fann'd with the eastern wind, turns to a crow
107 When thou hold'st up thy hand: O, let me kiss
108 This princess of pure white, this seal of bliss!

109 HELENA: O spite! O hell! I see you all are bent
110 To set against me for your merriment.

111 If you were civil and knew courtesy,
112 You would not do me thus much injury.
113 Can you not hate me, as I know you do,
114 But you must join in souls to mock me too?
115 If you were men, as men you are in show,
116 You would not use a gentle lady so;
117 To vow, and swear, and superpraise my parts,
118 When I am sure you hate me with your hearts.
119 You both are rivals, and love Hermia;
120 And now both rivals, to mock Helena.
121 A trim exploit, a manly enterprise,
122 To conjure tears up in a poor maid's eyes
123 With your derision! None of noble sort
124 Would so offend a virgin, and extort
125 A poor soul's patience, all to make you sport.

126 LYSANDER: You are unkind, Demetrius; be not so;
127 For you love Hermia; this you know I know.
128 And here, with all good will, with all my heart,
129 In Hermia's love I yield you up my part;
130 And yours of Helena to me bequeath,
131 Whom I do love, and will do till my death.

132 HELENA: Never did mockers waste more idle breath.

133 DEMETRIUS: Lysander, keep thy Hermia; I will none.
134 If e'er I loved her, all that love is gone.
135 My heart to her but as guest-wise sojourn'd,
136 And now to Helen is it home return'd,
137 There to remain.

138 LYSANDER: Helen, it is not so.

139 DEMETRIUS: **Disparage** not the faith thou dost not know,
140 Lest, to thy peril, thou aby it dear.
141 Look where thy love comes; yonder is thy dear.

142 [Enter HERMIA.]

143 HERMIA: Dark night, that from the eye his function takes,
144 The ear more quick of **apprehension** makes;
145 Wherein it doth impair the seeing sense,
146 It pays the hearing double recompense.
147 Thou art not by mine eye, Lysander, found;
148 Mine ear, I thank it, brought me to thy sound.
149 But why unkindly didst thou leave me so?

NOTES

150   LYSANDER: Why should he stay, whom love doth press to go?

151   HERMIA: What love could press Lysander from my side?

152   LYSANDER: Lysander's love, that would not let him bide—
153   Fair Helena! who more engilds the night
154   Than all yon fiery O's and eyes of light.
155   Why seek'st thou me? Could not this make thee know,
156   The hate I bear thee made me leave thee so?

157   HERMIA: You speak not as you think. It cannot be.

158   HELENA: Lo! she is one of this confederacy.
159   Now I perceive, they have conjoin'd all three
160   To fashion this false sport, in spite of me.
161   **Injurious** Hermia, most ungrateful maid!
162   Have you conspir'd, have you with these contriv'd
163   To bait me with this foul derision?
164   Is all the counsel that we two have shar'd,
165   The sisters' vows, the hours that we have spent,
166   When we have chid the hasty-footed time
167   For parting us—O, is all forgot?
168   All school-days friendship, childhood innocence?
169   We, Hermia, like two artificial gods,
170   Have with our needles created both one flower,
171   Both on one sampler, sitting on one cushion,
172   Both warbling of one song, both in one key,
173   As if our hands, our sides, voices and minds
174   Had been incorporate. So we grow together,
175   Like to a double cherry, seeming parted,
176   But yet an union in partition;
177   Two lovely berries moulded on one stem;
178   So, with two seeming bodies, but one heart,
179   Two of the first, like coats in heraldry,
180   Due but to one, and crowned with one crest.
181   And will you rent our ancient love asunder,
182   To join with men in scorning your poor friend?
183   It is not friendly, 'tis not maidenly.
184   Our sex, as well as I, may chide you for it,
185   Though I alone do feel the injury.

186   HERMIA: I am amazed at your passionate words.
187   I scorn you not; it seems that you scorn me.

THINK QUESTIONS

1. How do Titania's first impressions of Bottom differ from his true appearance? Cite evidence from the text to support your response.

2. Why is the character of Puck central to both scenes included in the selection? Cite evidence from the text to support your response.

3. How does Helena explain what is happening at the end of the scene? Support your answer with evidence from the text.

4. Use context to determine the meaning of the word **scorn.** Write your definition of the word here and identify a synonym in the surrounding text.

5. Use word parts and context clues to determine the part of speech and meaning of **apprehension.** Write your definition here and tell how you inferred the meaning.

CLOSE READ

Reread the excerpt from *A Midsummer Night's Dream*. As you reread, complete the Focus Questions below. Then use your answers and annotations from the questions to help you complete the Writing Prompt.

FOCUS QUESTIONS

1. Reread the excerpt from Act III, scene i. Why do you think Shakespeare placed this scene immediately before the reunion of Helena, Lysander, Demetrius, and Hermia in the woods? What kind of thematic context does this first scene establish?

2. Reread the conversation between Lysander and Helena. What does this exchange tell you about the nature of Helena's friendship with Hermia?

3. Consider Hermia's first words when she enters the scene. How do her comments about the setting relate to the action of the scene? In particular, how might Shakespeare intend a double meaning here for her use of the word "sense"?

4. Review the dialogue between Helena and Hermia at the end of scene ii. What effect has the potion had on their relationship? In what way does this further develop the theme of love in the play?

5. The character of Puck is widely recognized as a trickster archetype. (An **archetype** is a character, a conflict, a setting, or an idea that is common to human experience across cultures and throughout the world. Archetypes appear in oral storytelling, mythologies, and written works of literature. A **character archetype** refers to familiar individuals such as the wise leader, the rebel, the damsel in distress, etc. The **trickster archetype** is a mischievous character who enjoys playing tricks on others.) Find an example in the excerpt that supports this view of Puck. How do Puck's antics relate to or help develop other story elements, such as character, plot, setting, or theme?

WRITING PROMPT

Discuss different ways in which Shakespeare purposefully creates a sense of confusion in the characters' interactions with each other. What might Shakespeare be saying here about the nature of love and infatuation?

Please note that excerpts and passages in the StudySync® library and this workbook are intended as touchstones to generate interest in an author's work. The excerpts and passages do not substitute for the reading of entire texts, and StudySync® strongly recommends that students seek out and purchase the whole literary or informational work in order to experience it as the author intended. Links to online resellers are available in our digital library. In addition, complete works may be ordered through an authorized reseller by filling out and returning to StudySync® the order form enclosed in this workbook.

Reading & Writing Companion   355

LOVE IS NOT ALL

POETRY

Edna St. Vincent Millay

1931

INTRODUCTION

Edna St. Vincent Millay was one of the most famous American poets of her time, winning the Pulitzer Prize for Poetry in 1923. Millay's unconventional and bohemian lifestyle was representative of the liberated, modern woman of the Jazz era, and her frank commentary on taboo topics like feminism and sexuality earned her fans and critics alike. She was well known for dramatic and captivating live readings of her work. In "Love is not All," Millay contemplates the importance of love.

"Love is not all: it is not meat nor drink..."

FIRST READ

1 Love is not all: it is not meat nor drink

2 Nor **slumber** nor a roof against the rain;

3 Nor yet a floating **spar** to men that sink

4 And rise and sink and rise and sink again;

5 Love can not fill the thickened lung with breath,

6 Nor clean the blood, nor set the **fractured** bone;

7 Yet many a man is making friends with death

8 Even as I speak, for lack of love alone.

9 It well may be that in a difficult hour,

10 Pinned down by pain and moaning for **release,**

11 Or nagged by want past **resolution's** power,

12 I might be driven to sell your love for peace,

13 Or trade the memory of this night for food.

14 It well may be. I do not think I would.

Edna St. Vincent Millay, "Love is not all: it is not meat nor drink" from *Collected Poems*. Copyright 1931, © 1958 by Edna St. Vincent Millay and Norma Millay Ellis. Used with the permission of The Permissions Company, Inc., on behalf of Holly Peppe, Literary Executor, The Millay Society, www.millay.org.

THINK QUESTIONS

1. Refer to one or more details from the text to support your understanding of the poem's title and how it relates to the content of the sonnet.

2. How might you describe the author's reasons or purpose for writing this poem? Use details from the text to develop and support your answer.

3. What do the final lines of the poem tell you about the speaker? Support your answer with textual evidence.

4. Use context to determine the part of speech and meaning of the word **fractured.** Write your definition here and tell how you found and verified it.

5. Use the context clues to determine the meaning of **release** as it is used in the poem. Write what you think is the correct definition of "release" here and explain how it differs from other possible meanings of the word found in a dictionary.

CLOSE READ

Reread the poem "Love Is Not All." As you reread, complete the Focus Questions below. Then use your answers and annotations from the questions to help you complete the Writing Prompt.

FOCUS QUESTIONS

1. Reread the first two lines of the poem. What sort of tone or context is the speaker trying to establish with the figurative language of these lines?

2. Explain how the figurative language of lines three and four builds upon the first two lines. How does this progression further develop the theme of the poem?

3. Reread lines 7 and 8. How might you restate the figurative language in these lines? In particular, how might the poet's use of the word "lack" lead to multiple interpretations of these lines?

4. Consider the final six lines of the poem. How has the focus of this section shifted from the beginning of the poem? What effect does this have on the tone of the poem?

5. Reflect upon the poem as a whole. Do you think that the speaker truly understands the value of love? Does her final decision represent wisdom or potential folly in the context of the earlier imagery? How so?

WRITING PROMPT

Consider the figurative language of the sonnet and how it develops over the course of the poem. Based on your analysis, do you think that Millay considers love to be more of a physical or an emotional feeling? How does she address both aspects of love in the poem? Do you agree or disagree with her final opinion? Refer to strong and thorough textual evidence as you develop and support your argument.

Please note that excerpts and passages in the StudySync® library and this workbook are intended as touchstones to generate interest in an author's work. The excerpts and passages do not substitute for the reading of entire texts, and StudySync® strongly recommends that students seek out and purchase the whole literary or informational work in order to experience it as the author intended. Links to online resellers are available in our digital library. In addition, complete works may be ordered through an authorized reseller by filling out and returning to StudySync® the order form enclosed in this workbook.

Reading & Writing Companion   **359**

ON HER LOVING TWO EQUALLY

POETRY
Aphra Behn
1682

INTRODUCTION

Aphra Behn was a prolific English dramatist and poet from the seventeenth century who published subversive works on topics such as sexuality, society, and alternative relationships. As one of the first professional female writers, her literature offered a unique insight into the lives of women at the time. In "On Her Loving Two Equally," Behn challenges societal and cultural conventions on love. Torn between two men she loves equally, the poem's speaker

"For both alike I languish, sigh, and die."

 FIRST READ

I.

1 How strongly does my passion flow,
2 Divided equally 'twixt two?
3 Damon had ne'er **subdued** my heart,
4 Had not Alexis took his part;
5 Nor could Alexis powerful prove,
6 Without my Damon's aid, to gain my love.

II.

7 When my Alexis present is,
8 Then I for Damon sigh and **mourn;**
9 But when Alexis I do miss,
10 Damon gains nothing but my **scorn.**
11 But if it chance they both are by,
12 For both alike I **languish,** sigh, and die.

III.

13 Cure then, thou mighty winged god,
14 This restless fever in my blood;
15 One golden-pointed dart take back:
16 But which, O Cupid, wilt thou take?
17 If Damon's, all my hopes are **crossed;**
18 Or that of my Alexis, I am lost.

THINK QUESTIONS

1. Refer to one or more details from the text to describe the speaker of the poem.

2. Use details from the text to compare and contrast the time the speaker spends with Alexis to that spent with Damon. What possible inference might you draw from this observation?

3. What is the speaker actually wishing for in the third stanza of the poem? Explain how the figurative language of this section supports your interpretation.

4. Use context to determine the meaning of the word **languish.** Write your definition here and tell how you found it.

5. Use the context clues provided in the poem to determine the intended meaning of the word **crossed** as it is used in the poem. How were you able to distinguish this definition from other possible meanings of the word?

CLOSE READ

Reread the poem "On Her Loving Two Equally." As you reread, complete the Focus Questions below. Then use your answers and annotations from the questions to help you complete the Writing Prompt.

 FOCUS QUESTIONS

1. Consider the first stanza of the poem. Whom does the speaker blame for the situation in which she finds herself? How does this influence the tone at the start of the poem?

2. Reread the second stanza. Based on the word choice in the poem, is the speaker more or less content when both Alexis and Damon are present? How might you explain this?

3. Review the first two stanzas of the poem. From this, what might you infer about the relationship between Alexis and Damon? Do you think they are aware of each other and their interactions with the speaker? Why or why not?

4. Reread the third stanza of the poem. What tone does the speaker take when appealing to Cupid? What does this tell you about her attitude towards Cupid?

5. Consider the poem as a whole. Do you think the poet intends to show love in this context as inspiring folly or wisdom? How does the overall tone of the poem support your answer?

WRITING PROMPT

Why do you think the speaker appeals to Cupid in the final stanza of "On Her Loving Two Equally"? Do you think that she actually believes in the mythological god? How does this influence the tone of the poem as a whole? In your analysis of the poem, remember to include strong and thorough textual evidence that supports your central argument.

CYRANO DE BERGERAC

DRAMA
Edmond Rostand
1897

INTRODUCTION

studysynctv

In the late 19th Century, French poet and dramatist Edmond Rostand wrote this famous play loosely based on the life of Cyrano de Bergerac. Cyrano is a poet and swordsman living in Paris in 1640. His most prominent feature is an extraordinarily large nose, which he defends by word or sword against any who ridicule it. Yet his wit masks a deeper insecurity when it comes to winning over Roxane, the love of his life.

"I for your joy would gladly lay mine own down..."

FIRST READ

From Act I, Scene IV

1 CYRANO:
2 Take notice, boobies all,
3 Who find my visage's center ornament
4 A thing to jest at—that it is my wont—
5 An if the jester's noble—ere we part
6 To let him taste my steel, and not my boot!

7 DE GUICHE (who, with the marquises, has come down from the stage):
8 But he becomes a nuisance!

9 THE VISCOUNT DE VALVERT (shrugging his shoulders):
10 Swaggerer!

11 DE GUICHE:
12 Will no one put him down?. . .

13 THE VISCOUNT:
14 No one? But wait!
15 I'll treat him to. . .one of my quips!. . .See here!. . .
16 (He goes up to Cyrano, who is watching him, and with a conceited air)
17 Sir, your nose is. . .hmm. . .it is. . .very big!

18 CYRANO (gravely):
19 Very!

20 THE VISCOUNT (laughing):
21 Ha!

22 CYRANO (imperturbably):
23 Is that all?. . .

24 THE VISCOUNT:

25 What do you mean?

26 CYRANO:

27 Ah no! young blade! That was a trifle short!

28 You might have said at least a hundred things

29 By varying the tone. . .like this, suppose,. . .

30 Aggressive: 'Sir, if I had such a nose

31 I'd amputate it!' Friendly: 'When you sup

32 It must annoy you, dipping in your cup;

33 You need a drinking-bowl of special shape!'

34 Descriptive: ''Tis a rock!. . .a peak!. . .a cape!

35 —A cape, forsooth! 'Tis a peninsular!'

36 Curious: 'How serves that oblong capsular?

37 For scissor-sheath? Or pot to hold your ink?'

38 Gracious: 'You love the little birds, I think?

39 I see you've managed with a fond research

40 To find their tiny claws a roomy perch!'

41 **Truculent:** 'When you smoke your pipe. . .suppose

42 That the tobacco-smoke spouts from your nose—

43 Do not the neighbors, as the fumes rise higher,

44 Cry terror-struck: "The chimney is afire"?'

45 Considerate: 'Take care,. . .your head bowed low

46 By such a weight. . .lest head o'er heels you go!'

47 Tender: 'Pray get a small umbrella made,

48 Lest its bright color in the sun should fade!'

49 **Pedantic:** 'That beast Aristophanes

50 Names Hippocamelelephantoles

51 Must have possessed just such a solid lump

52 Of flesh and bone, beneath his forehead's bump!'

53 **Cavalier:** 'The last fashion, friend, that hook?

54 To hang your hat on? 'Tis a useful crook!'

55 Emphatic: 'No wind, O majestic nose,

56 Can give THEE cold!—save when the mistral blows!'

57 Dramatic: 'When it bleeds, what a Red Sea!'

58 Admiring: 'Sign for a perfumery!'

59 Lyric: 'Is this a conch?. . .a Triton you?'

60 Simple: 'When is the monument on view?'

61 Rustic: 'That thing a nose? Marry-come-up!

62 'Tis a dwarf pumpkin, or a prize turnip!'

63 Military: 'Point against cavalry!'

64 Practical: 'Put it in a lottery!

65 Assuredly 'twould be the biggest prize!'

66 Or. . .parodying Pyramus' sighs. . .

67 'Behold the nose that mars the harmony

68 Of its master's phiz! blushing its treachery!'

69 —Such, my dear sir, is what you might have said,

70 Had you of wit or letters the least jot:

71 But, O most lamentable man!—of wit

72 You never had an atom, and of letters

73 You have three letters only!—they spell Ass!

74 *From Act III, Scene IV*

75 CHRISTIAN:

76 Come to my aid!

77 CYRANO:

78 Not I!

79 CHRISTIAN:

80 But I shall die,

81 Unless at once I win back her fair favor.

82 CYRANO:

83 And how can I, at once, i' th' devil's name,

84 Lesson you in. . .

85 CHRISTIAN (seizing his arm):

86 Oh, she is there!

87 (The window of the balcony is now lighted up.)

88 CYRANO (moved):

89 Her window!

90 CHRISTIAN:

91 Oh! I shall die!

92 CYRANO:

93 Speak lower!

94 CHRISTIAN (in a whisper):

95 I shall die!

96 CYRANO:

97 The night is dark. . .

98 CHRISTIAN:

99 Well!

100 CYRANO:

101 All can be repaired.

102 Although you merit not. Stand there, poor wretch!

103 Fronting the balcony! I'll go beneath

104 And prompt your words to you. . .

105 CHRISTIAN:

106 But. . .

107 CYRANO:

108 Hold your tongue!

109 THE PAGES (reappearing at back—to Cyrano):

110 Ho!

111 CYRANO:

112 Hush!

113 (He signs to them to speak softly.)

114 FIRST PAGE (in a low voice):

115 We've played the serenade you bade

116 To Montfleury!

117 CYRANO (quickly, in a low voice):

118 Go! lurk in ambush there,

119 One at this street corner, and one at that;

120 And if a passer-by should here intrude,

121 Play you a tune!

122 SECOND PAGE:

123 What tune, Sir Gassendist?

124 CYRANO:

125 Gay, if a woman comes,—for a man, sad!

126 (The pages disappear, one at each street corner. To Christian):

127 Call her!

128 CHRISTIAN:

129 Roxane!

130 CYRANO (picking up stones and throwing them at the window):

131 Some pebbles! wait awhile!

132 ROXANE (half-opening the casement):

133 Who calls me?

NOTES

134 CHRISTIAN:
135 I!

136 ROXANE:
137 Who's that?

138 CHRISTIAN:
139 Christian!

140 ROXANE (disdainfully):
141 Oh! you?

142 CHRISTIAN:
143 I would speak with you.

144 CYRANO (under the balcony—to Christian):
145 Good. Speak soft and low.

146 ROXANE:
147 No, you speak stupidly!

148 CHRISTIAN:
149 Oh, pity me!

150 ROXANE:
151 No! you love me no more!

152 CHRISTIAN (prompted by Cyrano):
153 You say—Great Heaven!
154 I love no more?—when—I—love more and more!

155 ROXANE (who was about to shut the casement, pausing):
156 Hold! 'tis a trifle better! ay, a trifle!

157 CHRISTIAN (same play):
158 Love grew apace, rocked by the anxious beating. . .
159 Of this poor heart, which the cruel **wanton** boy. . .
160 Took for a cradle!

161 ROXANE (coming out on to the balcony):
162 That is better! But
163 An if you deem that
164 Cupid be so cruel
165 You should have stifled baby-love in's cradle!

166 CHRISTIAN (same play):
167 Ah, Madame, I assayed, but all in vain
168 This. . .new-born babe is a young. . .Hercules!

169 ROXANE:
170 Still better!

171 CHRISTIAN (same play):
172 Thus he strangled in my heart
173 The. . .serpents twain, of. . .Pride. . .and Doubt!

174 ROXANE (leaning over the balcony):
175 Well said!
176 —But why so faltering? Has mental palsy
177 Seized on your faculty imaginative?

178 CYRANO (drawing Christian under the balcony, and slipping into his place):
179 Give place! This waxes critical!. . .

180 ROXANE:
181 To-day. . .
182 Your words are hesitating.

183 CYRANO (imitating Christian—in a whisper):
184 Night has come. . .
185 In the dusk they grope their way to find your ear.

186 ROXANE:
187 But my words find no such impediment.

188 CYRANO:
189 They find their way at once?
190 Small wonder that!
191 For 'tis within my heart they find their home;
192 Bethink how large my heart, how small your ear!
193 And,—from fair heights descending, words fall fast,
194 But mine must mount, Madame, and that takes time!

195 ROXANE:
196 Meseems that your last words have learned to climb.

197 CYRANO:
198 With practice such gymnastic grows less hard!

199 ROXANE:
200 In truth, I seem to speak from distant heights!

201 CYRANO:
202 True, far above; at such a height 'twere death
203 If a hard word from you fell on my heart.

NOTES

204 ROXANE (moving):
205 I will come down. . .

206 CYRANO (hastily):
207 No!

208 ROXANE (showing him the bench under the balcony):
209 Mount then on the bench!

210 CYRANO (starting back alarmed):
211 No!

212 ROXANE:
213 How, you will not?

214 CYRANO (more and more moved):
215 Stay awhile! 'Tis sweet,. . .
216 The rare occasion, when our hearts can speak
217 Our selves unseen, unseeing!

218 ROXANE:
219 Why—unseen?

220 CYRANO:
221 Ay, it is sweet! Half hidden,—half revealed—
222 You see the dark folds of my shrouding cloak,
223 And I, the glimmering whiteness of your dress:
224 I but a shadow—you a radiance fair!
225 Know you what such a moment holds for me?
226 If ever I were **eloquent.** . .

227 ROXANE:
228 You were!

229 CYRANO:
230 Yet never till to-night my speech has sprung
231 Straight from my heart as now it springs.

232 ROXANE:
233 Why not?

234 CYRANO:
235 Till now I spoke haphazard. . .

236 ROXANE:
237 What?

238 CYRANO:
239 Your eyes
240 Have beams that turn men dizzy!—But to-night
241 Methinks I shall find speech for the first time!

242 ROXANE:
243 'Tis true, your voice rings with a tone that's new.

244 CYRANO (coming nearer, passionately):
245 Ay, a new tone! In the tender, sheltering dusk
246 I dare to be myself for once,—at last!
247 (He stops, falters):
248 What say I? I know not!—Oh, pardon me—
249 It thrills me,—'tis so sweet, so novel. . .

250 ROXANE:
251 How? So novel?

252 CYRANO (off his balance, trying to find the thread of his sentence):
253 Ay,—to be at last sincere;
254 Till now, my chilled heart, fearing to be mocked. . .

255 ROXANE:
256 Mocked, and for what?

257 CYRANO:
258 For its mad beating!—Ay,
259 My heart has clothed itself with witty words,
260 To shroud itself from curious eyes:—impelled
261 At times to aim at a star, I stay my hand,
262 And, fearing ridicule,—cull a wild flower!

263 ROXANE:
264 A wild flower's sweet.

265 CYRANO:
266 Ay, but to-night—the star!

267 ROXANE:
268 Oh! never have you spoken thus before!

269 CYRANO:
270 If, leaving Cupid's arrows, quivers, torches,
271 We turned to seek for sweeter—fresher things!
272 Instead of sipping in a pygmy glass
273 Dull fashionable waters,—did we try

Reading & Writing Companion

274 How the soul **slakes** its thirst in fearless draught

275 By drinking from the river's flooding brim!

276 ROXANE:

277 But wit?. . .

278 CYRANO:

279 If I have used it to arrest you

280 At the first starting,—now, 'twould be an outrage,

281 An insult—to the perfumed Night—to Nature—

282 To speak fine words that garnish vain love-letters!

283 Look up but at her stars! The quiet Heaven

284 Will ease our hearts of all things artificial;

285 I fear lest, 'midst the alchemy we're skilled in

286 The truth of sentiment dissolve and vanish,—

287 The soul exhausted by these empty pastimes,

288 The gain of fine things be the loss of all things!

289 ROXANE:

290 But wit? I say. . .

291 CYRANO:

292 In love 'tis crime,—'tis hateful!

293 Turning frank loving into subtle fencing!

294 At last the moment comes, inevitable,—

295 —Oh, woe for those who never know that moment!

296 When feeling love exists in us, ennobling,

297 Each well-weighed word is futile and soul-saddening!

298 ROXANE:

299 Well, if that moment's come for us—suppose it!

300 What words would serve you?

301 CYRANO:

302 All, all, all, whatever

303 That came to me, e'en as they came, I'd fling them

304 In a wild cluster, not a careful bouquet.

305 I love thee! I am mad! I love, I stifle!

306 Thy name is in my heart as in a sheep-bell,

307 And as I ever tremble, thinking of thee,

308 Ever the bell shakes, ever thy name ringeth!

309 All things of thine I mind, for I love all things;

310 I know that last year on the twelfth of May-month,

311 To walk abroad, one day you changed your hair-plaits!

312 I am so used to take your hair for daylight

Please note that excerpts and passages in the StudySync® library and this workbook are intended as touchstones to generate interest in an author's work. The excerpts and passages do not substitute for the reading of entire texts, and StudySync® strongly recommends that students seek out and purchase the whole literary or informational work in order to experience it as the author intended. Links to online resellers are available in our digital library. In addition, complete works may be ordered through an authorized reseller by filling out and returning to StudySync® the order form enclosed in this workbook.

Reading & Writing Companion **373**

313   That,—like as when the eye stares on the sun's disk,

314   One sees long after a red blot on all things—

315   So, when I quit thy beams, my dazzled vision

316   Sees upon all things a blonde stain imprinted.

317   ROXANE (agitated):

318   Why, this is love indeed!. . .

319   CYRANO:

320   Ay, true, the feeling

321   Which fills me, terrible and jealous, truly

322   Love,—which is ever sad amid its transports!

323   Love,—and yet, strangely, not a selfish passion!

324   I for your joy would gladly lay mine own down,

325   —E'en though you never were to know it,—never!

326   —If but at times I might—far off and lonely,—

327   Hear some gay echo of the joy I bought you!

328   Each glance of thine awakes in me a virtue,—

329   A novel, unknown valor. Dost begin, sweet,

330   To understand? So late, dost understand me?

331   Feel'st thou my soul, here, through the darkness mounting?

332   Too fair the night! Too fair, too fair the moment!

333   That I should speak thus, and that you should hearken!

334   Too fair! In moments when my hopes rose proudest,

335   I never hoped such guerdon. Naught is left me

336   But to die now! Have words of mine the power

337   To make you tremble,—throned there in the branches?

338   Ay, like a leaf among the leaves, you tremble!

339   You tremble! For I feel,—an if you will it,

340   Or will it not,—your hand's beloved trembling

341   Thrill through the branches, down your sprays of jasmine!

342   (He kisses passionately one of the hanging tendrils.)

343   ROXANE:

344   Ay! I am trembling, weeping!—I am thine!

345   Thou hast conquered all of me!

346   CYRANO:

347   Then let death come!

348   'Tis I, 'tis I myself, who conquered thee!

349   One thing, but one, I dare to ask—

350   CHRISTIAN (under the balcony):

351   A kiss!

352 ROXANE (drawing back):

353 What?

354 CYRANO:

355 Oh!

356 ROXANE:

357 You ask. . .?

358 CYRANO:

359 I. . .

360 (To Christian, whispering):

361 Fool! you go too quick!

362 CHRISTIAN:

363 Since she is moved thus—I will profit by it!

364 CYRANO (to Roxane):

365 My words sprang thoughtlessly, but now I see—

366 Shame on me!—I was too presumptuous.

367 ROXANE (a little chilled):

368 How quickly you withdraw.

369 *From Act V, Scene VI*

370 CYRANO:

371 Look you, it was my life

372 To be the prompter every one forgets!

373 (To Roxane):

374 That night when 'neath your window Christian spoke

375 —Under your balcony, you remember? Well!

376 There was the allegory of my whole life:

377 I, in the shadow, at the ladder's foot,

378 While others lightly mount to Love and Fame!

379 Just! very just! Here on the threshold drear

380 Of death, I pay my tribute with the rest,

381 To Moliere's genius,—Christian's fair face!

382 (The chapel-bell chimes. The nuns are seen passing down the alley at the

383 back, to say their office):

384 Let them go pray, go pray, when the bell rings!

385 ROXANE (rising and calling):

386 Sister! Sister!

387 CYRANO (holding her fast):

388 Call no one. Leave me not;

389   When you come back, I should be gone for aye.

390   (The nuns have all entered the chapel. The organ sounds):

391   I was somewhat fain for music—hark! 'tis come.

392   ROXANE:

393   Live, for I love you!

394   CYRANO:

395   No, In fairy tales

396   When to the ill-starred Prince the lady says

397   'I love you!' all his ugliness fades fast—

398   But I remain the same, up to the last!

399   ROXANE:

400   I have marred your life—I, I!

401   CYRANO:

402   You blessed my life!

403   Never on me had rested woman's love.

404   My mother even could not find me fair:

405   I had no sister; and, when grown a man,

406   I feared the mistress who would mock at me.

407   But I have had your friendship—grace to you

408   A woman's charm has passed across my path.

409   LE BRET (pointing to the moon, which is seen between the trees):

410   Your other lady-love is come.

411   CYRANO (smiling):

412   I see.

413   ROXANE:

414   I loved but once, yet twice I lose my love!

THINK QUESTIONS

1. Use details from the text to write two or three sentences describing how Cyrano humiliates the Viscount de Valvert in Act I, scene iv.

2. When and why does Cyrano step out and take Christian's place under Roxane's window in Act III, scene iv? Refer to textual evidence to support your response.

3. In Act V, scene vi, why does Cyrano claim that the scene under Roxane's balcony was "the allegory of my whole life"? Support your answer with textual evidence.

4. Use context to determine the meaning of the word **pedantic.** Write your definition here and explain how you inferred the meaning of the word.

5. Use the context clues in the passage to infer the meaning of **wanton.** Consider how the word relates to the figurative language of the passage. Then write your definition here and explain how you arrived at your inferred meaning.

CLOSE READ

Reread the excerpt from *Cyrano de Bergerac*. As you reread, complete the Focus Questions below. Then use your answers and annotations from the questions to help you complete the Writing Prompt.

FOCUS QUESTIONS

1. Reread Act I, scene iv to find and highlight an example of verbal irony. Explain how the literal meaning of Cyrano's words differs from his intended meaning.

2. What are the similarities and differences between Act I, scene iv and Act III, scene iv? Consider what Cyrano says and his underlying motivations in each scene. What is ironic about Cyrano's speaking for Christian in Act III?

3. In Act III, scene iv, highlight a key moment that helps to develop the character of Cyrano and explain what is revealed about Cyrano in that moment.

4. Reread Cyrano and Roxane's conversation in Act V, scene vi. Does this scene provide a comedic or tragic resolution to the play? How does this choice by the author contribute to the meaning of the play as a whole?

5. Do you think that this play suggests that romantic love leads to wisdom or folly? Explain your answer using examples and textual evidence from the play.

WRITING PROMPT

Select a key moment from the play and discuss how that moment helps to establish the play as a comedy (a drama meant to be humorous), a tragedy (a drama based on human suffering), or a tragicomedy (a drama containing elements of both humor and human suffering). Then explain what that moment suggests about the idea of romantic love.

DUMPED!

NON-FICTION
Helen Fisher
2004

INTRODUCTION

Anthropologist Helen Fisher has studied the evolution of romantic love, brain activity, and interpersonal relationships for over 30 years. In her article "Dumped," which was originally published in *New Scientist* magazine, Fisher combines scientific and literary analysis to further our understanding of love and deep attachment, arguing that romantic love is a natural drive with effects similar to addiction. She goes on to describe what happens in the brain when we experience rejection.

"The opposite of love is indifference."

 FIRST READ

Why is it so painful when romance goes wrong? Blame the wiring of your brain and the harsh realities of evolution, says anthropologist Helen Fisher.

1   Emptiness, hopelessness, fear, fury: almost everyone endures the agony of romantic rejection at some point in their lives. Why do we suffer so? Sorrow and anger are **metabolically** expensive and time consuming. Why didn't humanity evolve a way to shrug off romantic loss and easily renew the quest to find a suitable reproductive partner?

2   I have been studying romantic love for 10 years or so and have come to see it as an evolutionary adaptation. The ability to fall in love evolved because those who focused their courtship attention on a preferred partner saved time and energy and improved their chances of survival and reproduction.

3   Unfortunately, the same applies to love's darker side. We humans are soft-wired to suffer terribly when we are rejected by someone we adore—for good evolutionary reasons.

4   Back in 1996 I decided to use a technique called functional MRI to study the brains of men and women who had just fallen madly in love. I and several **collaborators,** including neuroscientist Lucy Brown of the Albert Einstein College of Medicine in New York and psychologist Arthur Aron of the State University of New York at Stony Brook, asked our subjects, a group of seven men and 10 women, to look at a photograph of their beloved projected on a screen just outside the brain scanner. We also showed each participant an emotionally neutral picture—a photograph of an acquaintance for whom they had no positive or negative feelings. In between looking at these photos, we asked each to perform a "distraction task" to wash the mind clean of all emotion.

5   The resulting scans told us many things about the brain in love (*New Scientist,* 22 November 2003, p. 18). Most significantly, when subjects were looking at their sweetheart, their brain showed increased activity in two regions: the right ventral tegmental area (VTA) in the midbrain, and parts of the caudate nucleus, a large c-shaped region near the centre. The VTA is rich in cells that produce and distribute the powerful **stimulant** dopamine to many areas of the brain, including the caudate nucleus. It is part of the brain's network that controls general arousal, focused attention and motivation to acquire rewards.

6   The fact that intense, early-stage romantic passion is associated with areas rich in dopamine suggested to us that romantic love is not, in fact, an emotion, but primarily a **motivational** state designed to make us pursue a preferred partner. Indeed, romantic love appears to be a drive as powerful as hunger. No wonder people around the world live—and die—for love.

7   But we weren't interested in just the lovey-dovey side of romance. We wanted to understand every aspect. So in 2001 we began scanning the brains of people who were suffering the trauma of a recent rejection in love.

8   The study is still in progress, but we suspect we will find continued activity in the VTA and associated parts of the caudate nucleus, largely because lovers keep loving long after they have been spurned. I think we will find much more than that, however. Being rejected in love is among the most painful experiences a human being can endure, so many other brain regions may be involved as well.

9   Even before the results come in, there is a lot we can say about the biology of rejection which suggests that it is an evolved response with specific functions. Psychiatrists have long divided romantic rejection into two phases: "protest" and "resignation/despair." During the protest phase, deserted lovers become obsessed with winning back the object of their affections. They agonise over what went wrong and how to rekindle the flame. They make dramatic, often humiliating, appearances at their lover's home or workplace, then storm out, only to return to berate or plead anew. They phone, email and write letters. They revisit mutual haunts and mutual friends. And alas, as the adversity intensifies, so does the romantic passion. This phenomenon is so common in the psychological literature (and in life) that I coined a term for it—frustration attraction. When romantic love is thwarted, the lover just loves harder.

But I love you more than ever.

10   What brain systems might underlie these odd behaviors? Psychiatrists Thomas Lewis, Fari Amini and Richard Lannon, all of the University of California, San Francisco, have argued that protest is a basic mammalian

Please note that excerpts and passages in the StudySync® library and this workbook are intended as touchstones to generate interest in an author's work. The excerpts and passages do not substitute for the reading of entire texts, and StudySync® strongly recommends that students seek out and purchase the whole literary or informational work in order to experience it as the author intended. Links to online resellers are available in our digital library. In addition, complete works may be ordered through an authorized reseller by filling out and returning to StudySync® the order form enclosed in this workbook.

Reading & Writing Companion   **381**

response to the rupturing of any social tie. They believe it is associated with dopamine, as well as with the closely related neurotransmitter norepinephrine. Elevated levels of both these chemicals lead to heightened alertness and stimulate the forlorn animal to call for help and search for its abandoner—generally its mother.

11 The rising level of dopamine may help explain the biology of frustration attraction. Since our research suggests that the dopamine system is activated during early-stage romantic love, one would think that as dopamine activity increased during protest the rejected lover would feel even greater passion. And another brain mechanism kicks in during the protest phase that could add to this frustration attraction—the stress system. In the short term, stress triggers the production of dopamine and norepinephrine and suppresses serotonin activity, that heady combination of neurotransmitters that I maintain in my book, *Why We Love,* is associated with romantic love.

12 But frustration attraction may be due to other brain activities as well. Neuroscientist Wolfram Schultz at the University of Fribourg in Switzerland reported in 2000 that when an expected reward, such as love, is delayed, "reward-expecting" neurons prolong their activities (*Nature Reviews: Neuroscience,* vol. 1, p. 199). These neurons do not make or distribute dopamine, but they are central components of the brain's reward system, the system associated with focused attention and motivation—the very behaviours that characterize romantic love.

13 What irony! As the beloved slips away, the brain networks and chemicals that most likely create the potent feelings of love increase.

14 The protest phase of rejection may also trigger activity in the brain's panic system. Neuroscientist Jaak Panksepp of Bowling Green State University of Ohio believes that this brain network generates the well-known "separation anxiety" response in infant mammals abandoned by their mother. When their mother leaves, infants become troubled. They express their alarm with a pounding heart, sucking gestures and distress calls.

15 Yet another brain system often becomes active as one protests against the departure of a lover: anger. Even when the departing lover severs the relationship with honesty and compassion and honours social and parental obligations, many rejected lovers swing violently from heartbreak to fury. Psychologist Reid Meloy of the University of California, San Diego, calls this reaction "abandonment rage." I use a different term: "love hatred." Whatever you call it, it's a curious reaction. Hate and rage don't generally entice a lover to return. Why does love turn to hate?

16 At first I assumed that hate was the opposite of love. But it isn't. The opposite of love is **indifference.** Moreover, it occurred to me that love and anger might

NOTES

be linked in the brain, and indeed they are. The basic rage network is closely connected to centres in the prefrontal cortex that anticipate rewards, including the reward of winning a beloved. In fact, experiments in animals have shown how intimately these reward and rage circuits are intertwined. Stimulate a cat's reward circuits and it feels intense pleasure. Withdraw the stimulation and it bites. This common response to unfulfilled expectations is known as the "frustration-aggression hypothesis."

17 So romantic love and love hatred are probably well connected in the brain. And when the drive to love is thwarted, the brain turns passion into fury.

18 Why did our ancestors evolve brain links that enable us to hate the one we cherish? Rage is not good for your health: it elevates blood pressure, places stress on the heart and suppresses the immune system. So love hatred must have evolved to solve some crucial reproductive problems. Among these, I now believe that it developed to enable jilted lovers to extricate themselves from dead-end love affairs and start again.

19 Abandonment rage also motivates people to fight for the welfare of their offspring. This certainly occurs in divorce proceedings: men and women who are otherwise well adjusted turn vicious to get the best deal for their children. In his book *Why We Hate* (New York, Contemporary Books, 2002), science writer Rush Dozier tells of a judge who regularly presides over child custody cases and trials of violent criminals, and reports that he is much more worried about his personal safety during the custody cases. He and other judges have even installed panic buttons in their chambers in case arguing spouses become violent.

20 Sadly, abandonment rage does not necessarily extinguish love. In a study of 124 dating couples, psychologists Bruce Ellis of the University of Canterbury in New Zealand and Neil Malamuth of the University of California, Los Angeles, found that romantic love and feelings of anger are independent, and can operate simultaneously. Hence, you can be terribly angry but still be very much in love.

21 Eventually, however, the jilted lover gives up. Then he or she must deal with new forms of torture: resignation and despair. Drugged by the potent liquor of sorrow, they cry, lie in bed, stare into space, drink too much or hole up and watch TV. Feelings of protest and anger of the desire for reconciliation sometimes resurface, but mostly they just feel deep **melancholy.** In 1991, sociologists at the University of California, Los Angeles, assessed 114 people who had been rejected by a sweetheart within the previous eight weeks. More than 40 per cent of them were clinically depressed. Of these, 12 per cent were suffering moderate to severe depressions. Some people even kill themselves, and some die of a broken heart. Psychiatrist Norman Rosenthal

of Georgetown University in Washington DC has reported that broken-hearted lovers can expire from heart attacks or strokes caused by their depression.

22   Resignation and despair are well documented in other mammalian species. When infant animals are abandoned by their mother, first they protest and panic. Later they slump into what psychologists call the "despair response."

23   Despair has been associated with several different networks in the brain. One is the reward system. As the abandoned partner realises that the expected reward will never come, the dopamine-making cells in the midbrain scale down their activity. And diminishing levels of dopamine produce **lethargy,** despondency and depression. The stress system also plays a part. As the stress of abandonment wears on, it suppresses the activity of dopamine and other potent neurotransmitters, contributing to feelings of depression.

24   Like abandonment rage, the despair response seems counterproductive. Why waste time and energy moping? Some scientists now believe that depression evolved millions of years ago as a coping mechanism. Theories on this subject abound. One I particularly like has been proposed by anthropologist Edward Hagen of Humboldt University in Berlin, biologists Paul Watson and Paul Andrews of the University of New Mexico in Albuquerque and psychiatrist Andy Thomson of the University of Virginia in Charlottesville. They argue that the high metabolic and social cost of depression is actually its benefit: depression is an honest, believable signal to others that something is desperately wrong. It is a cry for help which compels stressed people to request support in times of intense need.

25   Imagine a young woman living in a Palaeolithic tribe whose mate openly mated with another woman. First she protested, grew angry and tried to persuade her partner to give up his love. She also appealed to her friends and kin for help. Unable to influence her mate or relatives with words or tantrums, however, she became depressed. Eventually her despondency motivated her family to drive out her unfaithful partner and console her until she could recover her vitality, find a new mate and start contributing food and childcare again.

26   Depression is evolutionarily advantageous for another reason: it gives you insight. Depressed people suffer what psychologist Jeffrey Zeig of the Milton H. Erickson Foundation in Phoenix, Arizona, calls a "failure of denial," allowing them to make honest assessment of themselves and others. Severe depression can push a person to face **unpalatable** truths and make difficult decisions that ultimately promote their survival and reproductive success.

27   Not everyone suffers to the same degree, of course. Still, we human beings are intricately wired to suffer when we have been rejected by a loved one,

NOTES

and for good evolutionary reasons. I believe romantic love is one of three primary mating drives. The sex drive evolved to enable our ancestors to seek intercourse with any remotely appropriate individual. Romantic love developed to enable our forebears to focus their attention on preferred partners, thereby conserving precious mating time and energy. And long term attachment evolved to motivate mates to rear their babies as a team. So falling in love is one of the most important (and powerful) things we do; it profoundly affects our social and genetic future.

28   As a result, we are built to suffer terribly when love fails—first to protest the departure and try to win the beloved back, and later to give up utterly, dust ourselves off and redirect our energy to fall in love again. We are likely to find evidence of any combination of these myriad motivations and emotions as we examine the rejected brain in love.

THINK QUESTIONS

1.   Use details from the text to write one or two sentences describing dopamine and its effects on the brain. In a separate sentence, explain how this relates to the main idea of the article.

2.   Refer to one or more details from the text to explain why Fisher concludes her analysis of the term "frustration attraction" with the exclamation "What irony!"

3.   What biological link does the author establish between love and anger in the essay? Support your answer with textual evidence before summarizing this connection in your own words.

4.   Use your knowledge of word parts and context clues to determine the meaning of the word **motivational.** Write your definition here and tell how you verified it.

5.   Use word parts and the context clues in the passage to determine the meaning of **unpalatable.** Write your definition here and tell how looking it up in the dictionary might help you better understand its figurative use in this sentence.

CLOSE READ

Reread the excerpt from *Dumped!* As you reread, complete the Focus Questions below. Then use your answers and annotations from the questions to help you complete the Writing Prompt.

FOCUS QUESTIONS

1. What evidence does the author provide to support the assertion that romantic love is not an emotion, but a drive?

2. According to the article, what is "frustration attraction" and what brain activities are involved in creating this state?

3. Reread the later paragraphs about depression. Does the author present depression in a positive or negative way? Explain.

4. Reread the paragraph about the "young woman living in a Paleolithic tribe." How does this fictional story fit into Fisher's argument? Do you think this story helps make Fisher's points clear, convincing, and engaging?

5. Consider Fisher's remarks in the last two paragraphs. Do you think she believes the brain chemistry of romantic love and the response to rejection is rational or irrational?

WRITING PROMPT

The author claims that we are "soft-wired to suffer terribly when we are rejected by someone we adore." Do you think it would be beneficial or detrimental if we could "rewire" the human brain to avoid suffering after romantic rejection? Do you think the author would agree with your position? Include textual evidence to support your assertions.

WHAT IS LOVE?

NON-FICTION
The Guardian
2012

INTRODUCTION

ove is a complex aspect of human identity. We all experience it and intuitively know what it is without being able to explain it clearly. This news article from British newspaper *The Guardian* compiles the perspectives of writers, scientists, philosophers, and seekers from across the globe. From love of one's community to passionate commitment, these viewpoints offer varying definitions

"Love is more easily experienced than defined."

FIRST READ

1   "What is love" was the most searched phrase on Google in 2012, according to the company. In an attempt to get to the bottom of the question once and for all, the Guardian has gathered writers from the fields of science, psychotherapy, literature, religion and philosophy to give their definition of the much-pondered word.

The physicist: 'Love is chemistry'

2   Biologically, love is a powerful **neurological** condition like hunger or thirst, only more permanent. We talk about love being blind or unconditional, in the sense that we have no control over it. But then, that is not so surprising since love is basically chemistry. While lust is a temporary passionate sexual desire involving the increased release of chemicals such as testosterone and oestrogen, in true love, or attachment and bonding, the brain can release a whole set of chemicals: pheromones, dopamine, norepinephrine, serotonin, oxytocin and vasopressin. However, from an evolutionary perspective, love can be viewed as a survival tool—a mechanism we have evolved to promote long-term relationships, mutual defence and parental support of children and to promote feelings of safety and security.

—*Jim Al-Khalili is a theoretical physicist and science writer*

The psychotherapist: 'Love has many guises'

3   Unlike us, the ancients did not lump all the various emotions that we label "love" under the one word. They had several variations, including:

4   *Philia* which they saw as a deep but usually non-sexual intimacy between close friends and family members or as a deep bond forged by soldiers as they fought alongside each other in battle. *Ludus* describes a more playful affection found in fooling around or flirting. *Pragma* is the mature love that

develops over a long period of time between long-term couples and involves actively practising goodwill, commitment, compromise and understanding. *Agape* is a more generalised love; it's not about **exclusivity** but about love for all of humanity. *Philautia* is self love, which isn't as selfish as it sounds. As Aristotle discovered and as any psychotherapist will tell you, in order to care for others you need to be able to care about yourself. Last, and probably least even though it causes the most trouble, *eros* is about sexual passion and desire. Unless it morphs into philia and/or pragma, eros will burn itself out.

5 Love is all of the above. But is it possibly unrealistic to expect to experience all six types with only one person. This is why family and community are important.

—Philippa Perry is a psychotherapist and author of Couch Fiction

The philosopher: 'Love is a passionate commitment'

6 The answer remains elusive in part because love is not one thing. Love for parents, partners, children, country, neighbour, God and so on all have different qualities. Each has its variants—blind, one-sided, tragic, steadfast, fickle, **reciprocated,** misguided, unconditional. At its best, however, all love is a kind a passionate commitment that we nurture and develop, even though it usually arrives in our lives unbidden. That's why it is more than just a powerful feeling. Without the commitment, it is mere **infatuation.** Without the passion, it is mere dedication. Without nurturing, even the best can wither and die.

—Julian Baggini is a philosopher and writer

The romantic novelist: 'Love drives all great stories'

7 What love is depends on where you are in relation to it. Secure in it, it can feel as **mundane** and necessary as air—you exist within it, almost unnoticing. Deprived of it, it can feel like an obsession; all consuming, a physical pain. Love is the driver for all great stories: not just romantic love, but the love of parent for child, for family, for country. It is the point before **consummation** of it that fascinates: what separates you from love, the obstacles that stand in its way. It is usually at those points that love is everything.

—Jojo Moyes is a two-time winner of the Romantic Novel of the Year award

The nun: 'Love is free yet binds us'

8 Love is more easily experienced than defined. As a theological virtue, by which we love God above all things and our neighbours as ourselves for his sake, it seems remote until we encounter it enfleshed, so to say, in the life of another—in acts of kindness, generosity and self-sacrifice. Love's the one

NOTES

thing that can never hurt anyone, although it may cost dearly. The paradox of love is that it is supremely free yet attaches us with bonds stronger than death. It cannot be bought or sold; there is nothing it cannot face; love is life's greatest blessing.

—Catherine Wybourne is a Benedictine nun

Copyright Guardian News & Media Ltd 2012. Used by permission.

THINK QUESTIONS

1. Refer to one or more details from the text to explain why true or romantic love is more complex than lust.

2. Based on the psychotherapist's explanation of love, what inferences can you make about the types of subjects she has studied in addition to psychology?

3. Based on the romantic novelist's response to the title question, what can you infer about the kinds of story elements she is likely to include in her fiction?

4. Use context clues to define the word **infatuation.** Write your definition and tell how you determined both its denotation and connotation in this context.

5. Use context to determine the meaning of the word **mundane.** Then compare your inferred meaning to the dictionary definition.

CLOSE READ

Reread the excerpt from *What Is Love?* As you reread, complete the Focus Questions below. Then use your answers and annotations from the questions to help you complete the Writing Prompt.

FOCUS QUESTIONS

1. Compare and contrast the first and last sections of the text. Why do you think the article begins with the physicist's comments and ends with the nun's? How does this relate to the structure of the article as a whole?

2. Reread the philosopher's paragraph. How would you describe the text structure that he uses to organize his answer? How does this relate to his central argument?

3. Identify the parallelism in the last part of the philosopher's response. (**Parallelism** is the use of words, phrases, or clauses with a similar grammatical structure.) Do you think the use of parallelism helps make the writer's point that love is "a passionate commitment" clear, convincing, and engaging?

4. Identify one similarity and one difference that you find interesting between the ideas of any of the responders. Explain your thoughts about the similarity and the difference that you have identified.

5. Which excerpts might you use as support for the argument that love inspires wisdom? Which might you use as support for the argument that love inspires folly? Explain what text structure you might use if you were to incorporate both of these segments into a single essay.

WRITING PROMPT

Imagine that one of the authors in this unit has been asked the question "What is love?" What do you think the author would say? Take on the persona of that author and write a one-paragraph response to the question. Make sure that your response is consistent with ideas expressed about love in the work you have read in this unit by your chosen author. Before you write a response, plan to use an informational text structure that will help make your points clear, convincing, and engaging.

Please note that excerpts and passages in the StudySync® library and this workbook are intended as touchstones to generate interest in an author's work. The excerpts and passages do not substitute for the reading of entire texts, and StudySync® strongly recommends that students seek out and purchase the whole literary or informational work in order to experience it as the author intended. Links to online resellers are available in our digital library. In addition, complete works may be ordered through an authorized reseller by filling out and returning to StudySync® the order form enclosed in this workbook.

Reading & Writing Companion

391

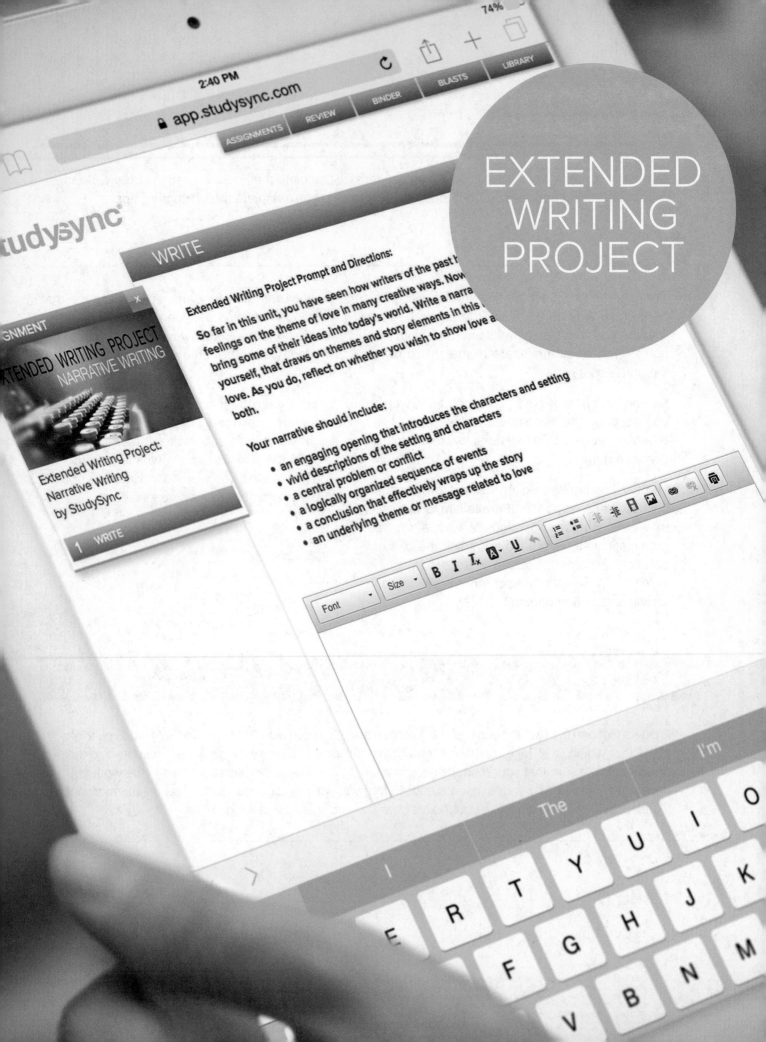

EXTENDED
WRITING
PROJECT

studysync

WRITE

ASSIGNMENT

EXTENDED WRITING PROJECT
NARRATIVE WRITING

Extended Writing Project:
Narrative Writing
by StudySync

1   WRITE

Extended Writing Project Prompt and Directions:

So far in this unit, you have seen how writers of the past have
feelings on the theme of love in many creative ways. Now
bring some of their ideas into today's world. Write a narra
yourself, that draws on themes and story elements in this
love. As you do, reflect on whether you wish to show love a
both.

Your narrative should include:

- an engaging opening that introduces the characters and setting
- vivid descriptions of the setting and characters
- a central problem or conflict
- a logically organized sequence of events
- a conclusion that effectively wraps up the story
- an underlying theme or message related to love

NARRATIVE WRITING

WRITING PROMPT

So far in this unit, you have seen how writers of the past have expressed their thoughts and feelings on the theme of love in many creative ways. Now you will have an opportunity to bring some of their ideas into today's world. Write a narrative for young adult readers, like yourself, that draws on themes and story elements in this unit to create a modern tale of love. As you do, reflect on whether you wish to show love as inspiring folly, wisdom, or both.

Your narrative should include:

- an engaging opening that introduces the characters and setting
- vivid descriptions of the setting and characters
- a central problem or conflict
- a logically organized sequence of events
- a conclusion that effectively wraps up the story
- an underlying theme or message related to love

Narrative writing tells a story of real or imagined experiences or events. Narratives can be fiction or nonfiction. Fictional narratives can take the form of novels, short stories, poems, or plays. Nonfiction narratives are true stories, often expressed in memoirs or diary entries, personal essays or letters, autobiographies or biographies, and histories. Many narratives have a clearly identified narrator who tells the story as it unfolds. In nonfiction narratives, the author usually tells the story. In fiction narratives, the narrator can be a character in the story or someone outside of the story. Effective narrative writing uses storytelling techniques, relevant descriptive details, and well-structured event sequences to convey a story to readers. The features of narrative writing include:

Please note that excerpts and passages in the StudySync® library and this workbook are intended as touchstones to generate interest in an author's work. The excerpts and passages do not substitute for the reading of entire texts, and StudySync® strongly recommends that students seek out and purchase the whole literary or informational work in order to experience it as the author intended. Links to online resellers are available in our digital library. In addition, complete works may be ordered through an authorized reseller by filling out and returning to StudySync® the order form enclosed in this workbook.

Reading & Writing
Companion

393

- setting
- characters
- plot
- conflict
- theme
- point of view

As you actively participate in this extended writing project, you will receive more instructions and practice to help you craft each of the elements of narrative writing.

Before you begin developing your own narrative, consider this story that one student wrote in response to the writing prompt. As you read, highlight and annotate the features of narrative writing that the student included in the story.

 STUDENT MODEL

The Overlook

For their class picnic, the seniors of Cedar City High chose a sprawling park at the base of Mojo Mountain. The bus ride there took a little over an hour, but it felt like four hours to Sam. As they neared the mountain, he imagined it might take another hour or more to hike up its evergreen slopes to the rocky top. Maybe there he could find some peace. Away from Cedar City's various cliques and groups. Somewhere he wouldn't have to feel so awkward around his classmates.

The bus pulled into the parking lot, where some local craft makers had set up folding tables and multicolored tents hoping to lure visitors into buying a carved wooden souvenir or plastic memento. Most of the other students made a beeline for the booths. All this natural beauty around them, and their first impulse was shopping, Sam thought. Typical.

P.J. was one of those other students. P.J., who never noticed that they took all the same science classes. Never attended one of the baseball games in which Sam played outfield. Never thanked Sam for a good deed or compliment. Probably didn't even vote for Sam when he ran for senior class vice president. Didn't even know Sam played drums. Why was Sam even interested in P.J.? Then again, wasn't that the story of Sam's life? Never noticed, passed by, overlooked. No wonder he lost the race for V.P.

Sam should have turned around and headed in the exact opposite direction, but instead he wandered toward the vendors. He pretended to inspect some hand-carved animal statues while keeping track of P.J., an easy-to-spot redhead, out of the corner of his eye. When a few other students glanced Sam's way, he turned his attention to a thumb-sized figurine of a coyote made of blue-green stone.

"You like that one there?" the vendor asked Sam. He was an old man with white hair that stuck up like little horns from his scalp. "Old Arapaho magic statue. Very strong, that one. Maybe too strong for you. Carry it with you, close as you can, and everybody notices you. Everyone pays attention. Everyone falls in love."

Something about the way the old man slurred the word "love" made Sam uneasy. He set the statue back down on the table, hoping to express disinterest, but the man stepped closer. "You're small, not yet full-size. For you, then, this one half price. Best deal here. Half price. One dollar."

Sam reached into his pocket and handed over a dollar bill. It was worth it to end the conversation and leave the tent, especially since P.J. had disappeared from view. As he scanned the crowd, Sam took the figurine from the vendor and dropped it without looking into his backpack. Oddly, just having the little coyote with him made Sam feel more sure of himself.

Sam stepped out of the shadows and into the light.

"Hey! Sam!"

It was P.J.

"Sam! You hike, right? I mean, you like nature and all that stuff, don't you? Like in our ecology class?"

"Yeah," Sam said. "I do, sort of. I mean, yes. Yes I do. Why?"

P.J. looked down. "You wore hiking boots. Everyone else wore fancy shoes for some stupid reason. I mean, Mojo Mountain is right here, and you wear high heels? What are these kids thinking? Am I right?"

Reading & Writing Companion

"Yeah. They're not thinking. So what are you thinking?" What a stupid question, Sam thought to himself. Focus. Stay calm. Think of the coyote, right there in the backpack. "I mean, why does it matter?"

"Look," P.J. said, pointing up toward the mountain. "There's a wicked cool spot up there that looks out over the whole valley. I want to hike up, but Mr. Fryson says I can't go alone. Go with me, OK? Wait, that sounded like an order. Right? Let me try again. Would you care to join me? Please?"

"Sure," Sam said. "O.K. No problem."

"If we hustle, we can make it up and back in time." P.J. strode across the parking lot. Sam followed, tightening the straps on his backpack to keep it from swaying, to keep the tiny coyote close to his body. It seemed silly, but P.J. had approached him as soon as he put it in his backpack.

The two of them scampered up a dirt trail that led into the woods. As they climbed, P.J. talked about their classmates, the schools' sports team, and some bands that were expected to visit Cedar City that summer. Sam imagined the coyote in his backpack telling him to mention that he played drums, but he stayed quiet. Let P.J. talk, he thought. Be a good listener, and don't mess things up by saying the most wrongest, most stupidest thing.

In what seemed like no time at all, they were at the summit. A granite ledge jutted out from the mountainside and offered a panoramic view of the valley. The refreshing scents of pine and cedar wafted up from the treetops below. "Whoa," Sam said, surprised by how high they were. His heart pounded in his chest. A hawk soared along the ridgeline, wings outstretched to catch the wind. Its sharp call sounded like a quick hello as it passed. In the distance, Cedar City sparkled in the sun like a pile of diamonds.

The two students stood side by side in silence, taking in the view. Finally, P.J. spoke.

"You look different today."

"Different? How?" Sam asked.

Copyright © BookheadEd Learning, LLC

"I don't know. Different." P.J. glanced quickly at Sam and then looked back out toward the city. "Like you're somebody now."

Sam's heart raced even faster and deeper, more like a booming bass drum than a snare. Had the coyote statue's magic worked after all? "I was somebody yesterday, too," he said at last.

P.J. laughed. "Yeah, yesterday. Everyone was somebody yesterday. But what about today? What about tomorrow?" P.J. turned to Sam. "Are you going to be somebody tomorrow?"

"I hope so!" Sam said. It sounded so weak, so lame. Who would he be? Did he even have a clue? Would he be some kind of superstar that P.J. would fall head over heels in love with, or would he just be a dull jerk wearing hiking boots with a stupid stone coyote in his backpack? "Maybe," Sam began, hesitant at first before listening to his heart beating madly in his chest, "I'll be a drummer in a rock band."

P.J. laughed. "I love it! I'll play bass. My sister's teaching me the basics. Get it? Bass-ics?"

Sam laughed. "Maybe together we can drum up some business in the music world."

For the next half hour, the two students talked about their favorite bands and songs they'd like to play. Before heading back, they each took pictures of themselves on the overlook with Cedar City in the distance behind them. By the time they had reached the parking lot, they had finalized the set list for their first concert, discussed possible artwork for their first album cover, and mapped out an itinerary of favorite cities for their worldwide tour.

It seemed impossible, but the whole day had already passed, and Sam had spent nearly every minute with P.J.

As they stood in line together to board the bus back home, the white-haired man from the sales area came dashing over. "Hey! There you are!" he shouted at Sam, drawing everyone's attention to him.

The man held out his hand to reveal the tiny blue-green coyote. "You took the wrong statue," the man explained. "You weren't even looking." He glanced at P.J. with a twinkle in his eye. "I think you were distracted."

NOTES

Sam opened his backpack and reached inside. Sure enough, what he thought was the magical coyote turned out to be nothing more than a hawk with folded wings.

"You don't need the hawk anymore," the man said. "That magic's flown away now." He took back the figurine and handed Sam the coyote. "Now you're ready for the stone coyote."

"Stone Coyote," P.J. said with a poke to Sam's ribs. "Great name for a band."

"Maybe," said Sam. "But I think that you and I can come up with something even better on our own."

THINK QUESTIONS

1. What is the setting of "The Overlook"? Who are the main characters? How are these two elements of the narrative related? Refer to two or more details from the text to support your understanding of why the writer might have placed these characters in this setting.

2. How is the plot of "The Overlook" organized? Does it follow a chronological sequence? Are there any flashbacks? If so, what purpose do they serve?

3. Describe the central problem or conflict in this narrative and how it is resolved. Use textual evidence to explain how the student has expressed this within the story.

4. Reflect on what you have read, listened to, and researched throughout this unit and the course of the entire school year. Combine this with your own personal experience and background knowledge to answer this question: What settings, characters, or plot events most relate to your own thoughts and feelings on the subject of love?

5. Which selections or other resources seem most relevant to the narrative writing prompt? What are some ideas that you may want to explore in more detail during the writing process? What resources might be most helpful to you as you consider these themes and ideas?

PREWRITE

WRITING PROMPT

So far in this unit, you have seen how writers of the past have expressed their thoughts and feelings on the theme of love in many creative ways. Now you will have an opportunity to bring some of their ideas into today's world. Write a narrative for young adult readers, like yourself, that draws on themes and story elements in this unit to create a modern tale of love. As you do, reflect on whether you wish to show love as inspiring folly, wisdom, or both.

Your narrative should include:

- an engaging opening that introduces the characters and setting
- vivid descriptions of the setting and characters
- a central problem or conflict
- a logically organized sequence of events
- a conclusion that effectively wraps up the story
- an underlying theme or message related to love

In addition to studying the language and stylistic techniques that authors use, you have been reading and learning about the various ways in which they approach and explore the theme of love. In this extended writing project, you'll use various writing strategies and techniques to compose your own narrative on the theme of love.

First you'll want to explore possible ideas that relate to the writing prompt itself. To do this, think back on prewriting strategies that you've used in the past, such as generating lists, brainstorming, mapping concepts, and free-writing. Keep in mind that different strategies might help you with specific parts of the prompt. For example, list-making might help you evaluate and

Please note that excerpts and passages in the StudySync® library and this workbook are intended as touchstones to generate interest in an author's work. The excerpts and passages do not substitute for the reading of entire texts, and StudySync® strongly recommends that students seek out and purchase the whole literary or informational work in order to experience it as the author intended. Links to online resellers are available in our digital library. In addition, complete works may be ordered through an authorized reseller by filling out and returning to StudySync® the order form enclosed in this workbook.

Reading & Writing Companion **399**

NOTES

rank which texts relate most closely to your own thoughts and feelings about love.

As you look back over the stories and poems you have read so far, consider how the authors have approached the theme of love in their work. Ask yourself:

- How do certain characters and their personality traits represent differing ideas or opinions about the topic? Which character or characters does the author seem to favor over the others?
- Where does the story or poem take place? How does this influence the action?
- What central problem or conflict drives the action forward?
- How do plot elements contribute to the development of the theme?
- How does the point of view influence and support the narrative?
- How do these narrative elements explore the theme of love?

Make a list of the answers to these questions for the Model or one of the reading selections that appealed to you. Look for strong ideas or details that you might include and explore further in your story. These points of inspiration can help you get started in developing ideas for your own characters, settings, plot elements, and themes. Then, use the outline below to organize ideas for your own narrative.

Complete this outline, putting in ideas you have for your own narrative:

Text: Ovid's *Metamorphoses*

Main Characters: Phoebus (foolish love), Cupid (spiteful love), Daphne (innocent love)

Secondary Characters: Peneus (Daphne's father)

Setting: Around the countryside

Main Conflict: Unrequited love between Phoebus and Daphne

Basic Plot: Cupid seeks revenge after Phoebus insults him and uses his poisoned arrows to make Phoebus fall in love with Daphne, whom Cupid has turned against him.

Point of View: Mostly third person

Central Theme: Love can be such a strong passion that it overpowers reason and leads heroic characters to act foolishly.

Copyright © BookheadEd Learning, LLC

SKILL:
ORGANIZE
NARRATIVE
WRITING

 ## DEFINE

Every **narrative,** be it a novel or a seven-word story, revolves around a **conflict,** or a problem that the characters must face or overcome. A conflict can be external—a knight fighting a dragon, or internal—a teenager struggling with the death of a friend.

To describe the events, a narrative needs a **narrator.** The narrator can be a character in the story, telling the story from the **first-person point of view,** or the narrator can be outside the story, telling it from the **third-person point of view.** If the narrator knows the thoughts and the actions of all of the characters, then that point of view is called **third-person omniscient.** When the narrator knows the thoughts and actions of only one character, then the point of view is called **third-person limited.** Whichever type of narrator you choose, make sure you are consistent throughout the story.

In a narrative, **characters** need to be introduced and developed. If they aren't, your audience will be confused. Details about the characters can be revealed slowly or all at once, but characters typically develop and change over the course of the narrative.

 ## IDENTIFICATION AND APPLICATION

- At the beginning of every narrative, it's important to establish a clear and consistent point of view. Effective narratives can use first-person, third-person, or third-person omniscient point of view.
  - › First-person point of view uses first-person pronouns, such as I, we, and my.
  - › Third-person point of view uses third-person pronouns, such as she, you, and ours.
- Provide strong introductions that identify the main characters for the readers.

Please note that excerpts and passages in the StudySync® library and this workbook are intended as touchstones to generate interest in an author's work. The excerpts and passages do not substitute for the reading of entire texts, and StudySync® strongly recommends that students seek out and purchase the whole literary or informational work in order to experience it as the author intended. Links to online resellers are available in our digital library. In addition, complete works may be ordered through an authorized reseller by filling out and returning to StudySync® the order form enclosed in this workbook.

Reading & Writing Companion

401

> › Establish your characters' motivations. Ask yourself: Why do they act the way they do? What background details or information will help the reader understand this character better?
> › Characters can be introduced all at once or over the course of the narrative.
> › In most narratives, the main character should grow or change in some way by the end of the story.

- Create a smooth progression of events built around a central problem or conflict. Use clear transitions and signal words that show how the action moves along and relates to the central problem or conflict.

 MODEL

The writer of the student model provides readers with a great deal of information in the first paragraph of the story. We meet the main character or protagonist—Sam, a high school student—almost immediately:

> For their class picnic, the seniors of Cedar City High chose a sprawling park at the base of Mojo Mountain. The bus ride there took a little over an hour, but it felt like **four hours to Sam.** As they neared the mountain, **he imagined it** might take another hour or more to hike up its evergreen slopes to the rocky top. **Maybe there he could find some peace.** Away from Cedar City's various cliques and groups. Somewhere he **wouldn't have to feel so awkward around his classmates.**

Because Sam is described as "he" and there are no first-person pronouns in the main narrative, the reader can tell that the story is being told in the third-person point of view. Clues tell us that the narrator is able to look inside Sam's mind and describe his thoughts. For example, the hour-long bus ride "felt like four hours to Sam." Words such as "he imagined" confirm the third-person point of view. At this time, we don't know whether we'll be able to hear other characters' thoughts or only Sam's, so we can't be sure if the author intends the point of view to be omniscient or limited only to Sam's thoughts.

The first paragraph also provides additional details about Sam's character as it sets up the central problem in the story. Sam worries about socializing with the members of his class and wishes he "wouldn't have to feel so awkward" around them. The writer of the student model develops this character trait even further in a subsequent paragraph:

> Sam **should have turned around and headed in the exact opposite direction, but instead he wandered toward the vendors.** He pretended to inspect some

Copyright © BookheadEd Learning, LLC

NOTES

hand-carved animal statues while keeping track of P.J., an easy-to-spot redhead, out of the corner of his eye. **When a few other students glanced Sam's way, he turned his attention to a thumb-sized figurine of a coyote made of blue-green stone.**

In this paragraph, major developments in the plot are related to Sam's perceptions of his classmates. Despite his awkward feelings around his classmates, Sam appears to be attracted to one of them, P.J. Because of this, his normal reactions to events change. Readers can see this in the first sentence. We go inside Sam's thoughts to learn that he feels he "should have turned around and headed in the exact opposite direction." Because P.J. is near the sales tents, however, Sam "wandered toward the vendors." Sam's uneasiness returns later in the paragraph to influence the plot further: "When a few other students glanced Sam's way, he turned his attention to a thumb-sized figurine of a coyote."

This small statue of the coyote will play an important role as the plot develops. Its introduction results directly from Sam's characteristic shyness, which shows that the writer of the "The Overlook" has given great thought to the organization of details and elements of the narrative.

 PRACTICE

Think about who might be the central character in your narrative. Write a short paragraph that introduces and describes this character from the third-person point of view. Then write another short paragraph that introduces and describes this character from the first-person point of view. Which version do you think works best in relation to the overall theme of your story? Which version do you think might engage the reader most effectively?

Please note that excerpts and passages in the StudySync® library and this workbook are intended as touchstones to generate interest in an author's work. The excerpts and passages do not substitute for the reading of entire texts, and StudySync® strongly recommends that students seek out and purchase the whole literary or informational work in order to experience it as the author intended. Links to online resellers are available in our digital library. In addition, complete works may be ordered through an authorized reseller by filling out and returning to StudySync® the order form enclosed in this workbook.

Reading & Writing Companion   **403**

SKILL: NARRATIVE SEQUENCING

⭐ DEFINE

A writer carefully crafts the **sequence of events** in a narrative—**exposition, rising action, climax, falling action,** and **resolution.** The events in a story build toward a specific **outcome,** which may be the full resolution of the story's conflict, the main character's growth over the course of the story, or an understanding that a lack of closure exists for a reason. The sequence of events also has to make logical sense. The writer has to provide details (or leave them out intentionally for a valid reason or effect) to make the story thought-provoking and entertaining for the reader.

⬤ IDENTIFICATION AND APPLICATION

- An outline such as a narrative sequence diagram can help writers plan the major events of a narrative before they begin to write the first draft of the story. In most narratives, this sequence will follow the time order or chronology of the main plot. It may also include cause-and-effect relationships, especially those that influence the outcome of the story. The outline should include the following elements in a logical framework: exposition, rising action (conflict), climax, falling action, and resolution.

  › The exposition provides essential information to help orient the reader, such as character names and descriptions, setting, and the central problem or conflict the characters will face.

  › In the rising action, a writer begins to develop both plot and character with important events related to the theme. There may also be a "trigger" event that sets the plot in motion, such as the arrival of an unexpected character or an event that interrupts the normal course of action. The trigger might signal the beginning of the rising action.

  › The climax represents the turning point in the story. This may be a dramatic plot event, such as an important revelation in a mystery, or a significant change in one of the characters.

> The details and events that follow the climax make up the falling action.
> Most stories end with a resolution of the main conflict or some other sense of closure related to the central theme.

MODEL

The author of "The Overlook" used a narrative sequence graphic organizer to outline and organize the main story elements and plot points.

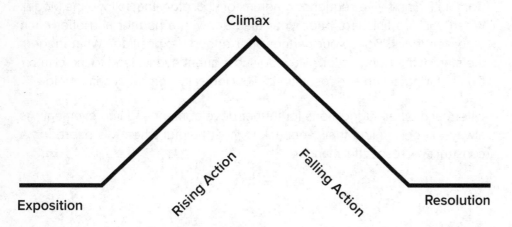

Look at how the writer has organized the sequence of events in the story. This may help you as you think about the narrative sequencing of your own short story.

Exposition:

- Introduce main character: Sam
- Introduce setting: senior class trip at Mount Mojo

Rising Action:

- Sam purchases coyote figurine (trigger)
- P.J. asks Sam to go on hike
- Sam and P.J. climb Mount Mojo

Climax:

- Sam and P.J. reach the summit and discover a common interest in music

Falling Action or Denouement:

- Sam and P.J. talk about music

NOTES

- Sam and P.J. rejoin their class
- The vendor finds Sam and swaps statues

Resolution:

- Sam realizes that he made friends with P.J. without the help of the coyote figurine

 ## PRACTICE

Complete a narrative sequence diagram for your story that follows the Model. When you are finished, trade your diagram with a partner and offer each other feedback. Does your partner offer enough exposition? What triggers the start of the rising action? How do subsequent events lead to the climax? Do the falling action and resolution follow logically from what came before?

Offer each other suggestions for further development and improvement. As always, keep in mind that feedback is most helpful when it is offered in a constructive, respectful manner.

SKILL:
NARRATIVE
TECHNIQUES

 DEFINE

To write a story, authors use a variety of techniques to develop the plot and characters. Narrative techniques include description, dialogue, pacing, reflection, and multiple plot lines.

Most narratives include **dialogue,** or the conversation between two or more characters. Dialogue can be used to develop characters or to move the plot forward.

Writers use **description** outside of dialogue to help readers picture the setting, characters, and events. Strong descriptions often include symbolism and figurative language.

Pacing is the speed at which a story is told. A writer can vary the pacing in order to achieve a desired effect. For example, a writer might speed up the pace as the story nears a suspenseful climax or slow down the pace to reflect a character's lingering indecision.

During a story written in the first-person point of view, the author or narrator might want to comment on the action. This technique is called **reflection** and sometimes sounds like a monologue as opposed to dialogue. Reflection can be quite effective in a personal narrative, especially in the introduction or conclusion. In a third-person story, reflection occurs when characters think or feel a certain way about what has happened but do not outwardly express their internal thoughts and emotions.

While most stories have one plot, some might have **multiple plot lines.** To create multiple plot lines, a narrator might spend one chapter or section following one character and then jump to another character engaged in separate but related activities.

IDENTIFICATION AND APPLICATION

- Dialogue is a great way to show characters interacting and allows them to speak in their own voices. A writer might use dialogue to explain what is happening in a scene or to develop a personality trait, such as shyness or arrogance, of an important character.

  › Use quotation marks to set off dialogue from descriptive text.
  › Include "tags," such as "he said" and "I whispered," that let the reader know who is speaking.
  › Sometimes it's best to summarize or paraphrase dialogue in order to move the plot along more quickly. This can help you avoid trivial or meaningless conversation as well.
  › Use precise and vivid description to engage readers and help them visualize the characters, setting, and other elements in the narrative. Descriptions can also help readers understand how the various story elements build upon one another, such as how a setting affects a particular character.

- Use pacing effectively to convey a sense of urgency or calm in a narrative. Short sentences or paragraphs can make the text move along at a quick pace, while compound and complex sentences in larger paragraphs can slow things down. Consider using a variety of syntax, sentence types, and paragraph lengths to create a range of effects that will hold the reader's attention and interest.

- Consider using reflection to show the reader how the narrator feels about the topic.

  › In the first-person point of view, the narrator can speak his or her thoughts and emotions directly to the reader.
  › In the third-person point of view, tags such as "he thought" or "they believed" can help to show what characters are thinking or feeling.
  › Some writers will briefly include the direct thoughts of characters without tags, even while writing in the third-person point of view. This is called "close third person" and should be used sparingly and only for a desired effect, such as to highlight or show deep emotion.

- Consider having multiple plot lines for stories in which separate events occur at the same time or multiple characters act independently to influence the climax or outcome. Section breaks or clear setting markers, such as noting a change in time and place, can help the reader clearly follow each story line.

MODEL

NOTES

In "The Overlook," the author provides the reader with some descriptive paragraphs at the beginning in order to establish the setting and the main character of the story, Sam. This also establishes that the story is told in the third-person point of view.

Before long, Sam comes face-to-face with P.J., a fellow student to whom he is attracted. The author allows the reader to listen in on their actual dialogue before providing Sam with a brief moment of reflection:

> P.J. looked down. *"You wore hiking boots. Everyone else wore fancy shoes for some stupid reason. **I mean, Mojo Mountain is right here, and you wear high heels? What are these kids thinking? Am I right?"***
>
> *"Yeah. They're not thinking. So what are you thinking?"* **What a stupid question, Sam thought to himself. Focus. Stay calm.** *Think of the coyote, right there in the backpack. "I mean, why does it matter?"*

These lines of dialogue allow the reader to actually "hear" P.J. and Sam talk. For that reason, the author includes a mixture of statements and questions that mimics real teenagers speaking, such as "I mean, Mojo Mountain is right here, and you wear high heels?" The reader can imagine P.J.'s voice rising up at the end of the sentence. When P.J. says, "Am I right?" the reader can visualize Sam being pulled back into the conversation.

Does this mean that Sam appeared distracted while P.J. spoke? The answer comes when it is his turn to speak. He responds to P.J. in a slightly confused tone before the author provides a moment of reflection or internal dialogue: "What a stupid question, Sam thought to himself. Focus. Stay calm." This shows Sam reflecting on what he has just said openly to P.J. and doubting himself. He knows he is overly excited and nervous about talking to P.J. and he wants to calm down so that it doesn't show.

Sam isn't the only character feeling nervous and excited. The author shows this in P.J.'s next line of dialogue:

> *"Look,"* P.J. said, **pointing up toward the mountain.** *"There's a **wicked cool spot up there** that looks out over the whole valley. I want to hike up, but Mr. Fryson says I can't go alone. **Go with me, OK? Wait, that sounded like an order. Right? Let me try again. Would you care to join me?** Please?"*

Please note that excerpts and passages in the StudySync® library and this workbook are intended as touchstones to generate interest in an author's work. The excerpts and passages do not substitute for the reading of entire texts, and StudySync® strongly recommends that students seek out and purchase the whole literary or informational work in order to experience it as the author intended. Links to online resellers are available in our digital library. In addition, complete works may be ordered through an authorized reseller by filling out and returning to StudySync® the order form enclosed in this workbook.

Reading & Writing Companion **409**

NOTES

Here, the dialogue is broken up with a short bit of description related to the setting, as P.J. is "pointing up toward the mountain." Rather than continue the description, the author includes additional details about a "wicked cool spot up there" in P.J.'s dialogue. Since the point of view is third-person and limited to Sam's interior thoughts, the author has to find another way to express how P.J. is feeling about talking with Sam. P.J. says, "Go with me, OK? Wait, that sounded like an order. Right? Let me try again. Would you care to join me?" The author doesn't provide direct access to P.J.'s thoughts and emotions, but the dialogue allows the reader to infer that P.J. is experiencing a mixture of over-eagerness and second-guessing, just like Sam.

By providing this dialogue, the author guides the reader toward making some important inferences about the characters and how they feel about one another. At the same time, the quick pace of the dialogue provides a snappy, comic tone that keeps the story moving along.

 ## PRACTICE

Write a short scene for your narrative that includes either dialogue or personal reflection. As you write, think about what the scene tells the reader about the characters, the setting, the theme, and/or the action of the story. You may choose to summarize or paraphrase sections of dialogue that don't feel meaningful or threaten to slow down the intended pace of the narrative. When you are finished, trade with a partner and offer each other feedback. Did your partner create a realistic conversation or moment of reflection? Were you interested and engaged in the scene? Did you want to continue reading to find out what happened next? Offer each other suggestions, and keep in mind that feedback is most helpful when it is offered in a constructive and respectful manner.

PLAN

WRITING PROMPT

So far in this unit, you have seen how writers of the past have expressed their thoughts and feelings on the theme of love in many creative ways. Now you will have an opportunity to bring some of their ideas into today's world. Write a narrative for young adult readers, like yourself, that draws on themes and story elements in this unit to create a modern tale of love. As you do, reflect on whether you wish to show love as inspiring folly, wisdom, or both.

Your narrative should include:

- an engaging opening that introduces the characters and setting
- vivid descriptions of the setting and characters
- a central problem or conflict
- a logically organized sequence of events
- a conclusion that effectively wraps up the story
- an underlying theme or message related to love

Review the information and ideas you have generated during the previous writing skills lessons. Check them against the original writing prompt to make sure that you are continuing to address all of the requirements for this assignment.

Use the information you included in your narrative sequencing plot diagram to write a one- paragraph summary that describes what will happen in your narrative. Don't worry about including all of the details now; focus only on the most essential and important elements. Your summary should also explain the sequence of events for your narrative. Note places where the story elements function most effectively in the context of your theme. You will refer

NOTES

back to this short summary when it is time to write a complete first draft of your narrative.

Consider the following questions as you write your summary:

- Which details and events figure most prominently in the rising action of the story?
- How are various plot elements related to one another? Do some events cause others to occur?
- How does the story's climax relate to the central conflict?
- How will you lead readers toward a resolution of a story?
- Are there any details or ideas you want to withhold from the reader? What purpose would that serve?
- What ideas about love do you hope readers will consider further after reading your story?

SKILL:
INTRODUCTIONS

 DEFINE

The **introduction** is the opening to a story. An introduction needs to grab the readers' attention and entice them to keep reading. In a short narrative, the introduction should introduce the central problem or conflict.

Some introductions reveal hints of an internal conflict, such as a character debating over which career to choose in life. Others may use descriptions and sensory language to throw readers right into the thick of an external conflict, such as two armies advancing against one another on a battlefield.

An introduction can present something unexpected to both the characters and the reader, such as a visit from a family member that everyone had assumed was dead.

All these examples engage the reader and pique his or her curiosity about what will happen next in the story.

 IDENTIFICATION AND APPLICATION

- The introduction provides a frame or context for the events of a narrative. Quite often, it will establish the point of view the author has chosen for the story.

- The introduction establishes the style or tone of the narrative. In many cases, this will be related to the genre and purpose for writing. For example, a mystery story might start off with questions and descriptions that create a suspenseful mood.

- When writing an introduction, make sure that you consider and/or address the following questions:

  › When and where does this story take place? Are there details about the setting that might intrigue the reader, such as a familiar landmark or an exotic foreign landscape?

NOTES

> Who is the central character, and what does the reader need to know about him or her right from the start?
> What situation does this character face that creates a problem or conflict, either internally or externally? Does this somehow relate to a broader theme that will be of interest to the reader?

 MODEL

The writer of "The Overlook" provides a lot of information in the introductory paragraph. This exposition helps to orient the reader in the world of the story and set the course for the narrative to come:

> For their **class picnic,** the **seniors** of Cedar City High chose a **sprawling park at the base of Mojo Mountain.** The bus ride there took a little over an hour, but it felt like four hours to Sam. As they neared the mountain, he imagined it might take another hour or more to hike up its evergreen slopes to the rocky top. **Maybe there he could find some peace.** Away from Cedar City's various cliques and groups. Somewhere he wouldn't have to **feel so awkward** around his classmates.

First, the writer establishes some details about the setting: a "class picnic" for "seniors" at "a sprawling park at the base of Mojo Mountain." The author also introduces us to the main character, Sam, who is most likely a member of the Cedar City High School senior class.

The reader briefly goes inside Sam's head as the bus nears Mojo Mountain. Sam imagines how long it might take "to hike up its evergreen slops to the rocky top." From this, the reader might predict that the plot of the story will involve a hike up the mountain. Some questions might arise: Why would Sam want to do this? What might happen to him while he's there?

So far, the writer hasn't identified a central problem or conflict in the story, but that comes soon enough. At the end of the introduction, the reader learns more about what Sam is thinking. He imagines that "maybe there he could find some peace" and that he "wouldn't . . . feel so awkward." These details point to an internal struggle or conflict. The reader can infer that something is bothering Sam, and he wants to spend some time away from his classmates to sort through it. The writer hasn't clearly identified exactly what is troubling Sam—and perhaps Sam himself can't fully express it yet, but the reader might be interested enough in the story to read on and learn more, especially if he or she is also of high school age and can identify with Sam's thoughts and emotions in this situation.

PRACTICE

Write an introduction for your narrative that invites the reader into the story. You may want to introduce the main characters, the setting, or the central conflict. When you are finished, trade with a partner and offer each other feedback. Did your partner evoke an interesting world with interesting characters? Were you engaged? Did you want to read the rest of the story based on what you have just read? Provide each other with helpful suggestions on how to improve and strengthen your introductions.

Reading & Writing
Companion

SKILL:
CONCLUSIONS

 DEFINE

The **conclusion** is the end of a narrative. The conclusion is the reader's final experience with the story. It should resolve the events of the story and provide a sense of closure to the central problem or conflict. A strong conclusion follows logically from what the characters have experienced or observed over the course of the narrative. It may also reflect on the happenings of the story.

 IDENTIFICATION AND APPLICATION

- Together with the introduction, a conclusion frames the events of a narrative. In most cases, the conclusion resolves the central conflict or problem of the narrative for the characters. It also leads the reader to think more deeply about the themes that the writer has explored.

- Writers may include descriptive details in the conclusion to evoke an emotional response, such as happiness or relief, in the reader. They may also want to leave the reader wondering or thinking more deeply about the meaning of the story as a whole as it relates to the central theme.

- When crafting your own conclusion, think back on the main characters and events of the story. Have they worked together to lead in a logical and believable way to this ending? Does the conclusion still contain enough twists or surprises to satisfy the reader's interest and curiosity? (In other words, was the story's ending unpredictable without being unbelievable?) Are there any plot lines or character development that remain unresolved? Does the language of the ending provide a sense of finality or closure to the narrative?

MODEL

At the end of "The Overlook," it would seem that Sam and P.J. have become close friends and will live happily ever after in love. Such an ending might not satisfy some readers, who may complain that it's too predictable and rather unoriginal. The writer seems to anticipate this, however, and so throws in a bit of a twist at the end:

> As **they stood in line together** to board the **bus back home,** the white-haired man from the sales area came dashing over. **"Hey! There you are!"** he shouted at Sam, drawing everyone's attention to him.

The clause "they stood in line together" signals that resolution has been achieved and Sam has been able to befriend the object of his affection, P.J. By mentioning "the bus back home," the writer also brings the story full circle; the class trip is over, and the students will now board the bus and return to their everyday lives. At that moment, however, a voice calls out: "Hey! There you are!" It seems there is more to this story after all.

This twist might surprise the reader and lead him or her to wonder what else the writer wants to say about the theme. Reading on, we learn some new information that may well influence how the characters reflect upon the events of the day:

> **"You don't need the hawk any more,"** the man said. "That magic's flown away now." He took back the figurine and handed Sam the coyote. "Now you're ready for the stone coyote."

> "Stone Coyote," P.J. said with a **poke to Sam's ribs. "Great name for a band."**

> "Maybe," said Sam. "But **I think that you and I can come up with something even better on our own."**

The vendor's first words, "You don't need the hawk anymore," confirm that Sam has resolved his self-doubt and found the inner confidence to become friends with P.J. Their friendship is further reinforced by P.J.'s "poke to Sam's ribs" and the reference to their shared musical interests. P.J. thinks that "Stone Coyote" would be a "great name for a band," and the reader might expect Sam to agree. Instead, Sam says, "I think that you and I can come up with something even better on our own."

Please note that excerpts and passages in the StudySync® library and this workbook are intended as touchstones to generate interest in an author's work. The excerpts and passages do not substitute for the reading of entire texts, and StudySync® strongly recommends that students seek out and purchase the whole literary or informational work in order to experience it as the author intended. Links to online resellers are available in our digital library. In addition, complete works may be ordered through an authorized reseller by filling out and returning to StudySync® the order form enclosed in this workbook.

Reading & Writing Companion **417**

NOTES

The reader might be surprised to hear this, as it signals even stronger growth in Sam's character. His statement also develops the themes of love and attraction a bit further, suggesting that magical figurines might be useful in some circumstances but that he is now ready to take full responsibility for his own actions. This leaves the reader with something to think about and a way of applying the story's central theme to his or her own life.

PRACTICE

Write a conclusion for your narrative. When you are finished, trade with a partner and offer each other feedback. How effectively did the writer wrap up the story? What final thoughts did the writer leave you with? Offer each other helpful advice or suggestions. As always, remember that comments are most helpful when they are constructive and offered with kindness and respect.

DRAFT

WRITING PROMPT

So far in this unit, you have seen how writers of the past have expressed their thoughts and feelings on the theme of love in many creative ways. Now you will have an opportunity to bring some of their ideas into today's world. Write a narrative for young adult readers, like yourself, that draws on themes and story elements in this unit to create a modern tale of love. As you do, reflect on whether you wish to show love as inspiring folly, wisdom, or both.

Your narrative should include:

- an engaging opening that introduces the characters and setting
- vivid descriptions of the setting and characters
- a central problem or conflict
- a logically organized sequence of events
- a conclusion that effectively wraps up the story
- an underlying theme or message related to love

You've already made substantial progress toward writing your own narrative. You've thought about your purpose, audience, and topic. You've reflected on the unit's reading selections and identified various ideas and details as your inspiration. You've decided on your central story elements and explored effective narrative techniques and sequences. You've also crafted potential introductions and conclusions.

Now it's time to write the first draft of your narrative.

Use your summary and your other prewriting materials to help you as you write your draft. Remember that narrative writing begins with an engaging opening and develops a central theme through the introduction and interaction of various story elements. A conclusion normally offers some sense of closure or resolution to the central conflict of the story. It should also leave your reader thinking about the central theme long after they've set the story aside.

When drafting, ask yourself these questions:

- How can I improve my introduction to make it more interesting or engaging?
- What can I do to make my central characters more vivid and believable?
- What descriptive details can I add to make the story more interesting and easier to visualize?
- Would dialogue, inner thoughts, or a different point of view make the characters or story more compelling?
- How well have I expressed the overall theme or message of my story?
- What final thought does my conclusion inspire in my readers?

Before you submit your draft, read it over carefully. You want to be sure that you've responded to all aspects of the prompt.

SKILL: DESCRIPTIVE DETAILS

 DEFINE

Descriptive details make writing more vivid and help readers visualize the various elements of a narrative, such as character, events, and setting. **Sensory language** appeals to one or more of the five senses (sight, hearing, touch, taste, and smell).

 IDENTIFICATION AND APPLICATION

- Descriptive details can help readers understand a character's physical appearance, the sound of his or her voice, and even the smell of his or her shampoo. With **direct characterization,** the writer makes explicit statements about a character and what that character experiences. Sometimes a writer will use **indirect characterization,** which reveals a character through his or her own words, thoughts, and actions or through what other characters think and say about him or her.

- Strong writers use concrete details to create believable settings and plots within the narrative. Vivid modifiers, such as adjectives and adverbs, can help to clarify descriptions and highlight important or telling aspects of a scene, such as color of a particular character's eyes or the smell of something burning in another room.

- **Sensory language** engages readers and provides an even richer, more deeply experienced association with the words on the page. As you develop or revise a scene, ask yourself: What can the characters see in this scene? What smells or aromas may be present in this setting? Can the characters feel something physical, such as the heat or the cold? What other sounds may be present that might draw their attention? You can use cluster maps or charts to help you think about the meaningful sights, sounds, smells, tastes, and physical sensations of a particular scene, especially one that is important to the narrative.

- **Figurative language** and **imagery** can help readers relate what is happening in the narrative to observations and events from their own lives.

 MODEL

The writer of "The Overlook" provides a great deal of information and detail about the setting of the story in the opening paragraphs. We know that the main character, Sam, is looking forward to experiencing the natural beauty of the park. However, this isn't the first thing that the writer describes as the students arrive for their class picnic:

> The bus pulled into the parking lot, where some local craft makers had set up **folding tables and multicolored tents,** hoping to **lure visitors** into buying a **carved wooden souvenir or plastic memento.**

These first descriptive details help the reader to visualize the scene, with its "folding tables and multicolored tents." The reader might imagine something like a flea market or yard sale and how much this would disappoint a character like Sam. The added details of "a carved wooden souvenir or plastic memento" support the idea that these are probably cheap tourist-trap items and not works of art inspired by nature. The writer might have been tempted to include additional sensory details—maybe the smell of fried junk food or the calls of vendors hawking their wares—but since this sales area isn't the major setting of the story, these details may have been deleted during the revision to make way for more meaningful or telling details later on.

Some of these details arrive in a moment of indirect characterization. The author hasn't provided a description of Sam yet, but when P.J. begins to talk with him, we learn more about his appearance and interests:

> "Sam! You hike, right? I mean, you like **nature and all that stuff,** don't you? Like in **our ecology class?**"

> "Yeah," Sam said. "I do, sort of. I mean, yes. Yes I do. Why?"

> P.J. looked down. "You **wore hiking boots. Everyone else wore fancy shoes** for some stupid reason. I mean, Mojo Mountain is right here, and you wear high heels? What are these kids thinking? Am I right?"

The reader could already guess from the opening paragraph that Sam liked "nature and all that stuff." P.J.'s indirect characterization reinforces this character detail. Sam had also mentioned that he and P.J. were enrolled in some of the same science classes, but P.J.'s more specific "ecology class" detail demonstrates an even greater interest in nature on both their parts. The writer also leaves it up to P.J. to tell the reader that Sam "wore hiking boots." From the comment "Everyone else wore fancy shoes," the reader can infer that P.J. is also wearing hiking boots or something similar. The writer incorporates these details into the action of the scene, providing character description without slowing the pace of the narrative or getting in the way of Sam and P.J.'s developing friendship.

 ## PRACTICE

Choose a meaningful paragraph or section from the draft of your narrative writing. Think of how you might incorporate one additional telling detail from each of the five senses (sight, sound, smell, taste, and touch) into the scene. You can insert these into existing sentences or create new sentences featuring the descriptive details. When you are finished, trade with a partner and offer each other feedback. Were you able to distinguish the new details from those already there? What added dimension or meaning did the new details offer? Has the writer introduced any new figurative language to make the details more evocative for the reader? Can you distinguish examples of either direct or indirect characterization in the revised selection? Provide each other with helpful feedback and suggestions on how to improve and strengthen your revisions.

REVISE

WRITING PROMPT

So far in this unit, you have seen how writers of the past have expressed their thoughts and feelings on the theme of love in many creative ways. Now you will have an opportunity to bring some of their ideas into today's world. Write a narrative for young adult readers, like yourself, that draws on themes and story elements in this unit to create a modern tale of love. As you do, reflect on whether you wish to show love as inspiring folly, wisdom, or both.

Your narrative should include:

- an engaging opening that introduces the characters and setting
- vivid descriptions of the setting and characters
- a central problem or conflict
- a logically organized sequence of events
- a conclusion that effectively wraps up the story
- an underlying theme or message related to love

You have written a draft of your narrative. You have also received input from your peers about how to improve it. Now you are going to revise your draft.

Here are some recommendations to help you revise:

- Review the suggestions made by your peers.
- Focus on large issues first, such as the clarity of major plot points or the relationships between important characters.
  - › Make sure your narrative has a substantive theme or message.
  - › Revise your introduction if it isn't engaging or if it doesn't orient readers with the characters and setting and properly introduce the conflict.

Copyright © BookheadEd Learning, LLC

NOTES

> › Check that the sequence of your narrative is clear. Add transition or time-order words to clarify any sections.
> › Determine whether the style and tone are appropriate for your intended audience.
> › Ensure that your conclusion neatly wraps things up and leaves the reader with something to think about.

- After you have revised major elements and resolved any lingering issues, think about smaller details that will better help your readers visualize the story.

  > › Should you add any descriptive details? For example, is there a detail about a character that relates to how other characters perceive of him or her?
  > › Would adding dialogue or interior thoughts help to make your characters come alive? If so, be sure to use correct formatting and punctuation.
  > › Consider the point of view in the story. If the story is in the first person, does the narrator have a clear voice? If the story is in the third person, is the point of view consistent throughout?

Please note that excerpts and passages in the StudySync® library and this workbook are intended as touchstones to generate interest in an author's work. The excerpts and passages do not substitute for the reading of entire texts, and StudySync® strongly recommends that students seek out and purchase the whole literary or informational work in order to experience it as the author intended. Links to online resellers are available in our digital library. In addition, complete works may be ordered through an authorized reseller by filling out and returning to StudySync® the order form enclosed in this workbook.

Reading & Writing Companion | **425**

EDIT, PROOFREAD, AND PUBLISH

WRITING PROMPT

So far in this unit, you have seen how writers of the past have expressed their thoughts and feelings on the theme of love in many creative ways. Now you will have an opportunity to bring some of their ideas into today's world. Write a narrative for young adult readers, like yourself, that draws on themes and story elements in this unit to create a modern tale of love. As you do, reflect on whether you wish to show love as inspiring folly, wisdom, or both.

Your narrative should include:

- an engaging opening that introduces the characters and setting
- vivid descriptions of the setting and characters
- a central problem or conflict
- a logically organized sequence of events
- a conclusion that effectively wraps up the story
- an underlying theme or message related to love

You have revised your narrative and received input from your peers. Now it's time to edit and proofread your narrative to produce a final version. Ask yourself: Have I addressed all of the valuable comments and suggestions from my peers? Is my writing clear and coherent? Have I used descriptive details and precise language? What more can I do to improve my narrative's structure and organization?

When you are satisfied with your work, move on to proofread it for errors. For example, check that you have used correct punctuation for dialogue and have used commas correctly throughout. Be sure to correct any misspelled words.

Once you have made all your corrections, you are ready to submit and publish your work. You can distribute your writing to family and friends, hang it on a bulletin board, or post it on your blog. If you publish online, consider including original artwork or other graphic elements to illustrate your narrative.

Please note that excerpts and passages in the StudySync® library and this workbook are intended as touchstones to generate interest in an author's work. The excerpts and passages do not substitute for the reading of entire texts, and StudySync® strongly recommends that students seek out and purchase the whole literary or informational work in order to experience it as the author intended. Links to online resellers are available in our digital library. In addition, complete works may be ordered through an authorized reseller by filling out and returning to StudySync® the order form enclosed in this workbook.

Reading & Writing
Companion

427